Very Innovative Parties Cookbook

For additional copies of **Very Innovative Parties Cookbook**, use the order blanks in the back of the book or write directly to:

Very Innovative Parties Cookbook
Loma Linda University Dental Auxiliary
P.O. Box 382
Loma Linda, California 92354
1-800-841-3838

Checks should be made payable to **Loma Linda University Dental Auxiliary**. The cost of the book is $24.95; $5.00 postage and handling U.S. residents; and $7.00 postage and handling non-U.S. residents; California residents please add applicable tax.

Copyright© 1987 by the **Auxiliary to the Alumni Association**

Library of Congress Catalog Number TX-2-233-265

Loma Linda University, School of Dentistry
P. O. Box 382
Loma Linda, California 92354

First Printing 1987
Second Printing 1988
Third Printing 1992

The profits from **Very Innovative Parties Cookbook** are for the expressed purpose of Loma Linda University School of Dentistry missions.

Printed in the United States of America
By Pacific Press, Nampa, Idaho

ISBN 0-8163-1118-8

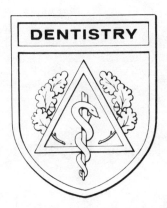

Purpose

The purpose of the Auxiliary to the Alumni Association, Loma Linda University, School of Dentistry, is for the advancement of philanthropy on behalf of missionary work conducted by the health professions.

Acknowledgments

Party Book Committee

Bakland, Jean
Baum, Alma
Cockrell, Ann
Davidian, Sally Jo
Johnson, Eunice
Jung, Janeece

Lofgren, Raye
Longfellow, Irene - Artist
Meckstroth, Carol
Rentschler, Sharon
Smith, Julie
Wacker, Charlene

Theme Chairmen

Banner, Betty
Beckner, Jeanne
Bonnet, Sandy
Darby, Joann
Dickinson, Darlene
Eddlemon, Dotty
Godfrey, Sondra
Libby, Pamela
Mathews, Darlene

McEwen, Sandra
Meyer, Michelle
Muncy, Patti
Osmunson, Kathy
Pence, Pat
Pfeiffer, Angie
Potts, Susan
Shipowick, Vicki

Contributors

Abbott, Dorothy
Abrew, Beverly
Acton, Julie
Adams, Marlene
Addison, Janyce
Allred, Charmay
Asgeirsson, Ruth
Baker, Clydella
Bakland, Jean
Ball, Susan
Banner, Betty
Barker, Ann
Barnes, Paige
Baum, Alma

Beams, Janie
Beckner, Ardis
Beckner, Jeanne
Benfield, Gladys
Betheu, Lisa
Bingham, Chris
Bishop, Patti
Bline, Darlene
Bloomquist, Willma
Bonnet, Sandy
Bounds, Venita
Brewser, Bonnie
Brizendine, Sally
Bryant, Barbara

Buck, Virgene
Byrd, Mary Ellen
Cafferky, Marlene
Catelli, Karen
Christensen, Nina
Chung, Helen
Churches, Connie
Clarke, Lorraine
Clifford, Cindy
Cochran, Mary Beth
Cockrell, Ann
Comm, Debbie
Conrad, Helen
Corbett, Peggy

Corbett, Rita
Cotton, Marilyn
Coulter, Bonneetah
Cutting, Jane
Darby, Joann
Davidian, Sally Jo
Davidson, Jan
Deeb, Helen
Dent, Donna
Dickinson, Darlene
Dillow, Judy
Diminyatz, Lois
Drayson, Grace
Drumwright, Kay

Drury, Dollie	Johnson, Eunice	Meilicke, Ethel	Sharp, Sheila
Dupont, LuAnne	Johnson, Fran	Mertz, Shirley	Shipowick, Vicki
Dwornik, Marilynn	Jones, Shirley	Meyer, Michelle	Shultz, Gertrude
Eddlemon, Dotty	Jung, Janeece	Mitzelfelt, Barbara	Smith, Julie
Elliston, Judy	Jung, Thana Ruth	Moss, Joanie	Smith, Marguerite
England, Nancy	Jutzy, Robin	Mounce, Vivian	Soper, Jean
Erickson, Wendy	Kann, Serena	Merrill, Alma	Staff, Toni
Ernston, Janice	Kaylor, Shelley	Muncy, Patti	Starkey, Doris
Everett, Kathleen	Kendall, Carol	Nelson, Esther	Steele, Mrs. Dennis
Finch, Bunny	Kerschner, Cheryl	Neufeld, Anabel	Stephens, Jerry
Foust, Georgia	Kiger, Betty	Neufeld, Tracey	Sundin, Marvil
Fowler, Twylla Lofgren	Kiger, Cheryl	Nixon, Donna	Swanson, Rheta
Francis, Betti	Kincl, Jeanne	Nugent, Charlene	Swenson, Katie
Freeman, Dorothy	Klooster, Arlene	Orser, Jessie	Taylor, June
Fritz, Judy	Knecht, Dorothy	Osmunson, Kathy	Taylor, Shaunie
Frey, Nancy	Krick, Beverly	Passion, Ida	Teed, Marion
Garner, Betty	Kunihira, Linda	Pence, Lynn	Theodorou, Georgia
Godfrey, Sondra	Larsen, Rue	Pence, Pat	Trefz, Evelyn
Goodacre, Ruth	Laspe, Marlys	Peters, Marolyn	Tomlinson, Mary
Grabow, Darlene	Lavelle, Jeanne	Peterson, Marty	Turk, Nancy
Grayson, Grace	Lawson, Brook	Pfeiffer, Angie	VanDenburgh, Chris
Griswold, Bethene	Leas, Barbara	Pierson, Gloria	Vega, Joanne
Hall, Diane	Leo, Carol	Pike, Connie	Vogt, Nancy
Hadley, Bonnie Rae	Lewis, Joan	Potts, Gail	Wacker, Charlene
Harder, Marjorie	Libby, Pamela	Potts, Susan	Watkins, Dixie
Hardesty, Marti Baum	Linebarger, Bankie	Prunty, Kay	Watkins, Gail
Hardy, Evelyn	Lindner, Carole Ann	Pyke, Carol	Weikum, Jeanne
Harris, Corinne	Lofgren, Becky	Quering, Glenda	Wells, Linda
Harris, LaVerne	Lofgren, Raye	Raines, Ruthe	Westphal, Carlla
Harris, Sally	Logan, Edie	Raitz, Vivian	Westphal, Elaine
Haskin, Sue	Longfellow, Irene	Reeves, Marie	Wheeker, Shirley
Heinrich, Ardis	Lowe, Carol	Rentschler, Sharon	Wheeler, Ruby
Henderson, Frances	Lucas, Dona	Revel, Joan	Williams, Doris
Henderson, Kay	McAnally, Dovie	Riger, Betty	Wilson, Mrs. Floyd
Hendrickson, Charlene	McAuliffe, Gail	Robertson, Darlys	Woesner, Jan
Herrick, Joann	McDonald, Marian	Rogers, Judy	Woods, Minnie Iverson
Henzer, Mrs. Fred	McDonald, Pearl	Roy, Aida	Yeager, Frances
Hirst, Arlene	McEwen, Sandra	Schaeffer, Dorothy	Yeatts, Helen
Hoffman, Loriann	McKinley, Gail	Schmitt, Jane	Ziegenhagel, Juanita
Hopkins, Juanita	Martin, Lynda	Schneider, Ardith	
James, Ruthie	Mathews, Darlene	Schnepper, Ladelle	
Jarrett, Darlyne	Meckstroth, Carol	Scott, Betty	

The contributors' list incorporates all persons who submitted party ideas and recipes. Even though some of these were not included in their entirety, an idea or combination of ideas may have been used. We regret that all ideas and recipes were not included, due to duplications and space limitations.

Thank you all for your contributions!

Foreword

Parties are like gifts waiting to be unwrapped, promising surprise, excitement, pleasure and satisfaction. The perfect party may be a warm gathering of family friends, a morning brunch with the ladies, a golden anniversary dinner, a sweet-sixteen party or a New Year's extravaganza. Whatever your party or holiday dream, it can be more than a figment of your imagination.

Very Innovative Parties Cookbook is a source book for party inspiration. It will take you through the calendar year and beyond. You will find a party plan for many special occasions and holidays.

The party plans are designed to simplify your entertaining. From invitations to menus, recipes to centerpieces, decorations to games, each party is planned. Artist's illustrations define many of the ideas. Each party may be used in its entirety or selected ideas may be borrowed from different parties to create one of your own.

V.I.P. is a collection of many wonderful cooks' private recipes, cuisine garnered from friends all over the world and previously unshared treasures from our own community's kitchen files. Some are tried and true favorites you have tasted before. Some are new and exciting and others were held in secrecy until now.

All the recipes in **V.I.P.** have been carefully tested. Noted in each recipe is baking or cooking time, yield or servings, and an occasional tip on freezing, advance preparation and variations.

V.I.P. is truly innovative! Not only have we created parties with complete menus and recipes, but these recipes contain no flesh foods or alcohol.

We regret that space limitations restricted the inclusion of many party ideas and recipes. Wording was altered occasionally for conciseness and clarity.

To the many dedicated volunteers who diligently worked on **V.I.P.,** patiently testing and tasting . . . to all our generous friends who took the interest and time to share recipes with us . . . to the Party Book Committee, whose enthusiasm and effort made an exciting idea an exciting reality . . . and to our husbands and families, whose patience and appetite for our creations were endless and invaluable . . . our heartfelt thanks and gratitude.

Celebrate with **Very Innovative Parties Cookbook**!

Table of Contents

TABLE OF CONTENTS

Parties

Bridal Shower by Mail

This is a special shower given for the bride who has moved away from her home community of friends. Even though these friends are far away, they will not miss out on the celebration. They will gather in the home of the hostess, eat and exchange cookies, wrap gifts, take pictures and write thank you notes! The hostess will mail packages with gifts and pictures. What a surprise awaits the bride at the post office!

Invitation

The invitations may be obtained from a party shop or card store. These may read:

> (Bride's Name) *is far away and can't be with us during this special time in her life. We want to let her know that we haven't forgotten her here at home. Let's surprise her with a "shower-by-mail." We will provide the drink and the wrappings. Bring a gift and a dozen cookies. It will be fun to wrap gifts, eat cookies and take candid pictures to be sent along with the gifts to the bride.*

Decorations or Setting the Mood

The mood is informal. The music is lively.

Table Setting and Centerpiece

The table setting may be simple.

Entertainment or Games

Gift Wrapping: Wrap gifts for the bride.

Guests Picture Taking: Candid pictures are taken so the fun may be shared with the bride.

Introduction of Bride and Groom: Share pictures of bride and groom for those who may not have met the groom.

Writing Thank You Notes: Each gift includes a thank you note which has been written, addressed and stamped. The fun part is writing one's own thank you note, using many superlatives. For example, "Thank you so much for the gorgeous, beautiful waffle iron. I know I will use it at least three times a day and dream about it at night! Never in my wildest dreams would I have expected such a lavish gift. I will keep it with my china and will pass it down to my children and their children!"

Signed *(bride's signature)*, The Perfect New Bride. (Space is left for the bride to add her own comments).

1

Elegant Bridal Shower

Invitation

On pastel cards, create an ink drawing of a parasol, ribbons and love birds. The border includes the bride's selection of gifts, such as pattern of china, silver and crystal, colors of bedroom, bath and kitchen, and stores where she is registered. The shower information is written in calligraphy.

A Shower For A Special Bride

Peggie Sue Miller

Open House: June 12th
Monday evening 7:00~9:30

5051 Sky Terrace Road
Yourtown
Regrets Only
359-7130   781-3302

Macy's ~ Silver: Gorham, "Grand Havana"/Crystal: Baccarat, "Flame"

China: Lenox, "Country Faire"/Stainless: Wallace, "First Colony"

Linens: Apricot and Grey/Bed: King-size/Bath: Turquoise ~ Bloomingdale's

Table Setting and Centerpiece

The buffet table is covered with a solid pastel tablecloth and top cloth. Solid or floral napkins add a lovely touch. The floral top cloth is drawn up at the corners and tied with bows at the table's edge. A fresh flower-decorated lace parasol, adorned with ribbon and doves, is a beautiful centerpiece.

Menu

Strawberries Dipped in Sour Cream and Brown Sugar
Asparagus Casserole
Layered Vegetable Salad
Nut Tree Bread
Bridal Ribbon Cake
Summer Champagne
or
Fruity Delight

BRIDAL RIBBON CAKE

12-14 pieces colored paper, cut into ½ x 2-inch strips
Aluminum foil
Several yards ⅟₁₆-inch ribbon, color to match theme
1 butter cake mix or favorite cake recipe
Butter cream frosting (your favorite), colored to match theme
1 8-ounce can almond paste
1 cup sifted powdered sugar
1 Tablespoon milk
1 teaspoon almond extract

1. Use colored poster paper or similar paper firm enough to slide into cake. Punch 1 hole in end of paper strips. With ball point pen, write advice to bride. Cover each piece of advice with aluminum foil to protect paper from moisture in cake. Tie 10-inch ribbon through foil and hole. Set aside.

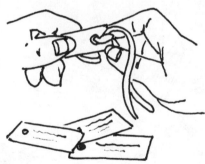

2. Prepare cake according to package directions, baking in 2 8-inch round cake pans. Let cool on wire racks.
3. Spread thin layer of frosting between layers and on sides of cake.
4. In large mixing bowl, combine almond paste, powdered sugar, milk and almond extract. Mix at low to medium speed until crumbly. Knead until well-blended. Mixture will be soft and pliable.
5. Roll out almond paste mixture on piece of waxed paper into strip about 29 inches long and 3½ inches wide. Using sharp knife, cut almond paste so it will fit evenly around sides of cake, about 28 x 3½ inches. Using waxed paper to help lift and guide almond paste strip, wind strip around side of cake, lightly pressing strip onto side of cake and pressing edges firmly to adhere.

6. Lightly notch top edge of almond paste strip with sharp knife to delineate slices of cake. Slide small paring knife vertically in center of each slice on side of cake to make cuts that will hold pieces of advice, alternating positional height of cuts so positions of ribbons will vary. Gently slide prepared foil-covered, cardboard pieces into cuts on cake.

7. Tie ribbons that extend from cake into bows.
8. Frost top of cake with remaining frosting, spreading it just over top of almond paste strip to make smooth border.
9. Tie additional ribbon into large bow and place on top of cake.

Preparation Time: **1½ hours**   **Serves:**   **10-12**

Entertainment or Games

A beautifully wrapped present is placed in a prominent place apart from the bridal presents. During the course of the party, someone will win this gift. A decorated sticker may be placed behind or under the winner's chair. The present contains something the bride-to-be can use, such as a travel kit. The recipient gives the present to the bride-to-be.

The chair of the bride-to-be is decorated with balloons or a large, pretty bow. A brand-new penny or a lucky sixpence to be worn in her shoe on the wedding day is tied with a ribbon and placed in her chair. Hidden under a glass or dessert plate is a lucky penny or wedding charm. The recipient is supposed to be the next bride.

Kitchen Bridal Brunch

Invitation

A pretty recipe card, preferably a doubled 3 x 5-inch card, is the bridal shower invitation. An extra recipe card is included for the guest to fill out and bring to the shower. The bride-to-be will surely appreciate this collection of proven recipes.

BRIDAL BRUNCH FOR *(name)*

(name of hostess)

Ingredients:

Food

Fun

Friends

Kitchen gifts for the bride-to-be: Her colors and theme are *(list)*.

Preparation: Mix ingredients together at   *(address)*.

Cooking Time: Place in oven and bake on *(date)* from 11 a.m. to 1 p.m. or until done.

Enclosed is a recipe card. Please fill it out with a "tried and true" recipe to be included in a special collection of recipes for the bride-to-be and her future husband.

Decorations or Setting the Mood

The guests are greeted with a wonderful aroma of cinnamon or stove-top potpourri (available at gourmet shops). The kitchen colors and theme chosen by the bride-to-be may be used for decorations. A ceramic strawberry cookie jar or a basket decorated with ribbons or flowers may be used to hold party favors or the recipe cards brought by guests.

Table Setting and Centerpiece

Brunch may be served buffet-style. The tablecloth is in the bride's colors or in a pattern matching her theme. Food, tableware and napkins are arranged in an attractive fashion so guests may serve themselves. The centerpiece is an assortment of kitchen utensils, attractively arranged in a salad bowl with flowers and ferns. This hostess gift is given to the bride-to-be.

Menu

Cheese Strada
Tossed Salad (your favorite)
Hot Curried Fruit
or
Fruit Salad (your favorite)
Zucchini Bread
Cream Puffs
Sparkling Cider

Entertainment or Games

Kitchen Contents: Type these scrambled kitchen articles on construction paper cut in shapes resembling item. Guests unscramble the words. The first guest completing the answers wins. A gift is given to the winner. Of course, a gracious recipient of a gift at a shower gives it to the honored guest.

1.	ate upc	*tea cup*
2.	resrewaliv	*silverware*
3.	aeptl	*plate*
4.	ndbreel	*blender*
5.	pnnkai dhrelo	*napkin holder*
6.	usrace	*saucer*
7.	msineagur cspu	*measuring cups*
8.	xmrie	*mixer*
9.	ttsreoa	*toaster*
10.	tecerlci ttelksi	*electric skillet*

A Love Letter: This letter is typed on construction paper in the bride's colors. Guests fill in the blanks with the name of a fruit or vegetable.

Dearest *(bride's name)*

First, I want you to know my heart *(beets)* only for you. If you *(carrot)* all for me, why not ask your parents if they will *(lettuce)* get married? Since we *(cantaloupe)*, I suppose you will want a big church wedding. Everyone knows I am *(plum)* crazy about you, and I'm sure we would make a happy *(pear)*. Please do not *(squash)* my hopes, because it is love like I have for you that makes a *(mango)* crazy.

You've been the *(apple)* of my eye for so long, and my love for you is as strong as an *(onion)*. I trust you will never *(turnip)* your nose at me. If you do, there is only one thing for me to do. I will go to the river *(endive)* in.

All my love,

(groom's name)

Rolling Pin: The guests are reminded of the old rhyme often written in youthful autograph books, "When you get married and your husband is cross, pick up a rolling pin and show him who's boss." As this is not the best way to handle a disgruntled mate, what is the best advice the guests might give the bride-to-be? Each advisor writes her advice and signs her name with a felt-tip permanent ink pen on the wooden rolling pin. This makes a truly unique gift, one the bride-to-be will treasure a lifetime.

Rice and Pins: Mix one pound rice and 100 brass safety pins in a large bowl. In one minute, a blind-folded player has to sort out as many safety pins as possible. Keep account of the number each person sorts. Each guest takes a turn sorting, and the person who sorts out the most pins wins. Sounds easy? Guess again! Give a gift to the winner.

Shivaree and Pound Party

SHIVAREE: *"A mock serenade with kettles, pans, horns and other noise makers given for a newly married couple,"* Webster. This is fun for a second-time marriage when two households are being combined. The honored couple's sense of humor must be taken into consideration. Neighbors should be alerted of the noisy "serenade" ahead of time. The object of the "shivaree" is to surprise the honored couple at their own home about the time the couple retires for the night. This MUST be a surprise!

Invitation

The invitation may be a simple note card with the definition of "shivaree" printed on the cover. Wording may read:

SH-H-H! It's a SURPRISE!

Come to a "Shivaree and Pound" Party
For Phoebe and John Smith
Saturday night, 10:00

Bring a noise maker (pie pan, lid, spoon, kettle, horn, bell, etc.).

Meet at Valley Church parking lot, 110 Maple Avenue at 9:45 p.m.
We will leave by 10:00 p.m. for the Smith's.

Gift suggestions: One pound item of choice, such as nuts, popcorn, beans, cake, butter, etc. A card may be included.

Decorations or Setting the Mood

This is an informal, fun party which begins with a boisterous celebration at the couple's front door. Quietly, with noise makers in hand, the guests sneak up to the front and sides of the house. On cue, they begin to "serenade." When one or both of the newlyweds come to the door, the guests call out "SURPRISE"! Invite yourselves into the house for more party fun.

Table Setting and Centerpiece

The hosts and hostesses bring attractively decorated paper plates, napkins and cups. As guests are seated, pass out the tableware. A basket filled with a variety of muffins and a tray of hot drink or punch may be served. Bring a heavy-duty garbage bag for clean-up so there is no mess for the newlywed couple.

Menu

Hot and Spicy Berry Bowl
Blueberry Muffins
Bran-Raisin Muffins
Cranberry Muffins

Entertainment or Games

Wedding Video: If a video of the wedding ceremony and/or reception is available, show this after refreshments.

Reading of "The W.C.":

THE W.C.

Before listening to this, understand that the "W.C." means bathroom or water closet to the British. A young couple from England about to marry were looking over a house in the country. After satisfying themselves that the house suited them, they started home. During the trip home, the bride-to-be asked her fiance where was the W.C. Her fiance, after laughing at her modesty, said he had not noticed. Upon their return home, they wrote the owner of the house. The owner figured the "W.C." meant Western Church and replied:

Dear Sirs:

Your kind letter was received. The W.C. is about nine miles from the house. This is quite a distance if you are used to going often. When in a hurry, the quickest way is to go by bicycle. It is nice to take a lunch and make a day of it. It seats 350 comfortably. Next year, it is planned to install plush seats as the present ones are quite cold in the winter. The W.C. has an excellent newspaper. It covers everything and is quite interesting. Special walls and ceilings pick up every sound. Soft organ music accompanies your duty. We first went there five years ago and it was very crowded. My wife sat, but, of course, I stood. We usually go once a week. It pains us we cannot go more often. Our daughter met her husband there. They go, as well as their children. Maybe next year we can share a pew. Come early as the overflow goes on the lawn.

Sincerely,

The Owner

Spelling Bee: Twenty-nine or more people are needed for this game. Divide into two teams of 14 people, 13 spellers and a leader for each team. The twenty-ninth person is the "teacher-scorekeeper." The 26 "spellers" remove their shoes and stockings. The leader of each team, using a felt-tip marker, writes letters of the alphabet on the bottoms of the feet of his 13 team members, one letter on each foot. For example, the first person will have an "A" foot and a "B" foot; the second person will have a "C" foot and a "D" foot, etc. When both teams have their feet marked, the spelling bee is ready to begin. The words are called by the "teacher-scorekeeper." The object is for a team to complete the word first by lining up the letters in correct order. It is easiest for the speller to sit on the floor as soon as he knows his 'place' in the word being spelled. The team leader calls out when his team has spelled the word. Do not call words that use the same letter twice. Suggested words are bride, lover, husband, zest, party, work, honey, quick, home, extra, jukebox, gravity, forget. Give a lollipop or piece of bubble gum to each winning team member.

Wedding Buffet or Dinner

A wedding reception is a very special party - a celebration of family and friends. The reception is a labor of love, one that will guarantee memories to last a lifetime.

Once the reception time, place, size and budget are decided, the setting or style may be selected. The hour alone will suggest a general menu. The personal taste of the bride will determine the specifics. The theme is influenced by the bride's choice of bridesmaid's dresses and seasonal aesthetics.

The wedding cake is the high point of the reception, a part of tradition that should always be present. It should be a very special treat. The traditional white wedding cake has now been replaced by carrot cake, lemon cake, spice cake, even chocolate cake or any combination of layers.

Wedding food should be particularly pretty - light, elegant, a delicate contrast of colors, textures and shapes.

A wedding reception may be either sit-down or buffet-style. It may be a breakfast or brunch, a luncheon or a tea reception, according to the time of day. A buffet reception is one in which the guests serve themselves. A dinner reception is usually started sometime between 6:00 and 9:00 p.m. The guests are served at the table. It usually, but not always, has a more formal feeling.

WEDDING BUFFET

Fresh Fruit Appetizers
Fresh Vegetable Appetizers
Avocado-Tomato Dip
Cheese Log
Dill-Sour Cream Dip
Garlic-Cheese Dip
Egg Chips
Stuffed Mushroom Caps
Bean Salad
Macaroni Salad
Walnut Meatballs with
Apricot Barbecue Sauce
or
Sour Cream-Mushroom Gravy
Rolls and Butter
Mints and Nuts
Lavendar Slush

WEDDING DINNER

Rainbow Fruit Salad
Rice Pilaf
Glazed Carrots with Orange Slices
Florentine Crepes
Rolls and Butter
Ruby Red Frosty Punch

HORS D'OEUVRE HOLDERS

Choose an attractive whole, unpeeled vegetable or fruit to serve as a base for hors d'oeuvres. Level bottom by cutting off a small flat slice. Bases may be:

Artichoke
Cantaloupe
Eggplant
Grapefruit
Green or red cabbage (hollowed)
Honeydew melon
Pineapple with foliage remaining

A hollowed artichoke, cabbage or eggplant may be used as a dip holder.

Spear food tidbits with toothpicks and stick into the fruit or vegetable base. Tidbits may be:

Apple wedges
Celery slices
Cheese cubes
Cherries
Cream cheese balls
Melon balls or cubes
Olives
Pickles
Mandarin orange segments

FRESH FRUIT APPETIZERS

3 pounds cantaloupe or honeydew melon	= 4 cups
1 pound green grapes	= 2 cups
1 pound Tokay grapes	= 3 cups
3 ounces kiwi	= ½ cup
4 pounds pineapple	= 5 cups
1 pint strawberries, blueberries or raspberries	= 2 cups
19 pounds watermelon	= 16 cups

Serves: 50

FRESH VEGETABLE APPETIZERS

2 pounds broccoli or cauliflower	= 32 (1¼-inch) flowerets
1 pound carrots	= 65 (3 x ½-inch) sticks
1¾ pounds celery	= 100 (4 x ½-inch) sticks
1 pint cherry tomatoes	= 25 (1-inch) tomatoes
1½ pounds cucumbers	= 50 (¼-inch) slices
1 pound zucchini	= 50 (¼-inch) slices

DIPS

1 cup dip   = 16 1 Tablespoon servings

Tips: Vary fruit shapes and colors. Include balls, spears, cubes and triangles. To get the most out of melons, cut chunks or cubes rather than balls. Use grapes, cherries and strawberries for round shapes. Blueberries and raspberries are best used as garnish as they are fragile and easily bruised when tossed with other fruits. Orange juice concentrate may be drizzled over or mixed lightly with fruit. Fruit such as bananas, apples and peaches should be sprinkled with lemon or pineapple juice to prevent discoloration.

VEGETABLE APPETIZERS

Asparagus spears
Broccoli flowerets
Carrot sticks or curls
Cauliflowerets
Celery fans
Cherry tomatoes
Cucumber slices
Green onion curls
Green pepper strips
Mushrooms
Radish roses
Snow peas
Zucchini slices

1. Prepare all vegetables. Keep in ice water until ready to serve.
2. Fill bottom of serving bowl with ice. Cover with plastic wrap.
3. Cover wrap with lettuce leaves. Arrange vegetables in an attractive presentation.

ROLLS, BUTTER, BEVERAGES, MINTS, NUTS

Servings	50	100
Rolls	60-75	125-150
Butter	1½ pounds	3 pounds
Decaffeinated coffee	1¼ pounds	2½ pounds
Cream	1½ quarts	3 quarts
Sugar	1 pound	2 pounds
Sparkling Apple Cider	10 bottles	20 bottles
Mints	2 pounds	4 pounds
Nuts	2 pounds	4 pounds

Open House Buffet
Silver Anniversary

Invitation

The front of the invitation may have a caricature of a young couple dressed in the style of the year the anniversary couple was married. The printed invitation is worded:

Twenty-five years ago
Martha and John Smith started a celebration.
You are invited to continue
with the festivity
by joining them on Sunday
September 1, 1987
between the hours of 3-7:00 p.m.
for an Open House.
A buffet will be served.
1001 Ninth Street
City, State

Decorations or Setting the Mood

Silver and white bells are hanging in various places. Several of the original wedding photographs are placed on a table with the guest book. A tape recording of popular tunes from the wedding year is playing during the anniversary celebration. Also include music that was played during the wedding ceremony.

The anniversary bride is given a corsage of flowers that were in her bridal bouquet.

Table Setting and Centerpiece

Twenty-five long-stemmed roses in the bride's colors are arranged in a silver vase and placed on a silver lamé tablecloth. Fine, white china reflects the beauty of the silver serving pieces and flatware. White cloth napkins are folded fancily and placed in the water goblets.

Menu II is adaptable to an outdoor buffet, using the topiary tree of fresh fruit as the centerpiece.

Menu

MENU I

Rice-Mushroom Pilaf
Artichoke-Parmesan Strudel
Green Beans (your favorite)
Mandarin Salad
Raspberry-Cranberry Salad
Chocolate Prune Cake
Champagne Cider

MENU II

Topiary Tree of Fresh Fruit
Almond-Poppy Seed Bread
Pumpkin Bread
Banana-Nut Bread
Orange-Nut Bread
Apricot-Nut Bread
with
Your Favorite Spreads
Cream Cheese-Nut Ball
Variety of Crackers
Mints and Nuts
Reproduction of Original Wedding Cake
Fruity Pink Punch

TOPIARY TREE OF FRESH FRUIT

1. Use gallon cans or large clay flower pots. If using flower pots with hole in the bottom, cover with piece of heavy cardboard.
2. Mix enough plaster to fill pot ¾ full.
3. Before plaster sets, place dowel in center of pot. Allow to dry.
4. Spray styrofoam green.
5. Spray pot and dowel with silver paint.
6. Gently push ½-inch dowel through center of styrofoam. Glue at dowel insertion points. Allow to dry.
7. Cover styrofoam with green leaves or lettuce, using U-shaped picks.
8. Arrange fresh fruit on covered styrofoam with toothpicks. Fresh fruit may include strawberries, grapes, melon balls, pineapple chunks, kiwi slices and cherries.

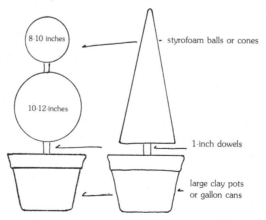

8-10 inches — styrofoam balls or cones

10-12 inches

1-inch dowels

large clay pots or gallon cans

Formal Dinner
Golden Anniversary

Invitation

A recent picture or wedding photograph of the "golden anniversary" couple is on the front of the invitation. Suggested wording is:

In honor of the
Fiftieth Wedding Anniversary
of Martha and John Smith,
their children and grandchildren
request the pleasure of your company
at a Formal Dinner.
Please join us for the
"Beginning of the Next Fifty Years"
on the tenth of June
Nineteen hundred and eighty-seven
at six o'clock
555 Rainbow Road
City, State

Enclose R.S.V.P. card with addressed and stamped return envelope.

Remembrance Album: As a very special surprise for the "golden" couple, compile a remembrance album. On the back of gold-trimmed stationery, the following letter is printed.

Dear Family and Friends,

In celebration of Martha and John Smith's fiftieth wedding anniversary, we, their children, would like you to participate in this happy occasion by sharing some personal memories with them. On the back of this letter, recount the day you met our parents, a special memory or a funny occasion and, if possible, include a picture or two.

This memorabilia will be compiled into an anniversary album for our parents, a remembrance of good times with special friends and family. The album will be presented to them during the party.

We hope to see you at the anniversary dinner. If you are unable to attend, please be a part of the celebration by writing your memories of John and Martha and returning them for inclusion in their album. Send to Sue and Bill Smith, 413 Golden Road, City, State, Zip Code.

We look forward to seeing you!

(children and spouses' names)

A white leather album (available from a photographer or stationery store) is entitled "Golden Wedding Anniversary," printed in gold foil lettering. Also printed in gold are the names of the honored couple and their anniversary date. The returned letters and old photos are compiled in the album along with pictures of guests taken at the party.

Decorations or Setting the Mood

A large mural displaying a rainbow is hung behind the head table. Painted at one end of the rainbow is a "Pot-of-Gold" with printed words, "Beginning of the Next Fifty Years." Displayed on a table are old wedding pictures, scrapbooks and family pictures. Next to the guest book is a large bouquet of rainbow-colored flowers in a "Pot of Gold" container. A second "Pot-of-Gold" may serve as a money tree for the anniversary couple. Old love songs playing in the background add to the nostalgic mood.

In the entry is an ivy-covered lattice arbor accented with a rainbow. As guests arrive, their picture is taken in front of the arbor. On a nearby table, pages are placed from the "Remembrance Album." Guests are asked to sign the space where their picture will be placed.

The original wedding gown or a copy may be worn by a grand-daughter or a special friend.

A chauffeur-driven car made in the anniversary year delivers the honored couple to the party. On their arrival, they are given rainbow-colored leis.

Table Setting and Centerpiece

Rainbow-colored flowers are arranged in a gold-painted container for the centerpiece. The handle is wired upright and wrapped with several colors of satin ribbon. Bows are tied on each side, leaving long streamers to decorate the table.

Nut and mint cups for each place setting are small clay flowerpots spray-painted gold and accented with a bow. The anniversary couple's name and wedding date is written with a felt-tip pen on each "Pot of Gold."

Rainbow-colored napkins folded in fan shapes are placed in the water goblets.

Several teenagers may be the waiters, dressed in black pants or skirts and white shirts with rainbow ties.

Menu

Rainbow Fruit Cup
Spinach Lasagne
or
Crustless Quiche
Tossed Green Salad (your favorite)
Ribbon Jello
Creamed Green Beans
Toasted Garlic Bread
or
Parmesan Bread Sticks
Mints and Nuts
Wedding Cake (purchased)
Champagne Cider
or
Coconut Punch

Entertainment or Games

"This is Your Life": A "This is Your Life" program is presented to the honored couple. Family members recall at-home days and a few surprise guests may highlight the program. A slide presentation may be included.

Renewal of Marriage Vows: A minister renews the marriage vows.

Cake Cutting: The finale for this memorable evening is the cutting of the wedding cake. The cake is beautifully decorated with 50 roses and 50 candles. "Happy Anniversary" is sung to the "golden anniversary" couple.

Mail Celebration
Golden Anniversary

Invitation

A special mail celebration may be done for the couple who, for health reasons or distance, is unable to attend a large party. On the front of the invitation is a recent picture or wedding photograph of the "golden anniversary" couple.

Martha and John Smith
will celebrate their
Fiftieth Wedding Anniversary
on the tenth of June.
In lieu of a party,
they would be delighted
to hear from their many
cherished friends and loved ones.

Remembrance Album: See party Golden Anniversary Formal Dinner on *page 17.*

Clothesline Baby Shower

Invitation

A blue sheet of stationery is folded in half. "Poles" are drawn on either side of the opened card and a twine "clothesline" is attached to the tops of the poles. Hanging on the clothesline are paper diapers, booties and a nightshirt large enough to include party details.

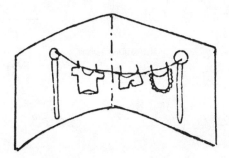

Decorations or Setting the Mood

Across the doorways are strung clotheslines with presents "clothes" attached with clothespins. A decorated laundry basket filled with gifts is placed near the chair of the mother-to-be. Her corsage is a miniature diaper with flowers tucked in the top. "Diaper" name tags may be a variation of this. In a laundry basket "bassinet" is a life-like newborn baby doll.

Table Setting and Centerpiece

A clothesline is strung across the table and filled with baby or doll clothes attached with pastel-colored clothespins. If these clothes are unavailable, use felt or paper cut-outs clothes. The clothesline is made using large dowel "poles" attached to heavy blocks of wood. Napkins are folded into kimono shapes, as illustrated, or pinned diapers. Flannel "diaper" nut and mint cups are dipped into paraffin wax and molded into shape as the wax hardens. Silverware is placed inside diaper-folded napkins.

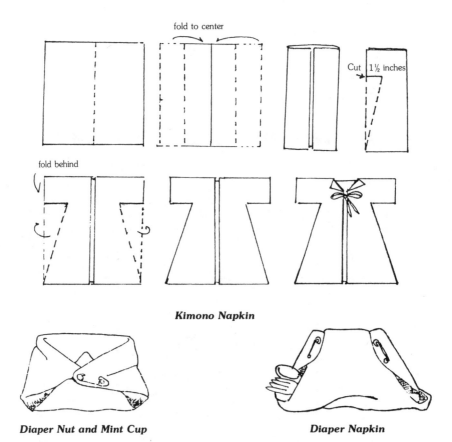

fold to center

Cut 1½ inches

fold behind

Kimono Napkin

Diaper Nut and Mint Cup   *Diaper Napkin*

Menu

Wrapped Baby Sandwiches
Pinwheels
Vegetables and Dips (your favorite)
Sour Cream Walnuts
Small Tarts (your favorite)
or
Pineapple Cream Delights
Mints and Nuts
Sugar Cookie Diapers
Strawberry Jello Punch

WRAPPED BABY SANDWICHES

Trim crusts from white bread slices. Flatten slices with a rolling pin. Spread slices with flavored cream cheese. Roll up with one corner overlapping the opposite corner. Garnish with "baby face" of sliced ripe olives and bits of marschino cherry, as if baby was wrapped in a blanket.

Tip: Place in waxed paper-lined box and store in refrigerator.
Filling Variations:
1. Cream cheese, sliced banana, coconut and chopped peanuts.
2. Cream cheese, jelly and chopped nuts.
3. Cottage cheese, chopped green pepper and onion salt.
4. Pimento cheese, sliced olives and mayonnaise.

SUGAR COOKIE DIAPERS

Use favorite sugar cookie recipe. Cut dough into triangle shapes and fold like diapers. Fill with jelly or other filling, if desired, before folding and baking.

Entertainment or Games

Fashions for Baby: Each guest is given an 8-inch oblong piece of colored crepe paper, a few white strips, lace doilies and some straight pins. From these materials, guests create a bonnet, bib, jacket or other baby clothes item.

Mail-Order Baby: Each guest is given an old magazine, a pair of scissors and an order list of baby articles. The list is filled by cutting out pictures of the items. The person whose order is most nearly complete when time is called is the winner. The list of baby articles may include a house, crib, blanket, curly hair, mother, children, toys, baby food, etc.

What is the Waist Size of the Mother-to-be? A ball of yarn is passed and each guest cuts a measured length of the estimated waist size of the mother-to-be. The person with the closest estimate wins.

Graduation Baby Shower

Invitation

A diploma-type invitation is created using heavy bond pink or blue paper. Hand write in calligraphy the following message:

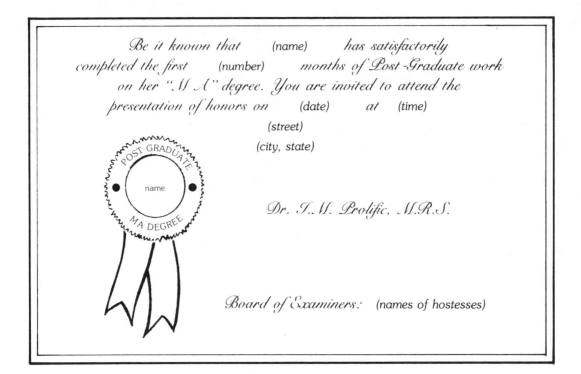

Be it known that (name) *has satisfactorily completed the first* (number) *months of Post-Graduate work on her "M A" degree. You are invited to attend the presentation of honors on* (date) *at* (time)

(street)

(city, state)

Dr. I. M. Prolific, M.R.S.

Board of Examiners: (names of hostesses)

A gold seal is placed in one of the lower corners of the invitation to give it an official look (available at a stationery store). This is rolled up diploma-style and fastened with a gold seal. Address labels and affix to mailing tube (available at a stationery store).

Table Setting and Centerpiece

The centerpiece is a baby doll dressed in a diaper, graduation hat, diploma in hand and draped with a banner reading "Fetus Graduate." Miniature baby books are placed at the baby's feet. Colored napkins are rolled diploma-style and tied with a ribbon. Matching plates and cups are also used.

Menu

Diploma Rolls
Graduation Caps
Honeydew Salad
Mints and Nuts
Italian Cream Cake
Ice Cream (your favorite)
Frosty Banana Punch

DIPLOMA ROLLS

With electric knife, trim crusts from white bread slices. Flatten slices with rolling pin. Spread slices with Pineapple-Cream Cheese Filling. Roll up jellyroll fashion and tie with green onion strip.

GRADUATION CAPS

Cut 2-inch squares from white bread and 1½-inch circles from dark rye bread. Spread 2 circles with Almond Sandwich Filling and top with 1 white bread square. Garnish with pimento strip for tassel.

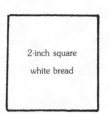
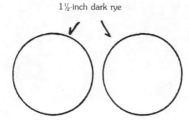
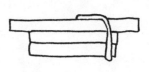

Entertainment or Games

Presentation of Candidate: Introduce the honoree and present her with a corsage.

Commencement Address: Humorous article on parenthood may be presented, although personal experiences may be enough material.

Charge to Candidate: Each guest or selected guests may give a piece of advice.

Conferring of Honors: Opening of gifts.

Guest and Gift List: A scroll large enough for names of guests and gifts is written during opening of gifts. At the top of the scroll, it reads, "This is to certify that the following individuals were present at the Graduation Exercise of Baby   *(name)*   ."

Mary Had a Little Lamb

Invitation

Lamb invitations are available at card shops. An alternate lamb invitation may be made by enlarging the illustrated pattern.

Decorations or Setting the Mood

A stuffed lamb decorated in a baby dress is sitting in a child's rocking chair placed in the entry. Attached to the chair is a bouquet of pastel-colored balloons. Sitting beside several chairs are stuffed lambs whose necks are encircled with floral wreaths or ribbons tied in bows. Baby and teenage pictures of the mother and father-to-be are set around the room.

Table Setting and Centerpiece

A "cauliflower lamb" is placed on a silver tray and surrounded with flowers, strawberries and baby's breath. Covering the table is a pastel-colored tablecloth accented with candles. The flatware is wrapped in matching napkins decorated with ribbons and baby's breath.

CAULIFLOWER LAMB

9-inch styrofoam egg
6-inch styrofoam egg
12-inch section of 1½-inch tube styrofoam
12-inch section of 2-inch tube styrofoam
Glue (florist glue, Tacky glue or white glue)
Toothpicks
Shredded coconut
Chocolate chips
3 heads cauliflower
Serrated knife
Butter knife

1. Form pieces of body by scraping away excess styrofoam with butter knife. Use a stuffed lamb as a model.

Body: 9-inch egg   Head: 6-inch egg

head

Ears, neck and tail: 2-inch tube   Front and back legs: 1½-inch tube

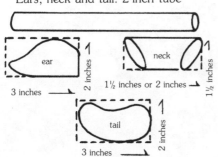

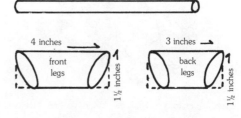

27

2. To assemble, holes are poked in body where toothpicks will hold body parts together. Fill holes with glue to give strength and stability. Place toothpicks halfway into carved piece with glue and stick into body. Glue joints for stability.

legs   neck

3. After assembly, do final shaping and level legs.

4. The face, legs, tail and ears are covered with coconut. Make mixture of coconut and glue. Glue on styrofoam, a little section at a time, then place coconut-glue mixture on glued styrofoam.
5. Melt chocolate chips. Make feet, nose and eyes.

6. Allow to dry overnight.
7. The next day, allow 3-4 hours to complete. Use the whitest, nicest cauliflower heads available. Wash cauliflower and cut off flowerets. Set aside smallest flowerets for head. Place half of toothpick into floweret and the other half into styrofoam body. Fit pieces like a jigsaw puzzle. Shape cauliflower to fit or shave off stem of floweret to give a nice finished look.

Tip: Assemble styrofoam lamb day before party to give glue time to dry.

This little lamb is so precious that it is worth the extra effort to make him!

Menu

Finger Sandwiches with
Pineapple-Cream Cheese Filling
Curry-Cream Cheese Filling
Nuteena Filling
Almond Sandwich Filling
Chicken Salad Filling with Cream Puffs
Fruit or Vegetable Tray
Petite French Rolls with Cheese
Lemon-Cheese Pudding Dessert
Mints and Nuts
Piña Colada Punch

Entertainment or Games

Genealogy: What relation to the Baby is . . .

1. his father's uncle's brother's sister? — grandaunt
2. his aunt's mother's father's wife? — great grandmother
3. his mother's nephew's daughter's son? — third cousin
4. his brother's son's sister's mother? — sister-in-law
5. his sister-in-law's father-in-law's grandson? — his son *(baby)*
6. his sister's father's stepson's mother? — stepmother
7. his uncle's father's only granddaughter? — sister
8. his brother-in-law's wife's grandmother's husband? — grandfather
9. his father's father's daughter's daughter? — his cousin

Baby Names: Beginning with each letter of the alphabet, compile two lists of names, one for boys and one for girls. The first person who completes the lists wins.

Baby Book: Each guest is asked ahead of time to write a letter or poem to the new baby. These are compiled in a baby book with a lamb cover. Guests may read their contribution aloud before the book is presented to the mother-to-be.

The first page reads, "Lisa's Debut" by hostesses *(list names)*.

The second page lists the table of contents.

Suggestions:

1. One Ticket to Smith's Production - Invitation
2. Meeting My Public - Guest's signatures
3. Feature Story - Games
4. Caught in the Shower - Gifts and givers
5. Tea for Two - Refreshments
6. Shower Pictures

Teddy Bear Picnic

Invitation

Teddy bear invitations are available at most card shops. An alternate bear invitation may be made by enlarging the illustrated pattern.

1. Cut one body, two arms and two legs.
2. Glue head to body.
3. Use paper fastener to hook arms and legs to body.
4. Write or type invitation on separate paper and glue on back.

Decorations or Setting the Mood

A teddy bear collection is placed at the front door to greet the guests. One bear is holding a cluster of helium-filled balloons. A similar bear grouping is placed near the chair by the mother-to-be or by the gifts. Other bears are sitting in various chairs. Large baskets tied with pretty ribbon bows are filled with the shower gifts.

Table Setting and Centerpiece

The centerpiece is a small picnic basket filled with artificial blueberries and strawberries. It is placed on a small gingham baby quilt which may be used as a hostess gift for the mother-to-be. Four small bears are sitting on the quilt. An alternate centerpiece may be a family of bears to include a daddy bear, a mother bear and a baby bear, dressed accordingly. The "picnic" is served in small baskets lined with various colors of tissue paper. Gingham or bear napkins add the final touch for this picnic.

Menu

Cottage Cheese-Potato Salad
Chicken Salad Filling with Cream Puffs
Mini-Bagels with Cream Cheese (your favorite)
Sugar Cookies (your favorite), made in Teddy Bear Shape
or
Teddy Bear Cake
May Day Punch

TEDDY BEAR CAKE

Bake package of cake mix in 9 x 1½-inch round baking pan and 6-ounce custard cup according to package directions. Cool. Cut "cupcake" horizontally in thirds. For nose, attach top cupcake slice to top of round cake with frosting. For ears, cut ½-inch piece from each of remaining cupcake slices and discard. Attach flat side of slice to edge of cake with frosting. Spread nose with white frosting and sprinkle with white coconut. Spread remaining cake with chocolate frosting. Toast coconut and sprinkle on chocolate frosting. Decorate face using marshmallow cut in half and 2 gumdrop slices for eyes, 1 gumdrop slice for nose and licorice for mouth.

Entertainment or Games

Animal Juniors: Write the baby's names of the animals listed below. Ten minutes are allowed to list the animal baby names.

1.	Bear	Cub
2.	Sheep	Lamb
3.	Duck	Duckling
4.	Frog	Tadpole
5.	Swan	Cygnet
6.	Chicken	Chick

7.	Hen	Chick
8.	Horse	Colt
9.	Mare	Filly
10.	Swine	Piglet
11.	Deer	Fawn
12.	Elephant	Calf
13.	Cat	Kitten
14.	Oyster	Set
15.	Seal	Calf
16.	Goose	Goslings
17.	Bull	Bullock
18.	Cow	Calves
19.	Cod	Codling
20.	Lion	Cub

Solo or Duet: "Teddy Bear Picnic."

How Well Do You Know The Mother-To-Be? Guests are asked to answer the following questions the way they think the mother-to-be would answer, circling one of the choices for each question. The mother-to-be fills out a sheet with her own answers, which are read to the guests. The winner is the player who guesses the most correct answers.

1. If the baby is a boy, would you most like him to become a doctor, artist, insurance agent, pro football star, social worker or plumber?
2. If the baby is a girl, would you most like her to become a fashion model, secretary, teacher, businesswoman, movie star or lawyer?
3. If you could choose the color of your baby's hair, would it be blonde, brown, red, sandy, auburn or black?
4. If you give birth to twins, would you prefer to have two boys, two girls or a girl and a boy?
5. If you had to choose from the following names, would you name your son John, Benjamin, Roger, Larry, Edward, Paul or Andrew?
6. If you had to choose from the following names, would you name your daughter Alice, Barbara, Nina, Emily, Joan, Patricia or Judy?
7. Would you sing your baby to sleep with a Brahm's lullaby, a Mother Goose tune, a Bob Dylan song or none of these?
8. If you had a problem with your baby, would you be most likely to seek advice from your mother, your mother-in-law, Dr. Spock, your husband or a friend?
9. Would you prefer to master the art of cooking Italian food, French food, German food, Chinese food or Mexican food?
10. If you were spending an evening at home, would you prefer to read a book, watch TV, listen to music or have a barbecue?
11. Would you prefer to own a French poodle, cocker spaniel, collie, dachshund, German shepherd or no dog at all?
12. Would you prefer to read a beautiful poem, an essay on current events, a home decorating magazine or a humorous novel?
13. Would your ideal residence be in the mountains, by the ocean, in a small town, in a large city or on a farm?

Story:

JUST AMONG OURSELVES

"All right fellows, everybody in and close the nursery door. That old head nurse is off the floor for a change, and now would be a good time to slip you a few ideas on what this life is all about."

"First off . . . Jones, put that bottle down! . . . Now . . . Most of us are at least two days old and about ready to go out into the world. You've got to go home with your parents. It's some kind of law. It's going to take you about two months to get your Mom and Pop straightened out and it's going to be two months of good work, but I don't think there's one of us here who can't handle it."

"Don't pat-a-cake with them and don't pamper them. A pampered parent will give you nothing but trouble! We might as well start out right. Get them on your schedule and keep them there. They'll go mooning around, biting their fingernails and pretending they can't understand what you want, but gradually they'll get the idea and then you're in clover. From there on in, it's just like room service."

"One thing you'll have to work out yourself is how to handle older brothers and sisters. They may get to poking their fingers through the crib at you. Just bide your time. Later on you'll get teeth. You'll have to stick around the house pretty close for a while, and if you work it right you can have everybody waiting on you hand and foot. Gradually, after you learn where things are, you can get up at night and help yourself, but for awhile lie low and play dumb. After the first month, they're going to start bothering you about saying something. This will get to be a pain in the neck, but there isn't much you can do about it. Wait until you're good and ready and slip them a 'Da-da' or 'Ma-Ma' or something simple, but keep it simple because they'll have everybody and his brother running in to hear you say it, and the whole business can get pretty tiresome. I know some little smart alecks who started out with complete sentences, and they didn't get any sleep for weeks. Serves them right!"

"You're going to get a lot of silly stuff to play with and, I might as well tell you, practically none of it will be good to eat. If you keep your eyes open, you can pick up one or two items that are fun. The first old guffer who dangles a round shiny thing on a chain in front of you . . . grab it! The thing ticks like mad, and you can keep it around to play with when they think you're taking a nap."

"It's better not to let things roll along too smoothly. No sense in letting your parents get in a rut. If the routine gets boring, pick the right time and roll off the bed. If that doesn't work, pretend to swallow something. This will get you a quick trip to the doctor, and it breaks up the day. But right here, let me warn you . . . don't try to pull anything on a doctor. It can be rough, brother, rough! Those boys have been around and they know too much. Just clam up and go along with them and you'll be a lot better off."

"Remember that parents are hereditary and you'll have to take what you get. Some of you seem to think you might get the wrong parent when you leave here! Don't believe it. They've got them fingerprinted and card indexed down in the office."

"Well, fellows, that's all I can think of right now. Anyway, it's about lunch time and we'd better stir things up. How about all cutting loose at once? All right, let's go! One . . . two . . . three . . ."

Search for Baby Items: In each sentence of the story, find an article which has something to do with a baby.

A STORY OF THE STORK

I shoe'es s'prised at what I just done seen.	shoes
Ol' Doc Stork is slippin' up on us again.	slip
It so appears that he's gettin' confused.	soap
Maybe he's gotten his addresses mixed.	dress
For he's hawling his bundle around over *(your town)*	shawl
Shh' Oodles of men are asleep and ladies too.	hood
The prattle of a baby might wake 'em up!	rattle
But Doc Stork shir thinks he knows his business.	shirt
He may look dumb and silly, but he's plenty smart.	band
He didn't plan to spend the night in galevantin' around,	nightingale
But he stubbed his toe while making a landing at the side road;	tub, bed
He broke out in a cold sweat ('er, perspiration)	sweater
And finding a sugar-coated pil, low in his bag, he took it.	pillow
Then he knocked loudly on the door. "Howdi! A person's supposed to be quiet here at night," comes a voice from within.	diaper
Then *(baby's name)* opens the door a crack and well nighties himself into a question mark in surprise.	nighties
"Sign here, sir," say Doc Stork, and *(baby's name)* takes the blank, etc.	blanket
And picks up his quil to sign the document.	quilt
"But you don't really mean this bundle is for us, Doctor?"	
"Oh yes! We've had to delay, Ette and I, in filling your order.	layette
But now, we're hopin' 's how we've found just what you wanted."	pins
"Ho, ho! See what we've got *(mother's name)* dear, it's a bundle from heaven!"	hose
"Do open it quick!" says *(mother's name)* with delight.	
"Doc says it's not quins, but maybe it's twins.	
Anyway, I'm sure it's just right!"	

Circus Clowns

Invitation

A large balloon is blown up but not tied. The invitation is written with a felt-tip pen on the balloon. Allow ink to dry, release the air, place in an envelope and mail.

Decorations or Setting the Mood

Brightly colored balloons are everywhere. A big circus tent is created by suspending a large sheet from the center of the ceiling, anchored with a nail, and attaching the corners to the walls. Curled crepe paper streamers hang from the corners of the tent.

Table Setting and Centerpiece

A white sheet serves as the tablecloth. Various colors of heavy construction paper are cut into animal shapes for place mats. The centerpiece is a cluster of balloons with clown faces. Balloons may be taken home as party favors.

Clown hats are made by cutting paper in a 24-inch circle. Cut a line from the edge of the paper to the center. Wrap ends around until a cone is formed, then staple together. Two pieces of yarn are stapled to the hat for ties. A pompon is made by wrapping yarn around four fingers 15 times, tying in the middle and snipping the ends. Staple pompon to cone tip of the hat. Decorate with star stickers and the child's name.

Menu

Hot Dogs
Popcorn
Carrot and Celery Sticks
Carnival Cake
Ice Cream Clowns

CARNIVAL CAKE

Bake an angel food cake. When cool, remove from pan and spread with white frosting. Dip animal crackers in melted chocolate and set aside. Sprinkle confetti candies in stripes resembling wheel spokes on top of cake. Stand animal crackers encircling the top of the cake. Decorate sides with crackers and confetti. For a birthday, insert colored candles in gumdrops and place between wheel spokes.

ICE CREAM CLOWNS

Place colored frosting in pastry bag. With large tip, make a 3-inch ruffly circle of frosting on baking sheet covered with waxed paper. Place ice cream ball on frosting. Decorate with clown faces using various candies. Attach cone. Must do ahead and freeze.

Entertainment or Games

Clown Faces: The faces of the children are painted with "grease paint" as they arrive. A picture of each child is taken with an instant camera and sent home as a party favor.

GREASE PAINT

2 Tablespoons white shortening
5 Tablespoons cornstarch
1 teaspoon white flour
Food coloring
Cocoa powder

Mix first 3 ingredients until smooth. Add desired food coloring and/or cocoa powder.

Yield: **Paint for 2 faces**

Pin the Nose on the Clown: This is similar to "Pin the Tail on the Donkey" except a red nose is used instead of a tail.

Balloon Blows: The children blow an inflated balloon along a race course without using their hands. The first child across the finish line is the winner.

Balloon Hop: The children hop with a balloon between their knees across the finish line.

Penny Pitch: Using a basket or hat, the children try to toss in ten pennies. The winner is the child getting the most pennies in the basket. Each child may keep their pennies as party favors.

Jungle Birthday Party

Invitation

Invitations are printed on stationery with a jungle theme or on green construction paper cut in leaf shapes. Solid-colored green note paper and envelopes may be decorated with jungle animal stickers. Inside the invitation reads:

> Join us in the jungle
> to celebrate David's birthday
> June 12 at 4:00 p.m.
> 743 Wildwood Lane
> R.S.V.P. *(phone number)*

If swimming is included in the party, invitation may read:

> David is celebrating his birthday
> Bring your bathing suit
> . and join the other wild animals
> at the watering hole*
> June 12 at 4:00 p.m.
> R.S.V.P. *(phone number)*

* "Watering hole" is at the party.

Decorations or Setting the Mood

The party room or patio is decorated with green and brown crepe paper streamers. Leafy jungle vines such as ivy may also be used. Stuffed animals are tucked in corners and hiding behind potted plants. A few plastic snakes are slithering across the carpet "grass." A live parrot is also a great addition to the atmosphere. Jungle music, animal calls or the sound track from "The Jungle Book" may be played during the party. An elephant or monkey costume is worn by the person who answers the door. The hostess may wear safari or jungle print clothes and the children may wear clothes with animal prints.

Table Setting and Centerpiece

A green or brown tablecloth is accented with a variety of bright, solid-colored paper plates and napkins. An assortment of small, leafy, potted plants and African violets with miniature plastic or stuffed animals is the centerpiece.

Menu

The menu is the birthday child's favorites.

Hamburgers, Hot Dogs and Sandwiches
Chips
Platters of Fresh Fruit
Cake and Ice Cream (your favorites)

Animal-shaped cakes may be made using a favorite cake recipe. Directions for decorating the animal cakes are usually included with the pan. A jungle scene may be created on a layer or sheet cake by using small plastic animals and trees.

Entertainment or Games

Jungle Masks: Provide large, brown paper bags, scissors, glue sticks, crayons, felt-tip pens and construction paper. As the children arrive, let them make masks of jungle animals, real or imaginary, or of the jungle witch doctor.

Jungle Hunt: Peanuts are scattered around the periphery of the room. The lights are turned out and the children are given flashlights and a bag. The hunt through the "jungle" for "elephant food" may begin.

Jungle Puzzle Race: Obtain two jigsaw puzzles which are identical in size, picture and number of pieces (less than 100). Hallmark makes an ideal small puzzle entitled "It's a Jungle Out Here." The children are divided into two teams and race to complete the puzzles. For a large group, more than two puzzles may be required.

Jungle Animal Charades: One jungle animal name per child is written on a separate slip of paper. Each child draws a slip and acts out the animal name while the other children guess what he is.

Jungle Pictures: Using a large piece of cardboard (from a furniture or appliance box), draw and color a lion or other jungle animal. Cut a hole for the animal's face about the size of a child's head. The animal should be about the height of the children. Pictures may be taken of each child peeking through the hole. If instant pictures are taken, the children may take them home.

Jungle Stories: The local library is a good source for stories or poems about the jungle. The age group and attention span, of the children must be considered, five to ten minutes maximum.

Jungle Party Favors: Any number of small jungle items may be given as party favors. Several of these placed in small, brightly colored bags may be given to each child. Suggestions for party favors include animal erasers, stickers, stamps, small toys, puzzles, pencils, whistles or paperback books about jungle animals. Gum and candy are always favorites, especially tropical fruit LifeSavers. Small packages of animal-shaped vitamins, bags of dried fruit or animal crackers may also be given. T-shirts with various stenciled animals are fun gifts for children.

Playtime

Invitation

Children love being involved in the preparation of a party. Let them help with the invitations by making their handprint or footprint on paper. This is done by dipping the child's hand or foot into poster paint. Allow print to dry and then print party information inside.

Decorations or Setting the Mood

The ceiling is covered with helium-filled balloons with strings attached, long enough for children to reach. Crepe paper curtains in the doorways are fun to walk through.

Table Setting and Centerpiece

The table is covered with a sheet. Children may make their own place mats by placing stickers on construction paper, coloring with crayons and writing their names. Upon completion of the mats, cover with clear contact paper so the children may take home. For tableware, use paper plates, napkins and cups in bright colors. The centerpiece may be a toy or stuffed animal and balloons.

Menu

Cheese Sandwiches, cut into quarters
Peanut Butter and Jelly Sandwiches, cut into quarters
Assorted Fruit, cut into bite-size pieces
Ice Cream Cone Cupcakes
Apple Juice

Entertainment or Games

Shoe Surprise: Each child leaves a shoe in one room, then goes to another room where the hostess reads a story or sings songs. Meanwhile, a helper leaves a prize in each shoe for the children to discover.

Bubble Blowing: Mix $\frac{1}{8}$ cup dishwashing liquid, 1 teaspoon sugar, 1 quart water and 4 Tablespoons glycerine. Each child is given a bubble pipe and a paper cup with soap mixture. The children make as many bubbles as they can.

Play Dough Art: Let the children sit on a large plastic tablecloth. They may roll out play dough and cut with cookie cutters or form into animals or other objects. Play dough, packaged in a sealable plastic bag, is given to each child to take home.

PLAY DOUGH

½ cup salt
2 cups water
Food coloring, desired color
2 Tablespoons powdered alum
2 Tablespoons vegetable oil
2½ cups flour

1. Combine salt, water and food coloring. Boil until dissolved.
2. Add powdered alum, oil and flour. Mix well.
3. Pour onto floured surface. Knead 5 minutes.

Tip: *Store in covered container.*

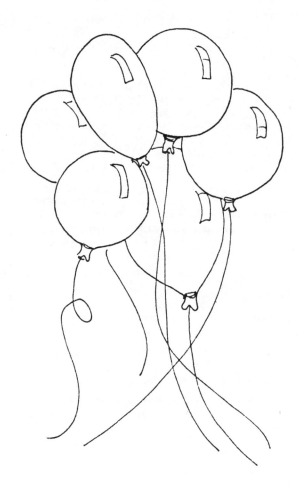

Space Age Blast Off!

Invitation

A rocket ship is cut from construction paper and party information is printed on the front.

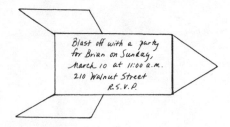

Table Setting and Centerpiece

A hanging rocket is made by taping together two ice cream tubs. (Empty tubs are available at many ice cream stores). Attach a nose cone made from gray construction paper. The rocket is sprayed silver. Attached to the tail section are "flame" streamers in yellow, red and orange. Place cards are 4-inch rockets cut from construction paper. Foil-covered, round cardboard serves as a "launching pad" place mat.

Menu

Moonwich (Burgers)
Comet Chips (Chips)
Bananaship (Bananas)
Saturn Soda
Rocket Cake

SATURN SODA

Scoop of orange sherbet in glass of orange soda.

ROCKET CAKE

Bake the birthday child's favorite cake in 2 square pans. Cut cake as illustrated. Place on foil-covered board and frost with yellow icing. Decorate with silver candles and child's name.

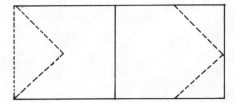

Entertainment or Games

Make A Space Helmet: Before the party, make the helmets by using empty ice cream tubs. Cut out a rectangular space for the eyes and spray paint silver. Allow to dry. When the children arrive, they are seated at a table so they can create their own helmet. Decorating items may include sequins, nails, screws, bolts, pipe cleaners, stickers, candy kisses and paper clips.

Airplane Sailing Contest: Children may make airplanes from colored construction paper. Have a contest to determine who can sail their plane the farthest distance. Give all children a prize.

Musical Moon Rock: Children sit in a circle and pass a "moon rock" around while the music plays. When the music stops, the child caught holding the "moon rock" is out.

Treasure Hunt

Invitation

A simple treasure map, as illustrated, is used as the invitation. Enclosed is an eye patch which the child guest may wear to the party.

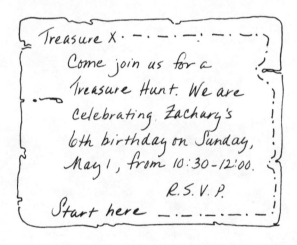

Treasure X · — · — · — : — · — ·
Come join us for a
Treasure Hunt. We are
Celebrating, Zachary's
6th birthday on Sunday,
May 1, from 10:30-12:00.
          R.S.V.P.
Start here — · — · — · — · —

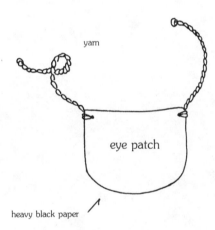

yarn

eye patch

heavy black paper

Decorations or Setting the Mood

A pirate's hat, skull and swords are placed on the front door. Nautical music or the sound track from "Pirates of the Caribbean" adds to the suspense of the children.

Table Setting and Centerpiece

A black or white tablecloth complements the treasure chest centerpiece. Small packages wrapped in silver and gold paper, coins, beads and trinkets fill the chest. Contrasting place mats complete this table setting. Black, white and silver helium-filled balloons with pirate faces are attached with silver ribbon to each child's chair.

Menu

Pizza Muffins
Fruit Salad (your favorite)
Monster Cookies
Ice Cream (your favorite)

Entertainment or Games

Treasure Hunt: The hostess accompanies the children and carries a cassette player. The tape recording outlines the clues for finding the treasure. Instructions may be, "Start at front door. Take five steps. Stop. Turn right. Take ten steps. Look for the next clue under the bush." Try to emulate the frightening laugh and sinister voice of a pirate, heightening the children's expectations. All clues lead to the "buried treasure." A sand box is the perfect place for the children to find a buried treasure box filled with toy prizes and foil-covered chocolate coins. Decorated and personalized, brightly-colored bags are provided for each child to fill with buried treasure.

Additional Children's Party Ideas

Dinosaur Party: Simple pictures are taken from coloring books to make invitations and decorations in dinosaur shapes.

Detective (Whodunnit?) Party: Decorate with foot prints, magnifying glasses, trench coat, etc. Games may include clues to hidden party favors, guessing objects by touch and sound or the board game "Clue." A short mystery story may be read to the children.

Hobo Party: This is a great alternative to trick-or-treating on Halloween and the costumes are easy to make. Serve simple foods such as hot dogs and baked beans. A neighborhood scavenger hunt is fun. Party favors are tied in bandannas on hobo sticks.

Circus Party: Hire a clown to do magic tricks and make balloon animals. Make-up is provided for making clown faces on the children. Snacks may include peanuts and popcorn. Boxes of animal cookies are sent home with the children.

Tea Party: This may be a "dress up like mommy" affair. Older girls might enjoy a demonstration on skin care and make-up by a cosmetologist. Serve dainty refreshments.

Cowboy Party: Roast hot dogs and marshmallows over a fire or grill. Sing cowboy songs and make a wigwam.

Holiday Parties: St. Patrick's Day, Easter, Fourth of July and Christmas are great times to have parties for children.

Driving Celebration

This party is great for a birthday party as well as when a teenager obtains his driver's license.

Invitation

An octagon is cut from red poster board and **"STOP"** is printed on it with a black or white pen. Inside it reads:

. . . to celebrate

Todd's 16th Birthday

Date _____

Time _____

Place _____

R.S.V.P. _____

Decorations or Setting the Mood

Road signs made from colored poster board are placed on doors throughout the house.

Table Setting and Centerpiece

On one side of the buffet table is the "Driver's License Cake." On the other side are three used oil cans tied with a bow. Flowers are placed in the punch-out holes. A fourth can is placed on top to form a pyramid and is filled with a variety of small traffic signs.

Menu

Soft Crepe Tortillas
Refried Beans
Soft Tacos
or
Haystack Special
Driver's License Cake
Ice Cream
Punch (your favorite)

DRIVER'S LICENSE CAKE

The cake is decorated to resemble a driver's license. A picture may be enlarged, wrapped in plastic and placed on the cake. The following information is printed on the cake:

\# _____

NAME _____

ADDRESS _____

CITY, STATE, ZIP _____

SEX   HAIR   EYES   HEIGHT   WEIGHT
M/F   Brn   Brn   5'4"   120

DATE OF BIRTH   _(month / day / year)_

X _____   _(Signature)_ _____

Entertainment or Games

Stuff a VW: The object is to get as many people as possible in a Volkswagen or other small car. Rules must be stated what body parts may be outside the car, but no body parts may be touching the ground.

Service Center Relay: For this relay, two cars and two teams are needed. It is fun to have the girls against the boys. At a given signal, teams must find the jack and a tire and place outside of the trunk, then check the oil and wash the windows. The team who finishes first is the winner. A BMW key chain or DMV driving booklet may be given as a prize.

Obstacle Course Relay: An obstacle course is created using traffic cones or similar objects. A "rider" sits in a wheelbarrow and a blindfolded "driver" pushes it. The "rider" gives directions to the "driver" telling him how to get to the end of the obstacle course. The team who completes the relay first wins.

Sweet 16 Birthday Party

Invitation

The invitation is made of pink and lavendar construction paper trimmed with white lace and a pink satin ribbon bow. Large white numbers are cut from construction paper. Party particulars are written inside. Cute gift suggestions are 16 one dollar bills, 16 packages of gum, a 16-ounce Hershey bar or 16 Hershey chocolate kisses.

Decorations or Setting the Mood

An English country garden atmosphere creates the mood for this special occasion. Silver balloons create a cloud-like effect and pink and lavendar crepe paper streamers line the ceiling. In a doorway is hung a Sugar Kissing Hoop encouraging the boys to kiss the birthday girl. A Sweet 16 Sugar Cube Corsage is pinned on the guest of honor.

Table Setting and Centerpiece

Baskets of fresh flowers are set on the tables covered with floral fabric tablecloths. Pink and lavendar napkins are folded fancily and placed on crystal plates at each setting. Serving pieces may be white or neutral baskets with plastic or glass liners.

SUGAR KISSING HOOP

Wrap surface of a 5¾-inch embroidery hoop with ribbon and decorate with lace. Sixteen sugar cubes are tied to ends of various lengths of ¼-inch pink or lavendar ribbon, which are attached to the decorated hoop, as illustrated. A ribbon hanging loop is attached to the center of the hoop and hung in a doorway.

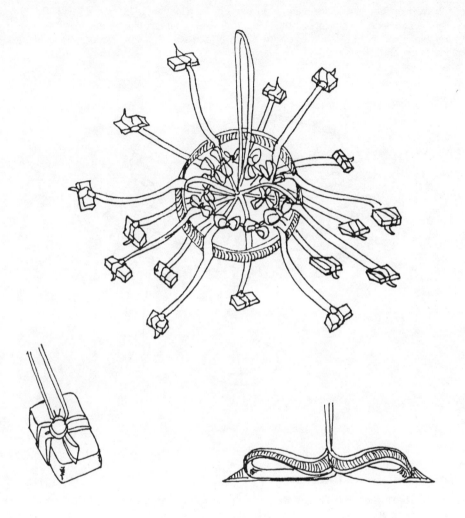

SWEET 16 SUGAR CUBE CORSAGE

Sixteen sugar cubes are tied to opposite ends of 8 1-yard strips of ¼-inch lavendar ribbon. Pick up each strip in the middle and tie into a bow. Sew through knots to connect all the strips, attaching a clasp-type pin. Fresh or silk flowers may be added to the corsage.

Menu

Rainbow Popcorn
Potato Salad (your favorite)
Stuffed Cheese Buns
Fresh Fruit Platter with Honey-Berry Dip
Sweet 16 Cake (Carrot Cake)
Frosty Banana Punch

SWEET 16 CAKE

Place 1 layer on pedestal cake plate lined with 12-inch paper doily. Spread with frosting. Place second layer. Frost sides and top of cake. Decorate like a hat, as illustrated. Position 1-inch wide ribbon to encircle the cake. Make ribbon bow and attach with hat pin. Decorate top of "hat" with a few tiny fresh or fabric flowers.

Entertainment or Games

True or False: Each guest must stand and relate three facts about herself. Only one fact is true and two others are false. Guests must decide which fact is true.

Teen Graduation

Invitation

Invitations are rolled-up white paper "diplomas," tied with class color ribbons. Inside the "diploma" is written the invitation which includes the officer's names, such as: "The Class President . . . announces class of . . . celebration at secretary . . . home."

Decorations or Setting the Mood

Decorate with balloons and streamers in class colors. A large poster is hung in a prominent place, displaying names of classmates under their baby pictures.

Table Setting and Centerpiece

The dining room table is decorated as the focal point. The tablecloth and napkins are in class colors and, of course, napkins are rolled diploma-style. Bookends enclosing school books are placed on either side of a large, fresh flower arrangement in the center of the table. Diplomas are interspersed among the flowers.

Menu

MENU I

Bean Dip
Salsa
Chips
Broiled Cheese Rolls
or
Mini-Pizzas
Onion Roulades
Orange-Lemon Custard Jello
Fresh Fruit Platter
Apple Cake
Vanilla Ice Cream
Raspberry Punch

MENU II

Fresh Vegetable Dip
Assorted Vegetable Tray
Green Salad (your favorite)
Cheese-Filled Manicotti
French Bread
Wild Raspberry Dessert
Assorted Bottled Drinks
or
Lime-Pineapple Punch

Entertainment or Games

Several of the class officers may initiate a few pantomimes. The first group portrays the major they plan to take in college. The second acts out a scene asking for a job. Each group guesses what the other group has pantomimed.

Up, Up and Away

Invitation

The invitation may be written on construction paper with colored felt-tip pens, then rolled up and inserted in a balloon. After the balloon is inflated, write with a felt-tip pen on the outside "Pop for Particulars." If unable to hand deliver, deflate balloon, place in envelope and mail.

Decorations or Setting the Mood

A miniature hot-air balloon is hung on the front door to greet the guests. Tethered to each chair and various other places around the room are helium-filled balloons held in place by brightly colored ribbons.

Table Setting and Centerpiece

Table is set with sky blue tablecloth and white paper place mats. On each place mat, a "hot-air balloon" is created with a brightly colored, dinner-size paper plate, a colored napkin folded in thirds for the basket and tethers of yarn connecting the balloon and basket. Glue ends of yarn to place mat and set plate and napkin, as illustrated.

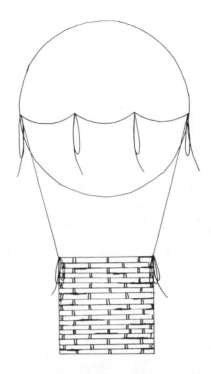

The centerpiece is made from a large, round decorated styrofoam ball. This is supported by dowels, simulating support ropes, placed in a square of styrofoam anchored to the inside bottom of a basket. The basket is lined with lettuce and filled with crisp, raw vegetables for dipping.

Menu

Lift-Off Appetizer with Vegetable Dip (Fresh Vegetable Dip)
High-in-the-Sky Salad (Layered Vegetable Salad)
Up, Up and Away Baked Beans (Baked Beans)
Ballooney Sandwiches (Mexican Rolls)
Basket Tarts (Cherry Tarts)
Helium Punch (Fruit Punch)

Entertainment or Games

Balloon Race 1: Divide guests into four teams. Each guest carries an inflated balloon on a spoon for a specified distance. The team finishing first wins.

Balloon Race 2: Each guest ties an inflated balloon to each ankle, then tries to pop everyone else's balloon while protecting his own. The last person with an unpopped balloon is the winner.

Goodwill Messages: A perfect ending to the party is to have each guest write a goodwill message which is inserted into a balloon. The balloons are filled with helium, tied with a ribbon and released as everyone says "good-bye."

Video Awards Night

Invitation

A clapboard invitation is made with white card stock and design is drawn with a black felt-tip pen.

Title: _____

Producer: _____

Location: _____

Date & Time: _____

Decorations or Setting the Mood

A larger version of the clapboard covers the front door. It reads:

> Location: HERE
> Time: TONIGHT

Table Setting and Centerpiece

On halved 3 x 5-inch colored note cards, write or print several popular commercial slogans. Glue cards to top of skewers and press into a carnation and daisy flower arrangement. Skewers may be cut in different lengths. Curly ribbon streamers and confetti may also decorate the arrangement. A white tablecloth is a nice contrast to the black paper plates and napkins.

Menu

Haystack Special
Brownie-Vanilla Ice Cream Dessert
Pepsi Generation (Pepsi Free, of course!)
Hi-C Punch

BROWNIE-VANILLA ICE CREAM DESSERT

Bake your favorite brownie mix in 9 x 9-inch pan. Soften ½ gallon vanilla ice cream to stirring consistency. Add large crumbled chunks of brownies. Spread into 11 x 14-inch pan and freeze. Must do ahead. Serve in individual bowls with Hot, Quick Chocolate Sauce.

HI-C PUNCH

Combine your favorite Hi-C Punch with 7-UP or Sprite.

Entertainment or Games

Commercial Slogans: As guests arrive, pin a commercial slogan on their back. While trying to discover the slogan, participants may ask three questions of any one person who may answer with only "yes" or "no." The slogan is moved to the collar or lapel when guessed.

Suggested slogans:

Kool-Aid, Kool-Aid - That's great!
Rice-A-Roni - A San Francisco Treat
Campbell's Soup is MmMmm Good
Wish I Were an Oscar Meyer Wiener
Mm, Ahh, Ohh, Poppin' Fresh Dough - Pillsbury
Fly the Friendly Skies with United
Nothing Says Lovin' Like Something from the Oven
If You Don't Look Good, We Don't Look Good - Sassoon
Put a Tiger in Your Tank - Texaco
Mikey Likes It - Life Cereal
Milk Has Something for Everybody
Finger Lickin' Good - Kentucky Fried Chicken
Nobody Doesn't Like Sara Lee
Snap, Crackle, Pop - Rice Krispies
How About a Hawaiian Punch?

Video Filming of Commercial: Divide the guests into small groups of four to six. Each group selects a favorite commercial to be video taped. The hostess may give ideas for commercials and allows certain areas and items to serve as props. Videos of each group are filmed separately in different rooms, out of sight from the other groups. A schedule for filming need not be set up as each group is ready at different times. Upon completion of the filming, the entire group is then brought into the viewing area where all may enjoy the creative craziness of their friends.

This is a fun activity for a freshmen high school class, with the plan to save the video to show again at their senior class party! The passing of time increases the comedy of it all.

Back From The Future
25th Class Reunion

Invitation

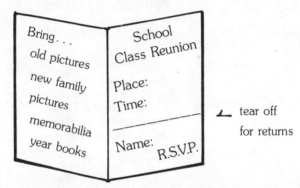

Bring...
old pictures
new family
pictures
memorabilia
year books

School
Class Reunion

Place:
Time:

Name:
R.S.V.P.

◢ tear off
for returns

Enclose R.S.V.P. card with addressed and stamped return envelope.

Decorations or Setting the Mood

Two large tables are set up. One may be filled with nostalgic memorabilia brought by the guests, such as band uniforms, sweaters, old love notes, programs, dried corsages, old pictures, etc. Another table is for everyone's yearbooks - have a resigning ceremony!

A basket is filled with lists of names and current addresses of as many classmates as possible. Roll the lists up diploma-style with ribbon tied around each - in class colors, of course. On departure, each guest is given a list to keep in touch for the 50th!

Up-to-date pictures of classmates with their families are displayed. Classmates bring eight to ten slides of home, family, etc. for a slide show. Each classmate and spouse should have a name tag. These may be made from cardboard or professionally made like a plastic-covered badge.

Plan nostalgic-type food.

If you don't
recognize me...I'm

Jane Doe

Class of '63
Orange High

If you don't
recognize me...I'm

John Doe

husband of
Jane Doe

Class of '63

25 years

Jane Doe

Reunion

Name of School

Table Setting and Centerpiece

Class colors should be used for tablecloth and napkins. Use class flowers for centerpiece. Pennants may be tucked into the centerpiece bouquet.

Menu

MENU I

Mushroom Tarts
Cheese Tempters
Asparagus Roll-Ups
Lime-Pineapple Salad
Mandarin Salad
Curried Rice-Mushroom Casserole
Petite Peas Piquant
Ice Cream Roll with Raspberry Sauce
Peach Delight

MENU II

Hot Artichoke Dip
Fresh Vegetable Tray
French Bread Pizza
Broccoli-Onion Pizza
Olive-Avocado Pizza
Mushroom-Artichoke Pizza
Zucchini Pizza
Coconutty Cake
or
Glazed Apple Pie Bars
Black Cows (Root Beer Floats)

Entertainment or Games

Class Reunion Phone Calls: A collect phone call is made to classmates who could not attend the reunion.

Class Reunion Picture: Before leaving, a class reunion picture is taken.

Class Reunion Momentos: As a parting gift for each classmate, visit a coin shop and buy enough quarters from the year of graduation for each classmate. Leave in the little plastic pouch to keep the gift special.

Big Kid's Birthday Party

Invitation

Invitations may be created with stickers on brightly-colored paper. Hand print the information, using the printing style a first grader might use. Instruct guests to dress as their favorite childhood character (Roy Rogers, Raggedy Ann, clowns, etc.) and to bring a small, wrapped gag or white elephant gift.

Decorations or Setting the Mood

Decorations should be very childlike with lots of balloons and crepe paper streamers. Stack in a corner large boxes covered with paper and "A B C's" painted on the sides to resemble blocks. Place bowls of bubblegum, gumdrops, pretzels and M&M's around the room. Have children's music playing on the stereo.

Table Setting and Centerpiece

Place mats are made in the shape of a fun object such as a kite. Fold napkins in kite shape. Small, colored paper kites glued to toothpicks and stuck into individually-wrapped pieces of bubble gum are used for place cards. For a fun centerpiece, different colored helium balloons are tied with ribbons to a heavy object. Small paper kites are tied to the ribbons. Write "Happy Birthday" with a felt-tip marker on the balloons or purchase "Happy Birthday" balloons. Allow some of the balloons to hang loosely from the ceiling.

Menu

Fruit Whiz With Fresh Fruit Garnish
Guacamole Dip
Vegetable Burritos
Chocolate Chip Chocolate Cake
or
Carrot Cake
Ice Cream (your favorite)

Entertainment or Games

Song Scramble: This game will organize the guests into choral groups and bring to light any latent vocal talent. All of the singing is so spontaneous that even the confirmed shower soloist will find himself joining in. Write out several songs, line by line, but only one line per slip of paper. The number of song lines must equal the number of guests (32 guests = 32 lines of song). Shuffle the papers and pass them out to guests. The fun begins when the guests enter into a mad scramble to find the holders of all the slips that will complete their song. As soon as the group assembles correctly, it can begin to sing its song. The first group to do this is the winner. Suggested songs are "You Are My Sunshine," "Bicycle Built For Two" and "I Love You Truly."

Balloon Popping: At least two teams of six or eight each are needed. Teams are seated in chairs facing each other. Each team member is given a balloon. At the signal, the first person of each team blows up his balloon, sits on it and bursts it. The next person blows up his balloon, sits on it and bursts it. Continue until all have burst their balloons. The first team to finish is the winner.

Chinese Auction: All guests are asked to bring a small wrapped gag or white elephant gift. Each person draws a number. The person with the lowest number selects and unwraps his gift. The next person may choose another wrapped gift or the one already unwrapped. If he chooses the gift the first person unwrapped, the first person chooses another one from the wrapped gifts and unwraps it. Each succeeding person may choose a gift of any other person or pick a wrapped one. At the end of the drawing, the first person may choose from all the gifts.

Bon Voyage

Whether your friends are planning a trip to the British Isles (the theme of this party), a cruise to Mexico or a visit to a special corner of the United States, there is no nicer way to express good wishes than by giving them a gala farewell. If you can make this a surprise, it is even more fun.

Invitation

An 8 x 12-inch, sturdy, navy paper is folded into a 4 x 6-inch "passport." This is written in gold lettering on the front of the invitation. Inside is a funny picture of the traveling person(s) under which the details of the party are written.

An alternate suggestion for an invitation is a ticket holder (available from a travel agency) with party information written inside. Mail in a business-size envelope.

Decorations or Setting the Mood

Masses of red, white and blue balloons, streamers and a Union Jack flag will capture the British spirit and set the mood.

Table Setting and Centerpiece

A large world globe surrounded with a wreath of red, white and blue flowers interspersed with small British flags is the centerpiece for the buffet table. Napkins are tied with red, white and blue ribbons. Posters of various "Ports of Call" (available from a travel agency) decorate the walls.

Menu

English Bibb Salad
Noodle-Broccoli Casserole
Tomatoes Stuffed with Mushrooms
Deviled Eggs (your favorite)
Popovers with Butter and Jelly
English Trifle
Sparkling Apple Cider

Entertainment or Games

Each guest is asked to bring a small gift item for a travel kit, such as needle and thread, folding scissors, shampoo, plastic rain hat, etc. The hostess may have pull-off labels available for guests' names and addresses, which the traveler(s) may take instead of an address book.

Detective's Dilemma
Crazy Party

Invitation

A black card is decorated with a large white question mark. Inside the invitation reads:

You are invited to a Mystery Dinner
Date:
Place:
Can you come? If so, call the
number below to discover
the name of your host.
(phone number)

Decorations or Setting the Mood

The front door is decorated with a large black question mark. The host and hostess are dressed in black and the hostess' face is covered with a black veil.

Table Setting and Centerpiece

The table is covered with a white cloth, and black place mats display large white question marks. A pencil is laid on each place mat. After all the guests are seated, explain that they will receive a menu filled with fictitious names.

Menu

The menu cover is a folded 8½ x 11-inch sheet of black construction paper. Displayed on the front is a large white question mark. On the inside are two menu-order forms, as printed below. A sheet of carbon is placed between the two forms. One form is given to the waiter and the guest keeps the other.

PRINTED INSTRUCTIONS

1. Guests sign name to their own menu.
2. Select entire four-course meal, five items per course, using all 20 names by number.
3. Do not suggest that the silverware is included in the menu. The surprise is yet to come!
4. There is to be no collaborating with dinner guests. Let them make their own mistakes!
5. No cover charge. Tipping is not only permitted, but encouraged!
6. Emily Post's rules of etiquette will not apply.
7. Please accept this menu following dinner with your complaints (our compliments).

SERVING SUGGESTIONS

1. If paper plates are used, only one per person per course is needed. If regular dinner service is used, affix waterproof name tags and rinse after each course.
2. The traffic pattern in the kitchen must be planned so that the food may be accessed efficiently. Write the number and name of each item on pieces of cardboard or heavy paper. Place these numbered guides beside the food items. The guests' menus are read and filled by number rather than by the name of the item.
3. Two people work together as a couple to serve; one person working in the kitchen to fill the plates and the other to serve as a waiter. One couple is needed for 8-12 people.
4. The menus are kept together by table. Each course is served and cleared by table.

MENU   ORDER FORM
          Order By Number

1. White Fog   Order Five Items Per Course By Number
2. Black Magic or Bug's Bunny Surprise
3. Gerber's Get-up   COURSE
4. Irish Trees
5. Necker's Menace   1. _____ _____ _____ _____ _____
6. Expensive Car
   Strip Teaser   2. _____ _____ _____ _____ _____
7. Boxer's Cut
8. Billy Goat   3. _____ _____ _____ _____ _____
9. Flubber Blubber
10. Expectant's Nibbler   4. _____ _____ _____ _____ _____
11. Driver's Dilemma
12. Dental Hygienist
13. Lazy Cabin
14. Chip Off the Old Block
15. Fruit of Antiquity
16. Lover's Delight
17. Sun Valley Steamer
18. Underground Icicle
19. Jack
20. Arctic Circle

MENU (Master Sheet for Kitchen Use)

1. Soup . . . . *White Fog*
2. Cake . . . . *Black Magic (devil's food)* or
                                                  Bug's Bunny Surprise (carrot)
3. Napkin . . . . *Gerber's Get-up*
4. Marinated Broccoli Salad . . . . *Irish Trees*
5. Green Onion . . . . *Necker's Menace*
6. Rolls . . . . *Expensive Car*
   French Bread . . . . *Strip Teaser*
7. Punch . . . . *Boxer's Cut*
8. Butter . . . . *Billy Goat*
9. Jello . . . . *Flubber Blubber*
10. Pickle . . . . *Expectant's Nibbler*

11. Fork .... *Driver's Dilemma*
12. Celery Stick .... *Dental Hygienist*
13. Cottage Cheese Loaf .... *Lazy Cabin*
14. Toothpick .... *Chip Off the Old Block*
15. Olive .... *Fruit of Antiquity*
16. Spoon .... *Lover's Delight*
17. Baked Potato .... *Sun Valley Streamer*
18. Carrots .... *Underground Icicle*
19. Knife .... *Jack*
20. Ice Cream .... *Arctic Circle*

Entertainment or Games

Of course, the mystery dinner itself is the entertainment. From the menu, guests do not know what they are ordering. The suspense is heightened as everyone awaits the first course, only to discover they may not have eating utensils or that their dessert is eaten with celery or carrot sticks serving as forks. Guests may not borrow anything from their neighbors. Watching the guests using toothpicks, celery sticks, olives or even fingers instead of utensils is hilarious! The evening is full of laughter and fun.

Farmer John's Garden Party

Invitation

In early spring, a package of seeds is sent with instructions to plant and harvest for a garden party in the fall. Then in the fall, send an invitation to the party and ask guests to bring a food dish made from their garden.

Seed packets are attached to folded construction paper with the heading, "Farmer's Garden Party." Inside the invitation reads:

Plant this seed in your backyard.
Be it peas or green swiss chard.
Now's the time to dig and plant,
So do it now before you can't!

Give water, sun and tender care,
And add to that your fervent prayer
That when your weeding's at an end
You have some plants that you can tend.

Now, when the peas have filled the pod
And leafy chard shades o'er the sod,
Go forth to reap with tools in hand
For harvest time is in the land!

Next, cut the chard and cook the peas
And make a dish that's sure to please;
Then make your way to (name)'s nest
To celebrate fall's harvest fest!

Decorations or Setting the Mood

In the front yard is a grouping of watermelon, cantaloupe, spaghetti squash and other garden vegetables. The host and hostess wear bib overalls, a red checked shirt and a bandanna around their neck or in their back pocket. A straw hat completes the look of "Farmer John." The setting for the party is on the lawn or patio. A wheelbarrow filled with ice holds the canned drinks. Garden tools are leaning against the side of the house.

Table Setting and Centerpiece

A white tablecloth is a perfect background to show off the bright colors of a vegetable ensemble from the garden or fresh cut garden flowers. Bandannas or red gingham napkins complement this setting.

Menu

Assorted Vegetable Dippers
Assorted Crackers and Chips
Spinach Dip
Baked Beans
Salsa
Potato Salad (your favorite)
Rolls and Butter
Canned Soft Drinks

Additional "garden" dishes are brought by the guests.

Entertainment or Games

Enjoy a wheelbarrow race or potato sack race, maybe even both.

Seems Like Only Polyesterday

Invitation

The front of the invitation is printed: "Seems like only polyester. . ." Inside the card reads, "We were celebrating *(name)*'s sixteenth birthday. Now it's time to count the candles and cut the cake for his/her *(number)*! 'Don't Leave It to Beaver' to help him/her celebrate. Be there!" Birthday gift suggestions may be items equal to the age of the birthday person, such as pennies in a denture container.

Decorations or Setting the Mood

The mood is reminiscent of the sixties. Of course, sixties music is playing, and the guests are wearing sixties styles. Momentos of that era are placed around the room.

Table Setting and Centerpiece

For this buffet-style party, the tablecloth is of double knit polyester fabric. The centerpiece may be a peace symbol surrounded by a bouquet of flowers. Ken and Barbie dolls may be used, dressed in the sixties' style or maybe even mousekateer hats.

Menu

Tossed Green Garden Salad (your favorite)
Asparagus-Leek Chowder
Stuffed Hot Dog Rolls
Chocolate Prune Cake
Vanilla Ice Cream
Spiced Pineapple Sparkle
or
Raspberry Crush

Entertainment or Games

Name That Tune: Using songs from the sixties, play the beginning of a song for one team. The team as a group tries to guess the tune. If the first team does not name the song within 30 seconds, the other team tries to guess.

Acting Charades: The game is played with two teams, whose object is to be the first team to collect 50 points. On each card, there are four charade categories from the sixties: (1) TV shows and characters, (2) movies, (3) books, plays and phrases and (4) songs. A player selects a charade card and relates to his team the category he has chosen. He has 30 seconds to think about how to perform the charade for his teammates and two minutes to complete the charade. If the team guesses the charade correctly in the allotted time, it receives ten points. If the team does not complete the charade in time, the next team player takes a turn.

Roasting the Birthday Person: Everyone is to relate a funny or embarrassing tale about the birthday person.

Stroke of Midnight
Surprise Birthday Raid

Invitation

Invitation is drawn to resemble the front of a refrigerator door, opening to the inside. The "door" reads: "Sh-h-h - It's a Surprise Midnight Birthday Raid! On the inside is written:

TO CELEBRATE *(name)*'s 40th BIRTHDAY

Time: Meet in front of the guest of honor's home at 11:30 p.m.

Dress: Night clothes preferred.

Gift ideas: Pamper yourself items such as soaps, sponges, magazines, chocolates, etc.

Decorations or Setting the Mood

This is a surprise to the birthday person, but the spouse or roommate needs to know of the plan so guests may help set up. Everyone comes in night clothes such as robes, pajamas, slippers, rollers, etc. The house is decorated quietly before the birthday person is awakened. Decorations may be as elaborate as desired. Lighting is kept very low and soft. The birthday guy or gal is awakened at 12:01 and brought to where the guests are waiting to wish him/her a very early Surprise Happy Birthday!

Table Setting and Centerpiece

Cover table with brightly-colored paper tablecloth and use paper plates and napkins.

Menu

Hot Artichoke Dip with Assorted Crackers
Fresh Vegetable or Fruit Platter
Glorious Berry Cheesecake
Iced Herbal Sleepy-Time Tea
Hot Chocolate

Entertainment or Games

Everyone brings something to go in a "Pamper Yourself" basket. A note in the basket reads: "Go ahead and pamper yourself today - you deserve it, after all, it's your birthday!!" Table games or old movies are appropriate for this early party.

The Good Old Days

Invitation

Old snapshots may be reduced and copies made. These are placed on yellowed parchment paper and party particulars written inside. An alternate invitation may be a "ticket," as illustrated.

To advertise "The Good Old Days," posters may illustrate a woman in a period costume standing next to an unrolled scroll with the date and time inscribed. Old English lettering is used to outline the party information.

Decorations or Setting the Mood

Pioneer-day costumes are very appropriate for this occasion and may include high-buttoned or tied shoes, gingham bonnets or other old hats, long dresses, aprons, etc.

Dried corn, corn stalks, dried gourds and bouquets of dried flowers set the mood for "The Good Old Days." Oil lamps and tallow candles in old-fashioned candle holders of pewter and wood are used for lighting. Old quilts drape the furniture or may be tacked on the walls. Other decorations might include an old coffee grinder, butter press or mold, antique musical instruments, old cameras, iron pots or kettles, crocks, copper pans or any other antique item.

Table Setting and Centerpiece

A quilt covers the table and handkerchiefs are used for napkins. An alternative is a gingham or checked tablecloth with matching napkins. The centerpiece may be several flowerpots of flowering plants placed in a large basket or a bouquet of dried flowers.

Tin, pewter or old china plates are used. Drinks are served in old jam jars or small canning jars. Hot cider is served from an old enamel coffee pot. If this is a sit-down dinner, small baskets filled with candies may be used as place card holders, which may be given as party favors.

Menu

Buttermilk Biscuits
Butter and Honey
Fresh Green Bean and Yellow Bell Pepper Salad
Cabbage Salad
Baked Potatoes with the following Toppings:
Broccoli-Cheese Sauce
Sour Cream and Chopped Green Onions
Sautéed Mushrooms
Grated Cheeses
Perk-Up-a-Potato
Apple-Pecan Cobbler
Molasses Taffy Squares
Hot Cider
Gingerale

Entertainment or Games

Old Movies: If using the "Bird Cage Theatre" theme, old-time movies starring W. C. Fields, Charlie Chaplin or other favorites may be shown.

Best Costume: Award prizes for best dressed, most original costume, etc. Prizes may be a 1890 Sears Catalogue, an "A-oo-gah" horn from an old car, an old iron, etc.

Baby Picture Guess Game: Everyone brings their baby picture. The person correctly identifying the largest number of pictures wins a prize.

Charades: Each guest is given a bag with an old object enclosed. Participants must act out an idea from the item in their bag. The charade is then guessed by the participants.

Character Analysis: Each person writes information about himself and does not include his name. Suggested information may include favorite food, middle name, hobby, favorite TV show, age when first kissed, favorite sports, favorite color or nickname. Everyone turns in the completed information which is shuffled and redistributed to the guests. Each person reads aloud the information slip. The group then tries to guess the described person. This is a fun way to get better acquainted.

Clothespin Relay: A clothesline is strung from one side of the room to the other, placement being shoulder high to the average person. Place clothespins on the line. The object is to run to the line, remove one clothespin with your teeth, using no hands, and bring it back to the team. The relay is continued until one team wins.

Birthday Turnover: This game is similar to the old game, "Fruit Basket Upset." Everyone sits in a circle with an equal number of chairs as people. "It" stands in the center without a chair and calls out three months of the year. Everyone who has a birthday during one of those three months gets up and tries to sit in a vacated seat. "It" also tries to find a vacant seat. The person left without a seat becomes "It." The big move is when "It" calls "Leap Year." Everyone gets up and finds another seat.

Paper Relay: By sucking on a straw, a piece of paper four inches square is picked up and carried around a goal and back. If the paper is dropped, the participant must start over.

Taffy Pull: Pulling taffy (see recipe) is lots of fun with a partner.

Baseball Party

Invitation

A baseball "cap" is cut from dark blue felt and stitched with white thread to highlight sections of the cap. Attached to the crown is a small button. The felt cap is stitched to a white card and party information is written inside.

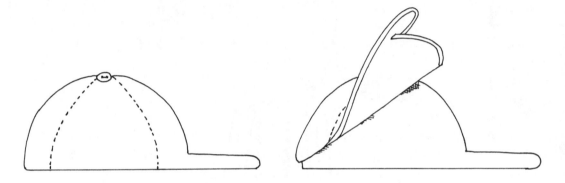

An alternate invitation is a baseball. Fold and double a white note card and cut into a round ball, leaving a 1-inch segment uncut. Zig-zag stitch outline of baseball in red. Party information is written inside.

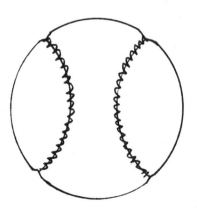
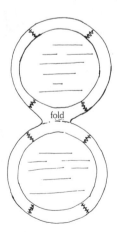

Guests are asked to wear a baseball uniform, if available, a major league souvenir shirt and cap or to carry a pennant.

Decorations or Setting the Mood

The house or back yard is decorated with red, white and blue crepe paper, balloons and major league souvenir pennants.

Table Setting and Centerpiece

A blue tablecloth, red napkins and white plastic utensils are used. The centerpiece is a baseball glove filled with an arrangement of red carnations, white mums and blue statice, with small American flags or small baseball pennants interspersed.

Menu

Hot Dogs with Mustard and Relish
Popcorn in Stadium-Size Bags
Canned Soda Pop
Carnation Frozen Malts

Entertainment or Games

Sing the National Anthem: A guest or all the guests may sing the national anthem.

The Wave: If the party is during the World Series and guests are watching the game on television, the "wave" may be done during commercial breaks.

Major League Speaker: A few major league teams provide a speaker free of charge. Contact the nearest team office for further information.

Party Favors: Bags of peanuts, baseball cards or small pennants are given to the guests as party favors, which may be traded if desired.

Hole-in-One

Invitation

Leather card stock (available from a printer) is used to make a brown golf bag with small clubs inside, bearing information about the party. Golf clubs are inserted into the golf bag.

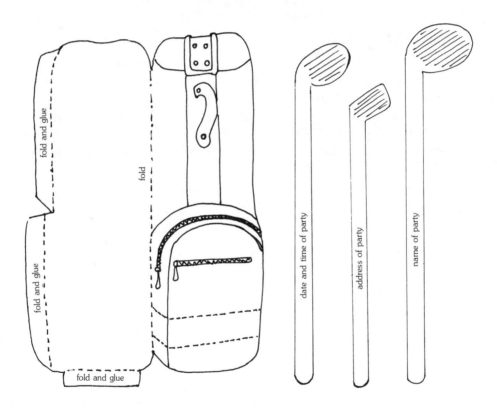

Decorations or Setting the Mood

A sign that reads "Clubhouse" is posted on the front of the house. The host and hostess wear Scottish golf attire, plus four's and knee socks. If guests park a distance from the house, transport them in a golf cart.

Table Setting and Centerpiece

In the center of the table is a "Golf Ball Cake."

A "golf course" is created with a green tablecloth and yellow "flagstick" napkins. To make flagsticks, open cocktail napkins, then refold point-to-point. Trim edge and fold to make a "flag." Attach an 8-inch small green plant stake (available from a nursery) by folding edge of napkin over stick and taping.

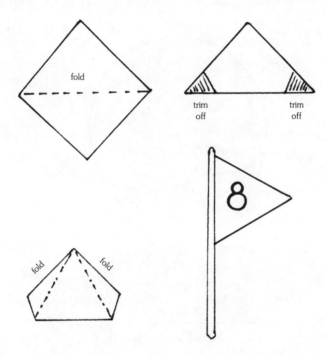

In the drinking glasses are "golf ball ice cubes" made in specialty trays (available from gadget shops or mail order catalogs).

Menu

Basket Filled with French Bread, Rolls and Croissants
Crock of Butter
Peach Bavarian Salad
Pasta Primavera Salad
Mandarin Salad
Hot German Potato Salad
Curry Chicken Salad
Tabouli
Golf Ball Cake
Perrier Water
or
Sparkling Apple Cider

GOLF BALL CAKE

Bake 2 halves of cake in medium-size, round stainless steel mixing bowls. Put 2 halves together with frosting and place on top of kitchen funnel (yellow plastic if available). Funnel is attached to a 12-inch square board with a long nail. If end of funnel is larger than nail, pack funnel with steel wool, then pour with mixture of flour and water. Let set until dry before moving. If available, use plaster of Paris. Using electric knife, shape cake until it is the shape of a golf ball. Cover with white frosting. Using the back of a teaspoon, make small "dimples" in the frosting.

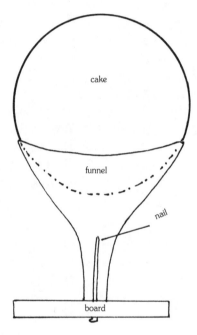

Entertainment or Games

Mixer: Hide golf items on guests as they arrive. Each guest is given a list of things to find. On the list beside each item is a place for the signature of the person wearing a hidden object.

Suggestions for items and possible hiding places:

Golf tee - through buttonhole
Green repairer - attached to belt like a buckle
Golf pencil - behind the ear of someone with long hair
Golf shoe kilties - on someone's shoe
Golf club - down a man's pant leg with only the "head" sticking out
Ball marker - taped to clothing
Score card - attached to inside of sweater
Golf sweater
Scotch tape - attached to eye glasses
Straight pin
Flesh-colored golf glove - keep hand in pocket as much as possible

Rent Video: Rent video of major golf tournament.

Golf Trivia: Play the game, "Golf Trivia".

Super Bowl Sunday

Invitation

Small, plastic footballs may be purchased at a toy store. Cut a slit in the top of each football and insert sheet with party information. Deliver in person. If a mailed invitation is preferred, use a solid red bandanna like the referees use, writing party information with a magic marker pen. Fold and mail in an envelope.

Decorations or Setting the Mood

Invite a local cheerleading team to come and do their routines on the front lawn. The cheerleaders are dressed in their team outfits and matching pompons.

Table Setting and Centerpiece

A deep bowl filled with chrysanthemums is placed inside a football helmet. The helmet is set in a cradle of ferns to balance it. A favorite team's colors are used for the tablecloth, paper plates, napkins and flowers.

Menu

Tex-Mex Dip
Cheese Enchiladas
Mixed Green Salad (your favorite) with Avocados and
"Good Seasons" Herb Dressing
Old South Pralines
Apricot-Nut Logs
Cream Cheese Bars
Crunchy Chocolates
Poppycock
Hot Chocolate and Assorted Canned Sodas

Entertainment or Games

Super Bowl on TV: Watch the Super Bowl on television.

Super Bowl Wager Pool: A "wager pool" may be done. Donate the money won to the favorite charity of the winner. "Odds" chart illustration:

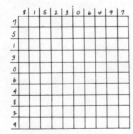

Each square represents a $1.00 wager. Person betting on a score signs his name in a square.

Olympiad

This party is great for a school class or youth group. Advanced preparation from the guests adds to the fun. The party emphasis is sports and the international aspects of the Olympic Games.

Invitation

White 3 x 5-inch note cards display the Olympiad insignia on the front and the party information is written inside. Each guest is assigned a nation to represent and must dress accordingly. Track clothes are worn underneath the costume.

Decorations or Setting the Mood

A gymnasium is an ideal party site. A local park or large yard is also a good choice. For decorations, use balloons and crepe paper in the five colors of the Olympic insignia - blue, yellow, black, green and red. Travel posters (available from travel agency) representing the assigned nations are hung on the walls.

Table Setting and Centerpiece

The white tablecloth reflects the vivid colors of the five Olympic rings as seen in the paper plates and napkins. Half a watermelon, cut side down, is placed on a large platter and used as a base for the centerpiece. The different country flags are drawn and colored on 3 x 5-inch cards, attached to skewers and inserted in the watermelon. International dolls and small trinkets representing the various countries surround the platter.

Menu

Tacos
Fruit Spears
Fortune Cookies
Olympiad Cake
Gatorade

An international menu may be simple or elaborate. Consider a menu that is assembled easily away from home. If the party is at a home, add a quiche and a green salad with feta cheese and Greek olives.

OLYMPIAD CAKE

Bake favorite cake in 9 x 13-inch pan. Frost with white icing and use decorator's gel to draw the 5 rings of the Olympic insignia.

Entertainment or Games

National Flags: Art supplies are set up at a table for guests to draw and color the flag of the country they are representing. The completed flags are covered with clear contact paper and used as place mats for the party.

National Anthems: An activity which older children may enjoy is listening to the national anthems of various countries and trying to match the song with the country.

Decathalon: A decathalon competition, indoors or outdoors, is planned according to the age of the guests and the facilities available. Choose ten events and keep cumulative team scores and/or individual scores for medals. Score five points for first place, four points for second place, etc.

Suggested events:

1.	Frisbee Throw:	Three tries to hit a target, measure and compare each competitor's closest effort.
2.	Balloon Kick:	Race kicking a balloon to the finish line without using hands.
3.	Bicycle Race:	Ride once around the block, timed or used as a relay.
4.	Backward Run:	If space is limited, use heats.
5.	Basketball:	Each player has five chances to throw a ball through the hoop or into a clean trash can.
6.	Relay Race:	Fun in a pool.
7.	Obstacle Course	
8.	Volleyball Game	
9.	Pillowcase Race	
10.	Duck Walk Race	
11.	Hopping Race	
12.	Broad Jump	

"Gold and silver medals" are gold or silver foil-covered chocolate coins attached to ribbon necklaces. Victory badges may be made by attaching short strips of crepe paper to flattened aluminum cupcake cups.

Party Favors: As party favors, guests are given their flag place mat and a small gift or candy from a foreign country. These international items are available from specialty or gourmet shops, foreign markets, delicatessens and shops such as Pier 1 Imports or Cost Plus.

After Eight

Invitation

Hand write invitation on ecru stationery, roll into a scroll and seal with wax. Drop into a dry, empty champagne bottle, recork and tie with a silver or gold bow. A messenger delivers the invitation. If champagne bottles are not available, send a long-stemmed red rose or a gourmet chocolate rose with invitation enclosed in the delivery box.

The invitation note should be handwritten in ink on personal informals, monogrammed or initialed note papers or just simple, elegant undecorated notes. Clearly state the time, place and date, and if formal or semi-formal attire is required. An R.S.V.P. number or card is included.

Decorations or Setting the Mood

Classical music is playing on the stereo. A local violinist or harpist provides the dinner music. Lights are dimmed and candles are lit. A few bouquets of fresh flowers may be placed around the room. Hors d'oeuvres and canapes are sitting on the coffee table.

Table Setting and Centerpiece

The table is draped in white satin moire. Chair cushions may also be wrapped. Mirrored place mats will reflect the beauty of fine china, glassware and silver. White napkins and silver napkin rings may be used or napkins may be folded fancily and placed in water goblets. Tall white candles are in silver or crystal candleholders. Arrange a low centerpiece of a few calla lilies or branches of white orchids, no higher than 12 inches. A bouquet of white roses in a silver bowl is also an elegant touch.

Menu

MENU I
Tomato-Cheese Salad with Cucumbers
Spinach and Mock Beef Dumplings
Mushroom-Onion Cream Sauce
Parsleyed Cauliflower
Green Beans with Cashews
Rolls and Butter
Oreo Cheesecake

MENU II
Curry-Carrot Soup
Spring Asparagus Salad
Creamed Chicken with Peas in Patty Shells
Tomatoes with Mushroom-Artichoke Filling
Broccoli with Parsley Vinaigrette
Rolls and Butter
Cheesecake with Raspberry Sauce

MENU III

Avocado Soup
or
Zucchini Soup
Spinach-Berry Salad
Stroganoff
Baby Carrots with Green Onions
Peas with Water Chestnuts
Rolls and Butter
Lemon Angel Torte

Entertainment or Games

Music is a must! It should be soft and muted, a good background for conversation.

The main entertainment of a formal gourmet dinner is usually the exchange of conversation between the host and hostess and their guests. It is a perfect time to enjoy the guests, the lovely dinner and the enchanting ambiance of a very special evening.

Backward Party

Think backward! The object is to do everything possible in a backward manner. Teens and adults find this to be a real challenge.

Invitation

Invitation is written backward starting in the lower right corner. Tracing paper is used to make a master copy, then photocopied. At the bottom of invitation, a suggestion is made to use a mirror for easier reading. Of course, the dress code is for everyone to wear their clothing backward.

Decorations or Setting the Mood

When the guests arrive, the host opens the door, backs out and greets the guests saying, "Good-bye, thanks for coming." The guests walk backward throughout the party. Each guest is given a name tag with his name printed backward.

Menu

The menu consists of recipes which may easily be served backward. Start with ice cream sundaes or banana splits - cherry at the bottom of the dish, then nuts, whipped cream, syrup, ice cream and bananas. The next course may be spaghetti and garlic bread. Parmesan cheese is sprinkled on the bottom of the plate, then the sauce and the spaghetti on top. The bread is placed butter-side down. End with salad, dressing on the bottom and beverage.

As guests leave, offer an appetizer such as cheese and crackers, tell them "Hello, it's good to see you," and show them out the door.

Entertainment or Games

Races: Many games are easily converted to backward play. A sack race which is run as a relay with teams may be done backward. With a large grocery bag on each foot, the players must shuffle to a given point and back, then pass the sacks to the next team member. At the end of the relay, a prize is given to the team finishing last. A three-legged race may also be run backward.

Scrambled Anatomy: Players are seated in a circle with a player who is "It" in the middle. "It" approaches another player and says, "This is my thumb" while touching his toe. While "It" counts backward from five to one, the approached player must do the same thing "It" did, only backward. He must say "This is my toe" while touching his thumb. If "It" finishes counting before the player finishes and does it correctly, the player becomes "It." The game continues with endless possible combinations.

Reverse Spelling: Divide guests into two equal teams and give each a set of letters consisting of file cards with one letter on each, written with a heavy felt-tip pen. A list of words is made ahead of time to be sure all sets have the correct number of letters. Each team places its set of letters on the floor. The word to spell is announced. Each team hurriedly scrambles to find the letters to form the word. The team members line up to spell the word backward, of course. The first team finished wins a point. Difficulty of selected words depends on the age group of guests.

Here's the Answer—What's the Question? The group is divided into several teams. Each team is given a number, a pencil and a paper pad. A secretary and a runner is designated for each team. The host reads the answer, the team members collaborate to decide the question, the secretary writes down the question and hands it to the runner, who rushes it to the host. The first correct question received is kept. The team's number is on the paper. At the end of the game, prizes are given to every team except the winners. After a different game is played, give the winners prizes.

Example answers and questions:

A: December 21
Q: What is the shortest day of the year?

A: Christopher Columbus
Q: Who discovered America?

Film "Back to the Future": The "backward" games liven the spirit and activity of the party, but if a more passive entertainment is desired, rent the film "Back to the Future."

Bag-a-Party

Invitation

A small lunch bag is the invitation and has the party information written on the outside. Use descriptive, catchy phrases such as, "It's fall! School has started, so let's have a 'bag of fun!' " or "bag a party." Place in an envelope and mail or hand deliver to guests.

Decorations or Setting the Mood

Carved pumpkins with candles inside or luminaries line the walkway to the front door and serve as outside lighting. Decorate with fall leaves, pumpkins and popcorn balls.

Table Setting and Centerpiece

The table is covered with a bright, fall-colored tablecloth accented with flattened "grocery bag" place mats. A pumpkin, filled with chrysanthemums, marigolds and asters, surrounded at the base with fall leaves, is the centerpiece. Food is served to each guest in a colored bag and sealed with various colored stickers. For a festive touch, seal the bag by punching two holes at the top, insert thin patterned or solid-colored ribbon, tie in a bow and curl ends. Dessert may be served in a separate decorated bag.

An alternate table setting may be a tablecloth in a bright color, covered with flattened paper bags of many sizes. If serving buffet-style, arrange "bags of eats" on one side of the table and bags of dessert on the other side. The punch bowl is placed in the middle.

Menu

Party Popcorn
or
Poppycock
Surprise Frenchies
Carrot and Celery Sticks
Wheat Sticks
Apple Dumplings
Orange-Cranberry Zing

Entertainment or Games

Paper Bag Relay: Divide the group into teams. If there is an unequal number of players on any team, one member must compete more than once during the relay. The leader of each team is given two large paper bags of equal size. At the signal, the leaders put a bag on each foot, shuffle their way to the goal line and then back. The second player steps into the bags and repeats the relay. Other players continue until one team finishes and is the winner.

Mystery Bags: Select 12-15 objects with distinctive shapes and place in separate numbered paper bags, one object per bag. Securely close the tops of the bags with a staple. Each player is given a pencil and paper and asked to sit in a circle. The bags are given to the players, which they will pass to the right. Players are allowed 30 seconds to feel the contents. At the end of 30 seconds, blow the whistle and the bags must be passed. After each bag is felt, players write the bag's number and their guess of its contents on their paper. When all the bags have been around the circle, their contents are revealed. Players check their guesses, and the one with the most correct identifications is the winner.

Throw-a-Bag: Air is blown into a paper bag and the opening fastened firmly so the air will not leak out. Players stand on a throwing line and each one, in turn, throws the bag in front of them, trying for distance. The player whose bag goes the farthest is the winner. If the group is large, have more than one player throwing a bag. The winners compete against each other to decide the final winner.

Bagged Advice: Give each guest a pencil and two slips of paper. On one slip is written a predicament and on the second slip its cure. The zanier the ideas, the better. Place the predicament slips in one paper bag, the cures in another. Give each bag a big shake to thoroughly mix the contents. Ask players to sit in a circle. Let them pass the two bags to the right, with each person drawing a slip from each bag. When everyone has a predicament and a cure, let them read the results aloud. The advice will be hilarious!

Blind Bag Race: Players line up against one wall of the room. They are instructed to put paper bags over their heads so they are unable to see. At the starting signal, players race to the goal at the far side of the room as best they can in this blind fashion. They touch the wall and then return to the starting line. The first to arrive back is the winner.

Bag and Baggage Quiz: Give each player a pencil and paper and ask them to answer the following quiz. Each answer is a variety of bag. Allow ten minutes for the quiz. The player with the most correct answers is the winner.

1.	Carried by a man of letters	Mail bag
2.	Oat tote	Nose or feed bag
3.	Tossing toy	Bean bag
4.	Useful equipment during a flood	Sandbag
5.	Knapsack	Sleeping bag
6.	Seen at tee time	Golf bag
7.	Cowboy equipment	Saddlebag
8.	Holds sailor's sewing equipment	Dirty bag
9.	Popular luggage after Civil War	Carpetbag
10.	Nickname for a rich person	Moneybag
11.	Carried by a soldier	Duffel bag
12.	A lady's personal property	Handbag

Everybody's Birthday Celebration

Invitation

Invitations may be as creative as desired. Bright-colored construction paper may be decorated with various fun stickers and the following verse may be printed or typed inside:

> Let's have a birthday party together,
> Right in the midst of this *wintry weather.
> For the date of your birthday we don't care a bit;
> But if you're longing to make a great hit,
> Wear something that shows just the time and the season
> That you were born in. Be sure there's a reason.
> We don't ask to know if 'twas night or 'twas morning,
> But merely the name of the month you were born in.
> Bring a picture to show how you looked when a baby
> For our great guessing contest, 'twill win a prize - maybe.

*Wintry may be substituted with adjectives such as picnicky, snowy, balmy, bleak or sunny.

Decorations or Setting the Mood

This party is in celebration of several birthdays and is great for a large group - the larger the better. The mood is lively, festive and creative with lots of balloons, crepe paper streamers and birthday banners. A live band may perform or recorded music may be played.

Table Setting and Centerpiece

Twelve tables are set up in the room. Each table is decorated to reflect an event or events occurring during one month. A decorated cake is the centerpiece. Flowers arranged with balloons may be placed on either side of cake. Bowls of popcorn, pretzels, peanuts and various other edibles may be placed on all the tables. If the party is for a large birthday group, it is best to assign committees to be responsible for each month's table.

Table ideas:

January	New Year's, confetti, streamers, fireworks on cake
February	Valentines Day, heart-shaped cake, President's Day
March	Kites, kite cake, spring colors, flowers
April	Umbrella, cake with flowers, Easter
May	Mayflower moving van model amidst flowers, May Day, tulips, Memorial Day
June	Formal wedding theme, summer, vacation
July	Fourth of July picnic, checked cloth, fireworks, flag
August	Summer camp fun, swim gear, beach, golf
September	Back to school, supplies, harvest time
October	Pumpkins, corn stalks, Halloween
November	Thanksgiving, fall colors, horn of plenty
December	Christmas lights, wreath, garlands, holly berries

Menu

MENU I

Spinach Dip
Potato, Cheese and Chile Soup
Marinated Broccoli Salad
Corny Cornbread
Super Bran Muffins
Whole Wheat Bagels (your favorite)
Double Chocolate Cake
or
Orange Blossom Cake
Ice Cream (your favorite)
Sparkling Grape Juice

MENU II

Salad Buffet
Onion Bread
or
French Bread Garlic Loaf
Cake(s) (your favorite)
Tropical Ice Cream
Fiesta Fruit Punch

SALAD BUFFET

Lettuce	Chopped eggs
Spinach	Mushrooms
Carrots	Artichoke hearts
Celery	Sunflower seeds
Cherry tomatoes	Imitation bacon bits
Broccoli	Croutons
Cauliflower	Several salad dressings

Entertainment or Games

Mixer: As each guest arrives, pin a famous person's name on his back. Each guest must ask "yes" or "no" questions while trying to discover whose name is pinned to his back. The name must be guessed before the guest may be seated at a table.

Sing Happy Birthday: Everyone sings "Happy Birthday To Us" as the candles are lit.

The Age Quiz: The following quiz may be taken at each table. The table with the most correct answers wins.

1.	What is the most traveled age?	Mileage
2.	What is the greenest age?	Foliage
3.	What is the most cruel age?	Carnage
4.	What is the most edible age?	Sausage
5.	What is an age a man dreads?	Mortgage
6.	What is a comfortable age?	Carriage
7.	What is a thieving age?	Pillage
8.	What is a condescending age?	Patronage
9.	What is the bravest age?	Courage
10.	What is the most barbaric age?	Savage
11.	What is a disgusting age?	Garbage

Baby Photo Contest: Baby pictures of the birthday persons are on display. The guests guess whose picture belongs to whom. The winner receives a prize.

Grab the Hankie: The people whose birthdays are from January to June are lined up on one side of the room. July to December birthday people are lined up on the other side. A hankie is placed in the middle. Call the name of a month from one side and the name of a month from the other side. Those whose birthdays are in the months called run to the middle to grab the hankie and hurriedly get back to their side without being tagged by an opponent. If a player is tagged while carrying the hankie, his side is penalized a point.

Tally Ho: At mealtime, each birthday person must sit at the table which represents the month of his or her birthday. During the meal, the following tallies may be done. Prizes may be awarded and are wrapped as birthday gifts.

1. The table with the highest shoe size. All shoe sizes are added together.
2. The table with the most surgeries.
3. The table with the birthdates that add to the highest number. Ten extra points are given to a table with someone born on a holiday.
4. The table with the most people born in a foreign country.
5. The table with the most people born within a hundred-mile radius of the party.

Hard Times

Invitation

Send folded notes with bright orange burlap "clothes" attached. A toothpick with a folded "knapsack" is enclosed for R.S.V.P.

A second invitation idea might be small paper bags on which party instructions are sloppily written.

A third idea might be a square of material pinked around the edges with party details written inside. This may be folded twice and the corners held with a toothpick or thin, wooden skewer.

Decorations or Setting the Mood

Luminaries line the walkway to the door. These are made by filling paper bags with two inches of sand and placing a votive candle inside. Guests are required to wear shabby, mismatched clothing with old hats. Candles and oil lamps are used for lighting. Furniture is covered with sheets as though the house has been abandoned. A sign is hung on the guest bathroom door, "Ye olde out-house," with a cut-out moon. A few small pieces of torn newspaper are on the floor below the regular toilet tissue.

A good time of the year to hold this party is in the fall or April 15 - income tax poverty time!

Table Setting and Centerpiece

The table is covered with a checked tablecloth or a combination of colored and designed fabrics that look old and faded.

Old lemonade cans or small canning jars are used for drinks. Mismatched plates, chipped china or plain white paper plates may be used. A crudely lettered sign is placed by old silverware that reads, "One utensil per guest." Place Band-Aids on small plate with sign, "For ye olde cut lip," to remind guests to be careful with lemonade cans. On the salad dressing bottles is a note reading, "For tax collectors only."

The buffet table centerpiece is an assortment of old, half-used candles in several different candleholders of varying sizes and shapes. Bouquets of wild flowers and weeds are arranged in canning jars and cans.

Menu

Buffet Salad Bowl
Chili Beans
or
Chili-Noodle Soup
Peanut Butter Cookies
Molasses Sugar Cookies
Zucchini Brownies
Fresh Lemonade

BUFFET SALAD BOWL

Diced celery
Red bell pepper strips
Green pepper strips
Shredded cabbage
Jerusalem artichoke slices
Water chestnut slices
Radish slices
Sunflower seeds
Chopped walnuts
Sesame seeds
Raisins
Julienned beets
Grated carrots
Jicama strips
Cucumber slices
Several salad dressings

Grated Parmesan or Cheddar cheese
Crumbled Roquefort or blue cheese
Lettuce, several varieties
Bean sprouts
Alfalfa sprouts
Cherry tomatoes
Kidney beans
Garbanzo beans
Green beans
Olives
Mushroom slices
Zucchini rounds
Red onion slices
Broccoli flowerets
Cauliflowerets

Entertainment or Games

Hard Luck Story: As each guest is brought through the back door, demand a hard luck story from them.

Who Is It?: Put a large numbered grocery sack over each person's head. The sack has a funny face and holes for eyes and nose. Each person is given a pencil and paper to write guessed names of persons behind the sacks.

Theme Prizes: Prizes are awarded for best costumes, best overall, most clever, best representing theme, most ragged, etc.

Drop the Blanket: This is a great way to have everyone get better acquainted. Before starting, all visitors are introduced so that everyone has at least heard everyone else's name. Divide into two teams and have each team huddle at opposite ends of the room. Two neutral people hold a blanket in a vertical position, fully opened and touching the floor. Each team sends one person to stand 12-inches from his side of the blanket. When both are ready, the blanket is dropped. The first person to say the other person's name correctly captures that person for his team. The game continues until only one person remains on one of the teams. In the event neither person knows the other's name, they are introduced and sent back to their teams.

Goody Guessing Game: Pass around containers such as jars, boxes, sacks, bowls, etc. of candy corn, jellybeans, cookies, peanuts, caramel corn, caramels, etc. Participants may guess number in each container, writing down the answers. The person with the most correct guesses wins.

Broomstick Relay: A player from each team attempts to sweep a balloon from the starting point to the finish line. If balloon pops, player must begin again. The first team to have all its players finish wins.

Pass It On: The entire group forms a circle. Each person is given an object, any size or shape, such as a bowling ball, a trash can, a shoe, etc. On signal, everyone passes the object to the person on the right, keeping the objects moving continuously. When a person drops an object, he must leave the game, but his object remains in. As the game progresses, more people leave the game, making it harder and harder to avoid dropping an object as there are more objects than people. The winner is the last person(s) to "drop out."

Cotton Balls: Have a person volunteer to see how fast he can pick up cotton balls with a spoon and place them in a bowl blindfolded. A dozen or more cotton balls are placed around the bowl. The volunteer must see them. Give volunteer a spoon and have him stand behind the table with the bowl on it. After volunteer is blindfolded, rearrange the cotton balls. Only one hand is used. For last player, blindfold and then remove all cotton balls off table into bowl. Watch the fun as player searches for non-existent balls.

Penny Toss: Who can toss the most pennies into a tin cup?

Ring Toss: Who can ring the leg of a chair, turned upside down, with a rubber ring?

Question and Answer Game: Two plain cards and a pencil are given to each guest. Everyone must write a question beginning with "how," such as "How do you peel a prune?" On the second card, guests write an answer beginning with "by," such as "By using pinking shears." Collect cars and then redistribute them at random, two per person. Each person reads the question and then the answer. The results will be hilarious.

Have Bike, Will Travel

Invitation

A small paper lunch sack is used as the invitation on which the picnic information is printed with a felt-tip pen. It reads, "You are invited to a pedaler's picnic. Please bring your knapsack and bike."

Menu

Box lunches must be prepared ahead of time to be distributed to each rider and placed in his knapsack. At the final destination, everyone may rest and enjoy their lunches. On the return trip, the group is routed by an ice cream parlor for a much-deserved treat.

MENU I

Wedges of Cheese
Yogurt
Croissant Sandwiches (your favorite filling)
Fresh Fruit
Canned Fruit Drink

MENU II

Tabouli
Pita Pocket Sandwiches (your favorite filling)
Baklava
Green Grapes
Boxed Fruit Drink

Entertainment or Games

Bike-Camera Rally: Divide guests into groups of 4-6 and explain the rules.

1. Each group is given one polaroid camera, one roll of film and a list of pictures to be taken. As only one roll of film is permitted, encourage riders to include combinations of ideas. A rider(s) must be in each picture.
2. There is a 1½-hour time limit.
3. Within the time limit, each group is to take the following pictures, with points given as shown, and meet the other groups at a predetermined destination at least 3 miles away.

   200 points:
       To arrive *exactly* on time and subtract 10 points for each minute of arrival before or after specified time.

20 points:
> By an Olympic license plate.
> Next to a boat.
> On a motorcycle.
> On playground equipment.

30 points:
> To hang upside down from a tree.
> For male member of group in a dress.
> For four pairs of feet without shoes or socks.
> By any city limit sign.

40 points:
> For group in Burger King crowns.
> With a senior citizen over 65.
> In front of a fire station.
> For group in togas.

50 points:
> With a cow.
> With a highway patrol officer.
> In front of a limousine.
> For group in a telephone booth.

60 points:
> Next to a juke box.
> Next to a windmill.
> With a statue.
> For member of group in a swimming pool.

Hobo Progressive Party

Invitation

Hand print as illegibly as possible the following message on either a brown bag or scraps of paper charred around the edges. "The annual Hobo Reunion is bein' planned 4 Saturday nite (date and time) - rain or shine. Kum with all earthly belongings strapped on yo back. Ain't no well-dressed tramps aloud. Be prepared to hop a freight 4 parts unknown. Late kumers will be left at mercy of cops. Meet at main RR track (address or directions) where red flag marks hobo junction. Remember patches and backpacks are a must."

Decorations or Setting the Mood

A great place to start the hobo progressive party is at a point by the railroad tracks where a freight train will pass. The group may wind up the party out-of-doors around a campfire, indoors at a home or in a barn. If indoors, the mood is set with railroad lanterns, candles and bales of hay for seating.

Table Setting and Centerpiece

Newspapers are spread over the table. A "hobo bundle," a stuffed red or blue bandanna tied on a stick, is attached to a lantern. Various sizes of tin cans hold bouquets of wildflowers and weeds. Old railroad signs and worn, shabby hats enhance the hobo atmosphere.

Plates may be tin or paper, slightly burned around the edges. Drinks are served in tin cups or empty tin cans. Napkins may be bandannas, paper napkins charred around the edges or a roll of toilet paper.

Menu

OUTDOOR MENU
Chips and Dip (your favorites)
Baked Beans
Roasted Hot Dogs
Buns, Mayonnaise, Catsup, Mustard, Relish
Roasted Corn-on-the-Cob
Doughnuts (your favorite)
S'Mores
Apples
Soda Pop
Hot Chocolate

INDOOR MENU

Herb Popcorn
Onion Rings
Cornbread
Old-Fashioned Vegetable Stew
or
Hobo Stew
Spicy Raisin Cookie Squares
Hot Spiced Nectar

S'MORES

Place hot roasted marshmallow and half of 1½-ounce Hershey chocolate bar between 2 graham crackers.

Entertainment or Games

The "hobos" meet at the time when the freight train will pass. A note is attached to the red flag, directing the group where to go next. At each destination, new direction notes are given. The notes are written as illegibly as possible, yet legible.

Before starting the journey, all "hobos" must repeat this pledge: "I pledge to stick with my fellow hobos sharing their troubles, embarrassments, trials and prison terms, not to leave the pack atal' 'til we've been fed."

Direction Note 1: Direct "hobos" to store's ice cream counter and order ice cream cones. The ice cream clerk gives them the next direction note.

Direction Note 2: Direct "hobos" to candy store to purchase a box of candy, then continue to the police station or sheriff's office to give a policeman the box of candy. The policeman gives them the next direction note.

Direction Note 3: Direct "hobos" to railroad station. The group identifies themselves to the train master, who gives them the next direction note. If a train station is not in the area, a bus station or other location may be used.

The final destination is a river bottom or other outdoor location where the "hobos" may eat around a campfire, sing songs, tell stories and play games. If an indoor destination is chosen, indoor games are played.

Singing: Sing songs relating to bums and gypsies, "I've Been Workin' on the Railroad" and "Tell Me Little Gypsy," maybe even a pun such as "Tramp, Tramp, Tramp the Boys Are Marching."

Skits: Members of the group may perform a skit such as "Oh, Those Hobos" or another fun skit.

Stories: Relate "hobo" stories.

Charades: Commercials are used as the categories. Guests, individually or in pairs, act out the charade.

Egg Toss: Standing close together in pairs, couples begin tossing raw eggs to each other. As the couples continue to catch the eggs, a referee gradually moves the partners farther apart, until all the couples have dropped out except the one who still has a whole egg.

Apple Paring Contest: Who can peel the longest continuous strip of peel from an apple? Reward with a prize.

The Point Game: A list, similar to the one below, is read aloud. Each person keeps track of his points. The person with the most points wins. Sample list:

1. 10 points if wearing red.
2. 10 points for each penny in a pocket or purse.
3. 10 points if person owns a white comb.
4. Points for shoe size, half sizes rounded off to next highest number.
5. 15 points if birthday is on a holiday.
6. 10 points if person has ridden on a train.
7. 10 points if person has a ball point pen, 25 points if pen has red ink.
8. 15 points if dressed in a hobo costume.
9. 10 points if patches are on costume.

Black Magic: This is a "mind reading" game which always works. While the mind reader is out of the room, the audience chooses an object. The mind reader returns and the leader points to many different objects. When he points to the chosen one, it is correctly identified by the mind reader. The secret is that the chosen object is pointed to immediately after a black object.

Rhythm: Everyone in the group is seated and numbered in a circle, with the #1 person sitting in the end seat. The "rhythm" is begun by the #1 person. Everyone joins in by first slapping thighs, clapping hands, snapping right hand fingers, then snapping left hand fingers in a 1-2-3-4, 1-2-3-4, 1-2-3-4 motion at a moderately slow speed. Rhythm may speed up as everyone learns how to play. The fun begins when the #1 person, on the first snap of the fingers, calls out his own number and, on the second snap of the fingers, calls out somebody else's number. For example, it might sound something like slap, clap, "one, six" and then the #6 person might go slap, clap, "six, ten." The #10 person would do the same thing, calling out someone else's number on the second finger snap, and so on. If anyone misses, they go to the end seating of the numbered progression and everyone moves up one chair. The object is to eventually arrive at the number one chair.

Home on the Range

Invitation

A boot invitation is made, as illustrated. Brown construction paper is folded in half and boot is drawn with left side on the fold. Cut out boot, leaving fold. Print information on the inside with a black felt-tip pen. Wording may be:

Join the stampede

to the

Western Jamboree

(date)

Round-up Time

Stompin' Grounds (address)

Western Duds

If ya'll can't be at the

corral, call (phone number)

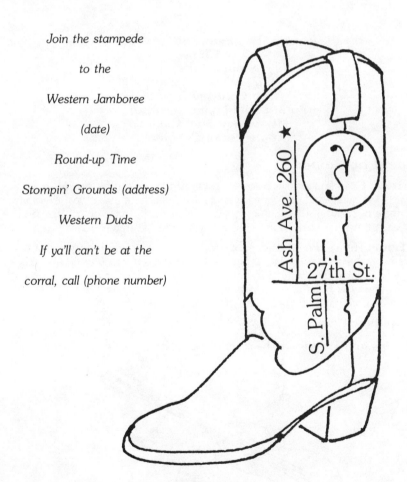

Decorations or Setting the Mood

If a barn is not available, the wide-open spaces of the backyard is great, adding items such as a chuck wagon, saddles, bridles, harnesses, whips, straw bales, lanterns, etc., to enhance the western atmosphere. "Wanted posters" may be made with enlarged pictures of individual guests.

In a grassy area or on cement, form a firepit with cement blocks and fill with sand. Logs are laid on top for the fire. Above the firepit, place a wrought iron tripod and hang a black iron kettle filled with spicy cider for sipping throughout the evening. The fire will keep it hot.

Bales of straw may be placed around the firepit for seating so guests may keep warm and toast marshmallows.

Table Setting and Centerpiece

Twelve bales of straw may serve as a table - two bales high, two bales wide and three bales long. Cover the "table" with red bandannas laid caddy-corner over the bales of straw.

Tin, blue enamel or paper plates are used with wicker holders. Bandannas or red and white checked paper napkins add a western flavor.

Menu

Hot Bean Dip
Corn Chips
Sloppy Joes
Chuck Wagon Beans
Coleslaw
Potato Salad (your favorite)
Mississippi Mud Cake
Apple-Pecan Cobbler

Entertainment or Games

Musical Straw: Place four or five bales of straw, depending on the size of the group, in a circle. Play music - live guitar and banjo music is great! When the music stops, everyone has to jump up onto a bale of straw. If they cannot get on the straw, they are out of the game. Take out a bale of straw each time the music stops until only one bale of straw is left.

Hobbled Horse Relay: Four boards 2 x 6 inches by 6 feet and eight pairs of old, large men's shoes are needed. Remove the laces. Nail or screw four left shoes to two boards and four right shoes to the remaining two boards. Repeat for second team. Four persons from each team get into the shoes and walk together up and around a bale of straw and return to the starting line. The next group of four continue the relay until all have participated.

Shoe the Stallion: Horseshoes.

Fireside Songs and Hayride: The evening is completed with singing around the fire and/or a hayride.

Indoor Beach Party

Tired of the snow and the long winter days? Homesick for the beach? Then, this party will be a perfect mood perker!

Invitation

Picture postcards of a beach scene or shell-shaped notecards may be used as invitations.

Decorations or Setting the Mood

To set the mood for a "beach party without the beach," display beach posters on the walls. Swim suits and beach towels are hung on doorknobs and draped over chairs, and even a few are tacked to the walls. There are several "beaches," depending on the size of the group. The "beaches" are identified with a sign, i.e., Laguna Beach, Waikiki Beach, Palm Beach, Myrtle Beach. The "inhabitants" of the different beaches comprise the teams for games. Music from the surfing era (Beach Boys, etc.) may be heard at this beach scene.

Table Setting and Centerpiece

A sea-blue or green tablecloth is covered with a fish net. If space allows, use separate card tables to represent each beach. A mermaid centerpiece may be created using a long-haired doll, such as a Barbie doll. Her gown and tail are shaped from aluminum foil. Place the mermaid on a pile of several small, jagged rocks draped with fish net and a few scattered seashells. Small sand pails hold flatware and rolled napkins.

Menu

Picnic foods are good for a beach party and may include burgers, hotdogs, potato salad, chips, soda pop, cupcakes and ice cream bars or cones. For something different, try:

Turkish Shish Kebabs
Layered Vegetable Salad
Golden Potato Casserole
Ice Cream Cone Cupcakes
Pink Lemonade (your favorite)

Entertainment or Games

Indoor Swimming Race: Select one "swimmer" from each "beach." Placed before each "swimmer" is a deep pie pan filled to the brim with water with four or five candy LifeSavers at the bottom. Each "swimmer" must remove the LifeSavers with his mouth. Hands may not be used.

High Dive: One "diver" is chosen from each "beach." On the floor at the feet of each "diver" is an identical-size, empty tumbler which he must attempt to fill from an erect standing position. Each "diver" is given a pitcher containing an equal amount of water, measuring a little less than tumbler capacity. The "diver" with the most water in his glass wins.

Clam Dig: One person from each "beach" participates in the dig. Small cardboard boxes, such as shoe boxes, are filled with sand and ten hidden pennies. Each participant is given a spoon and a bowl and on signal begins to dig for the pennies. This may also be a relay, using a larger box and hiding more pennies. Specify how many pennies each player must find. Only one spoon per team is permitted.

Sailboat Race: Stretch as many strings across the room as there are contestants. On each string is a paper cornucopia or cone. The "sailors" blow the "boat" from one end of the string to the other. The first "boat" across the finish line wins.

Rowing Race: Four or five "rowers" are chosen from each beach. They stand single file, close together. Each "rower" grasps the forearms of the "rower" in front of him by extending his arms on either side of that "rower." When all "rowers" are in place, the signal to start the race is given. The "rowers" race-walk to a specified point, working their arms like pistons all the way to the finish line.

Scull Race: Each beach works as a group and turns in one set of answers. Each answer is a word beginning with "sea" or "se." This may also be a match game, with answers listed out of order.

1.	A sea that is very old	Senile
2.	A sea that denotes an orderly succession	Series
3.	A sea that is quiet or calm	Sedate
4.	A sea that entices evil	Seductive
5.	A sea that is choice	Select
6.	A sea that follows as a continuous or related series	Sequence
7.	A sea that is placid	Serene
8.	A sea that is harsh	Severe
9.	A sea that few women can keep	Secret
10.	A sea that shuts itself off or apart	Sequester
11.	A sea that separates	Secession
12.	A sea that adds flavor	Seasoning
13.	A sea whose school days are ending	Senior
14.	A sea that is safe	Secure
15.	A sea that is half a year	Semester
16.	A sea that is shabby and run down	Seedy
17.	A sea that goes up-and-down	Seesaw
18.	A sea that is solemn	Serious
19.	A sea that is brown	Sepia
20.	A sea that churns and boils	Seethe

Party Favors: Beach balls, sand toys, LifeSavers, sun tan lotion and visors are fun party favors.

New Orleans Brunch

Invitation

The mood begins with the creation of special invitations. Fold a piece of white paper into thirds. Pen party information inside and draw pots of geraniums at random for decoration. Fold the invitation shut and draw wrought-iron gates on the front with black ink.

Decorations or Setting the Mood

Imagine moss-draped trees, bougainvillea clinging to intricately laced grill work, intimate courtyards of mossy brick closing out the twentieth-century world. This vision conveys the essence of New Orleans. The patio or terrace may be transformed into a "Deep South" celebration.

Table Setting and Centerpiece

A white tablecloth and geranium-colored napkins are used. The centerpiece may take the form of a geranium pyramid. Group three or four small pots of geraniums in a very large clay saucer. To form the top of the pyramid, place a fifth pot of geraniums in the center so that its bottom rests on the rims of the other pots. Each pot is tied with a black velvet ribbon just below the rim. The flower pots may be left natural or spray-painted black.

Menu

Seasonal Fresh Fruit with Raspberry-Lemon Cream
Coffee Cake
Southern Puffed Pancakes
or
Oven French Toast
Plantation Eggs
Cheese Grits
Orange Juice
Hot Beverage

SEASONAL FRESH FRUIT

1. Cut fruit in wedges, slices, balls and sticks.
2. Dip all fruit in orange or pineapple juice to prevent discoloration.
3. Decorate platter with leaf lettuce and place dressing surrounded by fruit.

Entertainment or Games

Entertainment may be in the form of a favorite Dixieland musical ensemble.

Spring Morning Brunch

Invitation

A strawberry, butterfly, tulip or daffodil-shaped invitation may be purchased from a stationery store. An alternative is a soft pastel blue, yellow or peach embossed note card with calligraphy-penned brunch information.

Decorations or Setting the Mood

Morning sunshine dappling the terrace or patio lends a perfect setting for a lovely brunch. Spring flower bouquets, either fresh or potted, may be placed beautifully around the patio.

Table Setting and Centerpiece

Fresh fruit is the focus of this brunch, and a Fresh Fruit Tree comprises the edible centerpiece. The fresh fruit theme may be enhanced by serving the fruit breads on silver platters, each decorated in a special way. For example, a loaf of Lemon Bread may be sliced, still retaining its loaf shape. Surround the bread with actual lemon leaves and lemon roses (roses made from the skin of the lemon). Strawberry bread may be sliced similarly, surrounded by fresh mint and long-stemmed, whole strawberries. Banana bread may be highlighted by clusters of meringue mushrooms and fresh greenery. Around the base of the punch bowl, arrange greenery with baby's breath. Bright-colored napkins, picking up the colors of the fresh flowers, may be used. A white tablecloth and crystal plates show the vividness of the luscious food, fruits and flowers.

Menu

MENU I

Cookie Crust Fruit Basket
Orange Gem Muffins
or
Apple Muffins
Cheese-Egg Casserole
or
Egg Scramble Surprise
Potato-Chive Squares with Special Applesauce
or
Tater Tots Supreme
Juice (your favorite)
Hot Beverage

MENU II

Fresh Fruit Tree
Strawberries and Cream Bread with Devonshire Cream
Blueberry Loaf with Blueberry Cream
Lemon Bread with Creamed Cheese
Banana-Nut Bread with Butter Molds
Meringue Mushrooms
Scrambled Eggs Supreme
Raspberry Frost

FRESH FRUIT TREE

4 red apples
2 pears
2 oranges
1 cantaloupe
1 honeydew melon
1 pineapple
6 plums
5 bananas
7 bunches red grapes
7 bunches green grapes
Fruit Fresh

24-inch cone-shaped styrofoam
Large platter
3 large bunches leaf lettuce
1 package wooden toothpicks
1 package wire U-shaped picks

1. Wash all fruit. Cut apples and pears in half. Dip in Fruit Fresh to preserve color. Set aside.
2. Cut oranges in half. Cut melons into 8 wedge slices. Cut pineapple in half lengthwise, including top. Cut in half lengthwise (4 wedges). Set aside.
3. Place cone on large platter. Starting at bottom, place fresh leaf lettuce to cover cone.
4. Place fruit on cone with toothpicks. Attach plums, bananas and grapes with wire picks.

Preparation Time: **2 hours**   **Serves:**   **35-40**
Tip: *Placement of fruit should be varied with colors and shapes. Lettuce leaves should show through for color balance.*

The Big Red Bash
New Year's Eve

Invitation

A phone invitation, followed by a mailing is the best way to reach everyone.

Invitations may be handwritten or printed on red paper. List all pertinent details and include a line tempting guests to "have a red-hot time." Write in bold letters, **"DRESS CODE RED."** Party should start about 9:00 p.m., no earlier.

An alternate invitation may be a scroll written on artist's tracing paper (looks similar to parchment). Burn the edges of the paper to give it an authentic look. Tuck scroll into a cardboard tube (use half of a small, empty aluminum foil tube). Fill with metallic confetti and small metallic red curled ribbon streamers, even a deflated balloon. Address and mail. Extra postage will be required.

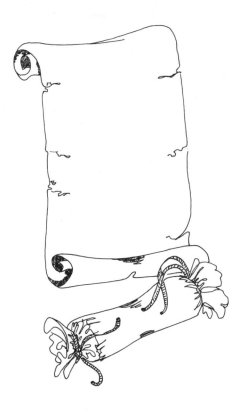

Decorations or Setting the Mood

Dozens of red helium and silver mylar balloons with matching ribbon streamers add an air of festivity. Tie red ribbons around throw pillows and lamp bases. Red towels and soaps are placed in the guest bathroom. Clusters of different sized and shaped red candles are everywhere. Lively, fast-paced music creates energy and excitement. Several potted red and white poinsettias are sitting around the house. Silver bowls of red hot cinnamon balls and peppermint candies may be placed on tables.

Table Setting and Centerpiece

A white tablecloth is the best contrast for the red decorations. Swirl red and silver metallic ribbon around the table. Use disposable plates, napkins and glasses of red, clear or white plastic.

The centerpiece is a large red basket or a large clear bowl filled with multi-colored hats, noise makers, kazoos, horns and poppers. These are passed around to the guests as midnight approaches.

Menu

Cherry Tomatoes with Artichoke and Hearts of Palm Stuffing
Cheese Appetizer Torte
Mushroom Turnovers
Spinach, Mushroom and Gruyère Cheesecake
Assorted Cheeses with Fresh Red Fruit
Display of Red Delicious Apples,
Red Grapes, Red Pears and Fresh Strawberries
Assorted Nuts
Silver Tray of Truffles and Turtles
Chocolate Cake with Buttercream Frosting
Sparkling Apple Cider
or
Eggnog Without Eggs

Entertainment or Games

Dress Code "Red": With the dress code "RED," the imagination of the guests will be interesting and create conversation. Most guests will rise to the occasion by wearing a red dress, tie or shirt or by dying their hair. Give a prize of a baby doll in a diaper for the most original "red" idea.

Resolutions: Hostess writes resolutions on small scrolls and ties each with a red ribbon. These are placed in a large glass bowl or red basket. Each guest selects a resolution and reads it aloud. After the drawing is complete, the guests may exchange resolutions.

"Auld Lang Syne": After the midnight countdown, sing a rousing rendition of "Auld Lang Syne."

Heart to Heart
Valentine's Day

Invitation

The invitation is written on small note paper and attached with ribbon to a silk or dried floral nosegay. This is nestled in pink and red tissue paper and placed in a small mailing box.

Table Setting and Centerpiece

The table is covered with a red cloth which is fancily adorned with large, white doilies for place mats. The white napkins are folded in the shape of a fan and placed in stemmed goblets. For place cards, bake 6-inch, heart-shaped sugar cookies and decorate with icing of different colors. The name of each guest is written with decorator gel on the cookies. Each cookie is placed on a small doily above the place setting.

An attractive centerpiece is created by stacking three round tiers of white styrofoam in graduated sizes. Edges of each tier are covered with wide red ribbon. Thin pink ribbon is woven through the white lace which is used to cover the ribboned tiers. A large styrofoam heart is covered with baby's breath interspersed with pink and red rosebuds. Two white doves, facing each other and linked with thin pink ribbon, are perched on top of the heart. A sturdy floral wire is inserted through bottom of heart to firmly attach to the tiered base. Candles in glass votive cups are placed around the base of the centerpiece.

Menu

Zucchini Soup
Curried Toast
Mushroom-Artichoke Crepes with Lemon Butter
Snow Peas with Almonds
Broiled Tomatoes
Meringue Chocolate-Layered Hearts

Entertainment or Games

Each couple is given the opportunity to reminisce about their first date and first Valentine's Day together.

Bunny Brunch
Easter

Invitation

**Bunny
Brunch**

Home of_____

Easter Sunday
11:00 a.m.

Decorations or Setting the Mood

In the entry is a cart or wagon filled with hay or artificial grass. Stuffed bunnies, ducks and chickens are nestled in the grass. Easter eggs or colored, plastic eggs are scattered at their feet. At the base of the cart or wagon are clay pots of tulips, daffodils and other spring flowers. Pastel-colored ribbons are tied in bows at the necks of the stuffed animals.

Table Setting and Centerpiece

At each place setting is a small basket filled with an assortment of candy eggs, jellybeans, a decorated Easter egg and a miniature stuffed bunny or other Easter animal. A small bow is tied to the handle of each basket. The centerpiece is a decorated Easter basket filled with tulips. Pastel-colored place mats and napkins are used, alternating colors for variety. Napkins are folded in bunny shapes.

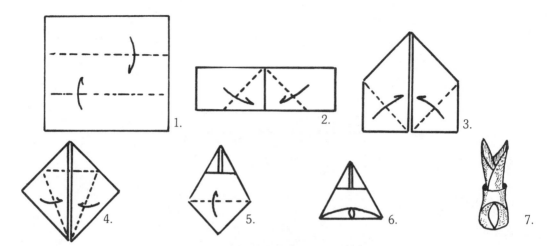

DIAGRAM

1. Fold the napkin into three parts as indicated.   2. Fold along the dotted lines to bring edges to the center.   3. Fold the corners up along the dotted lines.   4. Fold the left and right corners in along the dotted lines.   5. Turn napkin over and then upside down.   6. Turn up bottom point as shown.   7. Turn the left and right corners backwards, slip one corner into the other to fasten. Open out the ears first, then the base, and stand on the place mat.

Menu

Cheese Bread Ring
or
Almond-Poppy Seed Bread
Fruit Ring with Devonshire Cream
Deviled Eggs (your favorite)
Broccoli Casserole
Hash Brown Casserole
Fresh Orange Juice, Garnished with
Fresh Strawberries or Mint Leaves

FRUIT RING

Arrange different fruits on lettuce greens on a silver or crystal platter. Use a combination of fruits such as apples, bananas, cantaloupe, honeydew, oranges, peaches, pineapple or strawberries. Fruits may be served halved, sliced or cut in pieces. Serve with Devonshire Cream.

Entertainment or Games

Sunrise Service: Attend sunrise service before the brunch.

Decorate Easter Eggs: Cover a table or countertop with paper towels or newspapers. At each place are three or four hard-boiled eggs, egg dipper, gummed stickers and transfers. Cups of dye and a drying tray are placed in the center of table. A special Easter basket or stuffed Easter bunny is the prize for the best decorated egg.

Egg Hunt: Before brunch starts, hide colored eggs, chocolate eggs, candy and jellybean packets throughout the yard. Hide an elaborately decorated egg as a prize. Print the letters E - A - S - T - E - R on eggs before hiding. The first person to spell Easter wins a prize. There are enough eggs lettered to spell out the word at least twice. Also, numbers may be written on the eggs. Add up numbers at the end of the egg hunt and the largest score wins a prize. Prizes may be an Easter basket or stuffed animal.

Easter Dinner

Invitation

**Easter Sunday
Brunch**

Date:

Time:

Place:

Decorations or Setting the Mood

Easter lilies, baskets of tulips or spring bouquets are placed around the house. An arrangement including a porcelain or ceramic rabbit is a lovely addition. Crystal or silver bowls of jellybeans and chocolate eggs are placed on various tables.

Table Setting and Centerpiece

A pink tablecloth is used with a white or ecru lace cover, allowing pink to show through. If lace cover is unavailable, white or ecru place mats are used with contrasting pastel-colored napkins. Each napkin has a spring flower lying across it or is encircled with a flower ring. At each place setting is a silver or white porcelain egg cup filled with a pastel-colored egg candle to be lit at the beginning of dinner. For the centerpiece, an oblong mirror is placed in the center of the table. A silver candelabra or silver candlesticks with tall pink or other pastel-colored candles are placed on the mirror. At the base of the candlesticks are fresh cut spring flowers or rings of fresh flowers. Sitting at each end of the mirror is a porcelain rabbit with fresh flowers at the base of each. Or instead of fresh flowers, use artificial grass decorated with jellybeans, chocolate eggs and other decorated eggs.

109

Menu

Artichoke Hearts Stuffed with Camembert
Avocado Salad
Lemon-Buttered New Potatoes
Broccoli with Orange Sauce
Spinach Soufflé Ring with Mushroom Sauce
Easter Egg Nest Bread
Fresh Blueberries and Raspberries with Cream
Sugar Cookies (your favorite)
Lemon-Lime Soda
or
Water with a Twist of Lemon or Lime

Entertainment or Games

Inside Easter Egg Hunt: Before guests arrive, hide colored, plastic eggs filled with goodies, cellophane-wrapped chocolate eggs and bunnies. Also hidden are marshmallow chickens and ducks and decorated hard-boiled eggs.

Jellybean Guess: Fill a basket or jar with jellybeans. All participants must guess the number of jellybeans. The person who guesses closest to the actual number wins the filled basket.

Easter Movie: As an alternative to games, an Easter movie may be shown.

Red, White and Blue Picnic
4th of July

Invitation

The invitation is written in white ink on a red card outlined with blue and gold star stickers. A small American flag may be included.

A firecracker invitation is created by covering an empty tissue roll with red paper. Information is inside and attached to an 8-inch wick of heavy string with tag that reads, "Pull." Hand deliver.

Decorations or Setting the Mood

Several American flags line the entrance of the home to greet guests with a patriotic spirit.

Clusters of red, white and blue balloons with crepe paper streamers decorate the party area.

Table Setting and Centerpiece

The buffet table is covered with a red or white tablecloth. Blue paper napkins are encircled with napkin rings made of white construction paper, affixed with a large gold star. Red and white paper plates and cups complete the table setting.

An "Uncle Sam" hat filled with red and white petunias is the patriotic centerpiece. A small toy drum with one end removed may be used as a serving dish. Place small flags around the rim. The table is also enhanced by a watermelon cannon.

Menu

Vegetable Torta
Watermelon Cannon with Fruit Salad (your favorite)
Grilled Corn in Husks
Tomato and Red Onion Slices with Vinaigrette Dressing
Flag Cake
Three-Layer Chocolate Bars
Banana-Walnut Ice Cream
Fresh Lemonade

WATERMELON CANNON

Cut off one-third of the melon, from which two thick slices are cut for wheels. The longer section is hollowed to serve as a container for the fruit salad. Affix the wheels and prop the cannon at a 45-degree angle. Insert a rope wick at base end of the cannon. For a patriotic touch, add small American flags.

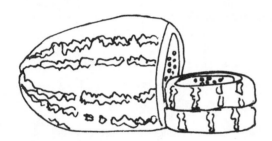 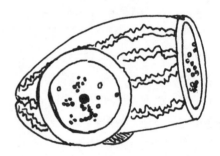

Entertainment or Games

Game of the U.S.A.: As guests arrive, a question or answer is pinned to their shirt. Each guest is given a card on which to write the names of the people who have corresponding questions and answers. The questions correspond with answers written as abbreviations of states in the U.S.A.

1.	Is the cleanest	WASH
2.	Is most religious	MASS
3.	Never forgets itself	ME
4.	Saved Noah and family	ARK
5.	Is a physician	MD
6.	Is a grain	RI
7.	Seems to be in poor health	ILL
8.	Is an exclamation	OH or OK
9.	Is a parent	MA or PA
10.	Is to cut long grass	MO
11.	Is a number	TENN
12.	Is a metal	ORE
13.	Is the happiest	HA

Races and Games: Other games may include relay races such as a three-legged race, wheelbarrow race, sack race, horseshoes, tug of war, raw egg toss and volleyball.

Fireworks: This fun-filled day is ended with fireworks. A large supply of sparklers are provided for your guests to enjoy.

The Great Cover-Up
Halloween

Invitation

The invitation information is printed in black on heavyweight 8½ x 11-inch orange paper. This is folded into thirds and fastened with a black seal.

You're Invited to
"THE GREAT COVER-UP"
Those summer days have come and gone,
We've all been here and there,
Let's get together - have some fun,
Give everyone a scare.
But first we'll gather, in disguise
Behind the masks we wear,
To win the prize, so coveted,
For scarey mask or fair.
You don't need to come in costume,
Unless you really dare,
But cover up those cheeks of tan—
Your face must not be bare!

DAY	DATE	TIME
Saturday Night	October 31	7:00 p.m. sharp!

(name)
(address)
R.S.V.P. (phone number)

An alternate invitation may be a cat cut from black construction paper with orange eyes and whiskers attached, as illustrated.

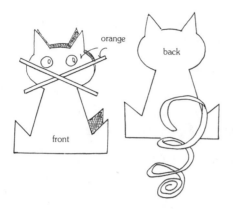

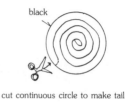

cut continuous circle to make tail

Decorations or Setting the Mood

Line driveway or front sidewalk with jack-o'-luminaries. One of these is easily made by cutting a face in one side of a brown paper lunch bag, then filling with two inches of sand and placing a votive candle inside. Near the front door is a jack-o'-lantern pole. This is a carved pumpkin, lantern-pole style, securely attached to a mop or broom handle which is pushed several inches into the ground. A tape recorder playing "The Haunted House" is hidden inconspicuously.

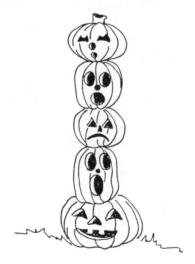

A "ghost" silently greets the guests and solemnly points to white footprints on the floor, directing guests.

Table Setting and Centerpiece

The table is covered with a black cloth. A six-foot paper skeleton is the guest of honor and is covered with clear plastic. Using the skeleton as an outline, arrange the buffet food, as illustrated. The head is a large round glass bowl filled with potato salad, the eyes and mouth are created by olives and strips of pimento. Large leaf greens are arranged around the base of the bowl, creating a collar. Sandwich meat slices are rolled up and secured with toothpicks. These are arranged on the torso of the skeleton, forming the ribs.

Bread triangles and crackers are used to form the arms.

114

Place one small glass bowl at each elbow, one filled with mayonnaise and the other filled with mustard. The paper hands are left uncovered.

Select a pumpkin large enough to hold a gallon container. Cut the top off the pumpkin and clean out the pulp. Place gallon container in the pumpkin, then fill with Pumpkin-Leek Soup and place in the skeleton's tummy. Overlap cheese slices down both legs. Small bowls of mustard and mayonnaise are placed at each knee. Extra food decorations may be added. As the evening progresses, keep the skeleton filled with fresh food. Other table props may include black candle tapers, gourds, squash of various shapes and sizes, candy corn, trick-or-treat bags and rubber masks.

Menu

Swamp Water
Pumpkin-Leek Soup
Potato Salad (your favorite)
Sandwiches (See Table Setting and Centerpiece)
Apple on a Stick
Pumpkin Cake Squares

SWAMP WATER

Equal amounts of orange slush and root beer.

Entertainment or Games

Balloon Bounce: Give volunteer a balloon and an overcoat. Place a glass of water on the floor and scatter 20 matches around the volunteer. The object is to keep the balloon bouncing with one hand while putting on the overcoat, drinking the water and picking up all 20 matches in two minutes.

Decorate Pumpkins: Each person or couple may decorate a pumpkin as desired. If many guests are present, divide into several groups. Instead of carving pumpkins, vegetables may be used to decorate or a combination of both. Toothpicks are used to secure the vegetables. Plenty of newspaper and plastic tablecloths should be available.

Dead Mouse: This game is best with female participation and male observation. The girls form a circle around the hostess who is holding a gaily-tied gift box. Participants are told a dead mouse is in the box. As the music starts, the girls must move in a circle. The hostess tosses the box to one of the girls who tosses it to another girl, and so on. When the music stops, the girl holding the box must open it, remove the mouse and bury it in the back yard. The joke is that the "dead mouse" is actually a pretty present.

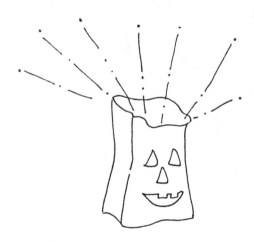

Cookies Make It Christmas

Invitation

A Christmas tree is cut from green construction paper, using a cookie cutter for a pattern. The tree invitation is trimmed with small pieces of lace and beads.

Inside the invitation reads, "Christmas cookies hold a special magic during this holiday season. Come and exchange favorite cookies and recipes with friends." Instruct guests to bring five or six dozen cookies, using only one recipe, and send the recipe on a card at least one week before the cookie exchange. Invitations must be mailed at least a month in advance so everyone has time to send their recipes. This also allows time for notification of guests if there is recipe duplication.

Decorations or Setting the Mood

As the guests arrive, they are greeted with the wonderful aroma of Holiday Fragrance and the sound of Christmas music. A white tablecloth covers the cookie table, set up to display all the cookies. On one side of the cookie table is an exquisitely decorated gingerbread house and on the other side is a silver or crystal punch bowl.

HOLIDAY FRAGRANCE

½ sliced orange
¼ cup whole cloves
2 small cinnamon sticks
½ sliced lemon
¼ cup whole allspice
1 Tablespoon cinnamon
2 cups water

Heat slowly on stove. Add water as necessary.

Table Setting and Centerpiece

The buffet table is draped with a vintage lace tablecloth or handmade quilt. An arrangement of antique porcelain dolls and white roses in silver bud vases give the table a nostalgic look. Candles are everywhere in non-matching candlesticks. Antique silver bowls reflect the brightness of this Christmas buffet.

Menu

Jellied Cranberry Salad
or
Cinnamon Jello
Florentine Crepes
or
Broccoli Muffins with Cheese Sauce
Baby or Frozen Parisienne Carrots
Herb Bread
or
Rolls
Red Cinnamon Holiday Punch

CHRISTMAS PACKAGES

Cut Jellied Cranberry Salad into squares. Spread softened cream cheese "wrapping paper" over each square. Using red decorator gel, form ribbon and bow on "package."

Another "package" may be red. Trim with softened cream cheese using small, round pastry tip to form ribbon and bow around "package."

Entertainment or Games

Cookie Exchange: Christmas tins, decorative gift boxes, colored tissue paper, cellophane and ribbons are provided for the cookie exchange. Each guest shares half a dozen or so cookies with each of the other guests.

Cookie Recipe Booklet: Each guest is given a ribbon-tied recipe booklet, inclusive of all recipes used for the cookie exchange, a momento of the "special magic of this holiday season."

Cranberries, Carols and Cookies
Christmas

Invitation

On a song sheet of parchment paper with singed edges, the following verse is printed.

Come ye all in great apparel
Join in chorus for a carol.
Tis' the season to be jolly
To our house all decked with holly.
Follow all in Merry Measure
Lots of food for you to savor.
December *(date)*, that's the date
Come at *(time)* with your mate.

The Smith's
Sunshine Lane
Happy Town, USA
R.S.V.P. *(phone number)*

Decorations or Setting the Mood

To create a nostalgic atmosphere, a large yuletide log decorated with holly and holly berries is placed on the porch or in the entry. An evergreen wreath with jingle bells and a beautifully tied red Christmas bow adorns the front door. Large, flat baskets are filled with cuttings from pines, junipers, magnolia and ivy, plus holly berries and pine cones. The basket handles are decorated with large festive bows.

On a taffeta-covered round table, a steaming wassail bowl is surrounded with boughs of pine, spruce and holly, entwined with plaid ribbon and accented with lemons, limes, oranges, red apples and pine cones.

The song "12 Days of Christmas" is the mixer for this party. As the guests arrive, each is given a name tag with his name and a word or day number from the song. For example, "Jody Jones - Day 3" is on a name tag and "Jon Robinson - French Hens" is on another. Each person finds the person whose number or phrase matches his own. The partners formed in this mixer will be partners when the "12 Days of Christmas" is sung later.

Table Setting and Centerpiece

The table is covered with a white tablecloth. Plaid ribbon, five inches wide, criss-crosses the table in a lattice-look and is tied in bows at the table's edge. Tucked amidst Christmas evergreens are red candles and caroler figurines, with accents of miniature brass horns and other musical instruments. Tiny red and green baskets are filled with candies and set at each place. This table setting is brightened by the reflection of traditional Christmas china. Red napkins are tied with plaid ribbons and a candy cane.

Menu

Hilo Franks
Garbanzo Dip with Crackers
Crocked Cheese with Crackers
Curry Dip with Fresh Vegetables
Egg Salad Mold
Yams in Orange Cups
or
Sweet Potatoes with Coconutty Topping
Broccoli Soufflé Roll
Parsley Rice with Almonds and Monterey Jack Cheese
Cranberry Cobbler
or
Pound Cake
Wassail Bowl

Entertainment or Games

Christmas Carols: After dinner, a quartet of carolers, dressed in winter attire, arrive at the front door and join in a chorus. The hostess invites the carolers in to lead guests in singing Christmas carols. Before each song, the unusual name description is read. When the song title is correctly guessed, the carol is then sung.

1. Invite hitherward the entire assembly of those who are consistent in their belief - O Come All Ye Faithful
2. Listen, the heavenly messengers create harmonious sounds - Hark, the Herald Angels Sing
3. Nocturnal timespan of continuous quietness - O Silent Night
4. Happiness to our global sphere - Joy to the World
5. Decorate the inside passageways - Deck the Halls
6. Exalted celestial messengers to whom we listened - Angels We Have Heard on High
7. Twelve o'clock on a sparkling night witnessed its arrival - It Came Upon a Midnight Clear
8. The Christmas before all others - The First Noel
9. Tiny municipality southeast of Jerusalem - O Little Town of Bethlehem
10. Small masculine master of epidermis-covered noise maker - Little Drummer Boy
11. Omnipresent being who calms jovial distinguished males - God Rest Ye Merry Gentlemen
12. Stout personification fabricated of compressed globes of minute crystals - Frosty the Snowman
13. Anticipation of arrival to populated area by imaginary masculine perennial gift-giver - Santa Claus is Coming to Town
14. An albino natal celebration - White Christmas
15. In awe of the most religious and sacred nocturnal time span - O Holy Night
16. Geographic state of fantasy during the time of mother nature's frozen dormancy - Winter Wonderland
17. The first person nominative plural of a triumvirate of Far Eastern royalty - We Three Kings of Orient Are

18. Tintinnabulation of oscillating pendulums in inverted, metallic, resonant spheres - Jingle Bells
19. In a distant location the existence of large animals masticating slumber furniture - Away in a Manger
20. Proceed forth declaring upon a specific fortification - Go Tell it On the Mountain
21. Jovial yuletide desired for a designated character - We Wish You a Merry Christmas

Twelve Days of Christmas: As the evening draws to a close, the "12 Days of Christmas" is sung. The partners selected in the mixer line up in front of the group in order, beginning with the first day, "partridge in a pear tree." All the guests sing and, as each "day" is sung, the partners pantomime their "day of Christmas." Everyone will anticipate seeing the partners' interpretation of each day of Christmas!

Trim-a-Tree
Christmas

Invitation

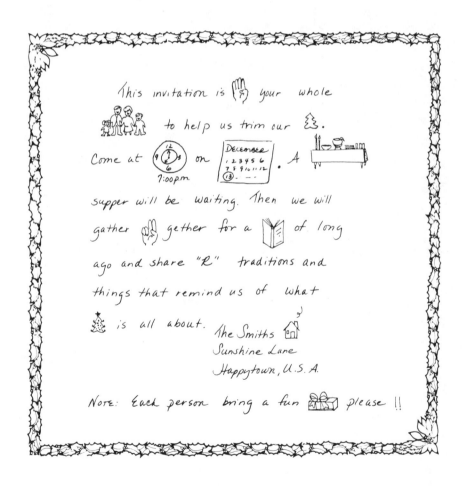

Decorations or Setting the Mood

The Christmas tree, standing statuesque and beautiful, is filled with twinkling lights. Dozens of balls, yards of ribbons and garlands are sitting nearby. Strings of crystals and pearls intertwined in multiple strands may fill the tree and add elegance. Wooden ornaments and bows are great accent pieces. Old ornaments covered with lovely fabrics are contemporary and stunning. Three to five balls may be clustered together, giving fullness, volume and color to the tree. Any theme for trimming the tree may be chosen, even an old-fashioned look with garlands of popcorn and cranberries and ornaments of gingerbread cookies and candy canes.

On a red-draped serving table is a teddy bear, dressed in a wool scarf and hat, riding a sleigh. Pine boughs, holly berries and brass jingle bells accent this centerpiece. Sitting to one side of the sleigh is a large bowl of eggnog and on the other side is a crystal bowl filled with poppycock.

Table Setting and Centerpiece

The table is covered with a forest green cloth, accented with several brass candlesticks. The centerpiece is reminiscent of Christmas past with its whimsical train filled with miniature presents, baskets filled with evergreens, toy soldiers and bright splashes of candy in all shapes and sizes. A small, fancily wrapped present is set at each place. Placed in the center of each plate is a forest green napkin folded to resemble a Christmas tree with a red ribbon bow at the top. Napkins may also be rolled up and tied with gold cord.

On completion of the tree trimming, the overhead lights are dimmed and the tree lights are lit. The setting is now complete for a candlelight dinner.

Menu

Spinach Balls
or
Feta Cheese with Crustadés
Stuffed Cheese Roll with Crackers
Mushroom Appetizers
Cranberry Jello
Gift of the Magi
or
Lasagne Swirls
Marinated Green Beans
Spiced Peaches
Butterhorn Rolls
or
Sour Cream Yeast Rolls
Persimmon Pudding with Lemon Sauce
Buttermilk Brownies with Peppermint Frosting
Fruity Punch

Entertainment or Games

Christmas Story: After dinner, the guests gather around the Christmas tree for "The Christmas Story" or another story from years past.

Gift Exchange: Guests are asked to bring a small, fancily wrapped gift, something special (may set price limit). Each person draws a number. The person with the lowest number selects and unwraps his gift. The next person may choose another wrapped gift or the one already unwrapped. If he chooses the gift the first person unwrapped, the first person chooses another one from the wrapped gifts and unwraps it. Each succeeding person may choose a gift of any other person or pick a wrapped one. At the end of the drawing, the first person may choose from all the gifts.

123

Come Home to Greece

Traditionally the Greek people are fun-loving and enjoy being with family and friends. A rich and elaborate feast sets the stage for this tradition.

Invitation

A flocked grape leaf is attached to a maroon card with thin silver or white ribbon. Party information is written in silver or white ink under the grape leaf.

Decorations or Setting the Mood

Lively Greek music sets the mood for this festive occasion.

Table Setting and Centerpiece

The table is covered with a maroon cloth accented with a basket filled with green and Tokay grapes, eggplants, artichokes and zucchini. This is placed on a large grape leaf mat created by overlapping grape leaves. Smaller grape leaf place mats and artichoke candleholders with ivory candles complete each place setting.

Menu

Egg-Rice Lemon Soup
Tiropites
Dolmas
Greek Salad with Garlic Dressing
Moussaka
Spanakopeta
or
Zucchini with Kasséri Cheese
Galatoboureko
Kourabiedes
or
Baklava
Sparkling Catawba

Entertainment or Games

After dinner, everyone remains at the table. Each person is given a plastic place mat and a can of play dough. The creativity and imagination of the guests are challenged as they form a Greek sculptured statue.

International Roots Party

Invitation

Decorations or Setting the Mood

Lively Swiss or other European-type music sets the mood for this ethnic mixer. Each guest is greeted and given a flower tied with a ribbon or a colored tassel.

The party area is alive with color. This may be achieved by any or all of the following:

1. Clusters of balloons tied with tassels of different colored ribbons are suspended from the ceiling.
2. Travel posters depicting different countries are on display.
3. Flags from different countries are hanging or draped appropriately.
4. Streamers in assorted, bright colors are draped around door arches and windows.
5. Different types of hats, such as Mexican or cowboy, or other articles, such as Oriental umbrellas or fans may be displayed around the room.

Table Setting and Centerpiece

Old crocks of different heights or an odd number of canning jars are filled with baby's breath and tied with brightly-colored ribbon. These are arranged in a cluster on a lace-crocheted tablecloth. Nostalgic items that are reminders of the past are interspersed in the arrangement. Napkins may be in different flag colors.

Menu

This is a perfect opportunity for a potluck buffet. The guests are asked to bring a dish that represents their ethnic background. A card may be placed by each dish with the title and origin of the recipe and the cook's name.

French Mushroom Tarts
Italian Party Lasagne
Turkish Shish Kebabs
Chinese Asparagus
International Salad with Parisian Dressing
English Cucumbers
American Toffee Ice Cream Pie

Entertainment or Games

Mixer: On large sheets of poster board, outline maps of various countries. Cut each map into six or more pieces, depending on number of guests. Mix the map pieces and pass them to the guests. Each guest finds the rest of his group by fitting the pieces together. The group who finishes first wins the prize. Guests should remain in "map" groups for the remainder of the activities.

Roots Game: Provide guests with pencils and paper to use for writing their names and the answers to the following questions:

1. Where were you born?
2. What was the occupation of your father?
3. Where was your grandfather born?

The answers are collected and then read to the guests. Each group ponders these and then records the person they think is responsible for the answers. The group with the most correct answers wins.

Musical Showdown: Each group makes a list of songs that include names of places or have an ethnic origin, such as "My Wild Irish Rose" or "The Yellow Rose of Texas." At a given time, the leader points to a group. The group must immediately begin to sing one of their selected songs. While the group is singing, the leader randomly points to another group who must sing a different song. Groups are eliminated if they sing a song that has been sung, if they do not start singing immediately when signaled or if they do not know the words to the songs they have started to sing. The group who remains in the game longest wins.

Oriental Buffet

Invitation

Invitations are written on rice paper fold-up fans (available at an import store) and inserted in cardboard tubing (available at a stationery store) for mailing. Assign guests one or two dishes to bring.

Decorations or Setting the Mood

Jade vases with fresh, red crysanthemums, silk screens, prints, paintings, paper fans, parasols, kimonos, bamboo novelties, lacquer trays and a display of Oriental curios are but a few suggestions for enhancing the mood of this buffet. Bonsai trees may be borrowed or rented and placed on various tables.

Table Setting and Centerpiece

A table setting with Oriental overtones is easily achieved with plain white dishes and napkins. As red symbolizes happiness in China, red napkins are used. For an authentic touch, use accessories such as rice bowls, soup bowls or teacups in various patterns. These may be purchased inexpensively at import stores.

Fold napkins in fan shapes and stand them in water goblets. An alternative is to fold napkins in half lengthwise, tie them in a loose knot, tuck chopsticks into the center of each knot and place above the plates. The chopsticks add authenticity to the meal, plus a little fun. Have forks handy in the event someone needs them.

An Oriental centerpiece should remain simple, but stately. One or two stalks of pussy willow branches may stand alone. A spray of flowering quince adds a touch of color. To shape the pussy willow branches, soak in warm water and bend in curved shape.

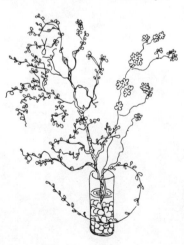

Menu

The endless array of dishes on an Oriental menu is always tempting. The more guests in the group, the greater the variety of dishes to tempt everyone. A menu of this size seems impossible, but becomes possible with the participation of all the guests. A planned potluck dinner buffet with five or six couples participating shares the responsibility of the food preparation. The hostess provides the setting, plans the buffet and prepares her part of the meal. Each invited guest is assigned one dish to prepare ahead and bring.

Egg Rolls with Apricot Dipping Sauce
Spicy Cashews
Fried Walnuts
Watercress Soup
Fried Rice
or
Steamed Rice (your favorite)
Moo Shu Vegetables with Plum Sauce
Egg Foo Yong
Asparagus Noodles
Stir-Fried Vegetables
Skallop Casserole
Pineapple-Cheese Casserole
Oriental Oranges
or
Kiwi Ice
Almond Cookies
Assorted Teas

Pasta Party

Invitation

To a 4 x 6-inch red card, attach a slightly smaller white card. With ⅛-inch green ribbon, tie together three to five dry spaghetti pieces to form a little bouquet. Affix the bouquet to the upper left side. The invitation may read "Pasta Party" at the Jones' Villa, address, time and date.

Decorations or Setting the Mood

The red, white and green of the Italian flag sets the theme for the party in bright table linens, fresh vegetable and bread baskets and colored pasta.

Table Setting and Centerpiece

White linens and dishes set off the colors and textures of the pasta and sauces. Red and green napkins are used with rigatoni dry noodle napkin rings. For the centerpiece, a large basket is lined with a large red or green napkin and filled with fresh whole vegetables such as eggplant, radishes (clean and leave root and greenery, if possible), zucchini, whole garlic bulbs, tomatoes, leaf lettuce and parsley. Another basket is lined with a large red or green napkin and filled with varied sizes and shapes of small bunches of dried or fresh herbs. A decorative cheese board filled with wedges of various cheese will complete this setting.

Menu

Zucchini Bites
Gruyère Cheese Fritters with Honey-Mustard Sauce
Parmesan Bread Sticks
Marinated Antipasto Platter
Italian Green Salad with Poppy Seed Dressing
Vegetable-Gorgonzola Sauce with Linguini
Spaghetti with Pesto
Pasta with Roasted Tomato-Basil Sauce
Sourdough Bread
or
Toasted Garlic Bread
Garlic Butter
Italian Cream Cake
or
Apricot Cheesecake with Apricot Sauce

At a pasta party, the pasta itself is King. Commercial pasta from the supermarket is excellent, but the taste and texture of homemade pasta is well worth the effort. A recipe for Homemade Pasta is included.

La Fiesta Grande
Mexican

Invitation

Yellow poster cardboard is used for the Mexican Man invitation and a piece of brightly-colored, striped material for the blanket. Colored felt-tip pens are used to color the hat and thongs.

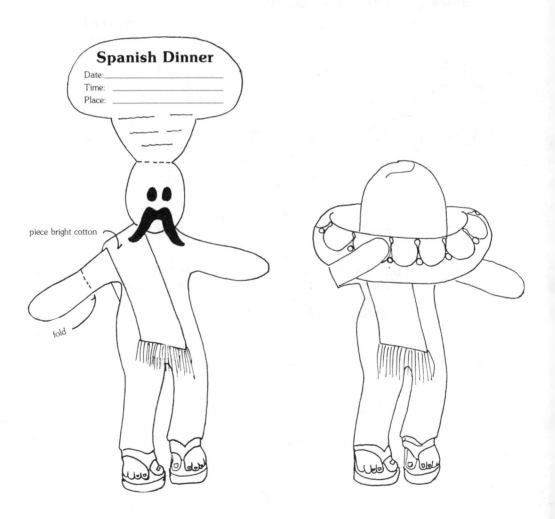

Decorations or Setting the Mood

This is a great party for the back yard. Guests are encouraged to come in Mexican dress. A Mariachi band or background music may be playing as guests arrive.

Bright colors and music are essential to establish the fiesta mood! White Christmas lights are strung in the trees and the patio is lined with luminaries and pots of brightly-colored flowers. Floating in the pool are votive candles in foil pie plates surrounded with flowers. A large piñata hung in a prominent place is a must!

Table Setting and Centerpiece

The buffet and individual tables are covered with brightly-colored burlap cloths with fringed edges. Individual place settings are enhanced by brightly-colored plates and napkin bouquets. Create each bouquet by unfolding three brightly-colored napkins (red, yellow, purple, green, etc.). Place one on top of the other, rotating corners, gather from the center and tuck into a stemmed goblet.

BURRO CENTERPIECE

2 watermelons
2 pineapples
1 orange
Red grapes
Lettuce
Large tray

On the watermelon, outline the area to be carved with a nut pick or something similar. First, carve the face, removing the rind down to the red meat of the melon (about ⅓ of the top). In the green-wedge area left for nose, cut out two holes for nostrils with a small, round canapé cutter. Carefully carve out the teeth, removing just enough of the green rind to expose the white underneath. Remove some of the red flesh of the melon in the mouth area, leaving enough in back of the teeth for support. On the opposite end of the melon, cut two triangle-shape holes. From the second melon, cut two long wedges for ears. Place these wedges in the prepared holes and secure with long wooden skewers. Attach pineapple tops just ahead of the ears with toothpicks and wooden skewers. Cut two round slices from the middle of the orange for eyes. Make eyelids with small wedges cut from the end of the orange and use two red grapes for eyeballs. Place the burro on a lettuce-lined platter surrounded with wedges of watermelon, slices of pineapple and bunches of grapes. This may be assembled the day before the party and covered with damp paper towels and plastic wrap.

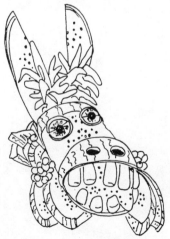

Menu

South of the Border Snack
Mexican Rice
Chile Relleno Casserole
Chimichangas
Guacamole Dip
Chocolate Orange Pie
or
Lemon Frost Pie with Raspberry Sauce
Mexican Fried Ice Cream
Mock Margarita Punch

Christmas "Sopa" Celebration

Invitation

A piece of burlap is cut into an envelope-size rectangle with fringed edges. An overlay of brightly-colored construction paper is attached with party information. Affix a small silk poinsettia to the upper left-hand corner, if desired.

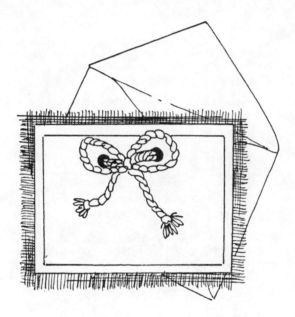

Decorations or Setting the Mood

Piñatas are hung in several places. Orange, red and yellow candles are lit everywhere. All the guests wear festive and colorful attire.

Table Setting and Centerpiece

A small Christmas tree decorated with multi-colored lights may be used for the centerpiece. Christmas bells, trees and wreaths are cut from tortillas with cookie cutters and hung on the tree with colored ribbon. Dried red chiles may also be added. Soup tureens are surrounded with greenery and small poinsettias. Red, green and white napkins, representing the Mexican flag, are overlapped in a decorative fashion.

Menu

Mexican Ruby and Emerald Jewels
Tortilla Dry Soup
Potato-Queso Chowder
Spicy Tomato-Rice Soup
Taco Bread Bites
Spanish Cornbread
Fresh Fruit Platter
Fresh Coconut Cream Pie
or
Lemon Caramel Flan
Chocolate Mexicano
Mineral Water with Twist of Lime

MEXICAN RUBY AND EMERALD JEWELS

Cream Cheese
Triscuits
Red and green jalapeño jellies

Spread cream cheese on each Triscuit and top each with dollop of jelly.

Entertainment or Games

Piñata Surprise: As the party begins to wind down, several of the guests may break the piñata which is filled with Christmas candies and small gifts.

Recipes

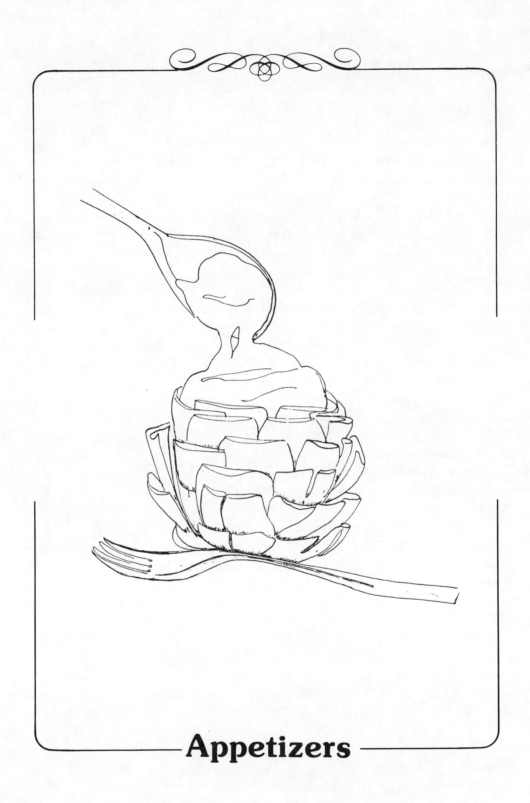

Appetizers

ARTICHOKE HEARTS STUFFED WITH CAMEMBERT
"This is definitely worth the trouble"

2 Tablespoons lemon juice
1 teaspoon flour
8 small to medium artichoke hearts, cut from fresh artichokes
1 6-ounce package Camembert cheese, rind discarded, cut into 1½-inch pieces

1. Add lemon juice to saucepan of boiling water.
2. Whisk in flour.
3. Cook artichoke hearts in boiling water 12-15 minutes or until tender.
4. Drain and pat dry.
5. Remove chokes, trim off edges and place in casserole.
6. Put cheese on chokes in 250-degree oven until cheese is melted.
7. Cover with foil and keep warm in low-temperature oven.

Sauce

¼ pound asparagus, cut into 1-inch pieces and cooked until tender
2 cups heavy cream
3 minced shallots
¼ cup unsalted butter
1 small to medium tomato peeled, seeded and diced
1 Tablespoon finely minced fresh basil

1. Purée asparagus with 2 Tablespoons cream. Set aside.
2. In saucepan, sauté shallots in butter.
3. Add remaining cream, asparagus purée and tomato.
4. Bring to boil until slightly thickened. Do not stir.
5. Add basil.

Garnish

1 small to medium tomato, peeled, seeded and diced
Additional minced basil

To serve, pour Sauce in small plate. Place artichoke hearts with melted cheese in middle of Sauce. Sprinkle diced tomato bits and basil on Sauce for Garnish.

Preparation Time:	**30 minutes**	**Serves:**	**8**
Cooking Time:	**30 minutes**	**May do ahead**	

Variations: *Brie cheese may be substituted for Camembert. Pimento may be substituted for tomato.*

ARTICHOKE NIBBLERS

"It will be hard to stop . . . nibbling, that is!"

2 7½-ounce jars diced, marinated artichoke hearts
1 cup finely chopped onion
1 minced garlic clove
4 eggs
¼ cup fine bread crumbs
¼ teaspoon salt
⅛ teaspoon oregano
⅛ teaspoon hot pepper sauce
2 cups sharp Cheddar cheese
2 Tablespoons minced parsley

1. Drain liquid from 2 jars of archichokes into frying pan.
2. In this liquid, sauté onion and garlic until onions are limp, about 5 minutes.
3. In separate bowl, beat eggs.
4. Add crumbs, salt, oregano and hot pepper sauce.
5. Stir in cheese, parsley, diced artichokes, onion and garlic.
6. Pour into 11 x 7-inch baking dish.
7. Bake at 325 degrees for 30 minutes. Cool.
8. To serve, cut into 1-inch squares.

Preparation Time:	**45 minutes**	**Yield:**	**50**
Baking Time:	**30 minutes**	**May do ahead**	

Tip: *May reheat at 325 degrees for 10-12 minutes.*

CHERRY TOMATOES WITH
ARTICHOKE AND HEARTS OF PALM STUFFING

2 8-ounce cans drained artichoke hearts
2 8-ounce cans hearts of palm
Juice of 1 lemon
¼ cup tarragon vinegar
⅓ cup olive oil
¼ cup chopped fresh basil
¼ cup chopped parsley
2 pints cherry tomatoes
Parsley for garnish

1. Chop artichoke hearts and hearts of palm into small pieces.
2. Combine lemon juice and vinegar. Add oil, beating constantly.
3. Add chopped artichoke-hearts of palm mixture, basil and parsley.
4. Cut off tops of cherry tomatoes. Use melon baller to scoop out middle of tomatoes.
5. Fill with artichoke-hearts of palm mixture.
6. Garnish with parsley. Replace tomato tops at an angle.

Preparation Time:	**30 minutes**	**Serves:**	**12-15**
Variation: *If using dry herbs, use ⅓ of listed amount.*		**Yield:**	**2½ cups stuffing**

ASPARAGUS ROLL-UPS

1 loaf white sandwich bread
¾ cup hollandaise sauce
½ cup grated, fresh Parmesan cheese
1 15-ounce can asparagus spears, 20 spears per can
Melted butter
Sesame seeds

1. Remove bread crusts. Roll bread slices with rolling pin until flat and thin.
2. Spread with hollandaise sauce.
3. Sprinkle with Parmesan cheese.
4. Place asparagus diagonally across each bread slice.
5. Roll corners and overlap at center. Secure with toothpicks. Place seam side down on baking sheet.
6. Brush with melted butter. Sprinkle with sesame seeds.
7. Bake at 400 degrees for 12-15 minutes or until golden brown.

Preparation Time:	**30 minutes**	**Yield:**	**20**
Baking Time:	**12-15 minutes**		

DILLED BABY CARROTS

¾ cup rice vinegar
¼ cup water
¼ cup honey
½ teaspoon dried, whole dill weed
½ teaspoon mixed pickling spice
Dash of salt
½ pound baby carrots, scraped
Sprigs of fresh dill, optional

1. In large saucepan, combine first 6 ingredients. Bring to boil.
2. Add carrots. Cover and reduce heat. Simmer 10-12 minutes or until crisp-tender. Remove from heat.
3. Pour mixture into plastic container. Set container in bowl of ice water to cool quickly. Chill.
4. Serve with slotted spoon. Garnish with sprigs of dill, if desired.

Preparation Time:	**15 minutes**	**Serves:**	**12-15**
Cooling Time:	**1 hour**		

CHEESE APPETIZER TORTE

"Serve with pride"

3 Tablespoons melted butter
1⅔ cups cheese cracker crumbs
2 cups sour cream
3 grated, hard-boiled eggs
¼ cup chopped green pepper
2 Tablespoons red bell pepper or pimento
3 Tablespoons chopped green onion
3 Tablespoons diced green chiles
2 Tablespoons lemon juice
2 mashed garlic cloves
½ teaspoon salt
½ teaspoon Beau Monde seasoning
1 teaspoon paprika
1 teaspoon Worcestershire sauce
Dash of hot pepper sauce
Parsley sprigs

1. Combine butter and cracker crumbs. Set aside.
2. Combine all other ingredients.
3. Spoon ⅓ of crumbs on bottom of buttered 9-inch springform pan.
4. Pour ½ mixture on top.
5. Gently spoon ⅓ of crumbs on top of mixture.
6. Repeat layers, ending with crumbs. Refrigerate 24 hours.
7. Remove sides of springform pan. Garnish with parsley.

Preparation Time:	**45 minutes**	**Serves:**	**15**
Chilling Time:	**24 hours**	**Must do ahead**	

CHEESE TEMPTERS

1 cup grated Cheddar cheese
½ cup butter at room temperature
½ cup flour
¼ teaspoon salt
1 cup cornflakes
Paprika

1. Combine cheese and butter until well-blended.
2. Add flour and salt.
3. Add cornflakes. Blend until mixture holds together.
4. Pinch off small amounts and roll into firm balls.
5. Place 2 inches apart on ungreased baking sheet.
6. Sprinkle with paprika.
7. Bake at 400 degrees for 12 minutes.

Preparation Time:	**40 minutes**	**Yield:**	**30**
Baking Time:	**12 minutes**		

CHEESE LOG

25 Servings

4 ounces cream cheese
2 Tablespoons margarine
¼ pound grated Colby cheese
2 Tablespoons smoked cheese spread
1 Tablespoon dried onions
¾ teaspoon Worcestershire sauce
¼ teaspoon paprika
Dash garlic powder
2 drops hot pepper sauce
¼ teaspoon dry mustard
¼ cup ground pecans

1. Mix all ingredients except pecans.
2. Form into log-shaped roll about 9 inches long. Roll in ground pecans.
3. Wrap in plastic wrap and chill.

Preparation Time: **30 minutes**   **May do ahead and freeze**
Serving Suggestion: *Serve on cheese board with favorite crackers.*
Tip: *Cheese log is more flavorful if refrigerated for at least 24 hours. May be frozen. Allow 8 hours to thaw in refrigerator before serving.*

50 Servings

1 8-ounce package cream cheese
4 Tablespoons margarine
½ pound grated Colby cheese
¼ cup smoked cheese spread
2 Tablespoons dried onions
1½ teaspoons Worcestershire sauce
½ teaspoon paprika
⅛ teaspoon garlic powder
4 drops hot pepper sauce
½ teaspoon dry mustard
⅓ cup ground pecans

Divide into 2 parts. Form each portion into log-shaped roll about 9 inches long.

100 Servings

2 8-ounce packages cream cheese
½ cup margarine
1 pound grated Colby cheese
½ cup smoked cheese spread
¼ cup dried onions
1 Tablespoon Worcestershire sauce
1 teaspoon paprika
¼ teaspoon garlic powder
8 drops hot pepper sauce
1 teaspoon dry mustard
½-¾ cup ground pecans

Divide into 4 parts. Form each portion into log-shaped roll about 9 inches long.

CREAM CHEESE-NUT BALL

2 8-ounce packages softened cream cheese
1 8-ounce can drained, crushed pineapple
2 cups chopped pecans
¼ cup chopped green pepper
2 Tablespoons chopped onion
1 Tablespoon seasoned salt

1. In bowl, place softened cream cheese. Gradually add crushed pineapple, 1 cup pecans, green pepper, onion and salt. Chill 1 hour.
2. Form into ball and roll in remaining 1 cup pecans.
3. Chill in foil, plastic wrap or sealed container.

Preparation Time:	20 minutes	Yield:	1 large ball or
Chilling Time:	1 hour		2-3 small balls
		May do ahead	

Serving Suggestion: *Good for finger sandwich filling and stuffed celery.*

GRUYERE CHEESE FRITTERS
"A most unusual appetizer"

1 egg white
1 pound grated Gruyère cheese
2 Tablespoons chopped parsley
¼ teaspoon grated nutmeg
½ teaspoon paprika
¼ cup flour
1 egg
2 Tablespoons milk
¾ cup bread crumbs
Oil for deep frying

1. Whisk egg white until foamy.
2. With hands, mix in cheese, parsley, nutmeg and paprika until well-blended. Chill 2-3 hours.
3. Mix together flour, egg and milk.
4. Shape cheese mixture into 1-inch balls and dip in egg mixture, then in bread crumbs. Refrigerate overnight.
5. Heat oil to 350 degrees. Fry balls approximately 3-5 minutes. Drain on paper towels.
6. Serve immediately.

Preparation Time:	20 minutes	Yield:	40 fritters
Chilling Time:	Overnight plus 2-3 hours		
Frying Time:	3-5 minutes		

Serving Suggestion: *Serve with Honey-Mustard Sauce.*

CROCKED CHEESE
"A delightful flavor"

½ pound finely grated, sharp Cheddar cheese at room temperature
1 8-ounce package cream cheese at room temperature
1 3-ounce package Roquefort cheese at room temperature
2 Tablespoons butter or margarine at room temperature

1. In food processor, combine all ingredients. Process until smooth.
2. Pack cheese mixture into crocks or other serving dishes. Seal tightly with plastic wrap and store in refrigerator.

Preparation Time: **10 minutes**   **Serves:**   **16**
                                                   Must do 3 days ahead
Serving Suggestion: *Sprinkle top of cheese with chopped parsley or nuts.*
Variation: *Substitute blue cheese for Roquefort cheese.*
Tip: *May store in refrigerator 1 month. Do not freeze.*

PIMENTO CHEESE ROLLS
"Serve . . . and purr!"

½ cup instant minced onion
1 cup water
1 cup butter
1 cup mayonnaise
4 pounds American cheese at room temperature, cut into chunks
2 4-ounce jars chopped pimento
1½ cups minced parsley
120-130 sandwich bread slices, crusts trimmed

1. Stir onions into water. Let stand 5 minutes.
2. Beat together butter, mayonnaise and cheese.
3. Mix in onion, pimento and parsley.
4. Spread 1 side of each bread slice with cheese mixture, reserving ⅓ cheese mixture for topping.
5. Roll each bread slice like jellyroll.
6. Place close together on baking sheet or jellyroll pan.
7. Spread tops with remaining cheese mixture.
8. Bake at 350 degrees for 10-12 minutes or until golden brown.
9. Serve hot.

Preparation Time: **1 hour**   **Yield:**   **120-130 rolls**
Baking Time: **10-12 minutes**   **May do ahead**
Variation: *Substitute Cheddar cheese for American cheese.*

STUFFED CHEESE ROLL

1 16-ounce package Velveeta cheese at room temperature
1 8-ounce package cream cheese at room temperature
1 7-ounce can drained, diced green chiles
1 2-ounce can drained, sliced pimentos
1 4-ounce can drained, chopped ripe olives
Green onion, optional
Lettuce leaves

1. Between 2 waxed paper sheets, roll Velveeta cheese evenly into rectangle about ⅓-inch thick. Remove 1 sheet of waxed paper.
2. Spread cream cheese over Velveeta.
3. Mix green chiles, pimentos and olives. Spread evenly over cream cheese.
4. Roll up cheese, keeping bottom sheet of waxed paper around cheese roll.
5. Refrigerate overnight.
6. To serve, trim off both ends of roll. Roll may be cut into 2 halves. Place seam down on bed of lettuce.

Preparation Time:	**30 minutes**	**Serves:**	**18-20**
Chilling Time:	**8 hours**	**Must do ahead**	

Serving Suggestion: *Garnish with pimento, green onion or pimento-stuffed olives. Serve with assorted crackers.*

TIROPITES
"Cheese triangles"

1 pound grated feta cheese
¼ cup grated Parmesan cheese
2 beaten eggs
1 teaspoon oregano
1 teaspoon olive oil
1 pound phyllo dough
2 cups melted butter

1. Combine feta cheese, Parmesan cheese, eggs, oregano and olive oil. Mix well. Set aside.
2. Lay 1 phyllo sheet on flat surface. Brush with melted butter.
3. Cover with second phyllo sheet. Brush with butter.
4. Repeat with 1 more sheet.
5. Cut 3 phyllo sheets lengthwise in equal size strips about 2½ inches wide.
6. Place heaping teaspoon of filling at bottom of each strip.
7. Fold flag fashion, folding phyllo over filling. Continue to fold strip, maintaining triangular shape.
8. Brush top with melted butter. Place on lightly oiled baking sheet.
9. Repeat with remaining phyllo sheets and filling.
10. Bake at 400 degrees for 15-20 minutes or until golden brown.

Preparation Time:	**40 minutes**	**Yield:**	**40 triangles**
Baking Time:	**15-20 minutes**	**May freeze**	

Tip: *When not using phyllo dough, keep covered with damp cloth to prevent drying out.*

EGG CHIPS

10 Servings

3 chopped, hard-boiled eggs
1 Tablespoon chopped ripe olives
¼ teaspoon salt
1½ teaspoons chopped dill pickle
2 Tablespoons mayonnaise
½ 2-ounce jar pimento, cut in strips
10 potato chips or whole wheat thins

1. Mix first 5 ingredients.
2. Place small teaspoons of egg mixture on chips or crackers. Garnish with pimento.
3. Serve immediately.

Preparation Time: 20 minutes

50 Servings

5 chopped, hard-boiled eggs
½ can chopped ripe olives
1 teaspoon salt
2½ Tablespoons chopped dill pickle
⅓ cup mayonnaise
2½ 2-ounce jars pimento, cut in strips
50 potato chips or whole wheat thins

Preparation Time: 30 minutes

100 Servings

10 chopped, hard-boiled eggs
1 small can chopped ripe olives
2½ teaspoons salt
5 Tablespoons chopped dill pickle
1 cup plus 2 Tablespoons mayonnaise
5 2-ounce jars pimento, cut in strips
100 potato chips or whole wheat thins

Preparation Time: 45 minutes

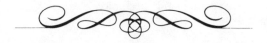

EGG ROLLS

2 cups plus 1 Tablespoon vegetable oil
1 teaspoon sugar
2 teaspoons soy sauce
1 minced garlic clove
½ teaspoon minced ginger root
1 cup finely shredded cabbage
½ cup shredded carrots
½ cup diced, fresh mushrooms
2 Tablespoons sliced green onions
¼ cup diced water chestnuts
1 package 4-inch square egg roll wrappers

1. In large skillet, combine 1 Tablespoon oil, sugar, soy sauce, garlic and ginger root. Heat until garlic and ginger root are fragrant.
2. Add cabbage, carrots, mushrooms, green onions and water chestnuts. Sauté until vegetables are crisp-tender, stirring occasionally. Remove from heat.
3. Place 2 Tablespoons vegetable mixture on each egg roll wrapper. Roll lengthwise into envelopes. Seal edges with drop of water.
4. Heat 2 cups oil to 400 degrees. Deep fry a few egg rolls at a time about 4 minutes or until golden brown.
5. Line cookie sheet with several paper towels. Place deep-fried egg rolls on towels to drain. Keep warm in 200-degree oven. Do not stack in pan or egg rolls will become soggy.

Preparation Time: 1 hour   **Yield:** 20 egg rolls
Cooking Time: 15 minutes
Variation: *Any combination of vegetables may be used, such as bamboo shoots, fresh bean sprouts and celery.*

HILO FRANKS
"A tasty surprise"

1 cup apricot preserves
½ cup tomato sauce
½ cup white vinegar
2 Tablespoons soy sauce
2 Tablespoons honey
1 Tablespoon vegetable oil
1 teaspoon salt
½ teaspoon ginger
2 pounds franks

1. Combine all ingredients except franks.
2. Cut franks on bias and insert toothpick in each piece.
3. Place franks in sauce and simmer ½ hour.

Preparation Time: 20 minutes   **Serves:** 20
Cooking Time: 30 minutes
Serving Suggestion: *Serve warm in chafing dish.*

FRENCH MUSHROOM TARTS

"You'll feel like a French chef serving this"

Pastry

½ **cup butter**
1 **cup flour**
1 **teaspoon baking powder**
Dash salt
1 **egg**
1 **Tablespoon milk**

1. Mix above ingredients.
2. Form pastry to cover bottoms and sides of 36 individual tart tins.

Mushroom Filling

¾ **cup chopped onions**
1 **Tablespoon butter**
1½ **cups chopped mushrooms**

1. Sauté onions in butter.
2. Add mushrooms to onions.
3. Place 1 Tablespoon mixture in each tart shell.

Filling

2 **beaten eggs**
3¼ **cups sour cream**
Dash hot pepper sauce
Chopped parsley

1. Mix all ingredients.
2. Pour over Mushroom Filling.
3. Bake at 350 degrees for 20 minutes.

Preparation Time:	**1 hour**	**Yield:**	**36 tarts**
Baking Time:	**20 minutes**		

MUSHROOM APPETIZERS

1 Tablespoon butter
1 crushed garlic clove
1 pound button mushrooms, washed and dried
1 teaspoon dill weed
½ teaspoon onion powder
½ teaspoon salt
1 Tablespoon lemon juice
1 cup sour cream

1. Melt butter.
2. Add garlic, mushrooms, dill weed, onion powder, salt and lemon juice. Mix well. Cook 20 minutes or until mushrooms are cooked through. Remove from heat.
3. Add sour cream.
4. Refrigerate overnight to marinate.
5. To serve, warm slowly. Place in chafing dish and eat with toothpicks.

Preparation Time:	15 minutes		Serves:	5-20
Cooking Time:	20 minutes			
Standing Time:	8 hours			

MUSHROOM TURNOVERS
"A crowd pleaser"

Filling

½ cup finely chopped onions
1 minced garlic clove
2 Tablespoons margarine or butter
1 cup chopped, fresh mushrooms
¾ teaspoon salt
1 chopped, hard-boiled egg yolk
1 3-ounce package cream cheese

Pastry

1½ packages pie crust mix
¾ cup sour cream
1 egg white

1. In medium skillet, sauté onion and garlic in margarine until tender. Add mushrooms and sauté 3 minutes.
2. Stir in salt, egg yolk and cream cheese. Cool.
3. In medium bowl, combine pie crust mix and sour cream. Mix until ball forms.
4. Divide in half. Roll lightly on floured surface to ⅛-inch thickness.
5. Cut into rounds with 3-inch cookie cutter.
6. Spoon rounded ½ teaspoon of Filling onto half circle Pastry.
7. Moisten edges with egg white or water. Press together with fork.
8. Bake at 400 degrees for 12-13 minutes.

Preparation Time:	40 minutes	Yield:	60
Baking Time:	12-13 minutes	May do ahead and freeze	

Suggestion: *Turnovers may be frozen on cookie sheet, then stacked in container with waxed paper between layers.*

MUSHROOM TARTS
"Worth the trouble"

Tart Crust

2 cups flour
1 teaspoon salt
¾ cup butter
4 Tablespoons ice water

1. Mix lightly.
2. Form into ball. Divide into 4 equal parts. Wrap in plastic. Chill 1 hour.
3. Roll out 1 section at a time to ¼-inch thickness.
4. Cut out 8 3-inch rounds with floured cookie cutter.
5. Line tart pans and prick well with fork.
6. Bake at 400 degrees for 10 minutes.

Filling

¾ cup chopped onion
2 Tablespoons butter
1 pound chopped, fresh mushrooms
1 Tablespoon lemon juice
½ teaspoon salt
1 Tablespoon cornstarch
1 Tablespoon water
1 cup heavy cream
¼ cup shredded Gruyère cheese

1. Sauté onion in butter.
2. Add mushrooms, lemon juice and salt. Set aside.
3. Combine cornstarch with water in cup.
4. In separate saucepan, heat cream until just boiling.
5. Stir in cornstarch mixture to thicken.
6. Add mushroom mixture.
7. Place 1 Tablespoon Filling in partially baked Tart Crust. Sprinkle with cheese.
8. Bake at 400 degrees for 10 minutes.

Preparation Time:	45 minutes	**Yield:**	**32 tarts**
Chilling Time:	1 hour		
Cooking Time:	10 minutes		
Baking Time:	20 minutes		

STUFFED MUSHROOM CAPS

MICROWAVE RECIPE

20 Servings

40 mushrooms, washed and dried
1 8-ounce package softened cream cheese
1 10-ounce package frozen, chopped spinach, thawed and squeezed dry
2 Tablespoons minced onions
½ cup shredded Cheddar cheese

1. Remove stems from mushrooms. Set caps aside and finely chop stems.
2. In medium bowl, combine cream cheese, spinach, onions and mushroom stems.
3. Fill mushroom caps and top with cheese.
4. Microwave 30 at a time at high power for 10 minutes.
5. Serve hot.

Preparation Time: **15 minutes**
Cooking Time: **10 minutes**

50 Servings

100 mushrooms, washed and dried
2 8-ounce packages softened cream cheese
2 10-ounce packages frozen, chopped spinach, thawed and squeezed dry
4 Tablespoons minced onions
1 cup shredded Cheddar cheese

100 Servings

200 mushrooms, washed and dried
4 8-ounce packages softened cream cheese
4 10-ounce packages frozen, chopped spinach, thawed and squeezed dry
½ cup minced onions
2 cups shredded Cheddar cheese

ONION RINGS

1 sliced, large onion
3 Tablespoons Wondra flour
1 cup buttermilk

1. Slice onions and separate rings.
2. Mix flour into buttermilk.
3. Dip onion rings in batter and fry quickly in very hot, deep oil.

Preparation Time: **10 minutes**   **Serves:**   **2**

NACHOS SUPREME

1 15½-ounce can Chilli Man Vegetarian Chilli
1 16-ounce can refried beans
4 small avocados, mashed, with 1 teaspoon lemon juice
Salt to taste
1 cup sour cream
6 Tablespoons mayonnaise
1 package taco seasoning
2 cups shredded Cheddar cheese
2 cups shredded Monterey Jack cheese
4 diced, small tomatoes
3 sliced green onions
2 large bags tortilla chips

1. Combine chili with beans. Set aside.
2. In separate bowl, combine mashed avocados, lemon juice and salt. Set aside.
3. In another bowl, combine sour cream, mayonnaise and taco seasoning. Set aside.
4. Layer in order listed:

   Bean dip
   Guacamole
   Sour cream mixture
   Cheddar cheese
   Monterey Jack cheese
   Tomatoes
   Onions

5. Serve with tortilla chips.

Preparation Time: **30 minutes**   **Serves:**   **15**

FRIED WALNUTS
"So delicious, they're indescribable"

6 cups water
4 cups walnuts
½ cup sugar
Salad oil
Salt

1. In 4-quart saucepan over high heat, bring water to boil. Add walnuts and heat to boiling. Boil 1 minute.
2. Rinse walnuts under running hot water. Drain. Wash saucepan and dry well.
3. In large bowl with rubber spatula, gently add warm walnuts into sugar. Stir until sugar is dissolved.
4. In same saucepan, heat 1 inch oil.
5. With slotted spoon, add half of walnuts to oil. Fry 5 minutes or until golden, stirring often.
6. Place walnuts in coarse sieve over bowl to drain. Sprinkle lightly with salt. Toss lightly to keep walnuts from sticking together. Transfer to paper towels to cool.
7. Fry remaining walnuts.

Preparation Time: **30 minutes**   **Yield:**   **4 cups**
Tip: *Store in tightly covered container.*   **May do up to 2 weeks ahead**

149

SPICY CASHEWS

1 teaspoon curry powder
¾ teaspoon cumin
1 teaspoon salt
3 Tablespoons unsalted butter
2 cups raw cashews

1. In small bowl, combine curry powder, cumin and salt. Set aside.
2. In heavy skillet, melt butter over moderate heat. Add nuts and sauté, stirring constantly, until pale golden.
3. Add seasonings. Continue to stir until lightly browned. Drain on paper towels.
4. Serve warm or at room temperature.

Preparation Time: **10 minutes**   **Yield:**   **2 cups**

ONION BITES
"Tasty and quick"

2 cups flour
1 cup softened butter
1 package onion soup mix
1 pound grated Cheddar cheese

1. Mix all ingredients. Form into log. Refrigerate or freeze.
2. When ready to serve, let stand at room temperature a few minutes.
3. Slice in ½-inch widths.
4. Bake at 375 degrees for 10 minutes. Serve immediately.

Preparation Time: **15 minutes**   **Yield:**   **100**
Baking Time: **10 minutes**   **May do ahead and freeze**

TACO BREAD BITES

⅔ cup finely chopped onion
⅓ cup butter
½-1 4-ounce can diced green chiles
1 pound loaf frozen bread dough, thawed
2 Tablespoons taco seasoning
1½-2 cups grated Monterey Jack cheese

1. In medium skillet, sauté onion in butter until tender.
2. Pat chiles dry on paper towels.
3. Add chiles to sauteed onions. Set aside.
4. Spread bread dough in greased jellyroll pan.

Continued

TACO BREAD BITES — Continued

5. Sprinkle with taco seasoning and onion-chile mixture.
6. Cover and let rise about 30 minutes or until almost double in bulk.
7. Top with cheese.
8. Bake at 400 degrees for 22-24 minutes or until browned.
9. Use kitchen shears to snip bread into serving-size pieces. Serve hot.

Preparation Time:	**20 minutes**	**Serves:**	**6-8**
Rising Time:	**30-60 minutes**		
Baking Time:	**22-24 minutes**		

HERB POPCORN

"A new twist for an old favorite"

¾ cup butter or margarine
1 teaspoon basil
1 teaspoon chervil
1 teaspoon thyme leaves
24 cups popped corn (about 1 cup kernels)
1 12-ounce can unsalted, mixed nuts

1. In small saucepan over low heat, melt butter. Remove saucepan from heat. Stir in basil, chervil and thyme leaves.
2. Place half of popped corn in large open roasting pan. Pour half of butter mixture over popcorn. With rubber spatula, gently toss to coat popcorn well. Pour popcorn mixture into large bowl. Repeat with remaining popcorn and butter mixture.
3. Add nuts. Toss to mix.

Preparation Time:	**30 minutes**	**Yield:**	**26 cups**

PARTY SNACK

"For the unusual fun snack"

½ cup melted butter
2 teaspoons soy sauce
1 teaspoon garlic salt
1 teaspoon ground ginger
2½ quarts popped corn
1 3-ounce can chow mein noodles
1 Tablespoon sesame seeds

1. Combine butter, soy sauce, garlic salt and ginger.
2. Mix with popcorn and chow mein noodles.
3. Sprinkle with sesame seeds.
4. Bake in 9 x 13-inch pan at 350 degrees for 30 minutes, stirring a few times during baking.

Preparation Time:	**25 minutes**	**Yield:**	**12 cups**
Baking Time:	**30 minutes**		

SOUTH OF THE BORDER SNACK

½ cup butter
1 envelope taco seasoning mix
1 8-ounce package soy nuts
2 cups pretzel sticks
2 cups small corn cereal squares
1 3-ounce can chow mein noodles
2 cups corn chips

1. Melt butter in saucepan. Stir in taco seasoning. Set aside.
2. In large baking pan, mix soy nuts, pretzel sticks, cereal squares, noodles and corn chips. Pour taco seasoning mixture over nut mixture. Toss gently to coat.
3. Bake at 300 degrees for 20 minutes or until crisp and hot. Cool.
4. Store in airtight container.

Preparation Time:	**10 minutes**	**Yield:**	**10-12 cups**
Baking Time:	**20 minutes**		

PINEAPPLE CREAM DELIGHTS

"Everyone wants this recipe"

2 packages Stella DeOro Anginetti Cookies
1 8-ounce package softened cream cheese
1 8-ounce can drained, crushed pineapple
1 8-ounce carton whipping cream, whipped, or 2 cups Cool Whip

1. Beat cream cheese until fluffy.
2. Mix in pineapple.
3. Fold in whipped cream.
4. Cut cookies in half, fill with mixture and replace cookie tops.
5. Cover tightly and refrigerate 24 hours.

Preparation Time:	**30 minutes**	**Serves:**	**15**
		Must do 1-3 days ahead	

SWEET POTATO CHIPS

"Great for a different snack"

3 long, narrow sweet potatoes
Shortening for deep frying
Powdered sugar or salt

1. Peel raw potatoes. Cut crosswise into paper-thin slices.
2. Soak slices in cold water 20 minutes.
3. Drain and dry thoroughly with paper towel.
4. Heat oil to 375 degrees. Fry ⅓ of chips at a time for 2-3 minutes, turning once or twice until golden brown on both sides. Drain.
5. Sprinkle with powdered sugar or salt.
6. Serve warm or at room temperature.

Preparation Time:	**30 minutes**	**Yield:**	**10-12 cups**
Cooking Time:	**6-10 minutes**		

FETA CHEESE SPREAD WITH CRUSTADES

"Disappears like magic"

Crustades

3 loaves white bread
1 cup melted margarine or butter

1. Roll bread slices with rolling pin to flatten.
2. Brush with melted margarine or butter.
3. Cut out circles with 2¾-inch cookie cutter.
4. Press into mini-muffin tins or individual tart pans.
5. Bake at 350 degrees for 8-10 minutes or golden.

Preparation Time:	15 minutes	**Yield:**	50
Baking Time:	6-8 minutes	**May do ahead and freeze**	

Variation: *May be used with your favorite fillings.*
Tip: *If frozen, rewarm in oven at 350 degrees for 3-5 minutes.*

Feta Cheese Spread

1 8-ounce package cubed cream cheese
4-6 minced green onions
⅓ cup frozen, chopped spinach, cooked and squeezed dry
⅛ pound grated Monterey Jack cheese
⅛ pound crumbled feta cheese
½ cup grated, fresh Parmesan cheese
Pimento for garnish

1. Place cream cheese and green onions in glass bowl.
2. Heat 2-4 minutes in microwave until cheese is creamy and onions are softened.
3. Add spinach, Monterey Jack cheese, feta cheese and Parmesan cheese.
4. Heat again until Spread is hot and bubbly. Spread may be thinned with a little milk.
5. Spoon into Crustade cups. Heat in 350-degree oven for 5-6 minutes. Garnish with pimento.
6. Serve warm or at room temperature.

Preparation Time:	30 minutes	**Yield:**	50 crustades
Baking Time:	5 minutes		

Variation: *Spread may be used on crackers.*

SPANAKOPETA

"Spinach phyllo squares"

2 Tablespoons olive oil
1 minced, small onion
15-20 minced parsley sprigs
1 cup crumbled feta cheese
6 lightly beaten eggs
Salt to taste
2 10-ounce packages frozen chopped spinach, thawed and squeezed dry or
  2 pounds fresh spinach, chopped, cooked and squeezed dry
12 sheets phyllo pastry (½ pound)
1 cup melted butter

1. In heavy skillet, heat olive oil. Add onion and stir until golden.
2. Mix with parsley, cheese, eggs and salt.
3. Add spinach. Mix thoroughly.
4. Brush 9 x 13-inch baking dish with melted butter. Line dish with 1 layer of phyllo pastry. Fold edges back over dough to fit dish. Brush generously with butter.
5. Repeat layering and buttering with phyllo dough, until there are 6 layers.
6. Spoon in spinach mixture and smooth it over pastry.
7. Cover with another layer of phyllo and brush with butter.
8. Continue adding 5 more layers, brushing each with butter.
9. Bake at 375 degrees for 45 minutes or until puffed and golden brown. Remove from oven.
10. Cool slightly. Cut into 24 squares. Serve warm.

Preparation Time:	**30 minutes**	**Yield:**	**24 squares**
Baking Time:	**45 minutes**		

Tip: *May use as entreé. Cut into 12 squares. May bake ahead and reheat.*

SPINACH BALLS

1 diced, large onion
1 cup softened margarine
2 10-ounce packages frozen chopped spinach, cooked and squeezed dry
2½ cups seasoned stuffing mix
1 cup grated, fresh Parmesan cheese
1 teaspoon garlic salt
½ teaspoon thyme

1. Sauté onion in ½ cup margarine.
2. Combine all ingredients.
3. Form into balls.
4. Bake at 375 degrees for 10 minutes.
5. Serve warm or at room temperature.

Preparation Time:	**20 minutes**	**Yield:**	**20-25 balls**
Baking Time:	**10 minutes**	**May freeze**	

FRESH VEGETABLE MARINADE

"Instead of a salad"

Herb Marinade
Fresh green beans, ends trimmed
Green and red bell peppers, cut into strips
Fresh cauliflower, separated into 1-inch flowerets
Eggplant, cut into 1-inch cubes, skin on
Fresh okra, ends trimmed
Fresh mushrooms, thickly sliced, stems on
Fresh broccoli, separated into 1-inch flowerets with stems
Frozen brussel sprouts, thawed
Carrots, pared and cut into 5-inch sticks
Frozen artichoke hearts, thawed
Fresh zucchini, diagonally sliced ¼-inch thick
Radish roses
Fresh snow peas
Cherry tomatoes

1. Make Herb Marinade.
2. Wash and prepare an assortment of vegetables from list. Use desired amounts to equal approximately 2 pounds.
3. To blanch vegetables, pour boiling water to cover green beans, red and green pepper and cauliflowerets. Let stand 10 minutes. Drain.
4. Pour boiling water to cover eggplant. Let stand 7 minutes. Drain. Remaining vegetables do not need to be blanched.
5. Arrange vegetables in single layer in shallow baking dish, plastic container or sealable plastic bag. Pour Marinade over vegetables, tossing gently to coat well. Refrigerate, covered, overnight, spooning Marinade over vegetables 4-5 times. If using sealable bag, turn several times.
6. To serve, drain vegetables. Arrange on platter.

Herb Marinade

1 8-ounce bottle Italian or herb-garlic salad dressing
2 teaspoons snipped, fresh dill weed
¼ cup lemon juice
½ teaspoon salt

Combine all ingredients. Mix well and refrigerate.

Preparation Time: **30 minutes**   **Yield:**   **1 cup marinade**
Standing Time: **Overnight**   **Must do ahead**
Tip: *Marinade will marinate 2 pounds fresh vegetables.*

MARINATED ANTIPASTO PLATTER

"Best if made one or two days ahead"

2 cups fresh broccoli flowerets
2 cups fresh cauliflowerets
2 cups fresh mushrooms
2 cups baby corn-on-the-cob
2 cups Italian or herbal Italian dressing
1 cup quartered, marinated artichoke hearts
½ cup pimento-stuffed olives
½ cup ripe olives
2 cups small cherry tomatoes

1. Combine broccoli, cauliflower, mushrooms and corn-on-the-cob.
2. Pour dressing over vegetables. Toss well. Refrigerate overnight to marinate.
3. Just before serving, add artichoke hearts, olives and cherry tomatoes.

Preparation Time:	**30 minutes**	**Serves:**	**12-15**
Marinating Time:	**6-8 hours**	**Must do ahead**	

ZUCCHINI BITES

"This boat will sail into your files"

4 small zucchini, cut into 1-inch thick slices
1 Tablespoon vegetable or olive oil
¼ cup chopped tomato
¼ cup chopped, fresh mushrooms
¼ cup chopped green or red bell pepper
2 Tablespoons minced ripe olives
1 Tablespoon grated onion
1 Tablespoon chopped, fresh basil or 1 teaspoon dried basil
1 teaspoon chopped, fresh oregano or ¼ teaspoon dried oregano

1. Place zucchini slices in steamer basket over boiling water for 3 minutes. Cool slightly and drain well.
2. Scoop out some of pulp, forming a small cup to hold filling. Set aside.
3. In large skillet, heat oil over medium heat. Add remaining ingredients and sauté 3 minutes. Drain well.
4. Fill zucchini cups with hot vegetable mixture.
5. Serve warm or at room temperature.

Preparation Time:	**30 minutes**	**Yield:**	**1½ dozen**
Cooking Time:	**6-8 minutes**		

APRICOT DIPPING SAUCE

1 cup apricot preserves
1½ Tablespoons grated fresh ginger or ½ Tablespoon ground ginger
1 teaspoon Dijon mustard
1 Tablespoon rice vinegar

1. Mix all ingredients in small saucepan.
2. Heat mixture over low heat, just to melt preserves.

Preparation Time: **10 minutes**   **Yield:**   **1¼ cups**
Serving Suggestion: *Serve with Egg Rolls.*

HOT ARTICHOKE DIP

"Easy and good"

4 4-ounce cans drained artichoke hearts
1 cup mayonnaise
1 cup grated, fresh Parmesan cheese
Hot pepper sauce to taste
Paprika

1. Place artichoke hearts, mayonnaise, Parmesan cheese and hot pepper sauce in food processor and blend.
2. Place in serving bowl. Top with paprika.
3. Bake at 350 degrees for 30 minutes.

Preparation Time: **10 minutes**   **Yield:**   **3 cups**
Baking Time: **30 minutes**
Serving Suggestion: *Serve with toasted, sliced sourdough bread, assorted crackers or fresh vegetables.*
Variation: *Add 4 ounces whipped cream cheese. Chop artichoke hearts. Do not use food processor to mix ingredients.*

MEXICAN ARTICHOKE DIP

MICROWAVE RECIPE

1 8-ounce can drained, diced artichoke hearts
1 6-ounce can drained, diced, marinated artichoke hearts
1 4-ounce can diced green chiles
1 8-ounce package cubed Velveeta cheese
½ cup sliced olives
3 Tablespoons mayonnaise

1. Combine all ingredients.
2. Microwave on medium heat until cheese is melted.

Preparation Time: **10 minutes**   **Yield:**   **4 cups**
Serving Suggestion: *Serve with tortilla chips.*

AVOCADO-TOMATO DIP

10-12 Servings

1 cup mashed avocado
1 Tablespoon lemon juice
¾ teaspoon salt
1½ teaspoons grated onion
1 Tablespoon chopped, fresh tomatoes
¼ teaspoon soy sauce

Mix all ingredients.

Preparation Time: 20-30 minutes

50 Servings

4 cups mashed avocado
¼ cup lemon juice
1 Tablespoon salt
2 Tablespoons grated onion
¼ cup chopped, fresh tomatoes
1 teaspoon soy sauce

100 Servings

8 cups mashed avocado
½ cup lemon juice
2 Tablespoons salt
¼ cup grated onion
½ cup chopped, fresh tomatoes
2 teaspoons soy sauce

SALSA

"Delicious low-calorie dip"

2 16-ounce cans chopped, whole tomatoes
2-3 chopped, fresh tomatoes
1 chopped, large red onion
1 7-ounce can diced green chiles
1 Tablespoon finely chopped, fresh cilantro
½ teaspoon basil
Hot pepper sauce to taste
Salt and garlic powder to taste

1. Mix all ingredients and refrigerate.
2. Serve chilled or at room temperature.

Preparation Time: 10 minutes   **Yield: 3 cups**
Chilling Time: 6 hours   **Must do ahead**

GUACAMOLE DIP

2 very ripe avocados
3 Tablespoons fresh lemon juice
2-3 Tablespoons finely minced onion
1 peeled, finely chopped tomato
3-4 dashes hot pepper sauce
¾ teaspoon salt
Sour cream
Finely minced scallions, including tops
Cayenne pepper
Sliced ripe olives

1. Peel avocados and mash until fairly smooth, reserving seeds.
2. Add lemon juice and blend well.
3. Add onion, tomato, hot pepper sauce and salt. Mix well.
4. Cover and chill in refrigerator until ready to serve.
5. To serve, place guacamole in bowl garnished with dollop of sour cream, scallions, cayenne pepper and olives.

Preparation Time:　　**15 minutes**　　　　　　　　**Serves:**　　**6-8**
Serving Suggestion: *Use corn or tortilla chips for dipping.*　　**May freeze**
Tips: *To prevent discoloration, place avocado seeds in guacamole until serving time. To freeze, place guacamole in airtight container. Cover guacamole with ⅓-inch layer of freshly squeezed lemon juice. Place plastic wrap over container and cover with tight-fitting lid.*

BEAN DIP
"A hit with teenagers!"

2 cups cooked pink beans
1 3-ounce can tomato paste
1 7-ounce can green chile salsa
½ teaspoon minced garlic
1 Tablespoon onion flakes
Salt to taste
¾ cup grated Monterey Jack cheese
1 16-ounce carton sour cream

1. Blend beans, tomato paste, salsa, garlic, onion flakes and salt.
2. Heat and stir bean mixture with cheese until heated thoroughly.
3. Remove from heat. Add sour cream.

Preparation Time:　　**10 minutes**　　　　　　　　**Serves:**　　**10**
Cooking Time:　　　　**15 minutes**

HOT BEAN DIP

2 16-ounce cans refried beans
1 8-ounce package softened cream cheese
1 cup sour cream
½ package taco dip mix
10-20 drops hot pepper sauce

1. Mix all ingredients.
2. Warm in 350 degree oven until bubbly.
3. Serve hot with chips.

Preparation Time:	10 minutes	**Yield:**	6 cups
Baking Time:	15 minutes		

GARBANZO DIP

1 15-ounce can drained garbanzos
⅓ cup lemon juice
⅓ cup sesame tahini
1 garlic clove
½ teaspoon salt

1. Combine all ingredients in blender. Process until smooth.
2. Chill overnight.

Preparation Time:	5 minutes	**Yield:**	1⅔ cups

Tip: *Reserve garbanzo liquid to thin mixture, if necessary.*

CURRY DIP

1 cup sour cream
1 cup mayonnaise
2 Tablespoons chopped onion
2 teaspoons curry powder
2 teaspoons dill weed
2 teaspoons seasoned salt

1. Combine all ingredients. Mix until smooth.
2. Refrigerate at least 6 hours.

Preparation Time:	10 minutes	**Yield:**	2¼ cups
Chilling Time:	6 hours	**Must do ahead**	

Serving Suggestion: *Serve with vegetables or serve in red cabbage. Microwave raw cabbage 2-3 minutes, then open and spoon dip into cabbage.*

TEX-MEX DIP
"Always a hit"

3 medium avocados
2 Tablespoons lemon juice
½ teaspoon salt
½ cup mayonnaise
1 8-ounce carton sour cream
1 package taco seasoning mix
2 9-ounce cans bean dip
1 6-ounce can drained, sliced olives
1 bunch sliced green onions
3 chopped, medium tomatoes
1 cup grated Cheddar cheese

1. Mash avocados with lemon juice, salt and mayonnaise.
2. In separate bowl, mix sour cream with taco mix.
3. Layer on large serving plate in listed order:

   Bean dip
   Avocado mixture
   Sour cream mixture
   Olives, green onions and tomatoes
   Grated cheese

Preparation Time: **20 minutes**   **Yield:**   **4½-5 cups**
Serving Suggestion: *Serve with tortilla chips or corn chips.*

HONEY-BERRY DIP

1 cup sour cream
2 large strawberries, washed and hulled
1 Tablespoon honey
Red food coloring, optional

1. Combine ¼ cup sour cream with strawberries and honey in food processor or blender. Puree until smooth.
2. Spoon into small bowl. Stir in remaining sour cream.
3. Chill until ready to eat.

Preparation Time: **10 minutes**   **Yield:**   **1¼ cups**
Chilling Time: **30 minutes**   **May do ahead**
Serving Suggestion: *Serve with green grapes or strawberries as dippers.*
Variation: *If darker color desired, add a few drops of red food coloring.*

HONEY-MUSTARD SAUCE

4 egg yolks
4 teaspoons vinegar
1 teaspoon salt
2 cups salad oil
1 Tablespoon lemon juice
2 Tablespoons mustard
2 Tablespoons honey

1. Beat egg yolks lightly with electric mixer.
2. Add 3 teaspoons vinegar and salt. Blend thoroughly.
3. Slowly pour in oil, beating continuously at medium speed.
4. Add last teaspoon of vinegar, lemon juice, mustard and honey. Blend until well mixed.

Preparation Time: **10 minutes**   **Yield:**   **2 cups**
Serving Suggestion: *Serve with Gruyère Cheese Fritters.*

PLUM SAUCE

1 cup plum preserves
½ teaspoon garlic powder
3 Tablespoons chicken-style broth
1 Tablespoon Dijon mustard
1 teaspoon dry mustard

1. Mix all ingredients in small saucepan.
2. Heat mixture over low heat, just to melt preserves.

Preparation Time: **10 minutes**   **Yield:**   **1½ cups**
Serving Suggestion: *Serve with Egg Rolls or Moo Shu Vegetables.*

DILL-SOUR CREAM DIP

20 Servings

½ cup mayonnaise
½ cup sour cream
2 teaspoons minced green onion
2 teaspoons chopped parsley
¼ teaspoon dill weed
¾ teaspoon seasoning salt

1. Mix mayonnaise and sour cream. Add remaining ingredients.
2. Chill at least 1 hour.

Preparation Time: **20 minutes**
Chilling Time: **1 hour**

50 Servings

1⅓ cups mayonnaise
1⅓ cups sour cream
2 Tablespoons minced green onion
2 Tablespoons chopped parsley
1 teaspoon dill weed
2 teaspoons seasoning salt

100 Servings

2⅔ cups mayonnaise
2⅔ cups sour cream
¼ cup minced green onion
¼ cup chopped parsley
2 teaspoons dill weed
4 teaspoons seasoning salt

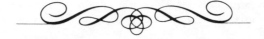

GARLIC-CHEESE DIP

10-12 Servings

1 cup cottage cheese
1 crushed garlic clove
1 teaspoon salt
¼ cup chopped ripe olives
¼ cup mayonnaise

1. Place cottage cheese in blender.
2. Add remaining ingredients.

Preparation Time: 15-20 minutes

50 Servings

1 quart cottage cheese
4 crushed garlic cloves
1 Tablespoon salt
1 cup chopped ripe olives
1 cup mayonnaise

100 Servings

2 quarts cottage cheese
8 crushed garlic cloves
2 Tablespoons salt
2 cups chopped ripe olives
2 cups mayonnaise

SPINACH DIP

"Popeye's special"

1 10-ounce package frozen, chopped spinach, thawed and squeezed dry
2 cups sour cream
1 cup mayonnaise
½ cup chopped parsley
½ cup chopped green onions
1 package leek soup mix
½ teaspoon dill weed
1 teaspoon Italian seasoning

Mix all ingredients. Chill.

Preparation Time: 15 minutes   **Yield:** 4 cups
Chilling Time: 5 hours   **Must do ahead**
Serving Suggestion: *Serve with raw vegetable tidbits or bread chunks.*
Variation: *To serve, hollow out a cabbage or large round bread and fill with dip. Reserve bread chunks for dipping.*

FRESH VEGETABLE DIP

"Fresh dill makes the difference"

1 cup mayonnaise
1 cup sour cream
4 minced green onions
1 Tablespoon chopped parsley
1 Tablespoon minced, fresh dill weed
2 teaspoons Beau Monde seasoning

Mix all ingredients. Chill.

Preparation Time:	10 minutes	**Yield:**	2½ cups
Chilling Time:	6 hours	**Must do ahead**	

Serving Suggestion: *Serve with fresh vegetables.*

BIG ROUND LOAF APPETIZER

1 10-ounce package frozen chopped spinach, thawed and squeezed dry
1 cup sour cream
1 cup mayonnaise
1 8-ounce can drained, chopped water chestnuts
1 bunch thinly sliced green onions
1 package dry vegetable soup mix
Garlic powder to taste
1 round loaf French or Italian bread

1. Combine all ingredients except bread. Set aside.
2. Cut top off bread and hollow out loaf. Reserve bread pieces.
3. Fill loaf with spinach mixture. Replace bread lid.

Preparation Time: 30 minutes   **Serves:** 8-10
Serving Suggestion: *Serve with reserved bread pieces. Break off pieces of lid and loaf sides.*
Variation: *To serve hot, wrap loaf in foil and bake at 350 degrees for 40 minutes.*
Tip: *When warm, wrap in layers of newspaper. This will keep loaf hot to take on a picnic or to the beach.*

Beverages

CHAMPAGNE CIDER

1 gallon apple cider
2 liters 7-UP

1. In large punch bowl, mix cider and 7-UP.
2. Add crushed ice.

Preparation Time: **10 minutes**   **Yield:**   **1½ gallons**
Serving Suggestion: *Pour into stemmed glasses.*

CHOCOLATE MEXICANO

1 circular tablet (3 ounces) Mexican spiced chocolate or 3 ounces
   semisweet chocolate
2 Tablespoons sugar
½ teaspoon cinnamon
¼ teaspoon vanilla
3 cups milk

1. In saucepan, combine all ingredients. Bring to boil.
2. When chocolate has melted, beat mixture until blended and mixture stops boiling.
3. Bring to boil again and beat well over heat.
4. Bring to boil a third time and beat over heat to produce as much foam as possible.
5. Pour into cups and serve immediately.

Preparation Time: **20 minutes**   **Yield:**   **4 cups**
Variation: *Each circle of Mexican chocolate is divided into 8 triangles. For individual serving of chocolate, melt 2 triangles with ¾ cup milk and beat as directed.*

CITRUS DELIGHT
"Light and refreshing"

2 cups sugar
1 cup water
½ cup fresh lemon juice
1 liter chilled carbonated water
½ cup fresh lime juice
½ cup fresh orange juice
2 cups fresh grapefruit juice
1½ quarts non-alcoholic wine

1. Combine sugar with water and lemon juice.
2. Bring to boil for 1 minute. Cool.
3. Add carbonated water and stir in lime, orange and grapefruit juice.
4. Pour into punch bowl over ice.
5. Add wine.
6. Garnish with lemon slices and mint leaves.

Preparation Time: **30 minutes**   **Yield:**   **1 gallon**

COCONUT PUNCH
"A knockout"

1 44-ounce can pineapple-coconut juice
2 12-ounce cans lemon-lime soda
2 ounces half-and-half
1 fresh pineapple

1. In large punch bowl, mix juice, soda and half-and-half.
2. Add crushed ice.
3. Pour into serving glasses.

Preparation Time: **30 minutes**   **Yield:**   **12 cups**
Serving Suggestion: *Garnish each glass with wedge of fresh pineapple.*

EGGNOG WITHOUT EGGS
"What a yummy surprise"

2 cups applesauce
1 pint half-and-half
1 6-ounce can frozen lemonade concentrate
1 pint lemon or lime sherbet
1 liter 7-UP
Nutmeg

Combine all ingredients except nutmeg. Sprinkle with nutmeg.

Preparation Time: **20 minutes**   **Yield:**   **10 cups**

FIESTA FRUIT PUNCH

1 12-ounce can frozen orange juice concentrate
1 12-ounce can frozen lemonade concentrate
9 cups water
1 quart canned peaches, undrained
2-3 Tablespoons Hawaiian Coconut Snow (coconut powder is better than syrup)
1 quart 7-UP

1. Mix juice concentrates with water.
2. In blender, mix peaches, Hawaiian Coconut Snow and 7-UP.
3. Add to orange-lemon mixture.

Preparation Time: **15 minutes**   **Yield:**   **20 cups**
Serving Suggestion: *To serve, float a Glamorous Ice Ring.*

FRESH LEMONADE

For each cup of water, use:

3-4 Tablespoons sugar
1½ Tablespoons lemon juice

1. Boil water and sugar 2 minutes. Chill.
2. Add lemon juice.

Preparation Time:	**15 minutes**	**Yield:**	**1 cup**
Cooking Time:	**2 minutes**		

FROSTY BANANA PUNCH

7 cups water
3 cups sugar
5 well-mashed bananas
1 6-ounce can frozen orange juice concentrate
1 6-ounce can frozen lemonade concentrate
1 46-ounce can pineapple juice
1 quart gingerale or 7-UP
Assorted fruit

1. Boil water and sugar for 5 minutes. Cool.
2. Add remaining ingredients, except for gingerale and fruit. Freeze.
3. Remove from freezer 2-3 hours before serving.
4. Mash slush mixture with potato masher and add gingerale.
5. To serve, float assorted fruit in punch bowl.

Preparation Time:	**30 minutes**	**Yield:**	**20 cups**
		Must freeze	

FROSTY FRUIT SURPRISE

1 cup sugar
1 quart buttermilk
1 teaspoon vanilla
4 cups whole, frozen fruit

1. In large bowl, combine sugar, buttermilk and vanilla.
2. Gently fold in fruit.
3. Serve as beverage or pour into 9 x 9-inch dish and freeze.

Preparation Time:	**15 minutes**	**Yield:**	**8 cups**
Freezing Time:	**Overnight**		

Tip: *Cherries and berries are best.*

FRUIT PUNCH

7 cups water
3 cups sugar
5 well-mashed bananas
1 6-ounce can frozen orange juice concentrate
1 6-ounce can frozen lemonade concentrate
1 46-ounce can pineapple juice
1 quart gingerale or 7-UP

1. Boil water and sugar for 5 minutes. Cool.
2. Add remaining ingredients except for gingerale. Freeze.
3. Remove from freezer 2-3 hours before serving.
4. Mash slush mixture with potato masher.
5. Add gingerale just before serving.

Preparation Time:	**30 minutes**	**Yield:**	**24 cups**
Freezing Time:	**Overnight**	**Must do ahead**	
Thawing Time:	**3 hours**		

Serving Suggestion: *Float assorted fruit in punch bowl.*

FRUIT WHIZ

1 46-ounce can pineapple juice
2 fresh bananas
2 Tablespoons frozen orange juice concentrate
Strawberries for taste and color

1. Blend 5 cups pineapple juice, bananas, orange juice and strawberries until smooth.
2. Pour into container and freeze overnight until solid.
3. When ready to serve, remove frozen juice and mash with potato masher.
4. Add remaining pineapple juice.
5. Blend a few seconds until just slushy.

Preparation Time:	**15 minutes**	**Yield:**	**8 cups**
Freezing Time:	**Overnight**		

Serving Suggestion: *Serve immediately with fresh fruit on decorated toothpick as garnish.*

FRUITY PINK PUNCH

¾ cup sugar
2 cups cranberry juice
1 cup pineapple juice
1 cup water

1. Mix all ingredients in punch bowl.
2. Add crushed ice.

Preparation Time:	**10 minutes**	**Yield:**	**6 cups**
Serving Suggestion: *Float lemon slice in each glass.*		**May do ahead**	

FRUITY DELIGHT

1 package unsweetened cherry Kool-Aid
1 cup sugar
1 6-ounce can frozen orange juice concentrate
1 6-ounce can frozen lemon concentrate
1 46-ounce can pineapple juice
4 overripe bananas
2 liters 7-UP or gingerale

1. Mix all ingredients except bananas and 7-UP in 6-quart sealable container (allow room for stirring and expansion of juice as it freezes).
2. Pour 2 cups juice mix in blender. Add bananas and purée.
3. Mix all juices and banana purée. Whisk until well-blended.
4. Place in freezer. Stir every 2 hours. Freeze solid.
5. Remove from freezer 4 hours before serving or partially thaw in microwave. Stir until slushy.
6. To serve, add 2 liters 7-UP or gingerale.

Preparation Time:	**20 minutes**	**Yield:**	**18 cups**
Freezing Time:	**6-8 hours**	**Must do ahead**	

Tip: *If need to refreeze, use only half of slush mixture initially, adding 7-UP to individual glasses, measuring ¾ cup slush with ¼ cup 7-UP.*

FRUITY PUNCH

3 12-ounce cans frozen Hawaiian punch concentrate
1 12-ounce can frozen pineapple juice concentrate
4 ripe bananas

1. Combine frozen juices. Dilute with water according to can directions.
2. Place 2 cups of diluted juice in blender with bananas. Purée. Add banana mixture to juice mixture.

Preparation Time:	**10 minutes**	**Yield:**	**2 gallons**

HOT AND SPICY BERRY BOWL

1 cup water
¼ cup red hot cinnamon candies
1 3-ounce package strawberry jello
7 cups cranapple drink or 4 cups cranberry juice and 3 cups apple cider

1. In 3-quart saucepan, mix water and cinnamon candies. Boil until candies are melted.
2. Stir in jello until completely dissolved.
3. Add cranberry juice.
4. Heat until punch is bubbly.
5. Serve hot.

Preparation Time:	**15 minutes**	**Yield:**	**2 quarts**

HOT CIDER
"A winter warmer"

2 quarts apple cider
2 cinnamon sticks
12 whole cloves
Grated nutmeg
1 Tablespoon brown sugar
½ cup lemon juice
1 orange

1. Place cider in saucepan. Add cinnamon, cloves, nutmeg and brown sugar. Simmer 1 hour.
2. Strain and add lemon juice.
3. Slice orange paper-thin and place 1 slice in bottom of each cup. Fill with cider. Serve hot or cold.

Preparation Time: **20 minutes**   **Yield:**   **8 cups**
Cooking Time: **1 hour**

HOT SPICED NECTAR
"Attention, apricot lovers"

3 cups apricot nectar
2 cups orange juice
1 cup water
2 Tablespoons lime juice
½ cup brown sugar
4-6 sticks cinnamon
1 teaspoon whole cloves

1. In crock pot, combine all ingredients except spices. Cook until very hot.
2. Tie spices in cheese cloth. Add to crock pot and cook 10-15 minutes.
3. Serve hot.

Preparation Time: **15 minutes**   **Yield:**   **6 cups**
Cooking Time: **1 hour**

LAVENDER SLUSH

10 Servings

2 cups grape juice
4 cups apple juice
2 cups water
1 12-ounce can frozen limeade concentrate
1 12-ounce can frozen lemonade concentrate
2 quarts gingerale

1. Mix all ingredients except gingerale.
2. Strain. Discard lemon and lime pulp.
3. Pour into 2 2-quart containers. Freeze until firm.
4. To serve, leave out of freezer about 30 minutes.
5. Mash and mix with approximately equal parts gingerale.
6. Serve immediately.

Preparation Time:	20 minutes		Yield:	1 gallon
Freezing Time:	24 hours			
Standing Time:	30 minutes			

50 Servings

2½ quarts grape juice
5 quarts apple juice
2½ quarts water
5 12-ounce cans frozen limeade concentrate
5 12-ounce cans frozen lemonade concentrate
10 quarts gingerale

Tip: *Freeze in 10 2-quart containers.*   Yield: 5 gallons

100 Servings

5 quarts grape juice
2½ gallons apple juice
5 quarts water
10 12-ounce cans frozen limeade concentrate
10 12-ounce cans frozen lemonade concentrate
20 quarts gingerale

Tip: *Freeze in 20 2-quart containers.*   Yield: 10 gallons

LIME-PINEAPPLE PUNCH

1 cup sugar
2 cups water
2 teaspoons grated lime peel
½ cup lime juice (about 4 limes)
1 pint lime sherbet
1 pint pineapple sherbet
3½ cups lemon-lime carbonated beverage

1. Combine sugar and 1 cup water. Cook and stir until dissolved.
2. Add remaining 1 cup water, lime peel and juice. Chill.
3. Pour into chilled punch bowl. Add scoops of sherbet and stir until partially thawed.
4. Pour in carbonated beverage, stirring with up and down motion. Serve immediately.

Preparation Time: **10 minutes**   **Yield:**   **2 quarts**

MAY DAY PUNCH

1 12-ounce can lemonade concentrate
4 12-ounce cans water
1 48-ounce can pineapple juice
1 quart pineapple sherbet
1 liter Sprite or 7-UP

1. Mix lemonade, water and pineapple juice.
2. Just before serving, add sherbet and Sprite.

Preparation Time: **10 minutes**   **Yield:**   **1 gallon**
Variation: *May add food coloring.*

ORANGE-CRANBERRY ZING

2 12-ounce cans frozen orange juice concentrate
6 cups water
2 quarts cranberry juice
1 quart 7-UP

1. Mix orange juice with water.
2. Just before serving, add cranberry juice and 7-UP.

Preparation Time: **10 minutes**   **Yield:**   **20 cups**

MOCK MARGARITA PUNCH

1 12-ounce can frozen lemonade concentrate
1 12-ounce can frozen limeade concentrate
1 cup powdered sugar
4 egg whites
6 cups crushed ice
1 quart club soda
Lime slices
Coarse salt

1. In 4-quart non-metal container, combine lemonade, limeade, powdered sugar, egg whites and crushed ice. Mix well. Cover and freeze, stirring occasionally.
2. Remove container from freezer 30 minutes before serving.
3. Spoon 2 cups slush mixture into blender. Add 1 cup club soda. Blend until frothy.
4. Repeat step 3 for further servings.
5. To serve, rub rim of glass with lime slice and dip rim in coarse salt. Fill glass.
6. Garnish with lime slices.

Preparation Time: **15 minutes**   **Yield:**   **10 cups**
Freezing Time: **6 hours**

PEACH DELIGHT

2 46-ounce cans peach Hi-C
1 12-ounce can frozen lemonade concentrate
2 liters chilled gingerale

1. Combine peach Hi-C and lemonade. Chill.
2. Just before serving, add gingerale.

Preparation Time: **5 minutes**   **Yield:**   **20 cups**

PINA COLADA PUNCH

2 quarts Pineapple-Coconut Juice
2 quarts 7-UP

1. Mix equal parts of Pineapple-Coconut Juice and 7-UP.
2. Add food coloring, if desired.

Preparation Time: **5 minutes**   **Yield:**   **1 gallon**

RASPBERRY CRUSH

1 envelope unsweetened raspberry-flavored soft drink powder
1½ cups sugar
4 cups water
1 6-ounce can frozen lemonade concentrate
1 10-ounce can frozen raspberries
1 12-ounce can lemon-lime carbonated beverage

1. Combine soft drink powder and sugar.
2. Add water. Stir until dissolved.
3. Stir in lemonade concentrate and raspberries. Chill.
4. When ready to serve, add carbonated beverage and serve over ice cubes.

Preparation Time: **30 minutes**   **Yield:**   **8 cups**

RASPBERRY FROST

2 16-ounce packages frozen raspberries
½ cup water
1 6-ounce can frozen orange juice concentrate
1 6-ounce can frozen lemonade concentrate
1 quart gingerale
Sugar to taste

1. Purée raspberries and water in blender.
2. Add juice concentrates.
3. Freeze until mixture forms ice crystals, but does not become solid.
4. Just before serving, mash mixture to slush and add gingerale and sugar to taste. Mixture will be thick.

Preparation Time: **10 minutes**   **Yield:**   **8 cups**
Freezing Time: **6-8 hours**

RASPBERRY PUNCH

"Special for any festive occasion"

1 12-ounce package frozen raspberries
¼ cup sugar
3 sprigs fresh mint or 2 drops mint extract
Grated peel of 1 lemon
¼ cup lemon juice
½ cup orange juice
1 quart chilled gingerale

1. Thaw raspberries. Press through sieve.
2. Slowly heat raspberry purée with sugar and mint, stirring until sugar is dissolved. Cool.
3. Remove mint. Add lemon peel, lemon juice and orange juice. Chill.
4. Just before serving, add chilled gingerale.

Preparation Time: **1 hour**   **Yield:**   **6 cups**

RUBY RED FROSTY PUNCH

8-10 Servings

1 quart cranberry juice
½ cup fresh lemon juice
½ cup sugar
1 quart chilled gingerale
1 cup raspberry sherbet

1. Mix fruit juices and sugar until sugar is dissolved.
2. Pour into punch bowl or large container.
3. Add chilled gingerale and sherbet. Serve immediately.

Preparation Time: 20 minutes   **Yield:**   10 cups

50 Servings

1 quart plus 1 cup cranberry juice
3 cups fresh lemon juice
2 cups sugar
4½ 28-ounce bottles chilled gingerale
1 quart raspberry sherbet

                                                          Yield: 1½ gallons

100 Servings

2½ quarts cranberry juice
6 cups fresh lemon juice
4 cups sugar
9 28-ounce bottles chilled gingerale
½ gallon raspberry sherbet

                                                          Yield: 3 gallons

RED CINNAMON HOLIDAY PUNCH

"A warming treat"

¼ cup sugar
½ cup red cinnamon candies
6 cups cranberry juice
3 cups pineapple juice
2 cups water
3 Tablespoons lemon juice

1. In large saucepan, combine all ingredients.
2. Cook uncovered 7 minutes or until hot, stirring occasionally.

Preparation Time: 10 minutes   **Yield:**   3 quarts
Cooking Time: 7 minutes
Serving Suggestion: *Garnish with orange slices.*

SPICED PINEAPPLE SPARKLE

"Great summertime drink"

⅔ cup sugar
1½ cups water
6 inches stick cinnamon
12 whole cloves
1 46-ounce can unsweetened pineapple juice
1½ cups orange juice
½ cup lemon juice
1 12-ounce can chilled gingerale

1. In large saucepan, combine sugar, water, cinnamon and cloves. Simmer 15 minutes. Strain.
2. Add pineapple juice, orange juice and lemon juice. Chill.
3. To serve, slowly pour juice over ice in punch bowl. Add gingerale.

Preparation Time:	30 minutes	Yield:	12 cups
Chilling Time:	4 hours		

STRAWBERRY JELLO PUNCH

"Straight from the berry patch"

4 10-ounce packages frozen unsweetened strawberries
3-4 mashed bananas
3 cups sugar
3 cups boiling water
1 6-ounce and 1 3-ounce packages strawberry jello
6 cups cold water
2 46-ounce cans pineapple juice
1 8-ounce can crushed pineapple
4 liters 7-UP
4 empty half-gallon milk cartons

1. Partially thaw strawberries and blend with bananas in blender. Set aside.
2. Add sugar to boiling water. Boil 2 minutes.
3. Add both packages strawberry jello and stir until dissolved.
4. Add cold water, pineapple juice, crushed pineapple and banana-strawberry mixture. Mix well.
5. Freeze in milk cartons.
6. Take out of freezer 2 hours before serving. Mash.
7. Add 1 liter of 7-UP per carton.

Preparation Time:	30 minutes	Yield:	2 gallons
Freezing Time:	6-8 hours		
Thawing Time:	2 hours		

Variation: *Use raspberry jello and frozen raspberries instead of strawberries.*

STRAWBERRY SLUSH

2 10-ounce packages frozen, unsweetened strawberries, drained
1 30-ounce can crushed pineapple with juice
3 cups orange juice
2 liters lemon-lime soda

1. In blender, mix half of strawberries and 15 ounces pineapple with juice. Blend until smooth.
2. Pour in ice cube trays. Freeze.
3. Repeat steps 1 and 2.
4. To serve, place 3 cubes in glass. Pour soda over cubes to fill glass. Stir gently to make slush.

Preparation Time: **20 minutes**   **Yield:**   **1 gallon**
Freezing Time: **Overnight**

SUMMER CHAMPAGNE

¾ cup sugar
1 cup water
1 cup canned grapefruit juice
½ cup canned pineapple juice
1 quart chilled gingerale

Combine all ingredients.

Preparation Time: **10 minutes**   **Yield:**   **7 cups**
Serving Suggestion: *Garnish with whole strawberries or pineapple chunks.*

TROPICAL SLUSH

2 1½-quart bottles Ocean Spray Mauna Lai Hawaiian Guava-Passion Fruit Drink
1 12-ounce can frozen orange juice concentrate
1 6-ounce can frozen pineapple juice concentrate
⅓ cup sugar
1½ quarts water
4 overripe bananas
2 liters 7-UP or gingerale

1. Mix all ingredients except bananas and 7-UP in 6-quart sealable container (allow room for stirring and expansion of juice as it freezes).
2. Pour 2 cups juice mix in blender. Add bananas and purée.
3. Mix all juices and banana purée. Whisk until well-blended.
4. Place in freezer. Stir every 2 hours. Freeze solid.
5. Remove from freezer 4 hours before serving or partially thaw in microwave. Stir until slushy.
6. Add 2 liters 7-UP or gingerale.

Preparation Time: **10 minutes**   **Yield:**   **2 gallons**
                                                 Must do ahead

Tip: *If need to refreeze, use only half of slush mixture initially, adding 7-UP to individual glasses, measuring ¾ cup slush with ¼ cup 7-UP.*

WASSAIL BOWL

2 sticks cinnamon
1 teaspoon whole allspice
1 small orange studded with cloves
2 quarts apple juice or cider
1 pint cranberry juice

1. Place cinnamon, allspice and orange in cheesecloth, tied securely.
2. Combine all ingredients in crock pot. Cover and simmer for 5 hours.
3. Serve warm.

Preparation Time:	**10 minutes**	**Yield:**	**12 cups**
Cooking Time:	**5 hours**		

GLAMOROUS ICE RING

Orange slices
Lemon slices
Lime slices

1. Fill ring mold with water, leaving ¾ inch at top. Freeze.
2. On top of frozen ring, arrange orange slices, lemon slices and lime slices. Fill to top with water. Freeze.
3. To serve, unmold. Float in punch bowl.

Preparation Time:	**15 minutes**	**Yield:**	**1 ice ring**
Freezing Time:	**5-6 hours**		

Breads

ALMOND-POPPY SEED BREAD

Bread

3 cups flour
1¾-2 cups sugar
1 cup plus 2 Tablespoons oil
1½ cups milk
3 eggs
2 Tablespoons poppy seeds
1½ teaspoons baking powder
1½ teaspoons salt
1 teaspoon vanilla
1 teaspoon almond extract
1 teaspoon butter flavoring

1. Mix all ingredients in listed order.
2. Pour into 2 9 x 5-inch loaf pans or 5 mini-loaf pans.
3. Bake at 350 degrees for 1 hour or until toothpick inserted comes out clean.
4. Remove from pan when cool.

Topping

½ cup orange juice
¾ cup sugar
1 teaspoon vanilla
1 teaspoon almond extract
1 teaspoon butter flavoring

1. Mix all ingredients.
2. Heat until boiling. Remove from heat.
3. With pastry brush, spread over top of cooled bread, allowing Topping to run down sides. Repeat.

Preparation Time: 15 minutes
Baking Time: 1 hour

Yield: 2 large loaves or 5 mini-loaves
May do ahead and freeze

APRICOT-NUT BREAD

"Delicious, tangy flavor"

1 16-ounce can apricot halves
⅓ cup shortening
½ cup sugar
2 eggs
1¾ cups sifted flour
1 teaspoon baking powder
½ teaspoon baking soda
½ teaspoon salt
½ cup chopped walnuts

1. Drain apricots, reserving syrup.
2. Sieve or purée apricots.
3. Add reserved syrup to apricots, if necessary, to make 1 cup.
4. In separate bowl, cream together shortening and sugar.
5. Add eggs, 1 at a time. Beat until light and fluffy.
6. In another bowl, sift together dry ingredients.
7. Add dry ingredients to creamed mixture alternately with apricot mixture.
8. Stir in walnuts.
9. Pour into well-greased 9 x 5-inch loaf pan.
10. Bake at 350 degrees for 50-60 minutes.
11. Cool 10 minutes before removing from pan. Cool completely on rack.

Preparation Time:	45 minutes	**Yield:**	1 loaf
Baking Time:	50-60 minutes	**May freeze**	

Serving Suggestion: *Spread with cream cheese for a tasty luncheon sandwich.*

BANANA-NUT BREAD

"Use those last ripe bananas your kids won't eat"

⅓ cup shortening
½ cup sugar
2 eggs
1¾ cups sifted flour
1 teaspoon baking powder
½ teaspoon baking soda
½ teaspoon salt
1 cup mashed, ripe banana
½ cup chopped walnuts

1. In bowl, cream together shortening and sugar. Add eggs and beat well.
2. In separate bowl, sift together dry ingredients.
3. Add dry ingredients to creamed mixture alternately with banana, blending well after each addition.
4. Stir in nuts.
5. Pour into well-greased 9 x 5-inch loaf pan.
6. Bake at 350 degrees for 40-45 minutes.
7. Cool 10 minutes before removing from pan. Cool completely on rack.

Preparation Time:	20 minutes	**Yield:**	1 loaf
Baking Time:	45 minutes	**May freeze**	

BLUEBERRY LOAF
"Spring special"

½ cup margarine
½ cup sugar
2 beaten eggs
2 cups flour
1 Tablespoon baking powder
½ teaspoon salt
¾ cup milk
1 cup fresh blueberries tossed with 1 teaspoon flour
1 teaspoon cinnamon-sugar

1. Cream margarine and sugar.
2. Add eggs. Beat until well-blended.
3. In separate bowl, mix dry ingredients.
4. Add dry ingredients alternately with milk to creamed mixture.
5. Gently fold blueberries into batter.
6. Pour into greased 8 x 4-inch loaf pan. Sprinkle with cinnamon-sugar.
7. Bake at 350 degrees for 50-55 minutes or until toothpick inserted in center comes out clean.
8. Cool on rack 10 minutes before removing from pan. Cool completely.

Preparation Time:	30 minutes	**Yield:**	1 large loaf
Baking Time:	50-55 minutes	**May freeze**	

Serving Suggestion: *Serve with Blueberry Cream.*

ORANGE-NUT BREAD

2 cups flour
¾ cup sugar
½ teaspoon salt
½ teaspoon soda
1 beaten egg
2 Tablespoons lemon juice
2 Tablespoons cooking oil
1 Tablespoon grated orange peel
¾ cup orange juice
¼ teaspoon grated lemon peel
½ cup chopped walnuts

1. In bowl, stir together flour, sugar, salt and soda.
2. In separate bowl, combine egg, lemon juice, oil, orange peel, orange juice and lemon peel.
3. Add to dry ingredients, stirring until just moistened.
4. Fold in walnuts.
5. Pour into greased 9 x 5-inch loaf pan.
6. Bake at 350 degrees for 50-60 minutes.
7. Cool 10 minutes before removing from pan. Cool completely on rack.
8. Wrap in foil and store overnight before serving.

Preparation Time:	30 minutes	**Yield:**	1 large loaf
Baking Time:	50-60 minutes	**Must do ahead**	
		May freeze	

Variation: *Glaze with ½ cup orange juice and ¾ cup powdered sugar mixed together.*

LEMON BREAD

"Yummy and oh, so easy!"

Bread

⅔ **cup sugar**
6 Tablespoons shortening
2 eggs
1½ cups flour
1 teaspoon baking powder
¼ **teaspoon salt**
½ **cup milk**
Grated peel of 1 lemon

1. Cream sugar and shortening.
2. Add eggs. Mix well.
3. Add dry ingredients alternately with milk.
4. Add grated lemon peel.
5. Pour into 8 x 4-inch well-greased glass loaf pan.
6. Bake at 325 degrees for 1 hour.

Lemon Glaze

⅓ **cup sugar**
Juice of 1 lemon

1. Combine sugar and lemon juice.
2. Spread over warm bread. Cool in pan.

Preparation Time: 30 minutes   **Yield:** 1 large loaf
Baking Time: 1 hour   **May freeze**
Serving Suggestion: *Serve with whipped cream cheese.*

PUMPKIN BREAD

"Be prepared - freeze ahead of time"

2⅔ **cups sugar**
4 eggs
⅔ **cup oil**
1 16-ounce can pumpkin
⅔ **cup water**
3⅓ **cups flour**
2 teaspoons soda
1½ teaspoons salt
½ **teaspoon baking powder**
1 teaspoon cinnamon
1 teaspoon cloves
1 teaspoon pumpkin pie spice
⅔ **cup chopped walnuts**

Continued

184

PUMPKIN BREAD — Continued

1. In large bowl, cream sugar, eggs and oil.
2. Add pumpkin and water.
3. Blend in dry ingredients.
4. Add walnuts.
5. Pour into ungreased bundt pan or 2 9 X 5-inch loaf pans.
6. Bake at 350 degrees for 1-1¼ hours.
7. Cool for 10 minutes before removing from pans. Cool completely on rack.

Preparation Time: **15 minutes**
Baking Time: **1-1¼ hours**
Variation: *⅔ cup raisins may be added.*

Yield: **2 large loaves or 1 bundt loaf**
May freeze

STRAWBERRIES AND CREAM BREAD

"Surprise your family with this moist bread"

1¾ cups flour
½ teaspoon baking powder
½ teaspoon baking soda
½ teaspoon salt
¼ teaspoon cinnamon
½ cup margarine at room temperature
⅔ cup sugar
2 eggs
½ cup sour cream
1 teaspoon vanilla
1 cup coarsely chopped, fresh strawberries

1. Combine all dry ingredients. Set aside.
2. Cream margarine and sugar until light and fluffy.
3. Beat in eggs.
4. Add sour cream and vanilla.
5. Add dry to liquid ingredients. Mix only until just moistened.
6. Fold in strawberries.
7. Pour into greased 9 x 5-inch loaf pan.
8. Bake at 350 degrees for 1 hour or until toothpick inserted in center comes out clean.
9. Cool on 10 minutes before removing from pan. Cool completely on rack.

Preparation Time: **30 minutes**
Baking Time: **1 hour**
Serving Suggestion: *Serve with Strawberry Devonshire Cream.*

Yield: **1 large loaf**

ZUCCHINI BREAD

"Where is the zucchini?"

2 cups finely grated zucchini
3 eggs
1½ cups sugar
1 cup oil
2 cups flour
3 teaspoons cinnamon
½ teaspoon cloves
1 teaspoon salt
2 teaspoons baking soda
3 teaspoons vanilla
1 cup chopped nuts

1. In large bowl, mix zucchini, eggs, sugar and oil.
2. In separate bowl, combine flour, spices, salt and soda.
3. Add dry mixture to zucchini mixture, blending just until moistened.
4. Add vanilla and nuts.
5. Pour into 3 greased and floured 5 x 3-inch loaf pans.
6. Bake at 350 degrees for 40-45 minutes.
7. Cool 10 minutes before removing from pans. Cool completely on rack.

Preparation Time:	**10 minutes**	**Yield:**	**3 small loaves**
Baking Time:	**40-45 minutes**	**May freeze**	

BREAKFAST MONKEY BREAD

1 cup chopped pecans
½ cup chopped dates
1 package Bridgeford frozen yeast rolls (16) or 1½ loaves frozen bread dough,
cut into small roll-size pieces
1 3-ounce box regular butterscotch pudding (not instant)
½ cup brown sugar
1 teaspoon cinnamon
½ cup melted butter

1. Place ½ nuts and ½ dates in bottom of greased bundt pan. Arrange rolls.
2. Sprinkle with dry pudding, brown sugar, cinnamon, remaining nuts and dates. Drizzle with melted butter.
3. Let stand overnight, covered with dinner plate.
4. Bake at 375 degrees for 25 minutes.
5. Invert immediately onto serving platter.

Preparation Time:	**20 minutes**	**Serves:**	**8**
Baking Time:	**25 minutes**	**Must do ahead**	

CHEESE BREAD RING

"Everyone who tastes it just loves it"

Bread

1 package hot roll mix
¼ cup warm water
¼ cup sugar
1 egg
½ cup sour cream
6 Tablespoons melted butter
Jam or powdered sugar

1. Soften yeast from hot roll mix in ¼ cup warm water.
2. Combine roll mix with ¼ cup sugar, yeast, egg, sour cream and butter. Mix well.
3. Place dough in greased bowl, turning once to grease surface. Cover and chill 2-3 hours or overnight.
4. Turn dough onto lightly floured surface and roll into circle 18 inches in diameter.
5. Gently fit into greased 6-cup ring mold, allowing some dough to hang over edges. Dough will cover center hole.
6. Pour Filling into mold.
7. Bring dough from sides over top of Filling. Seal securely to center of mold. Cut "X" in dough, covering center hole. Fold the 4 triangles back over top of ring, sealing to outer edges.
8. Let rise until almost double in size, about 1-1½ hours.
9. Bake at 350 degrees for 35-40 minutes or until toothpick inserted comes out clean.
10. Cool 10 minutes in pan. Turn out onto serving platter.
11. To serve, drizzle with any flavor of warmed jam and sprinkle with powdered sugar.

Filling

1 8-ounce package softened cream cheese
½ cup sugar
1 teaspoon vanilla
2 eggs

1. Beat cream cheese, sugar and vanilla until smooth.
2. Add eggs, 1 at a time, beating well after each addition.

Preparation Time:	**1-1½ hours**	**Serves:**	**10-12**
Chilling Time:	**2-3 hours**		
Rising Time:	**1-1½ hours**		
Baking Time:	**35-40 minutes**		

COFFEE CAKE

⅓ **cup brown sugar**
1¼ **cups white sugar**
1 **teaspoon cinnamon**
1 **cup chopped pecans**
½ **cup butter**
2 **eggs**
1 **teaspoon vanilla**
2 **cups flour**
1 **teaspoon baking powder**
1 **teaspoon baking soda**
1 **teaspoon salt**
1 **cup sour cream**

1. Mix brown sugar, ¼ cup white sugar, cinnamon and pecans.
2. Beat butter on high speed until creamy.
3. Gradually add 1 cup sugar. Beat until light and fluffy.
4. Add eggs, 1 at a time. Then add vanilla. Mix until well-blended.
5. Sift together, flour, baking powder, baking soda and salt.
6. At low speed, mix flour mixture alternately with sour cream into batter.
7. Spread half of batter in 8 x 8-inch baking dish.
8. Sprinkle with half of nut mixture.
9. Repeat layers.
10. Bake at 350 degrees for 40 minutes or until tested done.

| **Preparation Time:** | **30 minutes** | **Serves:** | **8** |
| **Baking Time:** | **40 minutes** | | |

GRAHAM STREUSEL CAKE

Streusel Cake

1 yellow cake mix
2 cups graham cracker crumbs
¾ cup chopped nuts
¾ cup packed brown sugar
1½ teaspoons cinnamon
¾ cup softened butter

1. Prepare cake according to package directions. Set aside.
2. Mix graham cracker crumbs and remaining ingredients. Set aside.
3. Pour ½ cake batter into well-greased 9 x 13-inch baking dish. Sprinkle ½ crumb mixture over cake batter.
4. Repeat step 3.
5. Bake at 350 degrees for 40-50 minutes or until tested done.

Glaze

1 cup powdered sugar
1-2 Tablespoons water or milk

1. Combine ingredients. Mix until smooth.
2. Drizzle over warm cake.

Preparation Time: **20 minutes**   **Serves:**   **12-15**
Baking Time: **40-50 minutes**
Variation: *Use any flavor cake mix.*

SOUR CREAM COFFEE CAKE WITH PECAN STREUSEL
"Worth waking up for"

Pecan Streusel

½ cup firmly packed brown sugar
4 Tablespoons rolled oats
1 teaspoon cinnamon
4 Tablespoons butter at room temperature, cut into pieces
4 Tablespoons chopped pecans

1. In bowl, combine brown sugar, oats and cinnamon.
2. With pastry blender, cut in butter until mixture is crumbly.
3. Add nuts. Set aside.

Coffee Cake

1⅔ cups flour
1 teaspoon baking powder
1 teaspoon baking soda
½ teaspoon salt
1 cup sugar
½ cup solid vegetable shortening
2 eggs
1 cup sour cream
1 teaspoon vanilla
1 egg white at room temperature
⅓ cup plum jam at room temperature

1. Sift together flour, baking powder, baking soda and salt. Set aside.
2. Using electric mixer, beat sugar and shortening until fluffy, about 4 minutes.
3. Add eggs, 1 at a time, beating well after each addition.
4. Stir in sour cream and vanilla.
5. Add flour mixture and stir until just moistened.
6. In separate bowl, beat egg white until stiff, but not dry.
7. Gently fold in plum jam 1 Tablespoon at a time.
8. Spoon half of batter into greased 8 x 8-inch baking dish, spreading evenly.
9. Sprinkle with half of Pecan Streusel.
10. Spoon egg white mixture over top in dollops. Do not spread.
11. Spoon remaining batter over egg white mixture, distributing evenly, allowing some egg white mixture to show through.
12. Sprinkle with remaining Pecan Streusel.
13. Bake at 350 degrees about 55 minutes or until toothpick inserted comes out clean.
14. Serve warm.

Preparation Time:	**30 minutes**	**Serves:**	**10-12**
Baking Time:	**55 minutes**		

APPLE MUFFINS

"A family and company favorite"

½ cup sugar
1½ Tablespoons softened butter
1½ cups brown sugar
⅔ cup oil
1 egg
1 cup buttermilk
1 teaspoon baking soda
1 teaspoon salt
1 teaspoon vanilla
2½ cups flour
1½ cups shredded apples
½ cup chopped pecans

1. Mix sugar and butter. Set aside for muffin topping.
2. In food processor, combine brown sugar, oil, egg, buttermilk, baking soda, salt and vanilla.
3. Add flour, apples and pecans. Pulse carefully, just until flour is incorporated.
4. Pour into cupcake liners in muffin tin, filling about ⅔ full. Place flattened piece of butter-sugar mixture on top of each muffin.
5. Bake at 325 degrees for 30 minutes.

Preparation Time:	20 minutes	**Yield:**	15-18 muffins
Baking Time:	30 minutes		

BLUEBERRY MUFFINS

1 cup fresh blueberries
1½ cups sifted flour
2 teaspoons baking powder
½ teaspoon salt
½ cup sugar
1 egg
2 Tablespoons melted butter
½ cup milk
Finely grated peel of 1 lemon

1. Wash berries. Spread on paper towel and gently pat dry with paper towel.
2. In large mixing bowl, sift dry ingredients.
3. In separate bowl, mix egg, melted butter and milk. Stir in lemon rind.
4. Add liquid to dry ingredients. Stir until dry ingredients are just moistened.
5. Gently fold in blueberries. Do not over-stir.
6. Spoon batter into greased muffin cups, filling about ⅔ full.
7. Bake at 350 degrees for 15-20 minutes.

Preparation Time:	20 minutes	**Yield:**	12 muffins
Baking Time:	15-20 minutes	May freeze	

BRAN MUFFINS
"Never fail"

4 eggs
3 cups sugar
1 cup oil
1 quart buttermilk
5 cups flour
5 teaspoons soda
2 teaspoons salt
1 15-ounce box raisin bran

1. Beat eggs, sugar and oil.
2. Add buttermilk.
3. Mix flour, soda and salt. Blend well.
4. Fold in raisin bran. Do not stir batter.
5. Pour into well-greased muffin tins, filling about ⅔ full.
6. Bake at 350 degrees for 12-15 minutes.

Preparation Time: **10 minutes**   **Yield:**   **50-60 muffins**
Baking Time: **12-15 minutes**
Tip: *Batter will keep for 6 weeks in refrigerator.*

BRAN-RAISIN MUFFINS

2 cups white or whole wheat flour
1½ cups bran
2 Tablespoons sugar
½ teaspoon salt
1¼ teaspoons soda
1½ Tablespoons grated orange rind
2 cups buttermilk
1 beaten egg
½ cup molasses
4 Tablespoons melted butter
1 cup coarsely chopped walnuts
⅔ cup raisins

1. Combine flour, bran, sugar, salt, soda and grated orange rind. Mix well.
2. Beat together buttermilk, egg, molasses and melted butter.
3. Combine dry and liquid ingredients until just moistened.
4. Fold in nuts and raisins.
5. Spoon into greased muffin cups, filling about ⅔ full.
6. Bake at 350 degrees for 20-25 minutes.

Preparation Time: **20 minutes**   **Yield:**   **24 muffins**
Baking Time: **20-25 minutes**

SUPER BRAN MUFFINS

"Deliciously healthy"

3 cups whole bran cereal
1 cup boiling water
2 slightly beaten eggs
2 cups buttermilk
½ cup oil
1 cup raisins
1 cup chopped prunes
1 cup chopped dates
1 cup chopped nuts
2½ teaspoons baking soda
½ teaspoon salt
½ cup brown sugar
2½ cups flour

1. Mix cereal and boiling water. Cool.
2. Add eggs, buttermilk, oil, fruit and nuts. Blend.
3. Mix dry ingredients and blend into other mixture.
4. Pour into muffin cups, filling about ⅔ full.
5. Bake at 425 degrees for 20 minutes.

Preparation Time:	30 minutes	Yield:	30 muffins
Baking Time:	20 minutes	May do ahead	

CRANBERRY MUFFINS

1½ cups flour
½ cup plus 1 Tablespoon sugar
2 teaspoons baking powder
½ teaspoon salt
1 Tablespoon grated orange peel
1 egg
½ cup milk
¼ cup oil
1 cup cranberries, cut into halves
¼ teaspoon cinnamon

1. Combine flour, ½ cup sugar, baking powder, salt and grated orange peel. Mix well.
2. In separate bowl, beat together egg, milk and oil.
3. Combine dry with liquid ingredients.
4. Gently fold in cranberries.
5. Spoon batter into greased muffin cups, filling about ⅔ full.
6. Mix 1 Tablespoon sugar with cinnamon.
7. Sprinkle batter lightly with sugar-cinnamon mixture.
8. Bake at 350 degrees for 20-25 minutes or until golden brown.

Preparation Time:	20 minutes	Yield:	12 muffins
Baking Time:	20-25 minutes		

ORANGE GEM MUFFINS
"Never enough"

Muffins

1 cup softened butter
1 cup sugar
2 eggs
3 cups flour
1 teaspoon soda
1 teaspoon baking powder
¾ cup buttermilk
Juice of 1 orange

1. Cream butter and sugar. Add eggs, 1 at a time.
2. Add dry ingredients, alternating with buttermilk and orange juice.
3. Spoon into greased muffin tins, filling about ⅔ full.
4. Bake at 350 degrees for 12 minutes.
5. Let cool for 3 minutes, then dip in Glaze and serve warm.

Glaze

1 cup sugar
Juice of 2 oranges
Grated rind of 2 oranges

Mix ingredients. Heat to boiling temperature, but do not boil until sugar is dissolved.

Preparation Time:	**15 minutes**	**Yield:**	**48 small-size muffins or**
Baking Time:	**12 minutes**		**24 regular-size muffins**

Tips: *May be frozen before dipping in glaze. Thaw thoroughly. On greased pan, reheat at 350 degrees for 3 minutes. Dip in glaze and serve warm.*

SPICY MANDARIN ORANGE MUFFINS

1 11-ounce can mandarin orange segments
1½ cups flour
2 teaspoons baking powder
½ teaspoon salt
¾ teaspoon nutmeg
¼ teaspoon allspice
Pinch of cinnamon
½ cup sugar
⅓ cup butter
1 slightly beaten egg
¼ cup milk
¼ cup melted butter
¼ cup sugar mixed with ½ teaspoon cinnamon

Continued

SPICY MANDARIN ORANGE MUFFINS — Continued

1. Drain mandarin orange segments well. Spread on paper towels while making batter.
2. Sift flour. Measure and sift with baking powder, salt, nutmeg, allspice, cinnamon and sugar into bowl.
3. Cut in butter until very fine.
4. Combine egg and milk. Add all at once.
5. Mix just until moistened.
6. Add orange segments. Mix lightly until evenly distributed.
7. Spoon into greased muffin tins, filling about ¾ full.
8. Bake at 350 degrees for 20-25 minutes until golden.
9. Remove from tins. Dip top in melted butter, then in cinnamon-sugar mixture.
10. Serve hot.

Preparation Time: **15 minutes**   **Yield:**   **12 muffins**
Baking Time: **20-25 minutes**

BUTTERMILK BISCUITS
"A real basic"

2 cups sifted flour
2 Tablespoons baking powder
2 teaspoons sugar
¼ teaspoon salt
⅛ teaspoon baking soda
1⅛-1¼ cups buttermilk
3-4 Tablespoons vegetable oil

1. In mixing bowl, combine flour, baking powder, sugar and salt.
2. Stir soda into 1⅛ cups buttermilk. Combine with dry ingredients, mixing well. If mixture is dry, add ⅛ cup buttermilk.
3. Turn dough out onto well-floured surface and knead gently about 5 times.
4. With floured hands, press dough into circle ¾-inch thick. Using 2-inch biscuit cutter or rim of glass, cut out biscuits. Press scraps of dough together to form circle. Do not over-flour. Continue cutting until all of dough is used.
5. Dip each biscuit into vegetable oil to coat completely.
6. Arrange biscuits with sides touching in 8-inch, round cake pan or pie plate.
7. Bake at 500 degrees for 10-12 minutes until biscuits are golden brown.

Preparation Time: **20 minutes**   **Yield:**   **16**
Baking Time: **10-12 minutes**   **May do ahead**
Serving Suggestion: *Serve hot with butter and honey or with gravy.*
Tip: *If baked ahead, cover with foil and reheat in oven at 300 degrees for 10 minutes or until hot.*

OVEN FRENCH TOAST

"C'est magnifique!"

4 eggs
⅔ cup orange juice
⅓ cup milk
¼ cup sugar
⅛ teaspoon nutmeg
½ teaspoon vanilla
1 8-ounce loaf Italian bread, cut into 1-inch slices
⅓ cup melted butter
½ cup diced macadamia nuts
Maple syrup
Butter

1. Beat together eggs, orange juice, milk, sugar, nutmeg and vanilla.
2. Place bread slices in single layer in casserole dish.
3. Pour milk mixture over bread.
4. Cover well and refrigerate overnight, turning once.
5. Pour melted butter in jellyroll pan, spreading evenly.
6. Arrange soaked bread slices in single layer in pan.
7. Sprinkle with macadamia nuts.
8. Bake at 400 degrees for 20-25 minutes or until golden.

Preparation Time:	**20 minutes**	**Serves:**	**4**
Standing Time:	**6-8 hours**	**Must do ahead**	
Baking Time:	**20-25 minutes**		

Serving Suggestion: *Serve with maple syrup and butter.*

STUFFED FRENCH TOAST

"Forget the calories and enjoy!"

1 loaf of sliced, day-old French bread
2 8-ounce packages softened cream cheese
2 10-ounce jars apricot jam or orange marmalade
8 eggs
2 cups milk
4 Tablespoons sugar
2 teaspoons vanilla
½ teaspoon nutmeg
1 cup butter

1. Cut pocket in the middle of each bread slice, ¾ of the way through, as illustrated.

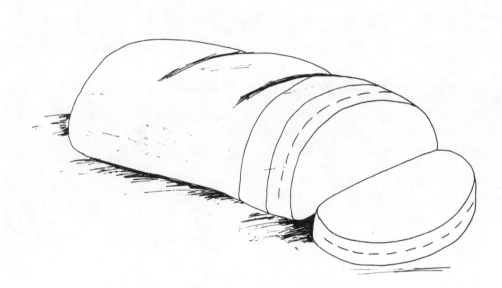

2. Spread cream cheese and jam in prepared pocket.
3. Beat together eggs, milk, sugar, vanilla and nutmeg.
4. Place stuffed slices in rimmed baking sheet or dish.
5. Pour half of egg mixture over slices and let stand. Turn slices and pour over remaining mixture until absorbed.
6. Fry with butter in heated skillet.

Preparation Time: **30 minutes**   **Yield:**   **10 slices**
Frying Time: **10 minutes**   **May freeze**
Serving Suggestion: *Serve with maple syrup.*
Tip: *Reheat in 500-degree oven for 8 minutes.*

SOUTHERN PUFFED PANCAKE

"Cinnamon and apples make it extra delicious"

4 Tablespoons butter
2 peeled, thinly sliced apples
6 eggs
1½ cups milk
1 cup flour
3 Tablespoons sugar
1 teaspoon vanilla
½ teaspoon salt
¼ teaspoon cinnamon
2-3 Tablespoons brown sugar

1. In oven, melt butter in 12-inch fluted porcelain quiche dish or 9 x 13-inch baking dish.
2. Add apple slices to baking dish.
3. Return to oven until butter sizzles. Do not let brown.
4. In blender or large bowl, mix eggs, milk, flour, sugar, vanilla, salt and cinnamon until well-blended.
5. Remove dish from oven and immediately pour batter over apples.
6. Sprinkle with brown sugar.
7. Bake in middle of oven at 350 degrees for 20 minutes or until puffed and golden brown.
8. Serve immediately.

Preparation Time:	**10-15 minutes**	**Serves:**	**6-8**
Baking Time:	**20 minutes**		

YEAST BELGIAN WAFFLES
"Light as a feather"

1 package yeast
$^1/_3$ cup warm water
$1^3/_4$ cups warm milk
1 cup whole wheat flour
1 cup plus 2 Tablespoons white flour
1 teaspoon salt
1 Tablespoon sugar
2 Tablespoons oil
2 eggs

1. Dissolve yeast in warm water and let stand until bubbles.
2. Pour warm milk into large bowl.
3. Add remaining ingredients except eggs.
4. Let stand $1^1/_2$ hours or more.
5. Beat egg yolks and stir into batter.
6. Beat egg whites to soft peaks and fold into batter.

Preparation Time:	**15 minutes**	**Yield: 5 $5^1/_2$ x 9-inch waffles**
Rising Time:	**$1^1/_2$ hours**	

SOUR CREAM BELGIAN WAFFLES
"Crispy-good"

3 separated eggs
$1^1/_2$ cups flour
2 teaspoons baking powder
$^1/_2$ teaspoon baking soda
1 Tablespoon sugar
$^2/_3$ cup sour cream
$^3/_4$ cup milk
$^1/_4$ cup melted butter
$^1/_4$ cup salad oil

1. Beat egg whites until stiff. Set aside.
2. In large mixing bowl, combine dry ingredients.
3. Beat together egg yolks, sour cream and milk.
4. Combine butter and oil.
5. Add liquid ingredients alternately with fats to dry ingredients. Stir until smooth.
6. Fold in beaten egg whites.
7. Bake in waffle iron until brown and crispy, about 4 minutes.

Preparation Time:	**20 minutes**	**Yield:**	**4 large waffles**
Baking Time:	**16 minutes**		

199

APRICOT BRAID
"Impressive"

Bread

3¼ cups unsifted flour
¼ cup sugar
1 teaspoon salt
1 Tablespoon dry yeast
⅔ cup milk
2 Tablespoons melted butter
2 eggs at room temperature
Apricot Filling
Topping
Glaze

1. In large bowl, mix flour, sugar, salt and dry yeast.
2. Combine milk and butter in saucepan and heat over low heat until very warm to touch, but not hot.
3. Add eggs and milk mixture to dry ingredients. Beat for 2 minutes with electric mixer or 5 minutes by hand.
4. Turn out onto floured surface and knead until smooth and elastic.
5. Place in greased bowl and let rise in warm place until doubled.
6. Punch down dough and divide in half. Let stand while preparing Apricot Filling.
7. Roll out each half of dough into 8 x 14-inch rectangle.
8. Place on 2 greased cookie sheets and spread half of Filling down middle of each.
9. Slit dough at 1-inch intervals down each side.
10. Lift and crisscross sides over top of Filling.
11. Cover loosely with towel and let rise until doubled.
12. Brush each braid with melted butter and sprinkle Topping on each loaf.
13. Bake at 350 degrees for 20 minutes.
14. Remove from cookie sheet and cool on racks.
15. Brush or drizzle with Glaze.

Apricot Filling

1½ cups chopped, dried apricots
1 cup water
1 cup brown sugar

1. Bring to boil and let simmer 20-25 minutes. Remove from heat.
2. Add brown sugar. Stir.

Topping

⅓ cup flour
2 Tablespoons sugar
1 teaspoon cinnamon
2 Tablespoons butter

Mix all ingredients until crumbly.

Continued

APRICOT BRAID — Continued

Glaze

⅔ cup powdered sugar
1 Tablespoon softened butter
1 Tablespoon milk

Stir all ingredients together until smooth. If thinner consistency is desired, add milk 1 drop at a time.

Preparation Time:	**45 minutes**	**Yield:**	**2 14-inch braids**
Rising Time:	**4-5 hours**	**Must do ahead**	
Cooking Time:	**25 minutes**		
Baking Time:	**20 minutes**		

CINNAMON ROLLS

2 packages dry yeast
2 Tablespoons honey
3 cups warm water
¼ cup vegetable oil
1 egg
5-6 cups flour
1 teaspoon salt
1 teaspoon mace
½ cup sour cream
½ cup brown sugar
1 Tablespoon cinnamon

1. Dissolve yeast in honey and ¼ cup warm water.
2. Mix in oil and egg.
3. Add flour, salt and mace.
4. Knead entire mixture, adding more flour if needed, until dough is firm and manageable.
5. Let rise covered in greased bowl until double in size.
6. Punch down. Let rise again.
7. On floured surface, roll into rectangle about ⅓-inch thick.
8. Spread with sour cream.
9. Mix brown sugar and cinnamon. Sprinkle over sour cream.
10. Roll up lengthwise. Cut into 1½-inch slices.
11. Place in greased 9 x 13-inch baking pan, allowing room for rising. Cover and allow to rise until double in size.
12. Bake at 350 degrees approximately 40-45 minutes.

Preparation Time:	**20 minutes**	**Yield:**	**36 rolls**
Rising Time:	**4-5 hours**		
Baking Time:	**40-45 minutes**		

CREAM CHEESE BREAD

Bread

1 8-ounce carton sour cream
½ cup sugar
1 teaspoon salt
½ cup melted butter
2 Tablespoons yeast
½ cup warm water (105-115 degrees)
2 beaten eggs
4 cups flour
Cream Cheese Filling
Glaze

1. Heat sour cream over low heat. Stir in sugar, salt and melted butter. Cool to lukewarm.
2. Sprinkle yeast over warm water in large bowl, stirring until yeast dissolves.
3. Add sour cream, eggs and flour. Mix well.
4. Cover tightly. Refrigerate overnight.
5. Divide dough into 4 equal parts. Roll out each quarter on floured surface into 12 x 18-inch rectangle.
6. Spread ¼ of Cream Cheese Filling on each rectangle. Roll up jellyroll fashion beginning at long sides. Pinch edges together and fold ends under slightly. Place rolls seam side down on greased baking sheets.
7. Slit each roll at 1-inch intervals about ⅔ of way through dough. Cover and let rise in warm place, free from drafts, until doubled in size, about 1 hour.
8. Bake at 375 degrees for 15 minutes. Spread with Glaze while warm.

Cream Cheese Filling

2 8-ounce packages softened cream cheese
¾ cup sugar
1 beaten egg
⅛ teaspoon salt
2 teaspoons vanilla

Combine all ingredients. Blend until smooth. Set aside.

Glaze

2 cups powdered sugar
4 Tablespoons milk
2 teaspoons vanilla

1. Combine all ingredients. Blend until smooth.
2. Drizzle over tops of bread loaves.

Preparation Time:	**45 minutes**	**Yield:**	**4 16-inch loaves**
Rising Time:	**6-8 hours**		
Baking Time:	**15 minutes**		

CORNMEAL ROLLS

"Completes a Mexican dinner"

1 cup boiling water
1¼ cups yellow cornmeal
1 cup milk
⅓ cup sugar
2 teaspoons salt
½ cup butter
1 Tablespoon yeast
2 eggs at room temperature
3 cups white flour

1. Combine boiling water and cornmeal. Stir well and let stand 10 minutes.
2. Mix milk, sugar, salt and butter. Heat to 110-115 degrees. Add yeast. Allow to stand until bubbly.
3. Add eggs. Mix well.
4. Add cornmeal mixture. Beat until smooth.
5. Add flour. Mix, keeping dough soft. Knead until dough is smooth. Allow to rise twice.
6. Form into small rolls and place on greased baking sheet.
7. Bake at 375 degrees for about 10 minutes.

Preparation Time:	15 minutes	Yield:	12-14 rolls
Rising Time:	2-3 hours		
Baking Time:	10 minutes		

BUTTERHORN ROLLS

2 cups milk
1 cup sugar
1 Tablespoon salt
1 cup oil
2 slightly rounded Tablespoons yeast
6 eggs at room temperature
8½-9 cups unbleached flour

1. Heat milk, sugar, salt and oil to 120-130 degrees.
2. Place milk mixture in large bowl. Cool to 105-115 degrees. Add yeast. Mix well. Allow to stand until bubbly.
3. Add eggs. Blend thoroughly.
4. Add 7 cups flour. Beat well.
5. Add 1½-2 cups more flour. Mix until thoroughly blended. Keep dough soft. Knead until smooth and elastic.
6. Allow to rise until double in size, about 2 hours. Punch down.
7. Allow to rise a second time until double in size.
8. Cut into 6 pieces. Roll each piece into circle. Cut into 8 wedges. Roll up to form crescent shapes. Place on greased cookie sheet.
9. Allow to rise 30-45 minutes.
10. Bake at 375 degrees for 8-10 minutes.

Preparation Time:	30 minutes	Yield:	48 rolls
Rising Time:	4 hours, 45 minutes		
Baking Time:	8-10 minutes		

EASTER EGG NEST BREAD

"You won't believe you made it yourself"

Bread

1 package active dry yeast
½ cup sugar
¼ cup warm water (105-115 degrees)
2 Tablespoons grated orange peel
1 cup milk
½ cup butter
5-5½ cups flour
1 teaspoon salt
2 eggs at room temperature
¼ cup orange juice

1. Sprinkle yeast and 1 Tablespoon sugar over warm water. Set aside.
2. Mix orange peel with 1 Tablespoon sugar and set aside.
3. In small saucepan, heat milk and butter until lukewarm.
4. In mixing bowl, place 2 cups flour. Add warm milk with butter, remaining sugar, salt and yeast mixture. Mix until blended.
5. Beat in eggs, 1 at a time.
6. Add orange juice and orange peel.
7. Beat 2 minutes, scraping down sides occasionally.
8. Mix in 3 additional cups flour. Dough should be fairly stiff. If it is too soft, add more flour. Knead on floured board or with dough hook, adding more flour if needed, until smooth and elastic, about 8 minutes, not more than 10 minutes.
9. Shape dough into ball, place in greased deep bowl and turn to grease all surfaces.
10. Cover dough with plastic wrap and damp towel. Let rise in warm place until double in size, about 1½ hours.
11. Punch dough down and let dough rest 10 minutes.
12. Use ⅓ dough to make eggs. Break off small balls of dough and shape into approximately ½-inch oval-shaped eggs. There should be at least 20 eggs. Place on greased baking sheet.
13. Use remaining ⅔ dough to make nest. Divide dough in half.
14. Spread half into bottom of greased 10-inch springform pan.
15. Roll remaining dough into rectangle ½-inch thick and about 12 inches long. Cut into 6½-inch strips. Braid 3 strips.
16. Stand braid up along inside of pan. It should go halfway around pan. Press braid into dough on bottom of pan.
17. Repeat with remaining 3 strips, making another braid. Attach to braid in pan, pressing ends together securely.
18. Press braid against sides of pan and flatten bottom dough, forming nest.
19. Cover nest and let rise 45 minutes to 1 hour or until nearly double in size.
20. Bake at 350 degrees. Bake eggs 15-20 minutes and nest 30-40 minutes or until golden brown.
21. Cool completely.

Continued

EASTER EGG NEST BREAD — Continued

Tinted Coconut

Green food coloring
1 teaspoon water
1 cup flaked coconut

1. Mix a few drops green food coloring and water.
2. Place coconut in small bowl. Add food color mixture a little at a time, until desired color is attained.
3. Place in bottom of cooled nest.

Glaze

¾ cup powdered sugar
Hot water
Red and yellow food coloring

1. Place sugar in small bowl.
2. Add 1 teaspoon hot water. Stir. Continue to add hot water a few drops at a time until sugar is thin, spreading consistency.
3. Divide sugar in thirds. Tint ⅓ pink, ⅓ yellow and leave ⅓ plain.
4. Brush or spread Glaze on cooled eggs. Let dry.
5. Place as many eggs as desired on coconut in nest.
6. Serve remaining eggs separately as rolls.

Preparation Time:	**2 hours**	**Serves:**	**10-12**
Rising Time:	**2½ hours**	**Nest and eggs may be frozen**	
Baking Time:	**30-40 minutes**		

PORTUGUESE SWEET BREAD

1¼ cups milk
1 cup sugar
¼ cup butter
1 teaspoon salt
2 slightly rounded Tablespoons yeast
4 eggs
5½-6 cups white flour

1. Heat milk, sugar, butter and salt to 120-130 degrees. Cool to 115 degrees.
2. Add yeast and allow mixture to bubble.
3. Mix in 3 eggs and 4 cups flour. Beat well.
4. Mix in 1½-2 cups more flour, as needed. Knead well.
5. Allow to rise until double in size, about 1½-2 hours.
6. Divide dough in half, then divide each half in thirds, 1½ inches in diameter. Braid together.
7. Place on greased cookie sheet. Allow to rise until double in size.
8. Brush with beaten egg.
9. Bake at 350 degrees for 25-30 minutes.

Preparation Time:	**25 minutes**	**Yield:**	**2 braids**
Rising Time:	**3-4 hours**		
Baking Time:	**25-30 minutes**		

DINNER ROLLS

"Light as a feather"

2 packages active dry yeast
1¼ cups warm water (105-115 degrees)
½ cup shortening
½ cup sugar
2 teaspoons salt
3 well-beaten eggs
4½ cups flour
Softened butter

1. Mix yeast and ¼ cup warm water. Let stand 5-10 minutes.
2. In large bowl, combine 1 cup water, shortening, sugar, salt and eggs.
3. Stir in yeast mixture and 2½ cups flour.
4. Add remaining flour.
5. Place in greased bowl. Cover and let rise in warm place until double in size, about 1-1½ hours.
6. Punch down and place in refrigerator overnight.
7. About 3½ hours before serving, divide dough in half. On lightly floured board, roll each half into rectangle about ¼-inch thick. Spread with softened butter.
8. Roll up jellyroll style and cut slices ¾-inch thick.
9. Place cut-side down in greased muffin tins. Cover and let rise 3 hours.
10. Bake at 400 degrees for 15 minutes.

Preparation Time:	**45 minutes**	**Yield:**	**24 rolls**
Rising Time:	**4½ hours**	**Must do ahead**	
Chilling Time:	**Overnight**		
Baking Time:	**15 minutes**		

NUT TREE BREAD

1½ Tablespoons sugar
1 envelope active dry yeast
1 cup lukewarm water (105-115 degrees)
3-3½ cups unsifted flour
1½ teaspoons salt

1. In warmed mixing bowl, add sugar and yeast to lukewarm water. Stir until dissolved.
2. Add 1½ cups flour and salt. Beat hard with spoon about 2 minutes.
3. Gradually add 1¼-1½ cups more flour, mixing first with spoon, then with hands, to make a smooth, elastic ball of dough. This takes about 5 minutes.
4. Cover with towel and let stand in warm place about 25 minutes until doubled in size.
5. Divide dough into 4 pieces to fit small 2½ x 5-inch pans. Flatten on oiled surface, shape into loaves and put into greased pans.
6. Again, cover and let rise in warm place about 25 minutes until doubled in size.
7. Bake at 400 degrees for 20 minutes or until golden brown.
8. Cool 10 minutes before removing from pans. Cool completely on rack.

Preparation Time:	**20 minutes**	**Yield:**	**4 small loaves**
Rising Time:	**50 minutes**	**May freeze**	
Baking Time:	**20 minutes**		

HERB BREAD

3 cups flour
1 Tablespoon sugar
1 Tablespoon chopped, dried chives
2 teaspoons dill weed
2 teaspoons salt
¼ teaspoon baking soda
1 package active dry yeast
1 cup creamed cottage cheese
¼ cup water
1 Tablespoon butter
2 eggs, 1 beaten slightly

1. Combine 1 cup flour with sugar, chives, dill, salt, soda and yeast in large mixer bowl.
2. Heat cottage cheese, water and butter. Place in blender and process while warm.
3. Add to flour mixture with 2 eggs. Blend 3 minutes.
4. Beat in remaining flour to make stiff dough. Cover and allow to rise until doubled in size, about 1 hour.
5. Punch down. Divide dough into 6 equal pieces. Place dough in 6 1-pound, well-greased coffee cans. Do not allow to reach top of can when rising.
6. Brush lightly with beaten egg.
7. Bake at 350 degrees for 35-40 minutes.
8. Cool 10 minutes before removing from containers. Cool completely on racks.

Preparation Time:	**30 minutes**	**Yield:**	**6 loaves**
Standing Time:	**1 hour**		
Baking Time:	**35-40 minutes**		

Variation: *May be made into rolls.*

SOUR CREAM YEAST ROLLS

2 slightly rounded Tablespoons yeast
½ cup lukewarm water (105-115 degrees)
1 cup sour cream
1 cup softened butter
2 beaten eggs
⅓ cup sugar
1 teaspoon salt
4-5 cups flour

1. Dissolve yeast in lukewarm water. Let stand 5 minutes.
2. Place sour cream in saucepan over low heat, warming to 110-115 degrees.
3. In large bowl, combine sour cream, butter, eggs, sugar, salt and yeast.
4. Gradually stir in flour. Stir well.
5. Place dough in well-greased bowl, turning to grease top. Cover and let rise in refrigerator at least 6 hours (may rise up to 24 hours).
6. Divide into 4 equal parts. Roll each into circle, then cut into 12 triangles. Roll up into crescents and place on baking sheet.
7. Allow to rise 30-40 minutes.
8. Place pan in upper ⅓ of oven. Bake at 375 degrees for 12 minutes.

Preparation Time:	**20 minutes**	**Yield:**	**4 dozen rolls**
Rising Time:	**6½ hours**	**May do ahead**	
Baking Time:	**12 minutes**		

SOURDOUGH BREAD

"It's worth it, so plan ahead"

Starter (Do 4 days in advance)

1 cup warm water (110-115 degrees)
½ cup flour
2 teaspoons yeast

1. Combine all ingredients in glass bowl. Do not use metal bowl. Beat together and let stand covered 24 hours at room temperature.
2. On day 2, add ½ cup flour and ½ cup water. Beat together and let stand as in step 1.
3. Repeat step 2 on day 3.

Bread

5 teaspoons yeast
1½ cups warm water (110-115 degrees)
1 Tablespoon sugar
The Starter
3 cups bread flour
3 cups unbleached flour
2 teaspoons salt
1 beaten egg

1. Mix yeast, warm water and sugar. To proof yeast, let stand until foamy, no more than 10 minutes.
2. In electric mixer with dough hook, add proofed yeast and Starter.
3. In separate bowl, mix bread flour, unbleached flour and salt.
4. Add flour mixture to liquid mixture gradually. Stop adding flour when bowl sides are clean. Knead 1 minute by machine.
5. Place dough in floured 1-gallon size plastic bag. Let rise 1-1½ hours until doubled in size.
6. Punch dough down. Divide into 4 equal sections. Roll 1 section into rectangle. Roll up and shape into baguette, pinching seams. Repeat with remaining 3 sections.
7. Sprinkle flour on towel. Place baguette on floured towel and roll up. Repeat with remaining 3 sections. Let rise 30-40 minutes.
8. Remove towels and place baguettes on greased baking sheet. Brush with egg wash.
9. Bake at 425 degrees for 25 minutes.

Preparation Time:	**Starter-3 days**	**Yield:**	**4 baguettes**
	Bread-30 minutes	**Must do ahead**	
Rising Time:	**2 hours**		
Baking Time:	**25 minutes**		

Tip: *If bread flour unavailable, substitute all-purpose flour and 2 Tablespoons gluten powder.*

CORNBREAD

"Indians should have known about this"

2 cups yellow cornmeal
4 cups flour
⅔ cup and 1 heaping Tablespoon sugar
3 Tablespoons baking powder
3 teaspoons salt
1 cup soft shortening
4 eggs
3 cups milk

1. Combine dry ingredients in bowl and mix well.
2. Cut in shortening until well-blended.
3. Beat eggs and milk together. Mix with dry ingredients until just blended.
4. Pour into well-greased 9 x 13-inch pan.
5. Bake at 400 degrees for 25-35 minutes or until tests done.

Preparation Time:	**15 minutes**	**Serves:**	**6-8**
Baking Time:	**25-35 minutes**		

CORNY CORNBREAD

"An extra touch to quick and easy"

1 15-ounce package cornbread mix
1 egg
1 16-ounce can creamed corn
2 bunches finely chopped green onions

1. Mix all ingredients and pour into greased 9 x 13-inch pan.
2. Bake at 400 degrees for 35 minutes.
3. Serve warm.

Preparation Time:	**10 minutes**	**Serves:**	**6-8**
Baking Time:	**35 minutes**		

SPANISH CORNBREAD

1 cup cornmeal
1 cup creamed corn
⅓ cup oil
¾ cup milk
1 4-ounce can diced green chiles
½ teaspoon soda
2 eggs
¾ teaspoon salt
1 cup grated Cheddar cheese

1. Mix all ingredients except ½ cup cheese.
2. Pour into 9 x 9-inch baking dish. Sprinkle with remaining ½ cup cheese.
3. Bake at 350 degrees for 35-40 minutes.

Preparation Time:	**15 minutes**	**Serves:**	**6**
Baking Time:	**50-60 minutes**		

CURRIED TOAST

"Dare you to try this!"

4 slices white bread
4 Tablespoons butter
¾ teaspoon curry powder

1. Using 2-inch cookie cutter, cut hearts out of bread, getting 3-4 per slice.
2. In small skillet, melt butter. Stir in curry powder. Cook on low heat until blended and bubbly.
3. Dip cut-out hearts into curry butter and place on cookie sheet.
4. Bake at 400 degrees for 7 minutes. Turn over and bake 3 minutes.
5. Drain on paper towel.
6. Before serving, reheat at 400 degrees for 3-5 minutes or until hot.

Preparation Time:	**15-20 minutes**	**Yield:**	**12-16 toasts**
Cooking Time:	**10 minutes**	**May freeze**	
Baking Time:	**10 minutes**		

Tip: *May store at room temperature overnight.*

PARMESAN BREAD STICKS
"Don't plan on leftovers"

6 slices white bread
½ cup coarsely crushed cornflakes
6 Tablespoons grated, fresh Parmesan cheese
¼ teaspoon garlic salt
¼ cup melted butter

1. Trim crust from bread and cut each into 4 strips.
2. Mix cornflakes, cheese and garlic salt.
3. Roll bread strips in butter and then in dry mixture. Place on cookie sheet.
4. Bake at 425 degrees for 7 minutes.

Preparation Time: **30 minutes**   **Yield:**   **24 bread sticks**
Baking Time: **7 minutes**
Tip: *Seal and store up to 2 weeks.*

POPOVERS
"Just like dining out"

2 eggs
1 cup milk
1 cup flour
2 Tablespoons melted butter or margarine
1 teaspoon salt
Butter for preparing cups

1. Mix eggs, milk, flour, melted butter and salt in blender or bowl until smooth.
2. Grease 2½-inch muffin cups or popover pan.
3. Place ½ teaspoon butter or margarine in each cup.
4. Place in 425-degree oven until butter sizzles.
5. Pour batter into sizzling hot cups, filling each ½ to ⅔ full.
6. Bake 25-30 minutes or until popovers are puffed and brown. Do not open oven door while baking.
7. Serve immediately with butter.

Preparation Time: **15 minutes**   **Yield:**   **6 popovers**
Cooking Time: **25-30 minutes**
Serving Suggestion: *Serve with peanut butter and jelly.*
Tip: *Batter may be refrigerated for 2 days.*

TOASTED GARLIC BREAD

"Smells so good"

1 long loaf unsliced French bread
½ cup butter
½ teaspoon minced, dried garlic
½ teaspoon Italian seasoning
2 Tablespoons grated, fresh Parmesan cheese

1. Slice bread loaf lengthwise.
2. Spread with softened butter.
3. Sprinkle with minced garlic, Italian seasoning and Parmesan cheese.
4. Place on cookie sheet.
5. Brown under broiler.

Preparation Time:	**15 minutes**	**Serves:**	**8-10**
Broiling Time:	**2-5 minutes**	**May do ahead and reheat**	

WHEAT STICKS

1 cup white flour
2 cups whole wheat flour
½ cup wheat germ
½ cup oatmeal
2 teaspoons salt
1 cup shortening or ⅔ cup oil
½-¾ cup brown sugar

1. Mix all ingredients with hands.
2. When mealy, add ½ cup water, a few Tablespoons at a time.
3. Divide dough into 3 sections. Gently form into balls. Knead half a minute.
4. Roll dough on floured board to ¼-inch thickness. Cut into ½-inch strips.
5. Bake at 400 degrees for 15-20 minutes.

Preparation Time:	**45 minutes**	**Yield:**	**200 4-inch sticks**
Baking Time:	**15-20 minutes**	**May do ahead**	

Variation: *Instead of cutting into strips, cookie cutters may be used.*

Desserts

ALMOST CANDY BARS
"Don't overdose on these"

¾ **cup melted butter**
1 **cup chopped nuts**
1 **Swiss chocolate cake mix**
¾ **cup evaporated milk**
1 **package caramels (50)**
1 **12-ounce package chocolate chips**

1. Mix butter, nuts, cake mix and ½ cup milk.
2. Place ½ mixture in greased 9 x 13-inch baking dish.
3. Bake at 350 degrees for 6 minutes.
4. Melt caramels and ¼ cup milk in top of double boiler.
5. Spread chips over baked mixture.
6. Pour melted caramels over chips.
7. Pour remaining cake batter over caramels.
8. Bake at 350 degrees for 15 minutes.
9. Let cool at least 30 minutes in refrigerator before cutting into squares.

Preparation Time:	30 minutes	**Yield:**	32 squares
Baking Time:	21 minutes		

PECAN DIAMONDS
"Can't stop eating"

½ **cup well-chilled butter**
1½ **cups flour**
¼ **cup ice water**
1½ **cups firmly packed, light brown sugar**
1 **cup butter**
½ **cup honey or light corn syrup**
⅓ **cup sugar**
1 **pound chopped pecans**
¼ **cup whipping cream or evaporated milk**

1. Cut butter into flour until mixture resembles coarse meal.
2. Add water and toss lightly with fork.
3. Form dough into ball. Wrap in plastic wrap. Chill.
4. On lightly floured surface, roll out dough to 10 x 14-inch rectangle. Place in buttered, floured 9 x 13-inch baking dish. Pierce dough with fork and chill.
5. Combine brown sugar, butter, honey and sugar in heavy saucepan over medium heat. Bring to boil, stirring constantly, about 4 minutes. Remove from heat.
6. Stir in pecans. Blend in cream.
7. Pour over dough in baking dish.
8. Bake at 400 degrees for 25 minutes.
9. Cool completely before cutting into 1-inch diamonds.

Preparation Time:	30 minutes	**Yield:**	65 diamonds
Baking Time:	25 minutes	**May do ahead and freeze**	

CREAM CHEESE BARS
"Better make a double batch"

Crumb Mixture

½ cup unsalted butter
¼ cup sugar
¼ cup unsweetened cocoa
1 teaspoon vanilla
1 well-beaten egg
¼ teaspoon salt
1½ cups graham cracker crumbs
¾ cup flaked coconut
½ cup chopped pecans

1. In heavy saucepan, combine unsalted butter, sugar, cocoa, vanilla, egg and salt. Cook over low heat, stirring constantly until mixture coats spoon.
2. Stir in graham cracker crumbs, coconut and pecans.
3. Press evenly into greased 9-inch square pan.

Cream Filling

½ cup softened, unsalted butter
1 3-ounce package softened cream cheese
2 Tablespoons instant vanilla pudding and pie filling mix
1 cup powdered sugar
2 Tablespoons milk

1. Cream butter, cream cheese and pudding mix.
2. Beat in powdered sugar and milk.
3. Spread over Crumb Mixture. Refrigerate 30 minutes or until Cream Filling is firm.

Chocolate Glaze

4 ounces semisweet chocolate
1 Tablespoon unsalted butter

1. In double boiler over hot, not boiling water, melt chocolate and butter.
2. Spread evenly over Cream Filling. Refrigerate until chocolate is firm.
3. Cut into 1½-inch squares. Refrigerate until serving time.

Preparation Time:	15 minutes		Yield:	36 bars
Cooking Time:	15 minutes		May do ahead	
Chilling Time:	30 minutes			

GLAZED APPLE PIE BARS

"A grandmother's recipe"

Apple Pie

1 22-ounce package pie crust sticks or 2 11-ounce packages pie crust mix
½ cup hot water
¼ cup cornflake crumbs
10 cups peeled, thinly sliced Granny Smith apples
2 Tablespoons lemon juice
1 cup sugar
1 teaspoon cinnamon
½ teaspoon salt
2 Tablespoons butter

1. In large bowl, combine 2 pie crust sticks and ¼ cup hot water. Mix and form into ball. Cover with plastic wrap.
2. Repeat with remaining 2 pie crust sticks and ¼ cup hot water. Set aside.
3. Roll 1 ball of pastry dough into rectangle and place in 9 x 13-inch baking dish, with dough draped over sides of dish.
4. Sprinkle cornflake crumbs over pastry dough.
5. In large bowl, toss apple slices with lemon juice.
6. In separate bowl, mix sugar, cinnamon and salt.
7. Toss apple slices with sugar-cinnamon mixture.
8. Layer apples evenly over pastry dough. Dot with butter.
9. Roll remaining ball of dough into rectangle. Place on top of apples. Pinch edges of dough together or use fork to seal edges.
10. Prick dough top with fork to allow steam to escape.
11. Bake at 350 degrees for 1 hour or until golden brown.
12. Cool completely before cutting into bars.

Glaze

1 cup powdered sugar
1-2 Tablespoons milk or water
1 teaspoon vanilla

1. In small bowl, combine ingredients until smooth.
2. Drizzle over warm Apple Pie.

Preparation Time: 1 hour
Baking Time: 1 hour

Serves: 18-20
May do ahead

MOLASSES TAFFY SQUARES
"Flavorful and chewy"

1 cup shortening
½ cup molasses
1½ cups packed brown sugar
1 teaspoon soda
1 teaspoon salt
4 beaten eggs
2 cups flour
2 cups coarsely chopped nuts
1 teaspoon vanilla

1. In 4-quart saucepan, combine shortening and molasses. Cook over low heat for 2 minutes, stirring constantly. Add brown sugar, cooking a little longer.
2. Remove from heat and add soda. Cool.
3. Mix in remaining ingredients.
4. Pour into greased 9 x 13-inch baking dish.
5. Bake at 325 degrees for 25-30 minutes or until tests done.
6. Cool before cutting into squares.

Preparation Time: **30 minutes**   **Yield:**   **16-20 squares**
Baking Time: **25-30 minutes**

SPICY-RAISIN COOKIE SQUARES
"Delicious and spicy!"

1 cup raisins
1 cup water
1 cup sugar
1 teaspoon soda
1 teaspoon cinnamon
½ teaspoon nutmeg
¼ teaspoon cloves
2 cups flour
½ teaspoon salt
1 egg
½ cup melted shortening
1 teaspoon vanilla
1 cup chopped nuts

1. Combine raisins and water. Cook mixture down to ½ cup liquid.
2. Add sugar. Cool.
3. Add dry ingredients, egg, melted shortening and vanilla. Blend well.
4. Stir in nuts.

Continued

SPICY-RAISIN COOKIE SQUARES — Continued

5. Pour batter into greased, floured 9 x 13-inch baking dish.
6. Bake at 350 degrees for 20-25 minutes until tested done.
7. Frost while hot with heavy glaze made by mixing powdered sugar with a little milk, butter and vanilla.
8. Cool before cutting into squares.

Preparation Time:	**30 minutes**	**Yield:**	**24 squares**
Baking Time:	**20-25 minutes**	**May freeze**	

Variation: *Substitute dates for raisins. Cut lengthwise and simmer with water. Cook mixture down to ½ cup liquid. Dates stay almost intact, so do not chop.*

PUMPKIN BARS

Crust

1 yellow cake mix (reserve 1 cup for Topping)
½ cup butter at room temperature
1 beaten egg
1 16-ounce can pumpkin

1. Combine cake mix (reserving 1 cup for Topping), butter and egg.
2. Press into greased 9 x 13-inch baking dish.

Filling

1 16-ounce can pumpkin
¾ cup sugar
¼ teaspoon salt
½ teaspoon ground ginger
¼ teaspoon ground cloves
1 teaspoon ground cinnamon
2 slightly beaten eggs
⅔ cup evaporated milk

Combine ingredients and pour over Crust.

Topping

1 cup yellow cake mix
¼ cup sugar
1 Tablespoon cinnamon
¼ cup butter at room temperature
1 cup chopped nuts

1. Combine and spoon evenly over Filling.
2. Bake at 350 degrees for 50 minutes.
3. Cool completely before cutting into squares.

Preparation Time:	**20 minutes**	**Yield:**	**12-15 bars**
Baking Time:	**50 minutes**		

THREE-LAYER CHOCOLATE BARS

"So good they're almost sinful"

Crust

½ cup butter
2 ounces unsweetened chocolate
1 cup sugar
1 cup flour
1 teaspoon baking powder
1 teaspoon vanilla
2 eggs
1 cup chopped nuts

1. Melt butter and chocolate.
2. Add remaining ingredients. Mix thoroughly.
3. Pour into greased 9 x 13-inch baking dish.

Filling

1 8-ounce package softened cream cheese
½ cup sugar
2 Tablespoons flour
¼ cup softened butter
1 egg
1 teaspoon vanilla
½ cup chopped nuts
1 6-ounce package semisweet chocolate chips

1. Combine and beat filling ingredients, except nuts and chocolate chips, until smooth, about 1 minute.
2. Stir nuts into Filling. Pour over Crust.
3. Sprinkle chocolate chips on top of Filling.
4. Bake at 350 degrees for 25-30 minutes.

Frosting

¼ cup butter
2 ounces unsweetened chocolate
2 ounces softened cream cheese
¼ cup milk
3 cups powdered sugar
1 teaspoon vanilla
2 cups miniature marshmallows

1. Melt butter and chocolate.
2. Add cream cheese and milk.
3. Stir in powdered sugar and vanilla.
4. Stir in marshmallows.

Continued

THREE-LAYER CHOCOLATE BARS — Continued

To Assemble

1. Frost while hot.
2. Cool and cut into bars.

Preparation Time:	**45 minutes**	**Yield:**	**18-20 bars**
Baking Time:	**25-30 minutes**	**May do ahead**	

ZUCCHINI BROWNIES
"You'd never know it's zucchini"

Brownies

2 cups flour
1¼ cups sugar
1 teaspoon salt
1½ teaspoons soda
½ cup cocoa powder
½ cup oil
1 beaten egg
½ cup chopped nuts
2 teaspoons vanilla
2 cups grated, unpeeled zucchini

1. Combine dry ingredients.
2. Mix oil and egg. Stir into dry ingredients.
3. Add nuts, vanilla and zucchini. Mix well.
4. Spread into greased jellyroll pan.
5. Bake at 350 degrees for 18-20 minutes or until done.

Icing

1 cup sugar
¼ cup milk
¼ cup margarine
1 cup chocolate chips

1. Mix all ingredients except chocolate chips. Cook for 1 minute or until sugar is dissolved.
2. Add chocolate chips. Beat and spread quickly on Brownies.

Preparation Time:	**45 minutes**	**Yield:**	**20 brownies**
Baking Time:	**18-20 minutes**		

BUTTERMILK BROWNIES
"Eat fast - won't last"

Brownies

2 cups sugar
½ teaspoon salt
1 teaspoon vanilla
2 cups flour
1 teaspoon soda
2 beaten eggs
½ cup buttermilk
½ cup margarine
1 cup water
¼ cup cocoa powder
½ cup oil

1. Combine sugar, salt, vanilla, flour, soda, eggs and buttermilk.
2. Melt together margarine, water and cocoa. Remove from heat. Add oil.
3. Add cocoa mixture to flour mixture. Blend thoroughly.
4. Pour into jellyroll pan.
5. Bake at 375 degrees for 15-20 minutes.

Frosting

½ cup margarine
¼ cup cocoa
⅓ cup buttermilk
1 pound powdered sugar
1 cup chopped nuts
1 teaspoon vanilla

1. Melt together margarine, cocoa and buttermilk.
2. Add powdered sugar and blend well.
3. Add nuts and vanilla.
4. Frost Brownies while warm.

Preparation Time: **15 minutes**   **Serves:**   **6-8**
Cooking Time: **15-20 minutes**   **May do ahead**
Serving Suggestions: *Top with Peppermint Frosting or Hot, Quick Chocolate Sauce.*
Variations: *Substitute ½ cup sour cream for buttermilk in brownies. Substitute ⅓ cup milk for buttermilk in frosting.*

APPLE CAKE

"Men enjoy this"

Cake

2 cups sugar
3 eggs
1¼ cups oil
¼ cup orange juice
3 cups flour
1 teaspoon baking soda
1 teaspoon cinnamon
½ teaspoon salt
2 cups unpeeled, shredded apples
1 cup chopped nuts
1 cup shredded coconut

1. Mix sugar, eggs, oil and orange juice.
2. Sift flour, baking soda, cinnamon and salt. Add to sugar-oil mixture.
3. Fold in apples, nuts and coconut.
4. Pour mixture into greased bundt pan.
5. Bake at 325 degrees for 1¼ hours or until tester comes out clean.
6. Remove from oven and place on rack. While cake is still in pan, punch holes in cake and drizzle with hot Buttermilk Topping.
7. Remove from pan when cool and place on serving platter.

Buttermilk Topping

1 cup sugar
½ cup buttermilk
½ teaspoon soda

Bring ingredients to boil, stirring constantly.

Preparation Time: **20-30 minutes**   **Serves:** **15**
Baking Time: **1¼ hours**
Serving Suggestion: *Serve with vanilla ice cream.*

CARROT CAKE

Cake

2 cups sugar
2 cups flour
1 teaspoon salt
2 teaspoons cinnamon
1 teaspoon soda
1½ cups oil
4 eggs
3 cups grated carrots
1 cup chopped nuts

1. Combine sugar, flour, salt, cinnamon, soda and oil.
2. Add eggs, 1 at a time, beating after each addition.
3. Add carrots and nuts.
4. Pour into 2 well-greased and floured 9-inch cake pans.
5. Bake at 375 degrees for 40 minutes.
6. Cool in pans 10 minutes. Remove and cool on rack.

Frosting

1 8-ounce package cream cheese at room temperature
¼ cup milk
1 teaspoon vanilla
2 cups powdered sugar
¾ cup chopped nuts

1. Blend cream cheese and milk.
2. Add vanilla and sugar. Mix until creamy.
3. Add nuts and mix.

Frost Cake between layers, sides and top.

Preparation Time:	**25 minutes**	**Serves:**	**10-12**
Baking Time:	**40 minutes**		

Variation: *Bake in bundt or loaf pans at 375 degrees for 1 hour, 20 minutes.*
Tip: *Better flavor and moistness if baked 1 day ahead.*

CHERRY DELIGHT

"When you're out of time"

2 21-ounce cans cherry pie filling
1 yellow cake mix
2¼ cups chopped nuts
¾ cup melted margarine

1. Pour pie filling into 9 x 13-inch baking dish and spread evenly.
2. Sprinkle cake mix evenly over pie filling.
3. Layer nuts. Do not mix.
4. Drizzle margarine evenly over top.
5. Bake at 350 degrees for 35 minutes.

Preparation Time:	15 minutes	Serves:	12-15
Baking Time:	35 minutes		

CHOCOLATE CAKE WITH BUTTERCREAM FROSTING

Cake

2 cups flour
2 cups sugar
1 teaspoon soda
1 cup margarine
1 cup water
¼ cup cocoa powder
½ cup buttermilk
2 eggs
1 teaspoon vanilla

1. In medium bowl, combine flour, sugar and soda. Set aside.
2. In large saucepan, combine margarine, water and cocoa. Bring to boil. Remove from heat.
3. Add flour mixture, buttermilk, eggs and vanilla. Using electric mixer, beat 2 minutes on medium speed.
4. Pour batter into greased and floured 9 x 13-inch baking dish or 3 8-inch cake pans.
5. Bake at 375 degrees for 20-30 minutes or until toothpick inserted comes out clean.
6. Cool completely.

Buttercream Frosting

⅔ cup softened butter
4 cups powdered sugar
1 teaspoon vanilla
4 Tablespoons milk

1. In large bowl, cream butter until light and fluffy.
2. Gradually add powdered sugar, beating well after each addition.
3. Add vanilla and milk. Beat until light and spreading consistency.
4. Frost Cake.

Preparation Time:	20 minutes	Serves:	12-15
Baking Time:	20-30 minutes		

Variation: For a red cake, use 2 ounces of red food coloring and 6 ounces of water.

223

CHOCOLATE CHIP CHOCOLATE CAKE

1 cup butter
2 cups sugar
4 eggs
2 teaspoons vanilla
1 cup milk
1 cup sour cream
3¼ cups sifted flour
1 teaspoon baking powder
1 teaspoon baking soda
4 squares melted chocolate
1 12-ounce package chocolate chips
Powdered sugar

1. In mixer, cream butter and sugar.
2. Add eggs, 1 at a time.
3. In separate bowl, combine vanilla, milk and sour cream.
4. Alternately add sifted dry ingredients and sour cream mixture.
5. Add melted chocolate and blend well.
6. Fold in chocolate chips.
7. Grease and flour bundt or 10-inch angel food cake pan. Pour in mixture.
8. Bake at 350 degrees for 1¼ hours.
9. Cool in pan for 15 minutes. Remove and cool on rack.
10. Top with dusting of powdered sugar.

Preparation Time:	**30 minutes**	**Serves:**	**15**
Baking Time:	**1¼ hours**	**May freeze**	

Variation: Top with Chocolate Glaze.

CHOCOLATE PRUNE CAKE
"So rich it makes your teeth itch"

Cake

¾ cup pitted prunes
¼ cup boiling water
⅔ cup oil
1 cup sugar
2 Tablespoons cocoa
2 teaspoons cinnamon
1 teaspoon salt
1 teaspoon vanilla
2 eggs
1 cup buttermilk
2½ cups flour
1½ teaspoons soda
2 teaspoons baking powder

1. Soak prunes 30 minutes in boiling water.
2. In separate bowl, combine oil, sugar, cocoa, cinnamon, salt and vanilla.
3. Add eggs and beat well for 2 minutes.
4. Combine prunes and buttermilk in blender and pureé.

Continued

CHOCOLATE PRUNE CAKE — Continued

5. Add to creamed mixture with flour, soda and baking powder. Beat well.
6. Pour into well-greased 9 x 13-inch baking dish or 2 8-inch cake pans.
7. Bake at 350 degrees for 30 minutes.
8. Cool and frost with Chocolate Fudge Icing.

Chocolate Fudge Icing

¼ cup water
¼ cup shortening
¼ cup light corn syrup
2 cups sifted powdered sugar
½ cup cocoa
¼ teaspoon salt
½ teaspoon vanilla

1. Bring water to boil. Remove from heat.
2. Beat in shortening and corn syrup.
3. Add powdered sugar, cocoa, salt and vanilla.
4. Cream well to spreading consistency.
5. Spread over cooled Cake.

Preparation Time:	30 minutes	**Serves:**	**16**
Baking Time:	30 minutes		

CHOCOLATE MOUSSE CAKE

"A chocoholic's delight"

7 ounces semisweet chocolate
½ cup butter
7 separated eggs
1 cup sugar
1 teaspoon vanilla
⅛ teaspoon cream of tartar
1 8-ounce carton Cool Whip

1. Melt chocolate and butter over low heat.
2. In separate bowl, beat egg yolks and ¾ cup sugar until very light and fluffy, about 5 minutes.
3. Gradually beat in warm chocolate mixture and vanilla.
4. In separate bowl, beat egg whites with cream of tartar until soft peaks form.
5. Add remaining ¼ cup sugar slowly, continuing to beat until stiff.
6. Fold egg whites into chocolate mixture.
7. Pour ¾ of batter into 9-inch springform pan.
8. Cover and refrigerate remaining batter.
9. Bake at 325 degrees for 35 minutes.
10. Remove from oven and cool on rack. Remove outside ring of springform pan.
11. Spread reserved batter onto cooled cake.
12. Refrigerate until firm.
13. Frost top and sides with Cool Whip.
14. Refrigerate several hours before serving.

Preparation Time:	1 hour	**Serves:**	**8-10**
Baking Time:	35 minutes	**May be frozen**	
Chilling and Standing Time:	6-8 hours		

GODIVA CHOCOLATE MOUSSE CAKE
"Rich and dense"

Cake

12 ounces semisweet Godiva chocolate
5 Tablespoons prepared decaffeinated coffee
1 cup unsalted butter
2 cup sugar
6 eggs, separated
1 cup flour
Glaze or powdered sugar

1. Melt semisweet chocolate and coffee over very low heat, stirring constantly. Set aside to cool.
2. Cream together butter and sugar.
3. Stir in egg yolks, 1 at a time, to blend thoroughly.
4. Stir in flour, just until blended.
5. Beat egg whites until stiff.
6. Fold chocolate into egg whites.
7. Fold chocolate-egg white mixture into creamed mixture.
8. Pour into lightly buttered 9-inch springform pan.
9. Bake at 350 degrees for 65-70 minutes. The top will be crusty and the middle will still be slightly moist. Cool.
10. Glaze cake or decorate with powdered sugar.

Glaze

4 ounces semisweet Godiva chocolate
2 Tablespoons melted unsalted butter

1. Melt chocolate in top of double boiler.
2. Completely stir in melted butter.
3. Pour Glaze over cooled Cake.

Preparation Time: **15-20 minutes**   **Serves:**   **12-15**
Baking Time: **65-70 minutes**   **May do up to 24 hours ahead**
Variations: *Any good quality chocolate may be substituted for Govida chocolate.*

DOUBLE CHOCOLATE CAKE

½ cup butter
2½ cups brown sugar
3 eggs
3 ounces unsweetened baking chocolate
2¼ cups cake flour
½ teaspoon salt
2 teaspoons baking soda
½ cup sour cream or buttermilk
2 teaspoons vanilla
1 cup boiling water

1. Cream butter and brown sugar.
2. Add eggs and beat thoroughly.
3. Add melted chocolate and stir until blended.
4. Combine and sift together the flour, salt and soda. Add alternately with the sour cream.
5. Stir in vanilla and boiling water.
6. Pour batter equally into 3 buttered and floured 8-inch cake pans.
7. Bake at 375 degrees for 25-30 minutes.
8. Cool 15 minutes. Remove and cool on rack.
9. Spread layers and sides with Chocolate Whipped Cream Frosting.

Preparation Time:	**30 minutes**	**Serves:**	**12-15**
Baking Time:	**25-30 minutes**		

Chocolate Whipped Cream Frosting

1 pint whipping cream
½ cup powdered sugar
5 Tablespoons cocoa powder

Whip all ingredients together to whipped cream consistency.

MISSISSIPPI MUD CAKE

"A small piece is all one can eat!"

MICROWAVE RECIPE

Cake

1½ cups sugar
1½ Tablespoons cocoa
¾ cup margarine
3 eggs
1¼ cups flour
1½ teaspoons baking powder
1 teaspoon vanilla
1¼ cups flaked coconut
1¼ cups chopped walnuts
1 7-ounce jar marshmallow cream

1. Combine sugar and cocoa. Cream together with margarine.
2. Add eggs, flour and baking powder. Mix until well-blended. Batter will be very stiff.
3. Mix in vanilla, coconut and nuts.
4. Pour into greased 10-inch quiche pan.
5. Microwave on high for 11-12 minutes, turning every 2-3 minutes.
6. Spread hot cake with marshmallow cream, adding cream by dollops and spreading evenly.

Frosting

4 Tablespoons margarine
¼ cup evaporated milk
¼ cup cocoa powder
2 cups powdered sugar

1. On high power, heat together margarine, milk and cocoa 1-1½ minutes in microwave.
2. Add powdered sugar, mixing well until smooth.
3. Spread on top of marshmallow creme.

Preparation Time: **15 minutes**   **Serves:**   **20**
Cooking Time: **11-12 minutes**

COCONUTTY CAKE
"Very good"

Cake

1 yellow cake mix
1 3½-ounces package vanilla instant pudding and pie filling mix
1⅓ cup water
4 eggs
¼ cup oil
2 cups flaked coconut
1 cup chopped pecans

1. Mix cake mix, pudding mix, water, eggs and oil. Beat at medium speed until well-blended.
2. Stir in coconut and pecans.
3. Pour into 3 greased and floured 9-inch cake pans.
4. Bake at 350 degrees for 35 minutes or until toothpick comes out clean.
5. Cool in pans 10 minutes. Remove and cool on rack.
6. Fill and top with Coconut-Cream Cheese Frosting.

Coconut-Cream Cheese Frosting

4 Tablespoons butter
2 cups flaked coconut
1 8-ounce package cream cheese at room temperature
2 teaspoons milk
3½ cups powdered sugar
1 teaspoon vanilla

1. Melt 2 Tablespoons butter.
2. Add ¼ cup coconut, stirring constantly over low heat until golden brown.
3. Spread coconut on paper towel to cool.
4. Cream 2 Tablespoons butter with cream cheese. Add milk. Beat in sugar gradually.
   Blend in vanilla. Stir in 1¾ cups coconut.
5. Spread on tops of Cake layers. Stack and sprinkle with golden brown coconut.

Preparation Time: **30 minutes**   **Serves:** **12**
Baking Time: **35 minutes**
Variation: *May toast all coconut.*

ITALIAN CREAM CAKE

"Excellent! They'll ask for seconds"

Cake

2 cups sugar
½ cup shortening
½ cup unsalted butter at room temperature
5 egg yolks
1 teaspoon vanilla
2 cups sifted flour
1 teaspoon soda
½ teaspoon salt
1 cup buttermilk
1 cup chopped pecans
½ cup flaked coconut
5 egg whites

1. Cream sugar, shortening and butter. Add egg yolks and vanilla.
2. Sift dry ingredients.
3. Add buttermilk alternately with dry ingredients to butter mixture.
4. Add pecans and coconut.
5. Beat egg whites until stiff and gently blend into cake batter.
6. Pour into 3 greased and floured 9-inch cake pans.
7. Bake at 350 degrees for 25 minutes.
8. Cool in pans 10 minutes. Remove and cool on rack.

Frosting

¼ cup unsalted butter at room temperature
1 8-ounce package cream cheese at room temperature
2 cups powdered sugar
1 teaspoon vanilla
1 Tablespoon cream or milk
1 cup chopped pecans

1. Cream butter and cream cheese.
2. Add powdered sugar, vanilla and cream. Beat until smooth.
3. Add pecans.
4. Spread Frosting over tops and sides of cake layers.

Preparation Time:	**45 minutes**	**Serves:**	**10-12**
Baking Time:	**25 minutes**		

ORANGE BLOSSOM CAKE

"Better the next day"

1 medium orange
1 yellow cake mix
1½ cups sugar
3 Tablespoons cornstarch
¼ teaspoon salt
¼ cup butter
1 cup water
3½ ounces flaked coconut
1 package fluffy white frosting mix

1. Cut unpeeled orange in chunks. Blend at low speed in electric blender until almost smooth, or put through food chopper using fine blade. (⅔ cup ground orange will be needed).
2. Prepare cake mix following package directions.
3. Fold ⅓ cup of ground orange into batter.
4. Pour batter into 2 greased and floured 8 x 1½-inch cake pans.
5. Bake according to package directions.
6. Cool in pans 10 minutes. Remove and cool on rack.
7. Combine sugar, cornstarch, salt, butter, water and remaining ⅓ cup ground orange.
8. Cook and stir until mixture thickens and boils. Cook 2 minutes. Cool completely.
9. Stir in coconut.
10. Split each cake layer once, making 4 layers.
11. Spread layers and top of cake with orange-coconut filling.
12. Prepare frosting mix according to directions. Spread on sides of cake. Decorate with orange sections.
13. Let stand overnight for flavor enhancement.

Preparation Time: **30 minutes**	**Serves:** **12-14**
Tip: *Navel oranges are best.*	**Must do ahead**

GOOEY BUTTER CAKE

1 package pound cake mix
4 eggs
1 teaspoon vanilla
½ cup butter at room temperature
1 8-ounce package cream cheese
1 pound powdered sugar

1. Combine cake mix, 2 eggs, vanilla and butter.
2. Pour into greased and floured 9 x 13-inch glass baking dish.
3. Combine cream cheese, powdered sugar and 2 eggs. Pour over top of cake batter.
4. Bake at 325 degrees for 35-40 minutes.

Preparation Time: **15 minutes**	**Serves:** **12-15**
Baking Time: **35-40 minutes**	

231

PUMPKIN CAKE ROLL
"A new twist for pumpkin"

Cake

3 eggs
1 cup sugar
⅔ cup pumpkin
1 teaspoon lemon juice
¾ cup flour
1 teaspoon baking powder
½ teaspoon salt
2 teaspoons cinnamon
1 teaspoon ginger
½ teaspoon nutmeg
1 cup finely chopped nuts

1. Beat eggs at high speed for 5 minutes.
2. Gradually beat in sugar.
3. Stir in pumpkin and lemon juice.
4. Stir flour, baking powder, salt and spices together.
5. Fold dry ingredients into pumpkin mixture.
6. Spread in greased, floured jellyroll pan. Top with chopped nuts.
7. Bake at 350 degrees for 15 minutes.
8. Turn out on towel sprinkled with powdered sugar. Starting with narrow end, roll towel with cake inside. Cool.

Filling

4 Tablespoons butter
1 cup powdered sugar
2 3-ounce packages cream cheese
1 teaspoon vanilla

1. Beat ingredients until smooth.
2. Unroll cooled Cake and spread Filling over Cake.
3. Roll and chill.

Preparation Time:	**1 hour**	**Serves:**	**20**
Baking Time:	**15 minutes**	**Must do ahead**	
Chilling Time:	**2-3 hours**		

PUMPKIN CAKE SQUARES
"So easy and so good"

2 slightly beaten eggs
1 30-ounce can pumpkin pie mix
⅔ cup evaporated milk
1 cup chopped walnuts or pecans
1 yellow cake mix
½ cup melted butter

1. Combine eggs, pumpkin pie mix and evaporated milk, mixing thoroughly.
2. Pour mixture into 9 x 13-inch pan.
3. Add nuts to cake mix and blend. Sprinkle dry mixture over pumpkin mixture and spread evenly.
4. Drizzle butter evenly over dry cake mixture.
5. Bake at 350 degrees for 1 hour.
6. Cool 30 minutes. Serve warm.

Preparation Time:	15 minutes	**Yield:**	20 squares
Baking Time:	1 hour		
Cooling Time:	30 minutes		

PUNCH BOWL CAKE
"Beautiful to behold"

1 yellow cake mix
1 6-ounce package instant vanilla pudding
1 21-ounce can cherry pie filling
1 20-ounce drained fruit cocktail
1 20-ounce can drained, crushed pineapple
1½ cups chopped nuts, plus extra for garnish
1 12-ounce package flaked coconut, plus extra for garnish
2 8-ounce cartons Cool Whip
Maraschino cherries for garnish

1. Make cake in 2 layers. Cool.
2. Prepare instant pudding according to package directions. Refrigerate until set.
3. Place 1 cake layer in bottom of 6-quart punch bowl.
4. Add in layers ½ of ingredients in order listed: prepared pudding, cherry pie filling, fruit cocktail, pineapple, nuts, coconut and Cool Whip.
5. Add second cake layer. Continue layering remaining ingredients in same order as in step 4.
6. Garnish with maraschino cherries, nuts and coconut.
7. Refrigerate at least 6 hours before serving.

Preparation Time:	25 minutes	**Serves:**	35
Baking Time:	30 minutes	**Must do ahead**	
Chilling Time:	6 hours		

BOHEMIAN CAKE

1 cup butter
2 cups sugar
½ cup brown sugar
4 eggs
2 cups flour
1 cup coconut
1 cup chopped pecans
1 teaspoon vanilla

1. Combine all ingredients.
2. Pour into greased 2-quart tube or loaf pan.
3. Bake at 300 degrees for 1¼-1½ hours.
4. Cool in pan. Dip pan in hot water to release.

Preparation Time: **15 minutes**   **Serves:**   **10-12**
Baking Time: **1¼-1½ hours**

FLAG CAKE
"Serve with pride"

1 white cake mix
1 cup heavy cream
1 Tablespoon sugar
½ teaspoon vanilla
½ cup fresh blueberries
2 cups sliced, fresh strawberries

1. Mix and bake cake according to package instructions in 9 x 13-inch baking dish.
2. Place cake on attractive serving dish or platter.
3. Beat cream until soft peaks form. Add sugar and vanilla.
4. Spread whipped cream in even layer over top of cake.
5. Place 2 lines of blueberries at right angles in top left-hand corner to form a 4-inch square. Fill square with additional lines of blueberries. Leave small amount of white cream showing between berries.
6. Use overlapping sliced strawberries to form horizontal red stripes from side to side on cake, allowing cream to show for white stripes.
7. Refrigerate cake until serving time.

Preparation Time: **45 minutes**   **Serves:**   **12-15**

POUND CAKE
"Best ever"

3 cups sugar
1 cup butter
6 separated eggs
3 cups flour
¼ teaspoon soda
1 cup sour cream
1 teaspoon vanilla
1 teaspoon almond extract
2 teaspoons butter flavoring
1 teaspoon lemon extract

1. Cream sugar and butter.
2. Add egg yolks, 1 at a time, mixing after each addition.
3. Combine flour and soda. Set aside.
4. Combine sour cream and flavorings.
5. Alternately add flour and sour cream mixture.
6. In separate bowl, beat egg whites. Fold gently into cake batter.
7. Pour batter into greased and floured bundt pan.
8. Bake at 325 degrees for 1¼ hours.
9. Cool 10 minutes. Remove and cool on rack.

Preparation Time:	15 minutes	**Serves:**	18-20
Baking Time:	1¼ hours	**May freeze**	

Serving Suggestion: *Top with fresh or frozen berries and dollop of whipped cream or favorite sauce.*

ICE CREAM CONE CUPCAKES
"Kids love them"

1 cake mix
1¼ cup water
⅓ cup oil
3 eggs
½ cup chopped nuts, optional
36 flat-bottomed ice cream cones
Ready-to-spread frosting
Decorating items such as sprinkles, coconut, etc.

1. In large bowl, combine cake mix, water, oil and eggs. Beat at low speed until moistened, then at high speed for 2 minutes.
2. Fold in nuts.
3. Place ice cream cones in muffin pan and fill to within 1 inch of top with batter.
4. Bake at 350 degrees for 20-25 minutes. Cool.
5. Spread frosting on top and decorate as desired.

Preparation Time:	15 minutes	**Yield:**	36
Baking Time:	25 minutes	**May do ahead**	

LEMON PECAN FRUITCAKE

"Freezing makes it moist"

Fruitcake

1 pound brown sugar
1 pound margarine
6 beaten egg yolks
4 cups flour
1 teaspoon baking powder
1 2-ounce bottle lemon extract
1 quart chopped pecans
½ pound chopped candied pineapple
½ pound chopped candied cherries
6 beaten egg whites

1. Cream together sugar and margarine until smooth.
2. Add beaten egg yolks and mix well.
3. Combine 2 cups flour and baking powder. Add to creamed mixture.
4. Add lemon extract.
5. Coat pecans, pineapple and cherries with remaining 2 cups flour and add to creamed mixture.
6. Fold in beaten egg whites. Cover and let stand overnight.
7. Pour mixture into greased tube pan.
8. Bake at 300 degrees for 1½-2 hours. Place pan of water in lower rack of oven while cake is baking.
9. Brush with Glaze, if desired.

Glaze

½ cup light corn syrup
¼ cup water

1. Combine and bring to boil.
2. Remove from heat and cool to lukewarm. Brush on cooled Fruitcake.

Preparation Time:	**45 minutes**	**Serves:**	**18-20**
Baking Time:	**1½-2 hours**	**May do ahead and freeze**	

CANDIED FRUITCAKE

1½ pounds (3 cups) pitted dates
1 pound candied pineapple
1 pound whole candied cherries
2 cups sifted flour
2 teaspoons baking powder
½ teaspoon salt
4 eggs
1 cup sugar
2 pounds (6 cups) pecan halves

1. Coarsely chop dates and pineapple. Add cherries.
2. Combine flour, baking powder and salt. Sift into fruit and mix well.
3. Beat eggs until frothy. Gradually add sugar. Beat until blended. Add to fruit mixture and mix well.
4. Add nuts and mix well.
5. Grease and line 2 9 x 5-inch loaf pans with brown paper. Grease paper.
6. Spoon into prepared pans.
7. Bake at 275 degrees for 1¼-1½ hours.
8. Remove from pans and cool 5 minutes. Peel off paper. Cool completely.

Preparation Time:	**30 minutes**	**Yield:**	**2 loaves**
Baking Time:	**1¼-1½ hours**	**Must do ahead**	

Tips: *Fruitcake has better flavor when made several weeks ahead. Store in plastic wrap. Do not freeze unless planning to store for several months.*

APRICOT CHEESECAKE
"No baking - no eggs"

Crust

½ cup butter
1 cup flour
½ cup chopped almonds
¼ cup sugar

1. In medium skillet over low heat, melt butter. Stir in remaining crust ingredients. Cook over medium heat until mixture is medium-golden brown and crumbly, stirring constantly. Cool slightly.
2. Press evenly into bottom of greased 9-inch springform pan. Refrigerate until firm.

Filling

1 envelope unflavored gelatin
1 16-ounce can drained apricot halves, reserving ⅓ cup liquid
½ cup sugar
2 8-ounce packages softened cream cheese
1 8-ounce carton plain yogurt
1 teaspoon grated lemon peel

1. In small saucepan, combine gelatin and reserved apricot liquid. Let stand 1 minute. Cook over low heat, stirring constantly, until dissolved. Cool.
2. In food processor bowl with metal blade or blender, purée apricots.
3. Add sugar, cream cheese, yogurt and lemon peel. Process until smooth.
4. Gradually stir in gelatin mixture.
5. Pour cream cheese mixture over prepared crust.
6. Refrigerate overnight or until set.

Preparation Time:	30 minutes	**Serves:**	10-12
Cooking Time:	5 minutes		
Setting Time:	6-8 hours		

Serving Suggestion: Serve with Apricot Sauce.

CHEESECAKE

"Lemony and light"

Crust

16 finely crushed graham cracker squares
6 Tablespoons melted butter
½ cup sugar

1. Combine graham cracker crumbs, melted butter and sugar.
2. Press into bottom of 9-inch springform pan. Set aside.

Filling

4 separated eggs
¾ cup sugar
Juice of ½ lemon
1 teaspoon grated lemon rind
1 teaspoon vanilla
2 8-ounce packages softened cream cheese

1. In large bowl with electric mixer at medium speed, beat egg yolks and sugar until well-blended.
2. Add lemon juice, lemon rind, vanilla and cream cheese. Continue beating at medium speed until smooth, about 8 minutes. Wash and dry beaters well.
3. In deep bowl with mixer at high speed, beat egg whites until stiff peaks form.
4. Using rubber spatula, gently fold ¼ of beaten egg whites into cheese mixture to lighten. Fold remaining egg whites into cheese mixture until thoroughly incorporated.
5. Spoon Filling onto prepared crumbs in springform pan.
6. Bake at 350 degrees for 25-30 minutes or until light brown on top.
7. Remove cake from oven. Cool on wire rack 15 minutes. Do not turn oven off.
8. Spread Topping over cake, not all the way to edges. Bake 10 minutes.
9. Cool cake on wire rack for 1 hour, then refrigerate several hours.
10. Remove sides of springform pan. Serve with favorite sauce.

Topping

1 cup sour cream
½ teaspoon vanilla
2 Tablespoons sugar

Combine ingredients, mixing well.

Preparation Time:	**30 minutes**	**Serves:**	**15-20**
Baking Time:	**40 minutes**	**Must do ahead**	
Chilling Time:	**3-4 hours**		

Variation: Cake may be topped with whipped cream instead of sour cream mixture.

GLORIOUS BERRY CHEESECAKE

"New Yorkers, eat your heart out"

Crust

¾ cup walnuts
¾ cup graham crackers
3 Tablespoons butter

1. Mix walnuts, graham crackers and butter in blender.
2. Press into 9 or 10-inch springform pan.

Filling

4 8-ounce packages softened cream cheese
4 eggs
1¼ cups sugar
1 Tablespoon lemon juice
2 teaspoons vanilla

1. Mix cream cheese, eggs, sugar, lemon juice and vanilla together until smooth.
2. Pour into unbaked Crust in springform pan.
3. Bake at 350 degrees in 9-inch pan for 50-55 minutes or 10-inch pan for 40-50 minutes.
4. Remove from oven and let stand at room temperature for 15 minutes.
5. Add Topping and bake 5 minutes longer.
6. Allow to cool completely before removing from pan.
7. Just before serving, garnish with strawberries.

Topping

2 cups sour cream
¼ cup sugar
1 teaspoon vanilla
1 10-ounce package frozen strawberries, drained, or 2 cups fresh strawberries

Combine sour cream, sugar and vanilla.

Preparation Time: **20-30 minutes**   **Serves:**   **10-12**
Baking Time: **40-60 minutes**
Tip: Cheesecake is best if made several hours before serving.

OREO CHEESECAKE

"For sincere cheesecake lovers"

Crust

30 Oreo cookies (about 2⅔ cups crumbs)
4 Tablespoons melted, unsalted butter

1. Place cookies in food processor fitted with metal blade. Process until mixture turns to crumbs.
2. Add butter and mix until blended.
3. Pour into 10-inch springform pan. Press evenly over bottom and up sides. Refrigerate.

Filling

4 8-ounce packages softened cream cheese
1¼ cups sugar
2 Tablespoons flour
4 eggs
4 egg yolks
⅓ cup whipping cream
1½ teaspoons vanilla
1½ cups coarsely broken Oreo cookies

1. Beat cream cheese in large bowl with electric mixer until smooth.
2. Add sugar, beating about 3 minutes until mixture is light and fluffy.
3. Beat continuously and add flour, eggs and yolks.
4. Beat in whipping cream and vanilla until well-blended.
5. Pour half of batter into prepared Crust.
6. Sprinkle with chopped Oreo cookies.
7. Pour remaining batter over cookies.
8. Place pan on baking sheet.
9. Bake at 425 degrees for 15 minutes.
10. Reduce oven temperature to 225 degrees and bake 50 minutes or until set.
11. Remove cake from oven. Increase oven temperature to 350 degrees.

Topping

¼ cup sugar
2 cups sour cream
1½ teaspoons vanilla

1. Mix topping ingredients together and spread evenly over cake.
2. Return to oven and bake 7 minutes or until sour cream begins to set.
3. Cool to room temperature.
4. Cover and refrigerate several hours.

Preparation Time:	**40 minutes**	**Serves:**	**20**
Baking Time:	**1¼ hours**	**May do 3 days ahead**	
Chilling Time:	**5-6 hours**		

Variation: *Substitute Hydrox cream-filled chocolate cookies for Oreo cookies.*

BANANA SPLIT PIE DESSERT
"For the top banana"

Crust

2 cups graham cracker crumbs
½ cup melted butter
¼ cup sugar

1. Mix all ingredients.
2. Press into bottom of 9 x 13-inch baking dish.
3. Chill 1 hour.

Filling

2 cups powdered sugar
2 eggs
1 teaspoon vanilla
1 cup butter

1. Cream together.
2. Spread over Crust.
3. Chill 1 hour.

Toppings

4-5 sliced, ripe bananas
2 cups sliced, fresh strawberries
1 16-ounce can drained, crushed pineapple
2 cups Cool Whip
1 cup chopped pecans
1 4-ounce jar drained, chopped maraschino cherries
1½ ounce grated Hershey chocolate bar

1. Layer Toppings over Filling in listed order.
2. Chill ½-1 hour.
3. Cut into squares to serve.

Preparation Time: **20 minutes**   **Serves:**   **12-15**
Chilling Time: **2½-3 hours**
Tips: *Best if toppings are added 30-60 minutes before serving, as pie does not hold overnight. Do not use whipped margarine for filling.*

LEMON-CHEESE PUDDING DESSERT

"You'll get rave reviews with this dessert!"

Crust

1 cup flour
½ cup butter
½ cup chopped nuts

1. Mix flour, butter and nuts with pastry blender. Spread in 9 x 13-inch pan.
2. Bake at 350 degrees for 12 minutes or until slightly brown.

Cheese Layer

1 8-ounce softened cream cheese
1 cup powdered sugar
1 8-ounce carton Cool Whip
2 Tablespoons lemon juice

1. Mix cream cheese, powdered sugar, Cool Whip and lemon juice.
2. Spread on cooled Crust.

Pudding Layer

¾ cup cornstarch
4 cups water
2 cups sugar
4 egg yolks
2 Tablespoons butter
2 teaspoons grated lemon peel
1 cup lemon juice

1. Mix cornstarch in 1 cup cold water. Add 3 cups water and bring to boil, stirring constantly until thickened.
2. Add sugar, egg yolks, butter and lemon peel. Cook on very low heat 5 minutes.
3. Add lemon juice. Cool.
4. Spread on Cheese Layer.

Topping

1 cup whipping cream
1 Tablespoon powdered sugar
1 teaspoon unflavored gelatin

1. Whip cream with powdered sugar and unflavored gelatin.
2. Spread layer of sweetened whipped cream on Pudding Layer or serve with dollop of whipped cream.

Preparation Time:	**1 hour**	**Serves:**	**16**
Baking Time:	**12 minutes**	**May do ahead**	
Cooking Time:	**30 minutes**		

WILD RASPBERRY DESSERT
"Very pretty, very delicious"

Crust

1 cup butter
2 cups flour
2 Tablespoons sugar

1. Combine all ingredients.
2. Press into bottom of 9 x 13-inch baking dish.
3. Bake at 350 degrees for 20 minutes.
4. Cool 30 minutes.

Filling

½ cup butter
1 8-ounce package cream cheese
2 cups powdered sugar
1 cup chopped nuts

1. Combine butter, cream cheese and sugar in food processor until creamy smooth.
2. Spread over cooled crust.
3. Top Filling with nuts. Refrigerate.

Topping

1 cup boiling water
1 3-ounce package wild raspberry jello
2 12-ounce packages frozen raspberries

1. Combine boiling water and jello.
2. Stir in raspberries. Continue to mix until berries are completely thawed.
3. Spoon mixture over cheese-nut Filling. Refrigerate until firm.
4. Serve plain or with whipped cream.

Preparation Time:	**2 hours**		
Chilling Time:	**4-6 hours**	**Serves:**	**12**
		Must do ahead	

BLUEBERRY DESSERT

"Berry, berry good"

1 cup flour
¼ cup brown sugar
1½ cups chopped nuts
½ cup melted butter
¾ cup powdered sugar
1 8-ounce package softened cream cheese
1 teaspoon vanilla
2 cups Cool Whip
1 20-ounce can blueberry pie filling

1. Mix flour, brown sugar and nuts. Combine with butter.
2. Press into 9 x 13-inch baking dish.
3. Bake at 350 degrees for 10-15 minutes.
4. In mixing bowl, combine powdered sugar, cream cheese and vanilla. Beat until smooth.
5. Fold in Cool Whip.
6. Spread cream cheese mixture over cooled crust.
7. Spread pie filling over cream cheese mixture. Refrigerate.

Preparation Time: **20 minutes**   **Serves:**   **12-15**
Baking Time: **10-15 minutes**
Serving Suggestion: *Top with dollop of Cool Whip.*

FIVE-POUND FUDGE

"Eighty years old and still THE favorite!"

4 cups white sugar
½ cup light corn syrup
½ cup butter
1 12-ounce can evaporated milk
2 teaspoons vanilla
1½ cup chopped nuts

1. In heavy saucepan, combine sugar, corn syrup, butter and milk. Mix well.
2. On medium-high heat, bring to rolling boil. Stir constantly with wooden spoon.
3. Turn heat to medium-low. Continue soft boiling for 50-60 minutes until mixture reaches soft-ball stage, 236 degrees. Stir occasionally, about every 5 minutes.
4. Remove from heat and let stand 3-5 minutes.
5. Add vanilla.
6. Beat on high with electric beater until thick and creamy, about 6 minutes. Do not overbeat as it will harden quickly.
7. Stir in nuts.
8. Pour into 9 x 13-inch greased dish. Cut into squares while warm.

Preparation Time: **20 minutes**   **Yield:**   **60 1-inch squares**
Cooking Time: **50-60 minutes**   **May do ahead**

OLD SOUTH PRALINES
"A touch of New Orleans"

3 cups firmly packed brown sugar
1 cup water
1 teaspoon lemon juice
1 Tablespoon margarine or butter
⅛ teaspoon salt
1 teaspoon vanilla
3 cups chopped pecans

1. Combine sugar, water and lemon juice.
2. Cook to soft-ball stage, 236 degrees.
3. Add margarine, salt, vanilla and nuts. Remove from heat. Beat until mixture starts to thicken.
4. Drop teaspoonfuls onto waxed paper.

Preparation Time:	**30 minutes**	**Yield:**	**36 pralines**
Cooking Time:	**15-20 minutes**		

Tips: *Do not place in tightly covered container. Do not freeze or place in refrigerator.*

REESE'S CUP SQUARES

¾ cup margarine or butter
1 cup chunky peanut butter
1 pound powdered sugar
1 8-ounce Hershey's chocolate candy bar

1. Melt margarine. Add peanut butter and powdered sugar. Mix well.
2. Spread peanut butter mixture in greased 9 x 13-inch dish.
3. Melt chocolate in double boiler.
4. Spread over peanut butter mixture.
5. Chill at least 30 minutes. Allow to rest a few minutes after removing from refrigerator before cutting into small squares. Store in refrigerator.

Preparation Time:	**15 minutes**	**Yield:**	**3 dozen squares**
Chilling Time:	**30 minutes**		

TIGER FUDGE

½ pound milk chocolate
½ pound white chocolate
½ cup peanut butter

1. Melt milk chocolate over hot, not boiling water, in double boiler. Set aside.
2. Melt white chocolate as in step 1.
3. Add peanut butter to melted white chocolate. Mix well.
4. Pour and swirl milk chocolate into peanut butter mixture.

Preparation Time:	**20 minutes**	**Yield:**	**1½ pounds**

Tip: *Do not cool in refrigerator.*

TAFFY
"Fun, fun, fun"

2½ pounds sugar
1½ pints light corn syrup
1 pint cream
1 envelope unflavored gelatin
1 cup water
½ cup butter
1-inch square paraffin

1. Mix sugar, corn syrup and cream. Boil a few minutes while stirring.
2. In separate bowl, dissolve gelatin in water. Combine with syrup and remaining ingredients.
3. Cook, stirring constantly, until mixture forms hard ball when dropped into cold water.
4. Cool on greased baking sheets until it can be handled comfortably.
5. Pull until white.

Preparation Time:	30 minutes	**Yield:**	1½-2 pounds
Cooking Time:	15-20 minutes		
Cooling Time:	45 minutes		

ALMOND COOKIES

1 egg
1¼ cups powdered sugar
Grated peel of 1 lemon
1 teaspoon vanilla
1⅔ cups ground almonds
1 teaspoon baking powder
Almond slivers

1. In medium bowl, beat egg with sugar 3 minutes.
2. Add lemon peel and vanilla.
3. Mix in ground almonds and baking powder. Stir well.
4. Dampen 18-inch sheet of plastic wrap. Place cookie mixture on plastic wrap. Form into 16-inch roll. Freeze 1 hour.
5. Cut dough into thin slices. Space on 2 parchment-lined baking sheets. Return dough to freezer.
6. Decorate slices with almond slivers.
7. Bake at 350 degrees for 15 minutes or until golden.
8. Cool on baking sheets 2 minutes or until crisp. Peel cookies off paper.
9. Repeat procedure with remaining dough.

Preparation Time:	20 minutes	**Yield:**	100 cookies
Freezing Time:	1 hour		
Baking Time:	15 minutes		

Tip: *Store in airtight container up to 2 weeks.*

ALMOND CRESCENTS

1¾ cups flour
¾ cup butter
⅔ cup creamed cottage cheese
⅓ cup powdered sugar
½ teaspoon almond extract
⅛ teaspoon salt
1 8-ounce package almond paste
1 beaten egg

1. In medium bowl, mix flour, butter, cottage cheese, powdered sugar, almond extract and salt. Knead ingredients until well-blended.
2. Form dough into ball. Wrap with plastic wrap and refrigerate 2 hours or until dough is firm enough to handle.
3. On lightly floured surface using floured rolling pin, roll half of dough ⅛-inch thick. Refrigerate remaining half of dough until ready to use.
4. Cut out cookies using floured 2-inch round cookie cutter.
5. Using spatula, place cookie rounds on 2 greased cookie sheets about ½ inch apart.
6. Place about ½ teaspoon almond paste in center of each dough circle.
7. Brush edges of dough circles with egg. Fold dough over filling. With floured fork, firmly press edges to seal. Brush crescents with remaining egg.
8. Bake at 375 degrees for 15 minutes.
9. Remove cookies with spatula to wire racks to cool.
10. Repeat with remaining dough.

Preparation Time:	60 minutes	Yield:	30 crescents
Chilling Time:	2 hours		
Baking Time:	15 minutes		

APRICOT FOLD-UPS
"Tasty little packages"

Dough

2 cups unsifted flour
1 teaspoon salt
1 8-ounce package softened cream cheese
1 cup butter
1 Tablespoon milk
1 Tablespoon white vinegar

1. In large bowl, combine flour and salt.
2. With pastry blender, cut in cream cheese and butter until mixture is crumbly.
3. Add milk and vinegar.
4. Work dough with hands until it holds together.
5. Divide into 4 balls and wrap in waxed paper.
6. Refrigerate at least 2 hours.

Filling

1½ cups dried apricots
2 cups water
1½ cups sugar

1. In medium saucepan, cover apricots with water.
2. Add sugar and bring to boil.
3. Turn off heat and let cool in liquid. Drain.

Fold-Ups

1. On lightly floured surface, roll out each ball of dough to ⅛-inch thickness.
2. Cut into 2½-inch squares.
3. Place apricot in center of each square.
4. Fold each corner into center and pinch together to seal.
5. Place on ungreased cookie sheets.
6. Bake at 400 degrees for 15 minutes or until golden brown.
7. Remove to wire racks to cool.

Glaze

¾ cup powdered sugar
1 Tablespoon water

1. In small bowl, mix powdered sugar and water until smooth.
2. Drizzle on squares when slightly cooled.

Preparation Time:	**60 minutes**	**Yield:**	**45 fold-ups**
Chilling Time:	**2 hours**	**May do ahead and freeze**	
Baking Time:	**15 minutes**		

Variation: *Raspberry or prune filling may be substituted for above filling.*

APRICOT-NUT LOGS
"Yummy!"

16 finely crushed graham crackers
½ cup coarsely ground walnuts
2 Tablespoons butter
1 cup finely chopped, dried apricots
2 eggs
½ cup sugar
½ cup brown sugar
1 teaspoon vanilla
1 cup shredded coconut

1. Combine graham cracker crumbs and walnuts. Set aside.
2. In large skillet over low heat, melt butter.
3. Add apricots and stir.
4. In separate bowl, beat eggs and sugars. Add to butter-apricot mixture.
5. Continue to stir and cook slowly until bubbly and thick, approximately 10-15 minutes.
6. Stir in vanilla and crumb-nut mixture.
7. Mold into 2 logs while warm. Roll in coconut.
8. Wrap in foil or plastic wrap and refrigerate until very firm. Slice logs into ¼-inch rounds.

Preparation Time:	**35 minutes**	**Yield:**	**3½ dozen rounds**
Cooking Time:	**10-15 minutes**	**Must do ahead**	
		May freeze	

CHOCOLATE-CHOCOLATE CHIP COOKIES
"A double hitter"

1 package devil's food cake mix with pudding
½ cup softened butter
1 teaspoon vanilla
2 eggs
1 6-ounce package semisweet chocolate chips
½ cup chopped nuts

1. Mix half of cake mix, butter, vanilla and eggs in large bowl until smooth.
2. Stir in remaining cake mix. Fold in chocolate chips and nuts.
3. Drop dough by teaspoonfuls about 2 inches apart onto ungreased cookie sheet.
4. Bake at 350 degrees for 10-12 minutes. Centers will be soft.
5. Cool 1 minute before removing from cookie sheet.

Preparation Time:	**15 minutes**	**Yield:**	**4-5 dozen cookies**
Baking Time:	**10-12 minutes**		

Variation: *Use any flavor cake mix. If using cherry chip or yellow cake mix, decrease butter to ⅓ cup.*

CANDY BAR COOKIES
"Great for Christmas"

Cookie Pastry

¾ cup softened butter
¾ cup powdered sugar
1 teaspoon vanilla
2 Tablespoons evaporated milk
¼ teaspoon salt
2 cups flour

1. Cream butter and sugar.
2. Add vanilla, milk and salt. Mix well.
3. Blend in flour. Chill 1 hour for easier handling.
4. Separate pastry into equal halves. Refrigerate half not being used. Roll out on floured surface. Cut into circles.
5. Bake on ungreased baking sheets at 325 degrees for 12-15 minutes.

Filling

28 caramels
¼ cup milk
¼ cup butter
1 cup powdered sugar
1 cup chopped nuts

1. In saucepan, melt caramels and milk over low heat.
2. Stir in butter, powdered sugar and nuts.
3. Spread 1 teaspoon filling on each cooled cookie.

Chocolate Icing

1 6-ounce package chocolate chips
⅓ cup milk
2 Tablespoons butter
1 teaspoon vanilla
½ cup powdered sugar
Chopped nuts, optional

1. Melt chocolate chips and milk over low heat.
2. Stir in butter, vanilla and sugar.
3. Spread over filling. Cool. Garnish with extra nuts, if desired.

Preparation Time:	1½ hours	**Yield:**	2 dozen cookies
Baking Time:	12-15 minutes		
Cooking Time:	15-20 minutes		

CHOCOLATE CHUNK COOKIES
"The best"

½ cup unsalted butter at room temperature
½ cup packed light brown sugar
¼ cup sugar
1 teaspoon vanilla
½ teaspoon salt
1 egg
½ teaspoon baking soda
1 cup flour
¾ cup coarsely chopped toasted walnuts
2 cups coarsely chopped, semisweet chocolate chunks
Vegetable shortening for baking sheets

1. In large mixing bowl, combine butter, sugars, vanilla and salt. Beat until fluffy.
2. Beat in egg and baking soda.
3. Stir in flour, walnuts and chocolate.
4. Transfer to bowl just large enough to hold dough. Cover and refrigerate until firm, about 4 hours or overnight.
5. Lightly coat 1-2 baking sheets with shortening.
6. Using 2-3 Tablespoons dough for each cookie, shape dough into balls and place 1 in center of cookie sheet and evenly space 4 others a few inches in from each corner.
7. Bake at 350 degrees for 10-12 minutes, until cookies spring back when very lightly touched.
8. Cool on baking sheets 2 minutes. Transfer to paper towels to cool about 2 minutes. Transfer to racks to cool.
9. Repeat baking procedure with cool baking sheets.

Preparation Time:	15 minutes	Yield:	18-24 cookies
Chilling Time:	4 hours		
Baking Time:	10-12 minutes		

COOKIE CRUNCH
"Very festive"

1 cup chopped dates
1 cup white sugar
½ cup butter
1 egg
¼ teaspoon salt
½ teaspoon vanilla
½ cup chopped nuts
2 cups Rice Krispies
1 14-ounce package Angel Flake coconut

1. Combine dates, sugar, butter, egg and salt. Cook in pan until thickened, stirring constantly. Remove from heat and cool slightly.
2. Add vanilla, nuts and Rice Krispies. Stir to blend.
3. Form into balls and roll into coconut.

Preparation Time:	1 hour	Yield:	60 cookie balls
Cooking Time:	15-20 minutes	May freeze	

CRUNCHY CHOCOLATES

"What did we do before chocolate chips?"

MICROWAVE RECIPE

1 pound powdered sugar
¾ cup butter or margarine
2 cups chunky peanut butter at room temperature
3 cups crushed Rice Krispies
⅔ bar paraffin
2 8-ounce milk chocolate bars
1 12-ounce package semisweet chocolate chips

1. Place sugar and butter in bowl. Microwave on high 1-2 minutes or until butter melts.
2. Stir in peanut butter, then Rice Krispies.
3. Form mixture into small balls. Place on waxed paper-lined cookie sheet. Refrigerate until chilled.
4. Using vegetable peeler or sharp knife, shave paraffin into small pieces in a small bowl. Set aside.
5. Break chocolate bars into small pieces into bowl.
6. Add chocolate chips. Microwave on high for 3 minutes, stirring every 30 seconds.
7. Add paraffin. Microwave on high 4-5 minutes or until paraffin is melted.
8. Insert toothpick in balls. Dip into chocolate-paraffin mixture, coating evenly.
9. Place on waxed paper-lined cookie sheet.
10. When cool and set, refrigerate in airtight container.

Preparation Time:	**1 hour**	**Yield:**	**50 chocolates**
Cooking Time:	**11 minutes**	**May do ahead**	

KOURABIEDES

"Sweet shortbread"

2 cups sweet butter
½ cup powdered sugar
2 lightly beaten egg yolks
⅔ cup finely chopped, blanched almonds
⅓ cup orange juice
1 teaspoon baking powder
4½-5 cups sifted flour
Powdered sugar for garnish

1. Cream butter until light and fluffy. Beat in sugar, egg yolks, almonds and orange juice.
2. Sift baking powder with flour. Carefully blend into butter mixture.
3. Shape into small crescents and place on baking sheets.
4. Bake at 400 degrees for 20 minutes.
5. Sift powdered sugar onto large sheet of waxed paper.
6. After removing cookies from oven, carefully place on sugar and sift additional sugar over tops and sides. Cool thoroughly before storing.

Preparation Time:	**1 hour**	**Yield:**	**10 dozen cookies**
Baking Time:	**20 minutes**	**May freeze**	

MOLASSES SUGAR COOKIES

"Yummy - just like Grandma used to make"

¾ **cup shortening**
1 cup sugar
¼ **cup molasses**
1 egg
2 cups sifted flour
2 teaspoons baking soda
½ **teaspoon cloves**
½ **teaspoon ginger**
1 teaspoon cinnamon
½ **teaspoon salt**

1. Melt shortening in a 3 or 4-quart saucepan over low heat. Remove from heat. Let cool.
2. Add sugar, molasses and egg. Beat well.
3. Sift together flour, soda, cloves, ginger, cinnamon and salt. Add to shortening mixture. Mix well. Chill.
4. Form into 1-inch balls. Roll in granulated sugar and place on greased cookie sheets 2 inches apart.
5. Bake at 375 degrees for 8-10 minutes.

Preparation Time:	**30 minutes**	**Yield:**	**4 dozen cookies**
Baking Time:	**8-10 minutes**		

MONSTER COOKIES

"All ages like these"

12 eggs
2 pounds brown sugar
4 cups sugar
1 teaspoon light corn syrup
2 Tablespoons vanilla
8 teaspoons baking soda
2 cups butter (or 1 cup shortening and 1 cup butter)
3 cups peanut butter
18 cups oatmeal
4 cups chocolate chips
1 16-ounce package M&M candies

1. In very large bowl, mix ingredients.
2. Drop by Tablespoonfuls onto cookie sheet.
3. Bake at 350 degrees for 10-12 minutes.

Preparation Time:	**25 minutes**	**Yield:**	**200 cookies**
Baking Time:	**10-12 minutes**		**May do ahead and freeze**

Variation: *For larger cookies, use ⅓ cup cookie dough. Bake for 20-25 minutes.*

ORANGE BALLS

1 6-ounce can orange juice concentrate
1 7-ounce package crushed vanilla wafers
½ cup softened butter
2 cups powdered sugar
1 cup chopped nuts
1 cup shredded, unsweetened coconut

1. Mix all ingredients except coconut.
2. Form into balls and roll in coconut.

Preparation Time: **45 minutes**   **Yield:**   **60 balls**
Tip: *Best to let stand a few days before serving. Store in airtight container.*

PEANUT BUTTER COOKIES
"Kids love these"

1 cup margarine
1 cup peanut butter
1 cup white sugar
1 cup brown sugar
2 eggs
1 Tablespoon milk
2 cups flour
½ teaspoon salt
1 teaspoon soda

1. Mix first 6 ingredients thoroughly.
2. Sift together and stir in remainder of ingredients. Mix well.
3. Roll dough into walnut-size balls.
4. Place 3 inches apart on lightly greased baking sheet.
5. Flatten with fork dipped in flour. Criss-cross for design.
6. Bake at 350 degrees for 10-12 minutes.

Preparation Time: **20 minutes**   **Yield:**   **5 dozen cookies**
Cooking Time: **10-12 minutes**   **May freeze**
Variation: *For less rich cookies, add additional ½ cup flour and 2 teaspoons baking powder.*

PECAN TASSIES

Pastry

¼ **cup softened butter**
1 3-ounce package softened cream cheese
1½ cups flour

1. Cream butter and cream cheese. Add flour.
2. Roll out pastry on floured waxed paper. Cut out 3-inch circles with biscuit cutter and line mini-muffin tins.

Filling

½ **cup butter**
1 cup sugar
2 eggs
1 cup chopped nuts
1 cup raisins or chopped dates
Powdered sugar

1. Cream butter and sugar. Add eggs, 1 at a time.
2. Add nuts and fruits. Mix thoroughly.
3. Fill pastry-lined mini-muffin tins.
4. Bake at 350 degrees for 15-20 minutes.
5. Remove from pan while hot and sprinkle with powdered sugar.

Preparation Time:	**30 minutes**	**Yield:**	**30 Tassies**
Baking Time:	**15-20 minutes**		

BANANA-WALNUT ICE CREAM

"Mmm - Good!"

2 cups sour cream
2 14-ounce cans sweetened condensed milk
4 cups half and half (may use half milk)
3 mashed or chopped bananas
½ **cup chopped walnuts**

1. Mix all ingredients.
2. Process in ice cream freezer.

Preparation Time:	**10 minutes**	**Yield:**	**1 gallon**
Freezing Time:	**30 minutes**	**May do ahead**	

FROZEN STRAWBERRY DESSERT

Butter Crunch Crust

½ cup margarine
¼ cup brown sugar
1 cup flour
½ cup chopped nuts

1. Combine margarine, brown sugar and flour. Mix until crumbly. Add nuts. Press into 9 x 13-inch dish.
2. Bake at 400 degrees for 12 minutes.

Strawberry Filling

2 10-ounce packages frozen strawberries, partially thawed
1 Tablespoon lemon juice
2 egg whites
1 cup sugar
2 cups whipping cream
1 teaspoon vanilla

1. In large mixing bowl, beat strawberries, lemon juice, egg whites and sugar. Continue beating until peaks form.
2. In separate bowl, beat whipping cream and vanilla. Fold into strawberry Filling.
3. Pour mixture over cooled crust. Cover and freeze overnight.
4. To serve, cut into squares.

Preparation Time:	**30 minutes**	**Serves:**	**12-15**
Baking Time:	**12 minutes**	**Must do ahead**	
Freezing Time:	**6-8 hours**		

Serving Suggestion: *Garnish with whipped cream, strawberries and fresh mint.*

KIWI ICE
"Chinese gooseberry sherbet"

12 peeled, cubed kiwi
2 cups orange juice
1⅓ cups corn syrup

1. In food processor bowl with metal blade or blender, combine kiwi and orange juice. Process until smooth.
2. Pour mixture through cheesecloth into non-metal container to remove seeds.
3. Stir in corn syrup. Freeze 3-4 hours or until almost firm.
4. Place in food processor bowl with metal blade. Process until fluffy. Return to freezer. Freeze until firm.
5. To serve, let stand at room temperature about 30 minutes. Spoon into serving dishes. Garnish with sliced kiwi or orange curls.

Preparation Time:	**15 minutes**	**Serves:**	**8-10**
Variation:	*May use any fruit.*	**Must do ahead**	

ICE CREAM ROLL

4 separated eggs
1 Tablespoon oil
½ cup cake flour
½ teaspoon baking powder
2 Tablespoons cocoa powder
¼ teaspoon salt
¾ cup sugar
Powdered sugar
½ gallon ice cream

1. Line jellyroll pan with greased waxed paper.
2. Beat egg whites until stiff.
3. In separate bowl, mix oil and egg yolks.
4. Sift dry ingredients together and mix with egg yolk mixture. This should be very stiff.
5. Mix small amount of egg whites into flour mixture. Fold into remaining egg whites.
6. Spread evenly in jellyroll pan, filling corners.
7. Bake at 400 degrees for 10-12 minutes.
8. Dust tea towel with powdered sugar.
9. When cake is done, immediately loosen edges with small spatula. Invert onto towel. Gently peel off waxed paper. Roll up cake and towel. Cool.
10. Unroll and fill with softened ice cream about ½ inch thick.
11. Reroll and wrap in towel. Freeze.
12. To serve, slice into 12 slices.

Preparation Time:	**45 minutes**	**Serves:**	**12 slices**
Baking Time:	**10-12 minutes**	**May do ahead**	
Freezing Time:	**4 hours**		

Serving Suggestion: *Place slice on dessert plate spread with 2 Tablespoons Raspberry Sauce.*

TROPICAL ICE CREAM

4 lemons
4 oranges
4 overripe bananas
3½-4 cups sugar
4 cups milk
4 cups cream

1. Juice lemons and oranges.
2. Mash bananas.
3. Mix all ingredients until well-blended.
4. Process in ice cream maker.

Preparation Time:	**20 minutes**	**Serves:**	**12-15**
Freezing Time:	**30 minutes**		

MEXICAN FRIED ICE CREAM
"Wow"

1 pint vanilla ice cream
½ cup crushed cornflakes or cookie crumbs
1 teaspoon cinnamon
2 teaspoons sugar
1 egg
Oil for deep frying
Topping, your favorite
Whipped cream

1. Scoop out 5 balls of ice cream. Return balls to freezer.
2. Mix cornflake crumbs, cinnamon and sugar.
3. Roll frozen ice cream balls in half of crumb mixture and freeze again.
4. Beat egg. Dip coated ice cream balls in egg. Roll again in remaining crumbs. Freeze until ready to use.
5. Heat oil to 350 degrees.
6. Place 1 frozen ice cream ball in fryer basket or perforated spoon. Deep fry for 1 minute.
7. Serve immediately with favorite topping and dollop of whipped cream.

Preparation Time:	**30 minutes**	**Yield:**	**5 ice cream balls**
Cooking Time:	**5 minutes**		

Tip: *For thicker coating, repeat dipping in egg and rolling in crumbs. Balls will be crunchy on the outside and just beginning to melt on the inside.*

VANILLA ICE CREAM
"Again, everyone's favorite"

8 cups half-and-half
6 egg yolks
½ teaspoon salt
2 cups sugar
3 Tablespoons vanilla

1. Heat half-and-half.
2. Whisk in remaining ingredients. Cook 7 minutes. Cool.
3. Process in ice cream maker.

Preparation Time:	**10 minutes**	**Serves:**	**12**
Cooking Time:	**5-10 minutes**		
Freezing Time:	**30 minutes**		

AMERICAN TOFFEE ICE CREAM PIE

". . . melts in your mouth!"

Pie

½ **gallon vanilla ice cream**
1 **prepared graham cracker crust**
½ **cup crushed toffee bars**

1. Place half of ice cream in graham cracker crust.
2. Sprinkle toffee bar pieces on ice cream.
3. Add remaining half of ice cream. Wrap securely.
4. Store in freezer until ready to serve.
5. To serve, pour cool Sauce over individual pie slices.

Sauce

1½ **cups sugar**
1 **cup evaporated milk**
¼ **cup butter**
¼ **cup light corn syrup**
½ **cup crushed toffee bars**

1. Mix all ingredients except crushed toffee bars.
2. Bring to boil over medium-low heat. Boil 1 minute.
3. Add toffee bar pieces. Cool.

Preparation Time:	**30 minutes**	**Serves:**	**6**
Cooking Time:	**5-8 minutes**	**May do ahead**	

CRANAPPLE COBBLER

"It evaporates"

4 **cups sliced Granny Smith apples**
1 **package fresh whole cranberries (do not chop)**
¾ **cup light corn syrup**
1½ **cups flour**
1 **cup sugar**
¾ **teaspoon cinnamon**
¾ **cup mayonnaise**
1 **cup coarsely chopped nuts**

1. Toss sliced apples and cranberries gently with corn syrup. Place in greased 9 x 13-inch pan.
2. In separate bowl, mix flour, sugar and cinnamon. Blend mayonnaise into flour mixture, ending with coarse crumbs.
3. Stir in nuts. Sprinkle flour mixture over fruit.
4. Bake at 400 degrees for 35 minutes.

Preparation Time:	**30 minutes**	**Serve:**	**15-20**
Baking Time:	**35 minutes**	**May do ahead**	

Serving Suggestion: *Serve warm with half-and-half, whipped cream or ice cream.*
Tip: *Reheat to serve.*

APPLE-PECAN COBBLER
"Scrumptious and easy"

Cobbler

2 Tablespoons butter
6 Granny Smith apples (2 pounds), cored and cut into ½-inch lengthwise slices
4 Tablespoons sugar
2 Tablespoons flour
½ teaspoon cinnamon
Dash of nutmeg
Dash of mace
½ cup golden raisins
1 Tablespoon lemon juice

1. Melt butter. Add apple slices. Sprinkle with sugar. Stir and sauté several minutes. Remove from heat.
2. Combine remaining ingredients. Mix gently with apples.
3. Place mixture in 8 x 8-inch baking dish.

Topping

4 ounces melted butter
½ cup half-and-half
1 large egg
1 cup flour
½ cup sugar
2 teaspoons baking powder
Dash of salt
½ cup chopped pecans

1. With electric mixer, beat all ingredients except pecans. Mix until smooth.
2. Pour evenly over apple mixture. Sprinkle with pecans.
3. Bake at 375 degrees for 45 minutes.
4. Cool at least 30 minutes before serving with Sauce.

Sauce

2½ Tablespoons cream
1 teaspoon light corn syrup
⅓ cup brown sugar
2½ Tablespoons butter
½ teaspoon vanilla

1. Combine all ingredients except vanilla. Bring to boil over moderately high heat and cook 5 minutes, whisking frequently.
2. Remove from heat and stir in vanilla.
3. Serve over Apple-Pecan Cobbler.

Preparation Time: **45 minutes**   **Serves:**   **6**
Baking Time: **45 minutes**
Serving Suggestion: *Serve with vanilla ice cream drizzled with sauce.*

CHOCOLATE ORANGE PIE
"Tantalizing"

Crust

36 chocolate cookie wafers
¼ cup butter

1. In food processor, crumb chocolate wafers.
2. Combine with softened butter.
3. Press crumb mixture into 2 8-inch pie plates, bottoms and sides.
4. Bake at 300 degrees for 3 minutes.

Filling

2 8-ounce packages softened cream cheese
1 14-ounce can sweetened condensed milk
1 cup frozen orange juice concentrate
2 Tablespoons grated orange peel
1¼ cups sugar
1 pint whipping cream
Chocolate decors

1. Combine cream cheese, sweetened condensed milk, orange juice concentrate, orange peel and 1 cup sugar. Mix until fluffy.
2. Combine ¼ cup sugar and whipping cream. Whip until stiff.
3. Fold into cream cheese mixture.
4. Divide filling equally into 2 pie crusts.
5. Top with chocolate decors.
6. Freeze overnight.
7. Let stand at room temperature for 20 minutes before cutting and serving.

Preparation Time:	**25 minutes**	**Yield:**	**2 8-inch pies**
Freezing Time:	**6-8 hours**	**Must do ahead**	
Standing Time:	**20 minutes**		

CHOCOLATE PIE

"Only for true chocolate lovers"

2 cups sugar
4 Tablespoons cocoa powder
4 rounded Tablespoons flour
4 beaten egg yolks
1½ cups milk
¼ teaspoon salt
1 teaspoon vanilla
1 baked 9-inch pie crust

1. In saucepan, mix together sugar, cocoa powder and flour.
2. Blend in egg yolks, milk and salt.
3. Cook over low heat, stirring continuously until thickened.
4. Stir in vanilla.
5. Pour into pie crust and cool completely.

Preparation Time:	**45 minutes**	**Serves:**	**16**
Cooling Time:	**3-4 hours**		

FRESH COCONUT CREAM PIE

"Mexican vanilla adds marvelous flavor"

MICROWAVE RECIPE

1 cup sugar (¾ cup if using packaged coconut)
⅓ cup cornstarch
¼ teaspoon salt
3 cups hot milk (4 minutes on high)
3 beaten egg yolks
1 teaspoon vanilla
½ teaspoon almond extract
2 cups grated, fresh coconut
9-inch baked pie crust
1 cup whipping cream, whipped

1. Combine sugar, cornstarch and salt.
2. Stir in hot milk. Microwave on high for 5 minutes, stirring every 1½ minutes. Mixture will be quite thick.
3. Slowly combine egg yolks. Mix thoroughly. Microwave on high for 2 minutes.
4. Add vanilla, almond extract and 1 cup coconut.
5. Refrigerate overnight.
6. Beat mixture and pour into baked pie crust. Refrigerate 3 hours.
7. Spread whipped cream over pie. Top with remaining 1 cup coconut.

Preparation Time:	**15 minutes**	**Serves:**	**6-8**
Cooking Time:	**15 minutes**	**Must do ahead**	
Chilling Time:	**9-11 hours**		

Variation: *Packaged coconut may be used.*

LEMON FROST PIE

"Lemon lover's delight"

1 cup sifted flour
½ cup butter
⅔ cup plus 2 Tablespoons sugar
¼ teaspoon salt
2 egg whites
2 teaspoons grated lemon peel
¼ cup lemon juice
5 drops yellow food coloring
1 cup whipping cream

1. Mix flour, butter, 2 Tablespoons sugar and salt until crumbly.
2. Place ⅓ crumb mixture in baking dish. Press remaining ⅔ crumb mixture into greased and floured 9-inch pie plate.
3. Bake both crumb mixtures at 350 degrees for 12-15 minutes.
4. Combine egg whites, ⅔ cup sugar, lemon peel, lemon juice and food coloring. Beat until stiff peaks form.
5. Whip cream. Fold into lemon mixture.
6. Turn filling into cooled pie crust. Top with remaining toasted crumbs.
7. Chill or freeze.

Preparation Time:	**30 minutes**	**Serves:**	**6-8**
Baking Time:	**12-15 minutes**	**May do ahead**	
Chilling Time:	**4-6 hours**		

Serving Suggestion: *Serve with Raspberry Sauce.*

SOUR CREAM-LEMON PIE

"This is too good"

1¼ cups sugar
6 Tablespoons cornstarch
½ teaspoon salt
3 slightly beaten egg yolks
2 Tablespoons grated lemon peel
⅓ cup lemon juice
2 cups hot water
1 Tablespoon butter
1 cup sour cream
1 baked 9-inch pie shell
1 cup whipping cream

1. Combine sugar, cornstarch, salt, egg yolks, lemon peel, juice, water and butter in saucepan.
2. Cook over medium heat, stirring constantly until thick and clear, about 10-12 minutes.
3. Cool thoroughly. Add sour cream and beat until smooth.
4. Turn into pastry shell.
5. Whip cream until stiff and sweeten, if desired.
6. Spread over pie filling. Chill until set.

Preparation Time:	**25 minutes**	**Serves:**	**6-8**
Cooking Time:	**2-3 minutes**		
Cooling Time:	**1-2 hours**		
Chilling Time:	**3 hours**		

PUMPKIN CHIFFON-PRALINE PIE
"Husbands love this"

Crust

2 unbaked, 9-inch pie crusts
⅔ cup butter
⅔ cup brown sugar
⅔ cup chopped nuts

1. Bake pie crusts 10 minutes at 350 degrees.
2. Cream butter, brown sugar and nuts.
3. Spread ½ sugar-nut mixture over bottom of each pie crust.
4. Bake 5 minutes longer.

Filling

¾ cup sugar
1 envelope unflavored gelatin
1½ teaspoons cinnamon
½ teaspoon salt
4 beaten egg yolks
¾ cup half-and-half
1 29-ounce can pumpkin
4 egg whites
¼ cup sugar
2 cups whipping cream, whipped

1. Combine sugar, gelatin, cinnamon and salt in top of double boiler.
2. Stir in egg yolks, half-and-half and pumpkin. Cook about 15 minutes. Cool.
3. Beat egg whites until foamy.
4. Add ¼ cup sugar to egg whites. Beat until stiff.
5. Beat cooled pumpkin mixture until fluffy.
6. Fold pumpkin mixture into egg whites.
7. Spoon pumpkin mixture into baked pie crusts.
8. Top with whipped cream.

Preparation Time:	**1 hour**	**Yield:**	**2 9-inch pies**
Baking Time:	**15 minutes**		
Cooking Time:	**15 minutes**		

CREAM PUFF PASTRY
"Easy"

1 cup water
½ teaspoon salt
½ cup butter
1 cup sifted flour
4 eggs

1. Bring water to boil with salt and butter.
2. As soon as butter melts and full boil begins, add flour all at once and stir rapidly. Remove from heat as soon as mixture holds together and looks like cornmeal mush.
3. Add eggs, 1 at a time, beating well after each addition.
4. Drop by tablespoon of mixture onto cookie sheet, allowing for expansion space.
5. Bake at 425 degrees for 20 minutes or until golden and crisp. Remove from oven.
6. Cut tops off. Cool on racks and fill.
7. Replace tops. Dust with powdered sugar to give finished look.

Preparation Time:	**20 minutes**	**Yield:**	**12 regular puffs or**
Baking Time:	**20 minutes**		**3 dozen bite-size puffs**

Variation: *For bite-size puffs, use 1 teaspoon dough.*
Tip: *To store, cool completely and place in airtight container. Fill as desired just before serving.*
Filling Suggestions: *Fill puffs with any flavor ice cream and top with fudge sauce and nuts. Use instant pudding or pie filling - flavors such as banana, coconut or chocolate. Vanilla filling may be made by using 3¾ ounces vanilla pudding mix, 1 cup sour cream and ¾ cup half-and-half. Chill until firm.*

CHERRY TARTS
"George Washington would approve"

2 8-ounce packages cream cheese
¾ cup sugar
2 eggs
1 Tablespoon fresh lemon juice
24 vanilla wafers
1 21-ounce can cherry pie filling
20-24 foil cupcake liners

1. In food processor or electric mixer, combine cream cheese, sugar, eggs and lemon juice. Process until smooth.
2. Place 1 vanilla wafer in each foil cupcake liner.
3. Fill about ¾ full with cheese mixture.
4. Bake at 350 degrees for 15-20 minutes.
5. After cooling, place spoonful of cherry pie filling on top of each tart.

Preparation Time:	**15 minutes**	**Yield:**	**20-24 tarts**
Baking Time:	**15-20 minutes**		

ELEGANT NUT TART

Crust

⅓ cup butter
¼ cup sugar
1 egg yolk
1 cup flour

1. In food processor, combine butter with sugar. Add egg yolk. Process only to combine.
2. Add flour. Mixture will be crumbly.
3. In 9-inch fluted tart pan, press dough evenly in bottom and up sides.
4. Bake at 375 degrees for 12 minutes or until light brown.
5. Cool on rack.

Filling

2 cups coarsely chopped nuts
⅔ cup light brown sugar
¼ cup butter
¼ cup dark corn syrup
2 Tablespoons whipping cream

1. Lightly toast nuts at 375 degrees for 5 minutes. Cool.
2. Sprinkle nuts over baked tart Crust.
3. In heavy 2-quart saucepan, combine sugar, butter, corn syrup and whipping cream.
   Boil 1 minute. Pour over nuts.
4. Bake at 375 degrees for 10 minutes or until bubbly.
5. Cool.

Topping

4 Tablespoons chocolate chips, melted
Whipped cream, optional for garnish

Drizzle melted chocolate chips over Filling.

Preparation Time:	**20 minutes**	**Serves:**	**12**
Baking Time:	**27 minutes**		
Cooking Time:	**3-5 minutes**		

Variation: *Use coarsely chopped walnuts, sliced almonds, whole filberts and pecan halves or a combination of any or all of these nuts.*

CHOCOLATE MACADAMIA TART

Tart Shell

1 cup flour
½ teaspoon salt
⅓ cup butter
1-3 Tablespoons ice water

1. Place flour, salt and butter in food processor. Process until crumbly.
2. Add enough ice water through tube for dough to form ball.
3. Press pastry into greased 9-inch tart pan with floured fingers. Chill.

Filling

3 eggs
¾ cup brown sugar
¾ cup light corn syrup
¼ cup melted butter
½ teaspoon vanilla
1 cup coarsely chopped macadamia nuts
3 Tablespoons chocolate chips

1. Place eggs in food processor bowl. Add sugar and syrup. Process.
2. Add melted butter through feeding tube.
3. Add vanilla and nuts. Pulse.
4. Pour Filling into chilled Tart Shell.
5. Bake at 375 degrees for 35-40 minutes, until tests done. Place in low position to insure brown bottom crust.
6. Melt chocolate chips. Drizzle over cooled tart.
7. Refrigerate up to 24 hours. Serve at room temperature.

Preparation Time:	25 minutes	**Serves:**	**8-10**
Baking Time:	35-40 minutes	**Must do ahead**	
Chilling Time:	1 hour		

APPLE DUMPLINGS

Pastry

2 cups flour
1 teaspoon salt
⅔ cup and 2 Tablespoons shortening
¼ cup water
6 medium Granny Smith apples
½ cup brown sugar
1½ teaspoons cinnamon
2 Tablespoons butter

Syrup

1 cup brown sugar
2 cups water
3 Tablespoons butter or margarine
¼ teaspoon cinnamon

1. Measure flour in mixing bowl. Blend in salt.
2. With pastry blender, cut in shortening until mixture is crumbly.
3. Sprinkle with water, 2 Tablespoons at a time, mixing lightly with fork until all flour is moistened.
4. Form dough into ball.
5. Keep dough wrapped in waxed paper in refrigerator until ready to use.
6. Pare and core apples.
7. Roll out Pastry a little less than ⅛-inch thick. Cut into 6 7-inch squares.
8. Combine brown sugar and cinnamon.
9. Place apple on each square of Pastry. Fill cavities of apples with mixture of brown sugar and cinnamon. Dot with butter.
10. Bring opposite points of Pastry up over apple. Overlap, moistening if necessary, and seal.
11. Lift each apple carefully and place a distance apart in 9 x 13-inch baking dish.
12. Pour Syrup around dumplings.
13. Bake immediately at 425 degrees for 40-45 minutes or until crust is browned and apples are cooked through.

Preparation Time: **1 hour**   **Yield:**   **6 dumplings**
Baking Time: **40-45 minutes**   **May do 1-2 days ahead**
Serving Suggestion: *Serve warm with syrup, whipped cream or ice cream.*
Variation: *Bake dumplings without syrup on cookie sheet. Serve with ice cream drizzled with warm Nutmeg Sauce.*

BAKLAVA

Syrup

2 cups sugar
1 cup water
1 Tablespoon fresh lemon juice
¼ cup honey, optional

1. Combine sugar and water. Cook over medium heat until mixture starts to boil.
2. Add lemon juice. Cook over low heat for 10-15 minutes. Stir in honey. Set aside to cool.

Filling

1 pound toasted, chopped walnuts
½ pound chopped almonds
½ cup sugar
1 teaspoon cinnamon
Cloves to taste
Freshly ground nutmeg to taste

In bowl, combine nuts, sugar and spices.

Assembly

1 pound phyllo pastry
1-1½ pounds sweet butter, melted at low temperature

1. Place thawed phyllo on work surface.
2. Brush bottom of 11 x 14-inch pan with melted butter.
3. Lay 1 sheet of phyllo in pan. Butter lightly. Continue layering until half the sheets have been used.
4. Spread Filling evenly over phyllo layers.
5. Place remaining sheets of phyllo as before, buttering lightly between each one. Brush last layer.
6. Use sharp knife and gently score, cutting through all layers, into square or diamond shapes.
7. Bake at 350 degrees for 30 minutes.
8. Lower oven temperature to 300 degrees and bake 30 minutes longer or until golden brown.
9. Remove from oven and pour cooled Syrup over hot baklava.
10. Let sit loosely covered until next day to allow flavors to blend.
11. Serve at room temperature.

Preparation Time:	1 hour	**Yield:**	**5 dozen**
Baking Time:	1 hour		**May do several weeks ahead**

Tip: *To store, place in airtight container in cool area. Syrup may be prepared day before assembly.*

ENGLISH TRIFLE
"Don't let licky-loos near the kitchen"

MICROWAVE RECIPE

Custard

½ cup cornstarch
1½ cups sugar
½ teaspoon salt
4 cups milk
4 Tablespoons melted butter or margarine
4 slightly beaten egg yolks
2 teaspoons vanilla

1. Mix cornstarch, sugar and salt in bowl.
2. Gradually add milk and butter.
3. On high power heat to boiling, or until mixture is thickened, approximately 9 minutes, stirring every 3 minutes.
4. To avoid curdling, add a little hot mixture to egg yolks. Stir in egg yolks and cook 2 minutes longer.
5. Add vanilla and stir. Cool thoroughly.
6. Before assembling trifle, beat custard until smooth.

Trifle

2 layers of sliced sponge cake, pound cake, jellyroll or lady fingers
Raspberry preserves
Sliced almonds
Custard
2 10-ounce packages frozen raspberries, thawed and drained
Whipped cream

1. Trim and slice sponge cake into ¼-inch widths.
2. Spread each slice with 2 Tablespoons raspberry preserves and sprinkle with 2 Tablespoons of sliced almonds.
3. In deep serving dish, place 1 layer of garnished cake slices.
4. Spread generously with Custard, approximately 1 cup.
5. Layer with raspberries.
6. Repeat to make 3 layers.
7. Top with whipped cream. Chill.

Preparation Time:	**15-20 minutes**	**Serves:**	**15**
Cooking Time:	**30 minutes**	**Must do ahead**	
Chilling Time:	**2-3 hours**		

Variations: *Custard may be used as a base for any cream dessert, such as banana cream pie, coconut pie or pudding.*

GALATOBOUREKO

2 quarts milk
12 lightly beaten eggs
1 cup regular farina
1 cup sugar
4 Tablespoons butter
1 teaspoon vanilla
1 pound phyllo dough
1 pound melted sweet butter

1. In saucepan, combine milk, eggs, farina, sugar and butter. Cook over low heat, stirring constantly, until mixture is very hot and thickened. Remove from heat. Stir in vanilla.
2. Place 10 sheets of phyllo in high-sided jellyroll pan, buttering each sheet evenly after placing it in pan.
3. Pour filling into pan and cover with 10 more sheets of phyllo, again brushing each sheet generously with butter.
4. With sharp knife, cut top pastry into diamond-shaped pieces.
5. Bake at 400 degrees for 50-60 minutes or until golden brown.
6. Remove from oven. Cover with cooled Syrup.
7. Cool in pan, letting Syrup absorb.

Syrup

3 cups sugar
2 cups water
1 slice lemon

In saucepan, combine sugar, water and lemon. Bring to boil for 5 minutes. Cool.

Preparation Time:	30 minutes	**Serves:**	36-48
Baking Time:	50-60 minutes		

LEMON ANGEL TORTE

Meringue Crust

3 egg whites at room temperature
¾ cup sugar (superfine sugar works well)
2 teaspoons lemon juice

1. Beat egg whites until soft peaks form. Gradually add sugar, beating until stiff but not dry. Blend in juice.
2. Line cookie sheet with parchment paper. Draw 10-inch circle and spread meringue evenly over pattern.
3. Bake at 275 degrees for 1 hour or until meringue is firm.
4. Turn off heat and let meringue dry in oven with door closed for at least 2 hours. Meringue may be kept at room temperature, uncovered overnight, if desired.
5. When ready to use, place meringue crust in 9-inch springform pan. Cut crust to fit.

Filling

4 egg yolks
½ cup sugar
¼ cup fresh lemon juice
Grated peel of 1 large lemon
1 cup whipping cream, whipped

1. Beat egg yolks with sugar and lemon juice until light. Cook in top of double boiler over boiling water, stirring until thickened.
2. Remove from heat. Add lemon peel. Cool thoroughly.
3. Fold in half of whipped cream. Spread over Meringue Crust and refrigerate at least 2 hours to set.

Glaze

½ cup sugar
½ cup water
1½ Tablespoons lemon jello
1½ Tablespoons cornstarch

1. Combine sugar, water and jello in small saucepan.
2. Mix cornstarch in small amount of water. When dissolved, add to sugar-water mixture. Cook over medium heat, stirring constantly until clear and slightly thickened. Cool.
3. Pour Glaze over Filling, gently turning to cover torte top. Refrigerate.

Preparation Time:	**1 hour**	**Serves:**	**8-10**
Baking Time:	**1 hour**		
Cooking Time:	**30 minutes**		
Standing Time:	**2 hours**		

Serving Suggestion: *To serve, remove side of springform pan and garnish with whipped cream and lemon slices.*

MERINGUE CHOCOLATE-LAYERED HEARTS
"This is so romantic"

Meringue Hearts

6 egg whites at room temperature
¼ teaspoon cream of tartar
1½ cups sugar
¼ teaspoon raspberry flavoring (available at specialty food store)

1. Draw 16 3-inch heart shapes on sheets of parchment, spacing 1½ inches apart. Invert onto baking sheets.
2. Beat egg whites with cream of tartar until soft peaks form.
3. Gradually add sugar and beat until stiff and shiny.
4. Mix in raspberry flavoring.
5. Transfer mixture to pastry bag fitted with large star tip. Pipe meringue in ½-inch layer over hearts, covering completely.
6. Bake at 200 degrees for 1 hour.
7. Increase temperature to 250 degrees and bake 10 minutes longer.
8. Turn off oven and let meringues stand in oven until crisp and dry, about 3 hours.

Chocolate

3 ounces chopped semisweet chocolate
3 ounces chopped unsweetened chocolate

1. Melt both chocolates in top of double boiler over simmering water. Stir until smooth. Remove from heat.
2. Dip top of 8 Meringue Hearts in chocolate. Transfer to baking sheet.
3. Refrigerate until chocolate is firm.

Tip: *These may be prepared 1 day ahead. Store in covered container at room temperature.*

Cream

3 cups well-chilled whipping cream
6 Tablespoons sugar
½ teaspoon raspberry flavoring or vanilla

1. Whip cream with sugar and raspberry flavoring until firm peaks form.
2. Transfer Cream to pastry bag fitted with medium star tip. Pipe Cream in ½-inch layer over top of chocolate-covered hearts.
3. Top with plain hearts. Pipe Cream over tops.

Raspberry Sauce

4 10-ounce packages frozen raspberries, thawed and drained

Purée raspberries in blender until smooth. Strain through fine sieve, pressing to extract as much pulp as possible.

Continued

MERINGUE CHOCOLATE-LAYERED HEARTS — Continued

To Serve

Seedless red raspberry jam

1. Just before serving, film plates with raspberry sauce. Set heart in center of each.
2. Spoon jam into pastry bag fitted with small plain tip. Pipe jam in diagonal line across each heart to resemble an arrow. Pipe cream on plate to form point and quills of arrow.

Preparation Time:	**2 hours**	**Serves:** **8**
Baking Time:	**1 hour, 10 minutes**	
Standing Time:	**3 hours**	

PERSIMMON PUDDING

1 cup sugar
1 cup flour
¼ teaspoon salt
1 Tablespoon soda
½ teaspoon cinnamon
½ teaspoon nutmeg
½ teaspoon ginger
½ cup milk
½ cup chopped nuts
½ cup raisins
1 cup persimmon pulp
1 teaspoon vanilla
1 Tablespoon melted butter

1. Mix dry ingredients. Add milk and mix well.
2. Add nuts and raisins.
3. Add persimmon pulp and mix thoroughly.
4. Stir in vanilla and butter.
5. Pour into greased 9 x 5-inch loaf pan.
6. Cover with foil and set in pan of water.
7. Bake at 375 degrees for 1 hour, 10 minutes.

Preparation Time:	**20 minutes**	**Serves:** **8-10**
Cooking Time:	**1 hour, 10 minutes**	
Serving Suggestion:	*Serve with hot or cold Lemon Sauce.*	

LEMON CARAMEL FLAN
"Caramel custard"

1¼ cups sugar
6 eggs
2½ cups milk or half-and-half
2 teaspoons vanilla
¼ teaspoon salt
½ teaspoon grated lemon peel
Whipped cream, optional

1. Melt ¾ cup sugar in small, heavy skillet over low heat. Do not stir before sugar is completely dissolved. When completely melted, increase heat and stir constantly to achieve even caramel color, approximately 10 minutes or more. Do not let caramel boil.
2. Pour approximately ¼ caramel sauce into buttered, warm 2-quart casserole dish. Tip and swirl dish until bottom and sides are evenly coated.
3. Add small amount of hot water to remaining caramel sauce and place in small pitcher.
4. In large bowl, beat remaining ingredients until well-blended.
5. Pour into prepared dish and set in pan of hot water. Water should come up halfway on dish.
6. Bake at 350 degrees for 1 hour or until knife comes out clean. Refrigerate.
7. To serve, invert on platter. Decorate with whipped cream and remaining caramel sauce.

Preparation Time:	**30 minutes**	**Serves:**	**6-8**
Baking Time:	**1 hour**	**May do ahead**	

ORIENTAL ORANGES

6 large navel oranges

Syrup

1 cup sugar
⅓ cup water
2 teaspoons grenadine syrup, optional

1. With citrus zester, carefully remove peel from oranges, being careful not to include any white pith.
2. Cut away pith from oranges with sharp knife.
3. Chill oranges until serving time.
4. Blanch peel in boiling water for 1-2 minutes. Repeat 3 times, using fresh water each time to remove bitterness. Set aside.
5. In saucepan, bring sugar, water and grenadine syrup slowly to boil. Stir until sugar is dissolved.
6. Add orange peel. Return to boil. Cook over low heat 5 minutes without stirring.
7. With slotted spoonn, transfer peel to plate covered with waxed paper. Cover and set aside until serving time. Reserve Syrup.
8. To serve, slice oranges, overlapping slices on individual plates and spoon Syrup over them. Arrange candied peel on top.

Preparation Time:	**30 minutes**	**Serves:**	**6**
Cooking Time:	**10 minutes**	**May do ahead**	

Tips: *If done ahead, do not assemble until just before serving. Peel may also be removed with knife and cut into thin julienne strips.*

APRICOT SAUCE

"Great - even on toast"

1¼ cups dried apricots
1 cup boiling water plus ½ cup water
1 Tablespoon lemon juice
2 teaspoons cornstarch
½ cup sugar

1. Place apricots in medium-size bowl. Pour 1 cup boiling water over apricots and set aside to soften overnight.
2. Transfer mixture to food processor fitted with metal blade. Process until puréed.
3. Pour mixture into medium-size saucepan and add lemon juice, ½ cup water, cornstarch and sugar.
4. Cook over moderate heat, stirring constantly, until mixture comes to boil and thickens, about 10 minutes.
5. Cool to room temperature.

Preparation Time: **10 minutes**   **Yield:** **2½ cups**
Setting Time: **Overnight**
Cooking Time: **10-15 minutes**
Serving Suggestion: *Spread over top of cheesecake or ice cream.*

HOT, QUICK CHOCOLATE SAUCE

"Good and chocolatey"

MICROWAVE RECIPE

1 14-ounce can sweetened condensed milk
½ cup semisweet chocolate chips
½ ounce unsweetened chocolate

1. Melt all ingredients in microwave for 2 minutes.
2. Stir until chocolate is melted.

Preparation Time: **5 minutes**   **Yield:** **2 cups**
Cooking Time: **2 minutes**   **May do ahead**
Serving Suggestion: *Serve over brownies or ice cream.*
Variation: *Add 1 large Tablespoon chunky peanut butter.*

LEMON SAUCE
"Great with Persimmon Pudding or Gingerbread"

½ **cup sugar**
1 heaping Tablespoon cornstarch
¼ **teaspoon nutmeg**
1 cup boiling water
2 Tablespoons butter
2-4 Tablespoons lemon juice or to taste
1 teaspoon grated lemon peel

1. Combine sugar, cornstarch and nutmeg.
2. Add boiling water, butter and lemon juice. Boil until thickened.
3. Add grated lemon peel.

Preparation Time: **5 minutes**   **Yield:**   **1½ cups**
Cooking Time: **5 minutes**

NUTMEG SAUCE

⅔ **cup sugar**
1¼ Tablespoons flour
¼ **teaspoon nutmeg**
⅛ **teaspoon salt**
1¼ cups boiling water
1 Tablespoon butter

1. Combine dry ingredients and mix well.
2. Add boiling water. Mix and bring to boil.
3. Add butter. Stir.

Preparation Time: **10 minutes**   **Yield:**   **2 cups**
Serving Suggestion: *Serve warm over apple dumplings or warm apple pie slices.*

RASPBERRY SAUCE
"A colorful addition"

2 10-ounce packages frozen raspberries in syrup, thawed
¼ cup seedless raspberry jam
1 Tablespoon cornstarch
1 Tablespoon Squirt soda pop

1. Place strainer over small saucepan. (Do not use fine strainer). Push raspberries through strainer with wooden spoon to extract as much juice as possible. Discard seeds.
2. Add jam to juice in saucepan and bring to boil. Remove from heat.
3. Dissolve cornstarch in soda pop. Whisk into sauce.
4. Cook over moderate heat, whisking or stirring constantly, until sauce comes to boil and thickens.
5. Refrigerate until ready to use. Serve chilled.

Preparation Time: **20 minutes**   **Yield:**   **3 cups**
Serving Suggestion: *Delicious over cheesecake.*
Tip: *Sauce may be refrigerated, covered, up to 1 week.*

STRAWBERRY SAUCE
"Just right for cheesecake"

1 cup fresh strawberries
1 cup water
½ cup sugar
1½ Tablespoons cornstarch
3 drops red food coloring, optional

1. Slice berries and place in medium-size saucepan with water. Bring to boil over moderate heat and cook 2 minutes.
2. Push berries with spoon through strainer to remove all pulp.
3. Return berries to saucepan and stir in sugar and cornstarch. Bring to boil over moderate heat, stirring constantly, until mixture thickens. Stir in food coloring, if desired.
4. Cool to lukewarm.
5. Refrigerate until set, about 1 hour, not more than 4.

Preparation Time: **20 minutes**   **Yield:**   **Topping for 1 cheesecake**
Cooking Time: **10 minutes**
Chilling Time: **1 hour**
Serving Suggestion: *Serve over cheesecake. Slice 3 cups fresh strawberries in half and arrange in concentric circles over top of cheesecake. Spoon warm sauce over berries.*

TOFFEE BAR SAUCE

"You'll find a reason to make this"

¾ **cup sugar**
½ **cup whipping cream**
¼ **cup light corn syrup**
2 **Tablespoons butter**
5 **large frozen, crushed toffee bars**

1. Combine first 4 ingredients. Boil 2 minutes.
2. Add toffee bar pieces. Stir.

Preparation Time: **10 minutes**   **Yield:**   **2 cups**
Cooking Time: **2 minutes**
Serving Suggestion: *Serve warm over fresh fruit and add dollop of sour cream.*

PEPPERMINT FROSTING

3 **cups powdered sugar**
½ **cup crushed peppermint candy**
¼ **cup softened butter**
1 **3-ounce package softened cream cheese**
6-8 **teaspoons milk**

In large bowl, combine all ingredients. Beat until light and fluffy.

Preparation Time: **10 minutes**   **Yield:**   **4 cups frosting**
Serving Suggestion: *Frost Buttermilk Brownies.*

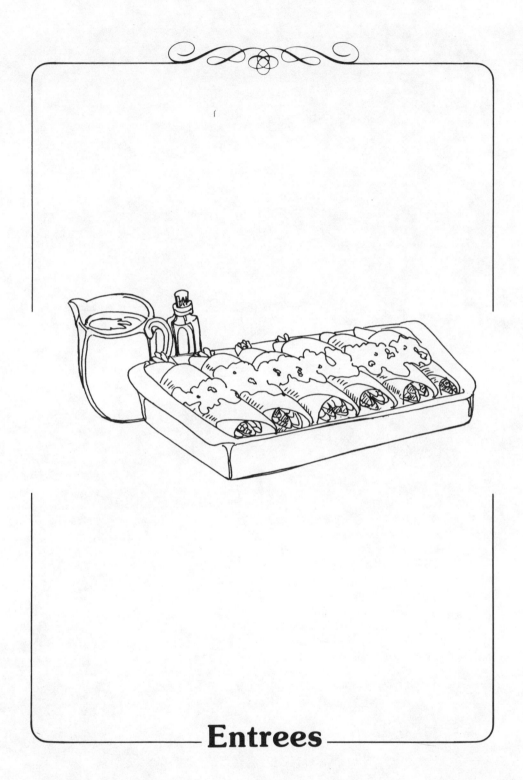

Entrees

Meat substitutes are commercially prepared vegetable protein products that simulate the texture and flavor of various kinds of meat. These products are available in an increasing number of markets and health food stores.

Two companies producing the largest volume of meat substitutes are: Worthington Foods, Worthington, Ohio 43085 and Loma Linda Foods, 11503 Pierce Street, Riverside, California 92502.

CHICKEN WELLINGTON

1 cup sliced carrots
2 sliced stalks broccoli
¼ cup butter
2 12½-ounce cans Worthington Fri-Chik, sliced
1 chopped onion
1 cup chopped, fresh mushrooms
2 packages G. Washington's Golden Seasoning and Broth
2 teaspoons garlic powder
1 teaspoon cumin seed
1 teaspoon caraway seeds
1 pound cream cheese at room temperature
2 eggs
¾ cup cracker crumbs
3 cups pie crust dough (your favorite)

1. Steam carrots and broccoli until crisp-tender. Sauté in butter with Fri-Chik, onion and mushrooms until tender.
2. Stir in seasonings, cream cheese, eggs and cracker crumbs. Mix well.
3. Pour filling into pie crust-lined 10-inch springform pan.
4. Cover with top crust. Decorate top with flowers or other decorations made from pie crust dough, if desired.
5. Bake at 350 degrees for 1-1¼ hours, covering crust with foil to prevent browning too rapidly.
6. After removing from oven, let stand for 20 minutes before removing from pan and serving.

Preparation Time:	40 minutes	Serves:	10
Baking Time:	1-1¼ hours		
Standing Time:	20 minutes		

CREAMED CHICKEN WITH PEAS IN PATTY SHELLS
"This will prove you're a great cook"

1 cup diced celery
1 finely chopped onion
¼ cup diced green pepper, optional
2 Tablespoons butter
1 cup sliced mushrooms
1 13-ounce can diced soyameat chicken
1 5-ounce can diced water chestnuts
½-1 cup grated sharp Cheddar cheese
1 cup mayonnaise
1 cup half-and-half (may use part sour cream)
1 Tablespoon fresh lemon juice
½ teaspoon salt
Garlic powder, Cavender's Greek Seasoning or other seasonings to taste
1 10-ounce package frozen green peas
6-8 Pepperidge Farm Frozen Patty Shells, baked according to package directions
Chopped parsley

1. Sauté celery, onion and green pepper in butter until vegetables are soft. Add mushrooms and sauté gently.
2. Add drained soyameat chicken, water chestnuts and cheese.
3. Stir in mayonnaise, half-and-half, lemon juice and seasonings. Stir until cheese melts.
4. Simmer over low heat about ½ hour. Thin with half-and-half, if necessary.
5. Before serving, add frozen peas. Cook until heated through.
6. To serve, fill shells and garnish with chopped parsley.

Preparation Time:	30 minutes	Serves:	6-8
Cooking Time:	35 minutes	May do ahead	

Tip: *May refrigerate creamed mixture. Reheat and fill shells before serving.*

COMPANY LOAF

2 chopped, medium onions
1 cup diced black olives
½ cup chopped celery
½ cup chopped green pepper
4 eggs
2½ cups cottage cheese
2 teaspoons sage
¼ cup vegetable oil
2½ cups bread crumbs
2 envelopes G. Washington's Golden Seasoning and Broth
1 cup vegetarian burger
½ cup half-and-half

1. In large mixing bowl, combine all ingredients.
2. Pour into well-greased 9 x 13-inch baking dish.
3. Bake at 350 degrees for 1 hour.

Preparation Time:	20 minutes	Serves:	12-15
Baking Time:	1 hour	May do ahead and freeze	

GIFT OF THE MAGI

"A special combination used again and again"

1 package hot roll mix
½ teaspoon celery seed
1 cup mayonnaise
2 Tablespoons milk
1 teaspoon curry powder
1 teaspoon soy sauce
2 cups shredded, frozen Chic-ketts
1 diced, medium apple
¾ cup halved, seeded, red grapes
½ cup golden raisins
½ cup slivered almonds
¼ cup chopped green pepper
2 diced, hard-boiled eggs
12-inch piece of twine
1 beaten egg
1 Tablespoon water

1. Prepare hot roll mix according to package directions, adding celery seed to dry ingredients. Cover dough and let rest 20 minutes.
2. In separate bowl, combine mayonnaise, milk, curry powder and soy sauce.
3. Add Chic-ketts, apple, grapes, raisins, almonds, green pepper and eggs.
4. On lightly floured surface, roll dough into 13-inch circle. Fold dough in quarters. Carefully transfer to greased baking sheet. Unfold circle.
5. Spoon filling into center of dough. Bring dough up and over filling, letting dough top flare loosely. Tie with twine. Let stand 20 minutes.
6. Brush with beaten egg mixed with water.
7. Bake at 350 degrees for 30 minutes.
8. Serve warm.

Preparation Time:	45 minutes	**Serves:**	6
Baking Time:	30 minutes		

Variations: *Serve filling as cold salad on lettuce leaves or halved cantaloupe. For individual servings, use crescent rolls. Roll out crescents. Do not separate into triangles, but leave in squares, pressing perforated line to seal. Place filling in center. Pull corners together and twist center to secure. Seal seams together. Brush with butter and sprinkle with crushed croutons. A third variation is to spoon filling into baked Pepperidge Farm Patty Shells. Two cups of diced, hard-boiled eggs may be substituted for Chic-ketts.*

Tip: *Before serving, decorate with red ribbon or according to party theme.*

VEGETARIAN CHICKEN CURRY
"Excellent entrée"

¾ cup butter
2 cups finely diced onions
2 cups finely diced, peeled, tart green apples
3 minced garlic cloves
2 teaspoons curry powder
2 teaspoons Beau Monde seasoning
½ teaspoon thyme
1½ cups chicken-style broth
1 cup whipping cream
1½ cups half-and-half
1½ Tablespoons cornstarch dissolved in ¼ cup cold water
1 12-ounce can diced soyameat chicken
2 cups cooked long-grain rice

Condiments

½ diced, fresh pineapple
1 cup toasted, flaked coconut
1 cup raisins
1 cup unsalted cashews or peanuts
Mango chutney

1. Melt butter in 4-quart saucepan.
2. Sauté onions, apples and garlic for 5 minutes or until onion is transparent.
3. Stir in curry powder, Beau Monde seasoning and thyme. Cook over medium-low heat 2-3 minutes.
4. Add chicken-style broth. Bring mixture to simmer for 15 minutes.
5. Stir in whipping cream and half-and-half. Bring to simmer.
6. Slowly pour in cornstarch-water mixture. Stir until thickened, about 1-2 minutes.
7. Gently stir in diced chicken.
8. Serve hot over rice. Add Condiments, as desired.

Preparation Time:	30 minutes	**Serves:**	12
Cooking Time:	30 minutes	**May do up to 4 days ahead and freeze**	

Tip: *For freezer storage, omit thickening step until after thawing sauce. Heat and add cornstarch as described.*

MOUSSAKA

"A choice Greek specialty"

1 medium eggplant
2 Tablespoons butter
1 20-ounce can vegetarian burger
2 Tablespoons instant onion or 2 finely chopped onions
3 8-ounce cans tomato sauce
¼-½ cup water
1 Tablespoon parsley flakes
1 Tablespoon oregano
1½ teaspoons salt
¼ teaspoon cinnamon
4 beaten eggs
¾ cup grated, fresh Parmesan cheese
¾ cup dry bread crumbs

1. Cut unpared eggplant crosswise into ½-inch slices. Cook in salted water 5-8 minutes until tender. Drain.
2. In large skillet, combine butter, vegetarian burger and onion. Stir until onion is slightly cooked.
3. Add 1 can of tomato sauce, water, parsley flakes, oregano, salt and cinnamon. Cook uncovered over medium heat until half of liquid is absorbed, about 20 minutes.
4. Add eggs, ½ cup cheese and ½ cup bread crumbs into burger mixture. Remove from heat.
5. Butter 11 x 7-inch baking dish. Sprinkle ¼ cup bread crumbs evenly in dish.
6. Arrange half of eggplant slices in baking dish. Cover with burger mixture.
7. Sprinkle with remaining cheese. Top with remaining eggplant slices.
8. Pour White Sauce over eggplant.
9. Bake uncovered at 375 degrees for 45 minutes.
10. Allow to stand for 20 minutes before serving.
11. To serve, cut into squares. Serve with tomato sauce prepared for heating the remaining 2 cans of tomato sauce.

White Sauce

3 Tablespoons butter
3 Tablespoons flour
½ teaspoon salt
¼ teaspoon nutmeg
2 eggs
1¾ cups milk
¼ cup Parmesan cheese

1. For White Sauce, melt butter in saucepan. Add flour, salt and nutmeg. Cook until smooth and bubbly.
2. Add eggs and milk. Heat to boiling, stirring constantly. Boil 1 minute. Add Parmesan cheese.

Preparation Time:	40 minutes	**Serves:**	6-8
Baking Time:	45 minutes	**May do up to 24 hours ahead**	

Variations: *Substitute 2 pounds zucchini, sliced lengthwise and fried, or substitute 2 pounds peeled potatoes, cut in ¼-inch slices and fried, for eggplant.*
Tips: *For thicker White Sauce, add 4 eggs. To reheat, place in 375-degree oven for 30 minutes. It is not necessary to cool before serving.*

TOMATO-RICE CASSEROLE
"Busy day dish"

½ cup chopped green pepper
½ cup chopped celery
½ cup chopped onion
2 Tablespoons oil
1 cup vegetarian burger
2 19-ounce cans tomatoes
1 cup uncooked rice
½ cup barbecue sauce
½ teaspoon salt
½ cup grated Cheddar cheese

1. In saucepan, sauté green pepper, celery and onion in oil.
2. Add remaining ingredients except cheese.
3. Cover and simmer 25 minutes, stirring occasionally.
4. To serve, top with grated cheese.

Preparation Time:	**15 minutes**	**Serves:**	**6**
Cooking Time:	**30 minutes**		

SKALLOP CASSEROLE

2 cups finely chopped celery
1 cup finely chopped onion
2 cups sliced, fresh mushrooms
1 Tablespoon oil
1½ Tablespoons soy sauce
2 11-ounce cans cream of mushroom soup
1 20-ounce can vegetable skallops, drained and cut into small pieces
1 2½-ounce can slivered almonds
1 5-ounce can sliced water chestnuts

1. In large skillet, sauté celery, onion and mushrooms in oil.
2. Stir in soy sauce.
3. Add soup, skallops, almonds and water chestnuts.
4. Heat until bubbly, about 8-10 minutes.

Preparation Time:	**25 minutes**	**Serves:**	**6-8**
Cooking Time:	**15 minutes**		

Serving Suggestion: *Serve immediately over rice or chow mein noodles.*
Tip: *Bake in 8 x 8-inch baking dish at 350 degrees for 20 minutes.*

SPINACH AND MOCK BEEF DUMPLINGS
"Truly different and delicious"

1 10-ounce package frozen, chopped spinach, thawed and squeezed dry
1 8-ounce package frozen Morningstar Farms Breakfast Patties, thawed
1 8-ounce package frozen Morningstar Farms Grillers, thawed
½ cup fresh bread crumbs
1 finely chopped, medium onion
2 eggs
¼ cup cracker crumbs
Salt and seasoning to taste
Flour

1. In food processor, combine all ingredients except flour. Mix until thoroughly blended.
2. Shape mixture into 1-inch balls. Roll in flour and flatten gently to ½-inch thickness.
3. Sauté dumplings in butter until browned on both sides.
4. Place dumplings in 1½-quart casserole and pour Mushroom-Onion Cream Sauce over top.
5. Place in 350-degree oven until heated through.

Preparation Time:	**30 minutes**	**Serves:**	**6**
Baking Time:	**30 minutes**		

Serving Suggestion: *Serve with brown rice.*

STROGANOFF
"Sensational"

1 19-ounce can vegetarian cutlets, sliced in strips
Flour
Oil
2 quartered, thinly sliced, medium onions
1 pound sliced, fresh mushrooms
3 11-ounce cans mushroom soup
1 package onion soup mix
1 Tablespoon beef-style seasoning
Season to taste with salt and garlic powder or 2 cloves of fresh minced garlic and
    Cavender's Greek Seasoning
1-1½ cups sour cream
1-2 pounds cooked fettuccine noodles
Chopped parsley or chives, optional

1. Squeeze out as much liquid as possible from cutlets. Toss cutlet strips in flour. Fry a few at a time in oil until brown. Set aside.
2. Sauté onions and mushrooms separately in butter. Set aside.
3. Mix soups in large saucepan. Add beef-style seasoning, onions, mushrooms and cutlets. Add remaining seasonings. Simmer 20-30 minutes.
4. Add sour cream and mix well. Heat thoroughly. Do not allow to boil. If more liquid is needed, add a little hot water and a little beef-style seasoning.

Preparation Time:	**30 minutes**	**Serves:**	**10**
Cooking Time:	**30 minutes**		

Serving Suggestion: *Serve over cooked noodles. Garnish with chopped parsley or chives.*

287

TURKISH SHISH KEBABS

Marinade

½ cup olive oil
¼ cup lemon juice
1 teaspoon marjoram
1 teaspoon thyme
1 minced garlic clove
½ cup chopped onion
¼ cup chopped parsley

Mix all ingredients.

Kebabs

2 pounds 1-inch cubed gluten pieces
1 pound fresh mushroom caps
6-8 cubed, fresh green peppers
2 pounds fresh cherry tomatoes

1. Marinate gluten pieces in Marinade 2-8 hours.
2. Arrange gluten pieces, mushroom caps and green pepper on water-soaked wooden skewers, alternating gluten with vegetables.
3. Broil 5 inches from heat for 8-10 minutes, turning occasionally.

Preparation Time:	30 minutes	**Serves:**	12
Marinating Time:	2-8 hours		
Broiling Time:	8-10 minutes		

Tip: *Gluten pieces may be prepared by omitting marinade.*

BAKED BEANS
"Tastes like Boston"

2 pounds small white beans
½ cup brown sugar
1 cup melted butter
2 16-ounce cans tomatoes
1-2 cups catsup
2 quartered, large onions
1 Tablespoon salt
¼ cup molasses

1. Cover beans with water and soak overnight. Do not drain.
2. Boil beans for 1 hour or until tender.
3. Add all ingredients to beans and bake at 350 degrees for 3 hours.

Preparation Time:	20 minutes	**Serves:**	20
Soaking Time:	6-8 hours	**Must do 1 day ahead**	
Cooking Time:	1 hour		
Baking Time:	3 hours		

CHILI BEANS

5 cups small red, pink or pinto beans
1 Tablespoon salt
2 quartered, large onions
3 Tablespoons cumin
3 minced garlic cloves
3 teaspoons chili powder
1 quart tomatoes
1 chopped green pepper
1 Tablespoon margarine

1. Soak beans overnight.
2. Cook for 2 hours in enough water to keep beans covered. If using a pressure cooker, cook with pressure up for 1 hour.
3. Add remaining ingredients. Simmer several hours.

Preparation Time:	20 minutes	**Yield:**	5 quarts
Cooking Time:	4-5 hours	**May freeze**	

Variation: *Brown favorite burger and add. Substitute Lawry's Chili Seasoning or Texas Chili for above seasonings.*

CHIMICHANGAS

6 8-inch flour tortillas
1 cup plus 2 Tablespoons refried beans
2 Tablespoons diced green onion
6 Tablespoons shredded Cheddar cheese
6 Tablespoons sour cream

1. Heat tortilla in large, ungreased griddle until hot and pliable, not dry.
2. Place 3 Tablespoons refried beans below center of 1 tortilla. Layer green onion, 1 Tablespoon cheese and 1 Tablespoon sour cream.
3. Fold sides of tortilla over filling to center. Fold bottom over filling and roll up, enclosing filling completely.
4. Deep fry in 1 inch oil on both sides. Repeat for each chimichanga.

Preparation Time:	45 minutes	**Yield:**	6 chimichangas
Frying Time:	20 minutes		

Serving Suggestion: *Serve immediately on platter garnished with guacamole and salsa.*
Tip: *May assemble ahead. Fry just before serving.*

CHUCK WAGON BEANS

2 15-ounce cans pinto beans, including bean liquid
¼ cup hickory barbecue sauce
¼ cup tomato paste
1 chopped onion
2 Tablespoons butter
¼ cup chopped green chiles
2 Tablespoons molasses or brown sugar

1. In large saucepan, combine all ingredients.
2. Slow cook for 1½-2 hours.

Preparation Time:	15 minutes	Serves:	8
Cooking Time:	1½-2 hours		

REFRIED BEANS

2 15-ounce cans pinto beans (1 can drained)
1-1½ teaspoons taco seasoning mix
3 chopped green onions
2-3 Tablespoons mild salsa
½ cup shredded Colby cheese

1. Cook beans, taco seasoning, green onions and salsa over low heat for 10-15 minutes, stirring frequently.
2. After beans thicken, mash with fork. Stir in cheese.
3. Serve warm.

Preparation Time:	20 minutes	Yield:	4 cups
Cooking Time:	10-15 minutes		

COTTAGE CHEESE PATTIES

"For the last minute guest"

2 beaten eggs
1 cup Italian-style bread crumbs
1 cup uncooked rolled oats
1 cup cottage cheese
1 grated medium onion
1 teaspoon salt
⅓ teaspoon chicken-style seasoning
2 Tablespoons melted butter
Oil

1. Mix all ingredients except oil.
2. Form into small to medium-size patties.
3. Lightly coat bottom of skillet with oil. Brown patties.

Preparation Time:	20 minutes	Yield:	16 patties
Cooking Time:	20 minutes	May be frozen	

Serving Suggestion: *Serve with favorite gravy or sauce.*

CREAM CHEESE MEATBALLS WITH MUSHROOM GRAVY
"Couldn't be easier"

Meatballs

5 eggs
4 ounces cream cheese
1½ cups bread crumbs
½ cup oatmeal
½ cup finely chopped nuts
1 chopped onion
1 teaspoon Accent
1 envelope G. Washington's Dark Seasoning and Broth
2 teaspoons garlic salt
Salt to taste

Mushroom Gravy

½ pound sliced, fresh mushrooms
1 11-ounce can cream of mushroom soup
1 cup sour cream
2 Tablespoons dry brown gravy mix

1. Combine all Meatball ingredients. Form into balls.
2. Fry until brown. Drain on paper towels.
3. Combine Gravy ingredients. Pour over meatballs.
4. Bake at 350 degrees for 30 minutes.

Preparation Time: 40 minutes   **Yield:** 36 meatballs
Baking Time: 30 minutes

MUSHROOM-NUT PATTIES

1 cup cottage cheese
1 cup cracker crumbs
½ cup chopped walnuts
1 chopped, medium onion
1 cup sliced, fresh mushrooms
6 eggs
¼ teaspoon poultry seasoning or sage
¼ teaspoon salt
2 packages G. Washington's Golden Seasoning and Broth
Oil

1. Mix all ingredients except oil.
2. Form into small to medium-size patties.
3. Lightly coat bottom of skillet with oil. Brown patties on both sides.

Preparation Time: 30 minutes   **Yield:** 15-20 patties
Frying Time: 10-12 minutes   May be frozen
Serving Suggestion: *Serve with your favorite gravy.*

ITALIAN CHEESE BALLS
"You can freeze these"

6 beaten eggs
1 cup bread crumbs
1 teaspoon salt
1 cup grated Colby cheese
⅓ cup cream or milk
1 finely chopped onion
1 cup chopped nuts
½ cup grated, fresh Parmesan cheese

1. Mix all ingredients except Parmesan cheese.
2. Form into walnut-size balls.
3. Deep fry in hot vegetable oil until lightly browned.
4. Arrange balls in buttered 8 x 8-inch dish.
5. Cover with favorite Italian tomato sauce.
6. Bake at 350 degrees for 30-45 minutes.
7. Sprinkle with Parmesan cheese.

Preparation Time:	**25 minutes**	**Serves:**	**6-8**
Frying Time:	**10 minutes**		
Baking Time:	**30-45 minutes**		

RITZ PATTIES
"The sauce makes the dish"

1 cup crushed Ritz crackers
½ cup finely chopped nuts
6 beaten eggs
1 cup grated sharp Cheddar cheese
½ teaspoon garlic salt
1 cup catsup
1 cup water

1. Mix all ingredients except catsup and water.
2. Form into patties by dropping heaping Tablespoon of mixture into hot oiled frying pan, pressing down to form rounded patty.
3. Fry until browned. Turn.
4. Arrange patties in buttered 11 x 17-inch baking dish.
5. Combine catsup and water to make sauce. Pour over patties. Let stand 30 minutes.
6. Bake at 350 degrees for 45-60 minutes.

Preparation Time:	**20 minutes**	**Serves:**	**6-8**
Standing Time:	**30 minutes**		
Baking Time:	**45-60 minutes**		

NUT BALLS

Nut Balls

5 eggs
1 cup shredded Cheddar cheese
½ cup cottage cheese
½ cup finely chopped onion
1 cup finely chopped nuts
1 teaspoon basil
½ teaspoon salt
½ teaspoon sage
2 cups crushed herb stuffing

Apricot Sweet and Sour Sauce

¼ cup oil
½ cup vinegar
1 cup apricot jam
1 cup catsup
¼ cup grated onion
1 teaspoon salt
1 teaspoon oregano
Dash hot pepper sauce

1. Mix all ingredients for Nut Balls.
2. Form into balls.
3. Combine Apricot Sweet and Sour Sauce ingredients. Pour over Nut Balls.
4. Bake at 350 degrees for 35-40 minutes.

Preparation Time:	25 minutes	**Yield:**	24 2-inch balls
Baking Time:	35-40 minutes		

COTTAGE CHEESE LOAF

2 cups cottage cheese
3 Tablespoons mayonnaise
3 Tablespoons food yeast flakes
1 chopped, small onion
2 packages G. Washington's Golden Seasoning and Broth
1½ cups fresh bread crumbs
3 Tablespoons chopped parsley
3 eggs

1. Mix all ingredients.
2. Bake at 350 degrees in well-greased 9 x 5-inch loaf pan for 30-40 minutes.

Preparation Time:	10 minutes	**Serves:**	6
Baking Time:	30-40 minutes	**May do ahead**	

Serving Suggestions: *This is good for sandwiches. Serve hot or cold or serve hot with your favorite gravy.*

SWEET AND SOUR TOFU PATTIES
"For tofu lovers"

Patties

1 pound mashed soft tofu
18 crushed Ritz crackers
3 eggs
1 chopped, medium onion
2 teaspoons chicken-style seasoning
1 teaspoon beef-style seasoning
1 package G. Washington's Brown Seasoning and Broth
1 teaspoon poultry seasoning
1 teaspoon salt
1 teaspoon dried parsley
Oil

Sweet and Sour Sauce

2 cups pineapple juice
¼ cup brown sugar
3 Tablespoons vinegar
½ teaspoon Accent
2 Tablespoons catsup
2 Tablespoons butter
3 Tablespoons cornstarch
¾-1 cup drained, chunk pineapple
⅓ cup toasted, sliced almonds

1. Mix all patty ingredients except oil.
2. Form into small to medium-size Patties.
3. Lightly coat bottom of skillet with oil. Fry Patties 10 minutes on each side. Place in 9 x 13-inch baking dish.
4. In saucepan, combine Sweet and Sour Sauce ingredients except pineapple and almonds. Cook and stir until thickened. Immediately pour over patties.
5. Sprinkle pineapple and almonds over top.

Preparation Time: **45 minutes**   **Yield:**   **15-18 patties**
                                                        May do ahead
Tip: *If done ahead, place patties in casserole dish, sprinkle lightly with water, cover with foil and bake at 225 degrees for 45 minutes. Add warmed sauce and serve.*

WALNUT MEATBALLS
"Pecans make a good alternate"

10 Servings

1¼ cups cracker crumbs
¾ cup ground walnuts
½ teaspoon salt
1 finely chopped, small onion
1½ teaspoons sage
¾ cup grated longhorn cheese
2 pressed garlic cloves
3 Tablespoons minced parsley
4 eggs
Apricot Barbecue Sauce (see recipe)

1. Mix all ingredients, except Apricot Barbecue Sauce. Form into walnut-size balls.
2. Pour Apricot Barbecue Sauce over meatballs in casserole dish.
3. Bake covered at 350 degrees for 30 minutes.

Preparation Time:	**20 minutes**	**Yield:**	**20 meatballs**
Baking Time:	**45 minutes**		**May do ahead and freeze**

Variation: *Substitute Sour Cream-Mushroom Gravy for Apricot Barbecue Sauce.*
Tip: *Freeze uncooked balls 2-3 hours on cookie sheet. When frozen bake 12 minutes at 350 degrees. Pour Apricot Barbecue Sauce over meatballs. Bake covered at 350 degrees for 30 minutes.*

20 Servings

2½ cups cracker crumbs
1½ cups ground walnuts
1 teaspoon salt
1 finely chopped, large onion
1 Tablespoon sage
1½ cups grated longhorn cheese
3 pressed garlic cloves
⅓ cup minced parsley
8 eggs
Doubled recipe of Apricot Barbecue Sauce

Yield:	**40 meatballs**

100 Servings

12½ cups cracker crumbs
7½ cups ground walnuts
1½ Tablespoons salt
5 finely chopped, large onions
¼ cup plus 1 Tablespoon sage
7½ cups grated longhorn cheese
15 pressed garlic cloves
2 cups minced parsley
3⅓ dozen (40) eggs
10 times recipe of Apricot Barbecue Sauce

Yield:	**200 meatballs**

PECAN LOAF

1½ cups grape-nuts cereal
1½ cups evaporated milk
2 chopped, large onions
2 cups chopped celery
¼ cup butter
1½ cups chopped pecans
1 teaspoon salt
4 eggs
1 teaspoon liquid smoke
1 package G. Washington's Golden Seasoning and Broth
1 teaspoon Worcestershire sauce
1 teaspoon garlic powder

1. Soak grape-nuts in milk until soft.
2. Sauté onions and celery in butter.
3. Combine all ingredients.
4. Line 8 x 8-inch baking dish with foil and grease.
5. Bake at 350 degrees for 45-60 minutes.

Preparation Time: **30 minutes**   **Serves:**   **8**
Baking Time: **45-60 minutes**
Serving Suggestion: *Serve with Gorgonzola Cream Sauce.*

CHEESE-EGG CASSEROLE

"Wonderful brunch entree"

1 cup butter
1 cup flour
2 teaspoons baking powder
12 eggs
2 teaspoons salt
2 pounds cottage cheese
1 pound grated Monterey Jack cheese
Any one or combination of:

  Chopped green chiles
  Green or black olives
  Mushrooms
  Marinated artichoke hearts
  Onion

1. Melt butter. Add flour and baking powder.
2. Mix eggs in bowl. Add remaining ingredients.
3. Pour into 9 x 13-inch baking dish.
4. Bake at 350 degrees for 1 hour.
5. Cut into 3-4-inch squares. Serve hot.

Preparation Time: **15 minutes**   **Serves:**   **15**
Baking Time: **1 hour**
Variation: *Cut into 1-inch squares for appetizers. Serve cold.*

CHEESE STRADA

"Excellent for a brunch"

16 slices white bread
1 pound grated Cheddar cheese
1 quart milk
6 eggs
1 teaspoon dry mustard
2 Tablespoons diced green chiles
1 teaspoon salt

1. Butter bread, 1 side only.
2. Place 8 slices bread, buttered side down, in 9 x 13-inch baking dish.
3. Sprinkle with ½ of cheese.
4. Place second layer of bread slices.
5. Mix milk, eggs, chiles, mustard and salt. Pour over second layer of bread.
6. Top with remaining cheese.
7. Bake at 350 degrees for 1 hour.

Preparation Time:	**15 minutes**	**Serves:**	**8-10**
Baking Time:	**1 hour**	**May do ahead and bake 1 day later**	

CRUSTLESS QUICHE

"Quick and easy"

10 eggs
1 quart cottage cheese
1 pound grated Monterey Jack cheese
¼ teaspoon seasoned salt
2 teaspoons baking powder
½ cup flour
½ cup melted butter
1 7-ounce can diced green chiles

1. Place ½ of mixture in food processor and mix 5 minutes. Repeat with remaining half.
2. Place in greased 9 x 13-inch baking dish.
3. Bake at 350 degrees for 45-60 minutes.

Preparation Time:	**20 minutes**	**Serves:**	**12-15**
Baking Time:	**45-60 minutes**		

PINEAPPLE-CHEESE CASSEROLE

"A bit unusual, but delicious"

2 16-ounce cans drained, chunk pineapple
1½ cups sugar
¾ cup flour
2 cups grated sharp Cheddar cheese
18 crushed Ritz crackers
1 cup butter

1. Spread pineapple in 11 x 17-inch baking dish.
2. Mix together sugar, flour and grated cheese. Add to baking dish, mixing into pineapple.
3. Spread cracker crumbs over top of pineapple-cheese mixture.
4. Melt butter and pour over crackers.
5. Bake at 350 degrees for 30 minutes.
6. Serve hot or cold.

Preparation Time:	**15 minutes**	**Serves:**	**12-15**
Baking Time:	**30 minutes**		

CHILE RELLENO CASSEROLE

"Cheese and chiles sharpen the flavor"

1 cup half-and-half
2 eggs
⅓ cup flour
1 12-ounce can whole green chiles
½ pound shredded Monterey Jack cheese
½ pound shredded Cheddar cheese
1 8-ounce can tomato sauce

1. Beat half-and-half with eggs and flour until smooth.
2. Split open chiles. Rinse out seeds and drain on paper towels.
3. Mix cheeses. Reserve ½ cup cheese for topping.
4. Alternate layers of remaining cheese, chiles and egg mixture in 8 x 8-inch baking dish.
5. Pour tomato sauce over top and sprinkle with reserved cheese.
6. Bake at 375 degrees for 1 hour or until cooked in center.

Preparation Time:	**20 minutes**	**Serves:**	**4-6**
Baking Time:	**1 hour**		

Tip: *Double recipe for 9 x 13-inch baking dish.*

CHEESE ENCHILADAS
"These are delicious"

Filling

3 11-ounce cans cream of celery soup
1 chopped medium onion
1 7-ounce can diced green chiles
2 cups sour cream
1 pound grated Cheddar cheese

Tortillas

18 flour or corn tortillas

1. Combine all Filling ingredients except cheese.
2. Spoon heaping Tablespoon of Filling on tortilla and add pinch of cheese. Roll tightly.
3. Place rolled tortillas close together in 9x13-inch baking dish.
4. Cover with remaining Filling and sprinkle with cheese.
5. Bake at 350 degrees for 30 minutes.

Preparation Time: **45 minutes**   **Serves:**   **8-10**
Baking Time: **30 minutes**   **May freeze**
Variation: *Add chopped olives to Filling.*

EGG SCRAMBLE SURPRISE
"Wonderful for company"

2 Tablespoons melted butter
2 Tablespoons flour
2 cups milk
½ teaspoon salt
1 cup shredded American cheese
¾ cup chopped green onions or 2 Tablespoons dried onions
3 Tablespoons melted butter
12 beaten eggs
½ cup milk
½ cup sliced, fresh mushrooms
¼ cup bread crumbs
Paprika

1. Combine butter and flour. Cook over low heat until bubbly.
2. Gradually stir in milk. Cook until smooth and thickened.
3. Add salt and cheese. Stir constantly until cheese melts. Set aside.
4. Sauté onions in butter.
5. Beat eggs and milk. Add to onions. Cook until set, stirring occasionally to scramble. Fold in mushrooms and cheese sauce.
6. Spoon into greased 9 x 13-inch baking dish.
7. Top with bread crumbs and sprinkle with paprika.
8. Bake at 350 degrees for 30 minutes.

Preparation Time: 30 minutes   **Serves:** 8-10
Baking Time: 30 minutes

EGGS RANCHO
"A favorite for a busy family"

⅓ cup oil
2 chopped, medium onions
2 16-ounce cans whole tomatoes
2 cups chicken-style broth
1 teaspoon salt
1 teaspoon sugar
8 eggs
2-3 ounces Monterey Jack cheese, cut into slices
1 7-ounce can whole green chiles, cut into strips

1. Heat oil in large skillet.
2. Add onions and cook until soft, but not brown.
3. Place tomatoes in blender and blend until just pulpy, not puréed.
4. Add chicken-style broth, salt and sugar. Cook 5 minutes.
5. Break each egg carefully into small plate. Slide eggs, 1 at a time, into hot mixture. Do not break yolks. Arrange slice of cheese and strip of chile on top of each egg. Cook on low for 5-8 minutes or until eggs are set and cheese is melted.

Preparation Time: 25 minutes   **Serves:** 8
Cooking Time: 15 minutes

PLANTATION EGGS

½ pound grated Monterey Jack cheese
6 eggs
1 pint whipping cream
½ teaspoon seasoned salt
½ teaspoon paprika
¼ teaspoon chili powder

1. Place layer of cheese on bottom of 9 x 9-inch baking dish.
2. Indent 6 areas in equal distribution in grated cheese. Place eggs in indentations.
3. Mix whipping cream, salt, paprika and chili powder. Pour over eggs.
4. Bake at 350 degrees for 30 minutes.

Preparation Time: 10 minutes   Serves: 6
Baking Time: 30 minutes

SCRAMBLED EGGS SUPREME

9 large eggs
1⅔ cups evaporated milk
½ teaspoon salt
1 teaspoon chopped chives
1 teaspoon butter
3 ounces cubed cream cheese

1. Beat eggs with milk, salt and chives until light and foamy.
2. Melt butter in frying pan.
3. Add egg mixture. On low heat, cook and stir constantly until eggs are almost set.
4. Fold cream cheese cubes into eggs. Stir until cheese begins to melt.
5. Serve immediately.

Preparation Time: 15 minutes   Serves: 6-8
Cooking Time: 15 minutes

ITALIAN PARTY LASAGNE

1 pound cooked lasagne noodles
4 8-ounce cans tomato sauce
1 cup minced onion
1 Tablespoon seasoned salt
1½ teaspoons herb seasoning
¼ teaspoon garlic powder
3 beaten eggs
1 16-ounce carton ricotta cheese
1 cup small curd cottage cheese
1 pound thinly sliced mozzarella cheese
½ cup grated, fresh Parmesan cheese

1. Cook noodles according to package directions.
2. In bowl, combine tomato sauce, onion, seasoned salt, herb seasoning and garlic powder. Set aside.
3. Blend eggs, ricotta and cottage cheese in small bowl. Set aside.
4. In 9 x 13-inch baking dish, arrange in layers half of each of the cooked noodles, ricotta mixture and mozzarella cheese slices. Repeat layers.
5. Sprinkle with Parmesan cheese.
6. Bake at 375 degrees for 40-45 minutes.
7. Let stand 10 minutes before cutting.

Preparation Time:	**30 minutes**	**Serves:**	**10-12**
Baking Time:	**45 minutes**	**May do ahead and freeze**	
Standing Time:	**10 minutes**		

Variation: *Two uncooked, thinly sliced zucchinis may be added to step 4.*

LASAGNE SWIRLS

"As pretty as they are delicious"

16 uncooked lasagne noodles
2 10-ounce packages frozen, chopped spinach, thawed and squeezed dry
2 cups grated, fresh Parmesan cheese
½ pound grated mozzarella cheese
2 cups ricotta cheese
1 teaspoon salt
½ teaspoon nutmeg
Tomato Sauce

1. Cook noodles according to package directions. Drain.
2. Rinse with cool water and drain again.
3. In bowl, mix spinach, 1½ cups Parmesan cheese, mozzarella cheese, ricotta cheese, salt and nutmeg.
4. Spread about ¼ cup of mixture along length of each noodle. Roll noodle up.
5. Pour half of Tomato Sauce into each of 2 greased 9 x 9-inch baking dishes.
6. In each baking dish, stand 8 rolled noodles on end.
7. Bake, covered, at 350 degrees for 30 minutes, or until heated through.
8. Remove from oven and sprinkle evenly with remaining ½ cup Parmesan cheese.

Tomato Sauce

2 minced garlic cloves
1 chopped, large onion
3 Tablespoons olive oil
2 15-ounce cans tomato sauce
¼ cup water
½ teaspoon dry basil
½ teaspoon oregano

1. In large frying pan over medium heat, sauté garlic and onion in olive oil until soft.
2. Add tomato sauce, water, basil and oregano.
3. Simmer, uncovered, 10 minutes.

Preparation Time:	**1 hour**	**Yield:**	**16 swirls**
Cooking Time:	**30-40 minutes**	**May do ahead**	
Baking Time:	**30 minutes**		

Tip: *If done ahead, cover and refrigerate before baking.*

SPINACH LASAGNE

"Spinach haters will love this"

10 cooked lasagne noodles
2 cups sliced, fresh mushrooms
½ cup chopped onion
1 Tablespoon vegetable oil
1 15-ounce can tomato sauce
1 6-ounce can tomato paste
½ cup chopped black olives
1½ teaspoons dried, crushed oregano
2 cups cottage cheese
1 pound fresh spinach, cooked and squeezed dry
1 pound sliced Monterey Jack cheese
½ cup grated, fresh Parmesan cheese

1. Cook lasagne noodles in boiling, unsalted water for 8-10 minutes or until tender. Drain.
2. In saucepan, cook mushrooms and onion in hot oil until tender, but not brown.
3. Stir in tomato sauce, tomato paste, olives and oregano.
4. In greased 9 x 13-inch baking dish, layer half of noodles, cottage cheese, spinach, Monterey Jack cheese and sauce mixture. Repeat layers, ending with several cheese slices on top.
5. Sprinkle with Parmesan cheese.
6. Bake at 375 degrees for 30 minutes.
7. Let stand 10 minutes before serving.

Preparation Time:	45 minutes	Serves:	8-10
Cooking Time:	10-15 minutes		
Baking Time:	30 minutes		

Variations: *Add 1 teaspoon minced garlic to step 2. Ricotta cheese may be substituted for cottage cheese.*
Tip: *May be frozen before baking.*

ASPARAGUS NOODLES

6 large, dried shitake mushrooms
½ pound fresh, pencil-thin asparagus
3 Tablespoons oil
1 Tablespoon minced garlic
1 Tablespoon fresh, minced ginger root
2 Tablespoons minced green onion
½ teaspoon red chili flakes
1 pound fresh, cooked Chinese Noodles (see recipe)

Sauce

6 Tablespoons hoisin sauce
2 Tablespoons soy sauce
2 Tablespoons chicken-style broth
2 teaspoons sesame oil
2 Tablespoons reserved mushroom liquid

1. Soak mushrooms in very hot water, covered, for 20 minutes. Drain, reserving 2 Tablespoons liquid. Cut into slices.
2. Slice asparagus on the diagonal. Roll asparagus ¼ turn and slice 2 inches down the stalk on the diagonal. Repeat.
3. Blanch asparagus in boiling water until crisp-tender. Place in ice water. Drain.
4. In wok or large skillet, heat oil until piece of garlic sizzles. Add garlic, ginger root, green onions and chili flakes. Stir fry for 45-60 seconds until very fragrant.
5. Add asparagus. Stir fry 1 minute.
6. Add Sauce ingredients.
7. Stir until slightly thickened. Add Chinese Noodles. Toss lightly.
8. Serve warm.

Preparation Time:	**30 minutes**	**Serves:**	**4**
Soaking Time:	**20 minutes**		
Cooking Time:	**5-8 minutes**		

Tip: *Hoisin sauce may be purchased at Oriental market.*

CHEESE-FILLED MANICOTTI
"Always a favorite"

Sauce

1½ cups finely chopped onion
1 crushed garlic clove
⅓ cup olive oil
1 35-ounce can undrained Italian tomatoes
1 6-ounce can tomato sauce
2 Tablespoons chopped parsley
1 Tablespoon salt
1 Tablespoon sugar
1 teaspoon dried oregano leaves
1 teaspoon basil leaves

1. In skillet, sauté onion and garlic in olive oil 5 minutes.
2. Add remaining ingredients. Bring to boil and reduce heat. Simmer 1 hour, stirring occasionally.

Manicotti

6 eggs at room temperature
1½ cups unsifted flour
¼ teaspoon salt
1½ cups water

1. Combine eggs, flour, salt and water. Beat with electric mixer until smooth. Let stand 30 minutes or longer.
2. Slowly heat 8-inch skillet. Pour in 3 Tablespoons manicotti mixture, tipping pan to cover bottom.
3. Cook until top is dry and then flip.
4. Cool on wire rack. When cool, stack between waxed paper.

Filling

1 32-ounce carton ricotta cheese
1 cup grated mozzarella cheese
⅓ cup grated, fresh Parmesan cheese
2 eggs
1 teaspoon salt
1 Tablespoon chopped parsley

Topping

¼ cup grated, fresh Parmesan cheese

1. Mix all filling ingredients.
2. Spoon 1½ cups Sauce into 9 x 13-inch baking dish.
3. Spread about ¼ cup Filling in center of each Manicotti and roll up.
4. Place filled Manicotti seam side down in baking dish. Cover with remaining Sauce. Sprinkle with ¼ cup Parmesan cheese.
5. Bake at 350 degrees for 30 minutes.

Preparation Time: **2 hours**   **Serves:**   **12**
Baking Time: **30 minutes**

MOSTACCIOLI-BROCCOLI BAKE

"Easy and flavorful"

2¾ cups mostaccioli
¼ cup margarine
¼ cup flour
2 cups milk
½ cup grated, fresh Parmesan cheese
½ teaspoon salt
½ teaspoon garlic powder
⅛ teaspoon thyme
⅛ teaspoon nutmeg
3 cups cooked, drained broccoli
½ cup shredded Swiss cheese

1. Cook mostaccioli according to package directions. Drain. Rinse with cold water.
2. In medium saucepan, melt margarine. Stir in flour until well-blended.
3. Add milk. Cook until thickened, stirring constantly.
4. Stir in Parmesan cheese, salt, garlic powder, thyme and nutmeg. Remove from heat.
5. In large bowl, combine mostaccioli, cheese sauce and broccoli.
6. Spoon into 9 x 13-inch baking dish. Sprinkle Swiss cheese over top.
7. Bake at 375 degrees for 10-15 minutes or until thoroughly heated.

Preparation Time:	30 minutes	Serves:	12
Baking Time:	10-15 minutes		

NOODLE-BROCCOLI CASSEROLE

"Broiling is the key"

1 8-ounce package egg noodles
4 Tablespoons margarine
2 finely chopped, medium onions
½ cup heavy cream or evaporated milk
½ cup grated, fresh Parmesan cheese
½ cup sour cream
1 teaspoon salt
½ teaspoon nutmeg
1 20-ounce package frozen or fresh broccoli, cooked and drained
1 cup grated Cheddar cheese
3 Tablespoons butter

1. Cook noodles according to package directions. Drain. Rinse with hot water.
2. Melt margarine in saucepan. Add onion and cook until golden.
3. Gradually pour in cream. Add Parmesan cheese and sour cream. Stir until hot, not boiling.
4. Add noodles to sauce.
5. Season to taste using salt and nutmeg.
6. Put broccoli in bottom of greased 9 x 13-inch baking dish.
7. Pour noodles over broccoli. Top with grated cheese and dot with butter.
8. Put under broiler and brown.

Preparation Time:	35 minutes	Serves:	8-10
Broiling Time:	5-6 minutes		

PASTA WITH ROASTED TOMATO-BASIL SAUCE
"Great flavor"

3 Tablespoons olive oil
Salt to taste
2 pounds tomatoes
2 Tablespoons minced garlic
½ bunch coarsely chopped, fresh basil
½ cup chicken-style broth
½ Tablespoon dried red pepper flakes or chili flakes
½-¾ pound pasta
3 Tablespoons toasted pine nuts, optional
Fresh basil leaves
Grated, fresh Parmesan cheese

1. Mix 1 Tablespoon olive oil and salt. Rub on tomatoes. Roast at 400 degrees until skins are lightly browned.
2. Peel tomatoes. Core and cut in wedges. Discard skins and seeds.
3. Sauté garlic in 2 Tablespoons olive oil. Add tomatoes, basil and chicken-style broth. Cook until slightly reduced. Season with red pepper flakes.
4. Cook pasta in large pot of salted water until done. Drain well.
5. Mix ½ cup of sauce into freshly cooked pasta.
6. Toss pine nuts into remaining sauce.
7. To serve, place pasta on platter. Pour sauce over pasta. Garnish with fresh basil leaves and Parmesan cheese.

Preparation Time:	30 minutes	Serves:	4
Roasting Time:	About 10 minutes		
Cooking Time:	10-15 minutes		

Variations: *Substitute shallots for garlic or use half garlic and half shallots. Use sun-dried tomatoes for sweeter flavor.*

SPAGHETTI WITH PESTO
"So easy and so good"

2 pounds cooked spaghetti, commercial or homemade
1 cup Pesto (see recipe)
¼ pound pine nuts
1 Tablespoon olive oil
Grated, fresh Parmesan cheese
Salt to taste
Fresh basil leaves

1. Put cooked spaghetti (may be hot or cold) in large bowl. Toss with Pesto, pine nuts, oil and Parmesan cheese.
2. Season with salt, additional oil and cheese, as desired.
3. To serve, arrange pasta on platter and decorate with basil leaves.

Preparation Time:	15 minutes	Serves:	4

SPAGHETTI CASSEROLE
"Freezes well"

1 11-ounce can cream of mushroom soup
1½ soup cans milk
Seasoned salt to taste
Sugar to taste
4 quarts water
1 12-ounce package thin spaghetti
1 pint sour cream
1½ pounds shredded sharp American cheese
1 minced onion
1 cup Ritz cracker crumbs
½ cup butter or margarine

1. Combine soup, milk, salt and sugar. Set aside.
2. Bring 4 quarts water to boil. Add spaghetti. Remove from heat and let stand until spaghetti becomes pliable, about 10 minutes. Drain.
3. Place layer of spaghetti in greased 9 x 13-inch baking dish.
4. Spread with thin layer of sour cream.
5. Sprinkle with thick layer of cheese and top with layer of onion. Repeat layers until all ingredients are used.
6. Pour soup mixture over spaghetti mixture.
7. Sauté crumbs in butter until golden. Sprinkle over casserole.
8. Bake at 325 degrees for 1 hour or until casserole is bubbly.

Preparation Time:	**30 minutes**	**Serves:**	**10**
Baking Time:	**1 hour**	**May freeze**	

VEGETABLE-GORGONZOLA SAUCE WITH LINGUINI
"A creamy, cheesy delight"

4 finely chopped shallots
¼ cup butter
3 thinly sliced zucchini
3 peeled, thinly sliced carrots
¾ pound thinly sliced mushrooms
½ diced red bell pepper
½ cup chicken-style broth
1 cup cream
2 Tablespoons finely chopped, fresh basil
¼ pound diced Gorgonzola cheese
1 pound linguini
Chopped, fresh parsley
½ cup grated, fresh Parmesan cheese

1. In large saucepan, sauté shallots in butter.
2. Add zucchini, carrots, mushrooms and red bell pepper. Stir-fry until crisp-tender, about 3 minutes. Reserve ¼ cup of vegetables for garnish.
3. Add chicken-style broth, cream and basil. Simmer 3 minutes.
4. Turn off heat. Stir in Gorgonzola cheese and melt into sauce. Cheese will thicken sauce.
5. Cook linguini according to package directions. Drain.
6. Pour vegetable sauce mixture over pasta and toss. Let pasta stand to allow absorption of cream mixture into pasta.
7. Top with reserved vegetable mixture, parsley and Parmesan cheese.

Preparation Time: 30 minutes   **Serves:** 4
Cooking Time: 20 minutes
Variations: *Swiss, Parmesan or feta cheese may be substituted for Gorgonzola cheese. Shitake mushrooms may be used. Green or yellow bell pepper may be substituted for red bell pepper.*

VEGETABLE STROGANOFF

2 cups broccoli flowerets
2 cups sliced carrots
1 cup creamed cottage cheese
¾ cup sour cream
½ cup grated, fresh Parmesan cheese
3 Tablespoons butter
½ cup chopped onion
1 minced garlic clove or ½ teaspoon garlic powder
½ cup sliced mushrooms
2 Tablespoons flour
1 teaspoon salt
2 cups milk
⅓ cup sliced olives
1 12-ounce package linguini

1. Steam broccoli and carrots until crisp-tender.
2. In separate bowl, combine cottage cheese, sour cream and ¼ cup Parmesan cheese.
3. In large saucepan, melt butter and sauté onion, garlic and mushrooms until onion is crisp-tender.
4. Stir in flour and salt. Cook until mixture is smooth and bubbly.
5. Gradually add milk. Cook until mixture is smooth and thickened, stirring constantly.
6. Add olives and steamed vegetables.
7. Stir about 1 cup hot vegetable mixture into sour cream mixture. Stir sour cream mixture into vegetable mixture. Heat thoroughly. Do not boil.
8. Cook linguini. Drain and rinse with hot water.
9. Combine hot linguini and vegetable mixture.
10. Place on serving platter. Sprinkle with remaining Parmesan cheese.

Preparation Time: 35 minutes   Serves: 6-8
Cooking Time: 30 minutes

CHEESE GRITS
"Kiss my grits"

1 cup grits
4 cups boiling water
½ cup butter
1 5-ounce jar sharp cheese spread
1 beaten egg and milk to equal 1 cup

1. Add grits to boiling water. Cook, covered, until thickened, approximately 5 minutes.
2. When thickened, add butter, cheese, egg and milk.
3. Pour mixture into greased 9 x 9-inch baking dish.
4. Bake at 350 degrees for 1 hour.

Preparation Time: 15 minutes   Serves: 6-8
Cooking Time: 5 minutes
Baking Time: 1 hour

CHILE-CHEESE RICE CASSEROLE

1 cup chopped onion
¼ cup butter
4 cups cooked, hot white rice
2 cups sour cream
1 cup cottage cheese
1 crumbled bay leaf
½ teaspoon salt
3 4-ounce cans whole green chiles, halved lengthwise, leaving seeds
2 cups grated sharp Cheddar cheese
Chopped parsley, optional

1. In skillet, sauté onion in butter until golden, about 5 minutes. Remove from heat.
2. Stir in hot rice, sour cream, cottage cheese, bay leaf and salt. Toss lightly, mixing well.
3. In lightly greased 9 x 13-inch baking dish, layer half of rice mixture in bottom of dish, then half of green chiles and cheese. Repeat.
4. Bake uncovered at 375 degrees for 25 minutes or until hot and bubbly.

Preparation Time:	**15 minutes**	**Serves:**	**8-10**
Cooking Time:	**5 minutes**		
Baking Time:	**25 minutes**		

Serving Suggestion: *Garnish with chopped parsley.*
Variations: *Substitute 1 cup sour cream and 1 11-ounce can cream of mushroom soup for 2 cups sour cream. Use 2 cans green chiles instead of 3 cans and remove seeds for milder taste.*

CURRIED RICE-MUSHROOM CASSEROLE

2½ cups water
1 teaspoon salt
1 cup uncooked, long-grain white rice (3 cups cooked rice)
¼ cup plus 2 Tablespoons margarine
1 2½-ounce jar drained, sliced mushrooms
1 chopped, medium onion
¾ teaspoon curry powder
¼ teaspoon paprika
3 peeled, sliced tomatoes
¾ cup finely crushed Rice Krispies
1 cup grated sharp Cheddar cheese

1. In heavy saucepan, bring to boil water. Add salt and rice. Cook, covered, for about 25 minutes on very low heat until rice is tender and water is absorbed.
2. Melt ¼ cup margarine in skillet. Add mushrooms and onion. Cook until almost tender.
3. Add cooked rice to mushroom-onion mixture.
4. Add curry powder and paprika. Mix well.
5. Arrange layer of ½ of tomatoes in bottom of buttered 11 x 7-inch baking dish.
6. Spoon rice mixture over tomatoes.
7. Cover with remaining sliced tomatoes.
8. Melt 2 Tablespoons margarine. Add cereal crumbs and cheese. Sprinkle over tomatoes.
9. Bake at 350 degrees for 25-30 minutes.

Preparation Time:	**45 minutes**	**Serves:**	**6-8**
Baking Time:	**25-30 minutes**		

DOLMAS

2½ cups chopped onions
1 cup olive oil
½ cup uncooked rice
½ cup finely chopped parsley
¼ cup currants
¼ cup pine nuts
¼ cup tomato purée
½ cup water
¼ teaspoon allspice
¼ teaspoon cinnamon
1 Tablespoon salt
35 canned grape leaves

1. Sauté onions in oil until golden.
2. Add rice and cook, covered, ½ hour.
3. Add remaining ingredients except grape leaves and cook 5 minutes. Cool slightly.
4. Place 2 teaspoons of mixture on each grape leaf and roll up like a package or envelope.
5. In bottom of 11 x 7-inch baking pan, place lettuce leaves or extra grape leaves to prevent dolmas from burning.
6. Stack dolmas side-by-side on lettuce leaves. Weight down dolmas with dinner plate. Pour on water to cover plate.
7. Cook, covered at 350 degrees for 1 hour.
8. Let dolmas cool in liquid, then place in refrigerator to chill.

Preparation Time:	1½ hours	**Yield:**	35 dolmas
Cooking Time:	1 hour		
Chilling Time:	6-8 hours		

Serving Suggestion: *Serve cold as appetizer or hot as entrée.*

FRIED RICE

2 eggs
3 Tablespoons oil
1 cup frozen green peas
½ cup sliced, fresh mushrooms
5 cups chilled, cooked rice
1 teaspoon garlic powder
½ teaspoon salt
4 Tablespoons soy sauce
½ cup finely chopped green onion

1. Scramble eggs in oil.
2. Add frozen peas and mushrooms. Stir-fry slightly.
3. Add rice and seasonings. Stir-fry.
4. Just before serving, add green onions.
5. Serve warm.

Preparation Time:	15 minutes	**Serves:**	6-8
Cooking Time:	15 minutes		

MEXICAN RICE
"Ole amigos"

1 diced onion
1 diced green pepper
3 minced garlic cloves
1½ cups rice
¼ cup oil
2 cups peeled, diced tomatoes
3 cups water
1 teaspoon cumin
1 teaspoon oregano
1 teaspoon paprika
1 envelope G. Washington's Golden Seasoning and Broth

1. In large saucepan, sauté onion, pepper, garlic and rice in oil until rice is golden.
2. Add remaining ingredients and stir, bringing to boil.
3. Simmer covered until rice is cooked, about 20 minutes.

Preparation Time: **20 minutes**   **Serves:**   **8-10**
Cooking Time: **30 minutes**
Variation: *After cooking, add ½ cup frozen peas.*

PARSLEY RICE WITH ALMONDS AND MONTEREY JACK CHEESE

4 cups chicken-style broth
2 cups raw, long-grain white rice
1 teaspoon salt
½ cup thinly sliced green onions
½ cup sliced almonds
¼ cup butter
½ cup chopped fresh parsley
2 cups sour cream
1 pound grated Monterey Jack cheese

1. In 2-quart saucepan, bring chicken-style broth to boil. Stir in rice and salt.
2. Cover and reduce heat to low. Simmer about 20 minutes, or until rice has absorbed liquid.
3. In small skillet, saute onions and almonds in butter over medium heat, stirring occasionally, until onions are soft and almonds are slightly toasted, about 5 minutes.
4. Fold parsley into rice. Add sour cream and onion-almond mixture.
5. Spread half of rice mixture into 9 x 13-inch baking dish.
6. Sprinkle half of cheese over rice mixture.
7. Repeat with remaining rice and top with cheese.
8. Bake at 350 degrees for 30 minutes until cheese is melted and golden on top.

Preparation Time: **20 minutes**   **Serves:**   **10-12**
Cooking Time: **25 minutes**
Baking Time: **30 minutes**

RICE PILAF

8-10 Servings

1 cup chopped onion
5 Tablespoons margarine
6 cups cooked, hot rice (2½ cups raw rice)
1 5-ounce package frozen peas, cooked
1-2 medium tomatoes, cut in wedges
½ cup slivered, toasted, blanched almonds
1 teaspoon salt or to taste
½ teaspoon paprika
1 teaspoon crushed rosemary

1. In large stockpot, sauté onion in margarine.
2. Add rice and remaining ingredients. Toss together lightly.
3. Serve hot.

Preparation Time:	15 minutes
Cooking Time:	5-10 minutes

50 Servings

3 cups chopped onion
1½ cups margarine
30 cups cooked, hot rice (12 cups raw rice)
2½ 10-ounce packages frozen peas, cooked
8 medium tomatoes, cut in wedges
2½ cups slivered, toasted, blanched almonds
1½ Tablespoons salt or to taste
1¼ teaspoons paprika
1 Tablespoon crushed rosemary

100 Servings

6 cups chopped onion
3 cups margarine
60 cups cooked, hot rice (24 cups raw rice)
5 10-ounce packages frozen peas, cooked
16 medium tomatoes, cut in wedges
5 cups slivered, toasted, blanched almonds
3 Tablespoons salt or to taste
2½ teaspoons paprika
2 Tablespoons crushed rosemary

TURKISH PILAF
"A snap for a working gal"

3 cups cooked rice
½ cup chopped green pepper
1 4-ounce can chopped mushrooms
1 chopped, small onion
1 cup grated Cheddar cheese
2 Tablespoons butter
¼ teaspoon thyme
1 11-ounce can cream of mushroom soup
1 11-ounce can tomato soup

1. Combine all ingredients.
2. Bake in greased 8 x 8-inch baking dish at 350 degrees for 35-45 minutes.

Preparation Time: **15 minutes**   **Serves:**   **6-8**
Baking Time: **35-45 minutes**

RICE-MUSHROOM PILAF
"This won't get sticky"

2 cubes chicken-style bouillon or 2 teaspoons chicken-style seasoning
1 cup hot water
1 cup uncooked rice
1 chopped, large onion
½ chopped green pepper
1 3-ounce can drained, sliced mushrooms
Dash of savory seasoning
Salt to taste
½ cup slivered, blanched almonds

1. Dissolve bouillon in hot water.
2. Combine remaining ingredients, reserving some almonds to garnish top.
3. Pour into 9 x 13-inch baking dish.
4. Bake at 350 degrees for 1 hour. Stir once or twice while baking. Rice should be crispy and brown.
5. Garnish with remaining almonds.

Preparation Time: **20 minutes**   **Serves:**   **6-8**
Baking Time: **1 hour**

HAYSTACK SPECIAL
"This sauce makes anything special!"

Sauce

1 chopped, medium onion
1 chopped green pepper
1 cup chopped celery
6-7 Tablespoons butter or margarine
Dash oregano
1¼ teaspoons cumin
¼ teaspoon garlic powder
Salt to taste
¼ cup flour
1 12-ounce can tomatoes
1 16-ounce can tomato sauce
1 4-ounce can diced green chiles

1. Sauté onion, green pepper and celery in 2-3 Tablespoons butter until tender.
2. Add oregano, cumin, garlic powder and salt.
3. Mix flour with 4 Tablespoons butter to form paste. Stir into vegetables.
4. Add tomatoes, tomato sauce and chiles. Cook and stir until mixture begins to boil.
5. Simmer for 15-20 minutes.

Preparation Time:	**30 minutes**	**Yield:**	**4 cups sauce**
Cooking Time:	**20 minutes**		**May do ahead 1-2 days**

Haystack

Crushed corn chips
Refried beans or chili
Toppings

   Grated Monterey Jack cheese
   Grated Cheddar cheese
   Guacamole
   Sour cream
   Chopped green onions
   Diced olives
   Sauce

Assemble as desired.

GORGONZOLA CREAM SAUCE

1 finely chopped onion
2 Tablespoons butter
½ pound softened cream cheese
3 ounces Gorgonzola cheese
3 cups heavy cream
1 cup milk

1. Sauté onions in butter until transparent.
2. Add cream cheese and Gorgonzola cheese. Stir until cheeses are melted and sauce is smooth.
3. Add cream and milk. Bring to soft boil and cook until sauce is reduced to creamy consistency.

Preparation Time: **20 minutes**   **Yield:**   **4 cups**
Cooking Time: **15 minutes**
Serving Suggestion: *Serve over Pecan Loaf or pasta.*

MUSHROOM-ONION CREAM SAUCE

"Makes beautiful gravy"

½ pound thinly sliced mushrooms
1 finely chopped onion
2 finely chopped shallots
2 minced garlic cloves
4 Tablespoons butter
2 Tablespoons flour
10½ ounces chicken-style broth
1 teaspoon beef-style seasoning
¾ cup cream
Salt to taste

1. Sauté mushrooms, onion, shallots and garlic in butter until onions are soft.
2. Add flour and cook for 2 minutes, stirring well.
3. Add remaining ingredients and cook, stirring until sauce is thickened.

Preparation Time: **10-15 minutes**   **Yield:**   **1½ cups**
Cooking Time: **15 minutes**

PESTO

"Distinct and flavorful"

1/2 cup pine nuts
4 garlic cloves
3-4 cups fresh basil leaves
1/4 pound grated, fresh Parmesan cheese
1/4 pound grated, fresh Romano cheese
1-1 1/2 cups olive oil

1. In food processor or blender, grind first 6 ingredients with 1/2 cup olive oil.
2. Add remaining oil and process until smooth.

Preparation Time: **15 minutes**   **Yield:**   **3 cups**
Variation: *Walnuts, butter, parsley or fresh spinach may be added.*

SOUR CREAM-MUSHROOM GRAVY

10 Servings

1 teaspoon oil
1-2 chopped green onions
1 crushed garlic clove
1 teaspoon soy sauce
2/3 cup sour cream
1/2 11-ounce can cream of mushroom soup

1. In oil, sauté onions until soft. Add garlic and continue to sauté 1 minute.
2. Add soy sauce, sour cream and mushroom soup. Heat through.

Preparation Time: **15 minutes**   **Yield:**   **1 1/2 cups**

20 Servings

2 teaspoons oil
4-5 chopped green onions
2 crushed garlic cloves
2 teaspoons soy sauce
1 1/3 cups sour cream
1 11-ounce can cream of mushroom soup

                                                  Yield: **3 cups**

100 Servings

3 Tablespoons plus 1 teaspoon oil
20-25 chopped green onions
10 crushed garlic cloves
3 Tablespoons plus 1 teaspoon soy sauce
6 2/3 cups sour cream
5 11-ounce cans cream of mushroom soup

                                        Yield: **3 3/4 quarts**

APRICOT BARBECUE SAUCE

10 Servings

¼ cup oil
¼ cup vinegar or lemon juice
¾ cup apricot jam
½ cup catsup
2 Tablespoons brown sugar
2 Tablespoons grated onion
½ teaspoon salt
½ teaspoon oregano
Dash hot pepper sauce

1. Mix all ingredients.
2. Bring to boil.

Preparation Time: **10 minutes**   **Yield:**   **2 cups**
Cooking Time: **5 minutes**
Serving Suggestion: *Pour over Walnut Balls and bake.*

20 Servings

½ cup oil
½ cup vinegar or lemon juice
1½ cups apricot jam
1 cup catsup
4 Tablespoons brown sugar
4 Tablespoons grated onion
1 teaspoon salt
1 teaspoon oregano
3-4 drops hot pepper sauce

                                         Yield: **4 cups**

100 Servings

2½ cups oil
2½ cups vinegar
7½ cups apricot jam
5 cups catsup
1¼ cups brown sugar
1¼ cups grated onion
4-5 teaspoons salt
4-5 teaspoons oregano
1½ teaspoons hot pepper sauce

                                         Yield: **5 quarts**

ASPARAGUS CASSEROLE

2 cups cubed, soft, brown bread
1 cup grated Cheddar cheese
4 Tablespoons butter
1 package frozen asparagus, cut in bite-size pieces
2 Tablespoons minced onion
2 Tablespoons flour
½ teaspoon salt
½ teaspoon Accent
1½ cups milk
1 large sliced tomato
Fresh minced dill weed

1. Mix bread cubes, ½ cup grated cheese and 2 Tablespoons butter.
2. Line greased 8 x 8-inch baking dish with half of bread mixture.
3. Add layer of asparagus.
4. Sauté onion in 2 Tablespoons butter.
5. Add flour, salt and Accent to onion. Remove from heat.
6. Stir in milk and ½ cup cheese.
7. Pour over asparagus.
8. Arrange tomato slices over top.
9. Cover with remaining bread mixture. Sprinkle with dill.
10. Bake at 350 degrees for 25 minutes.

Preparation Time: **30 minutes**   **Serves:**   **4-6**
Baking Time: **25 minutes**
Variation: *Use fresh asparagus or French style green beans.*

BROCCOLI MUFFINS

½ cup chopped onion
2 Tablespoons margarine
⅔ cup water
½ cup sour cream
2 cups buttermilk pancake mix
1 cup shredded Cheddar cheese
1 9-ounce package frozen cut broccoli, thawed and well-drained
1 4½-ounce can drained, sliced mushrooms

1. In small saucepan, sauté onion in margarine until tender.
2. In large bowl, combine water, sour cream and sautéed onion.
3. Add pancake mix and cheese. Blend well.
4. Fold in broccoli and mushrooms.
5. Spoon mixture into greased muffin tins, filling about ½ full.
6. Bake at 375 degrees for 35-45 minutes or until deep golden brown.
7. Cool 5 minutes. Remove from tins.

Preparation Time: **15 minutes**   **Yield:**   **20 muffins**
Baking Time: **35-45 minutes**
Serving Suggestion: *Serve warm with Cheese Sauce.*
Variation: *Mixture may be baked in greased 9-inch square pan or 6 10-ounce custard cups.*

ARTICHOKE-PARMESAN STRUDEL
"Always gets compliments"

1 finely chopped onion
2 minced garlic cloves
¼ cup butter
3 6-ounce jars drained, chopped, marinated artichoke hearts
1 5-ounce package grated, fresh Parmesan cheese
1 cup cottage cheese
1 8-ounce package softened cream cheese
3 eggs
½ cup cracker crumbs
1 teaspoon marjoram
1 teaspoon parsley
¾ teaspoon tarragon
1 teaspoon garlic salt
15 phyllo sheets
Butter for phyllo

1. Sauté onion and garlic in butter.
2. Mix together remaining ingredients except phyllo sheets and butter for phyllo.
3. Pick up 1 sheet of phyllo, spread thoroughly with melted butter. Add second, third, fourth and fifth sheets, buttering between each layer.
4. Place 2 cups of filling in log-type roll at bottom of sheets.

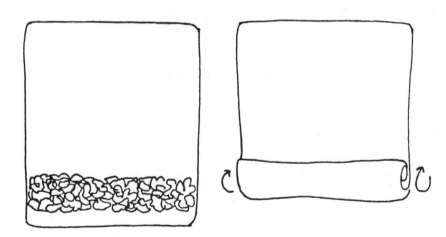

5. Tuck in sides and roll jellyroll fashion.
6. Butter top and sides of completed roll.
7. Continue with other sheets, forming 3 rolls.
8. Place roll on greased cookie sheet. Bake at 350 degrees for 30 minutes.

Preparation Time:	45 minutes	**Yield:**	3 rolls
Baking Time:	30 minutes		

Tip: *Before baking, rolls may be wrapped in waxed paper and frozen. Upon removing from freezer, unwrap and place on cookie sheets. Thaw and do not touch again until baked.*

BROCCOLI SOUFFLE ROLL

1 pound chopped broccoli
6 Tablespoons butter or margarine
¾ cup flour
1 teaspoon dry mustard
½ teaspoon salt
3½ cups milk
4 eggs
1 cup shredded Cheddar or longhorn cheese

1. Steam broccoli over boiling water just until crisp-tender, about 4-6 minutes.
2. Line bottom of greased jellyroll pan with foil. Grease and lightly flour foil and set pan aside.
3. Melt butter in 3-quart pan over medium heat. Stir in flour, mustard and salt. Cook, stirring, until flour is bubbly.
4. Gradually pour in 3 cups milk and continue cooking, stirring until sauce is smooth and thickened, about 8-10 minutes. Measure out 1 cup of this sauce and set aside.
5. Separate eggs. Beat yolks lightly and gradually beat in all but the 1 cup of reserved sauce.
6. Beat egg whites until stiff, moist peaks form. Fold in egg yolk mixture. Pour into prepared pan.
7. Bake at 325 degrees for 35-40 minutes or until soufflé is golden brown and center springs back when lightly touched.
8. In pan over medium heat, combine reserved sauce and ½ cup milk. Stir in cheese and cook, stirring, until cheese is melted. Add more mustard and salt, if desired.
9. Measure out 1 cup of cheese sauce and combine with chopped broccoli.
10. When soufflé is done, immediately invert onto clean towel. Starting at 1 narrow end, spread broccoli mixture over ¾ of soufflé. Using towel for support, roll up soufflé to enclose filling.
11. Place seam-side down on serving platter. If not served at once, place in 200-degree oven for as long as 30 minutes.
12. Reheat remaining cheese sauce over low heat, then pour over roll.

Preparation Time: **45 minutes**   **Serves:**   **8**
Baking Time: **40 minutes**
Serving Suggestion: *Garnish serving platter with cherry tomatoes or tomato wedges and watercress for festive color combination.*

CHILE-CORN CASSEROLE
"Make ahead - bake later"

2 cups fresh or frozen corn
¼ cup melted butter
2 beaten eggs
½ cup cornmeal
1 4-ounce can diced green chiles
½ teaspoon salt
1 cup sour cream
1 cup diced Monterey Jack cheese

1. Measure 2 cups of corn after corn has been slighted pulsated in food processor.
2. Combine all ingredients except cheese
3. Sprinkle cheese on top.
4. Bake in greased 8 x 8-inch baking dish at 350 degrees for 40-60 minutes.

Preparation Time:	**15 minutes**	**Serves:**	**6**
Baking Time:	**45-60 minutes**	**May do ahead**	

Tip: *May double recipe and bake in 9 x 13-inch dish.*

EGG FOO YONG

3 Tablespoons oil
1 cup chopped onion
½ cup chopped celery
1 cup thinly sliced mushrooms
¼ cup chopped green pepper
2 Tablespoons flour
½ teaspoon Accent
¼ teaspoon garlic salt
2 Tablespoons soy sauce
6 well-beaten eggs
1 14-ounce can drained, chop suey vegetables

1. In oil, sauté onion, celery, mushrooms and green pepper. Remove from heat.
2. Add remaining ingredients. Mix well.
3. Fry ⅓ cup mixture per patty in oiled pan.
4. Keep warm in 200-degree oven.

Sauce

1¼ cups water
2 Tablespoons soy sauce
2 Tablespoons flour
1 Tablespoon sugar

1. Combine all ingredients. Stir as mixture comes to boil.
2. Serve hot over Egg Foo Yong.

Preparation Time:	**45 minutes**	**Yield:**	**9-10 patties**
Cooking Time:	**20 minutes**		

MUSHROOM-ARTICHOKE CREPES
"Viva L'Amour"

½ **pound sliced, fresh mushrooms**
2 finely minced shallots or green onions
2 finely minced garlic cloves
3 Tablespoons butter
3 Tablespoons flour
1 cup cream
⅓ **cup non-alcoholic white wine**
1 6-ounce jar drained, chopped, marinated artichoke hearts
1 4-ounce jar drained, chopped water chestnuts
1 cup grated Swiss cheese
1 teaspoon dill weed
¼ **teaspoon Worcestershire sauce**
Fine herbs to taste
Salt to taste
8 crepes
Lemon Butter (see recipe)

1. Sauté mushrooms with shallots and garlic in butter.
2. Add flour and stir for 2 minutes, cooking on medium-low heat.
3. Stir in cream and wine. Continue cooking and stirring until sauce thickens.
4. Add remaining ingredients except crepes and Lemon Butter.
5. Place about 2 Tablespoons filling on each crepe and roll up jellyroll fashion.
6. Place crepes seam down in greased 9 x 9-inch baking dish. Brush tops with Lemon Butter.
7. Heat crepes at 350 degrees for 15-20 minutes.

Preparation Time:	**30 minutes**	**Serves:**	**8**
Heating Time:	**15-20 minutes**		

MUSHROOM FRITTATA

1 cup sliced, fresh mushrooms
⅔ cup chopped onion
⅔ cup chopped green pepper
1 cup thinly sliced zucchini
1 minced garlic clove
2 teaspoons oil
5 eggs
⅓ cup half-and-half
½ teaspoon salt
1½ cups Italian seasoned bread crumbs
1 cup grated Cheddar cheese
1 8-ounce package cream cheese, cut into ½-inch cubes

1. Sauté vegetables and garlic in oil.
2. Beat eggs, half-and-half and salt together. Combine with sautéed vegetables.
3. Add bread crumbs and Cheddar cheese.
4. Place in greased 8 x 8-inch baking dish.
5. Poke cream cheese cubes into mixture.
6. Bake at 350 degrees for 35-45 minutes.
7. Cool for 10 minutes before serving.

Preparation Time:	**25 minutes**	**Serves:**	**6**
Baking Time:	**35-45 minutes**		
Cooling Time:	**10 minutes**		

Tip: *To double recipe, place in 9 x 13-inch baking dish and bake 45-60 minutes.*

FLORENTINE CREPES

10 Servings

1 10-ounce package frozen, chopped spinach, cooked and squeezed dry
¼ teaspoon salt
⅔ cup ricotta cheese
3 Tablespoons plus 1 teaspoon half-and-half
2 slightly beaten eggs
Pinch of nutmeg
10 crepes
2 Tablespoons melted butter
2 Tablespoons grated, fresh Parmesan cheese

1. Mix spinach and salt.
2. Add ricotta, half-and-half, eggs and nutmeg. Mix well.
3. Fill crepes with spinach mixture.
4. Roll up and place in shallow baking dish.
5. Brush crepes with butter. Sprinkle with Parmesan cheese.
6. Heat at 350 degrees for 15-20 minutes.

Preparation Time:	30 minutes	Yield:	10 crepes
Assembly Time:	10 minutes		
Heating Time:	15-20 minutes		

50 Servings

6 10-ounce packages frozen, chopped spinach, cooked and squeezed dry
1½ teaspoons salt
3 cups ricotta cheese
1 cup half-and-half
8 slightly beaten eggs
⅓ teaspoon nutmeg
50 crepes
6 Tablespoons melted butter
¾ cup grated, fresh Parmesan cheese

| Yield: | 50 crepes |

100 Servings

12 10-ounce packages frozen, chopped spinach, cooked and squeezed dry
1 Tablespoon salt
6 cups ricotta cheese
2 cups half-and-half
17 slightly beaten eggs
¾ teaspoon nutmeg
100-108 crepes
¾ cup melted butter
1½ cups grated, fresh Parmesan cheese

| Yield: | 100 crepes |

SPINACH, MUSHROOM AND GRUYERE CHEESECAKE
"Rich and delicious"

½ cup melted, unsalted butter
1½ cups toasted, fine bread crumbs
5 8-ounce packages cream cheese, at room temperature
¼ cup whipping cream
½ teaspoon salt
¼-½ teaspoon freshly grated nutmeg
¼ teaspoon ground red pepper
4 eggs
½ cup shredded Gruyère cheese
1 10-ounce package frozen, chopped spinach, thawed and squeezed dry
2½ Tablespoons finely chopped green onion
½ pound finely chopped mushrooms
Salt to taste

1. Butter 9-inch springform pan with 1 Tablespoon unsalted butter.
2. Mix bread crumbs and 5 Tablespoons melted butter. Press mixture firmly into bottom and up sides of pan.
3. Bake at 350 degrees for 8-10 minutes. Cool.
4. Reduce oven temperature to 325 degrees.
5. Mix cream cheese, whipping cream, salt, nutmeg and red pepper in blender or food processor until smooth.
6. Blend eggs with cream mixture.
7. Divide mixture evenly between 2 medium bowls. Stir Gruyère cheese into 1 bowl. Mix spinach and onion into remaining bowl.
8. Pour spinach filling into greased springform pan.
9. Sauté mushrooms in remaining 2 Tablespoons butter in large skillet over medium-high heat. Cook until all moisture is evaporated, about 10 minutes, stirring frequently. Season with salt.
10. Spoon mushrooms over spinach filling.
11. Carefully pour cheese filling over mushrooms.
12. Set pan on baking sheet. Bake 1¼ hours.
13. Turn oven off. Cool cheesecake about 1 hour with door ajar.
14. Transfer cheesecake to rack. Remove sides of springform pan. Cool to room temperature before serving.

Preparation Time: **1 hour**   **Serves:**   **15**
Baking Time: **1¼ hours**
Variation: *Substitute Swiss cheese for Gruyère cheese.*

SPINACH SOUFFLE RING WITH MUSHROOM SAUCE
"Olive Oil should have had this for Popeye"

Soufflé Ring

4 Tablespoons butter
2 Tablespoons dry bread crumbs
1 Tablespoon diced green onions
3 Tablespoons flour
¼ teaspoon salt
¼ teaspoon nutmeg
1 cup half-and-half
1 pound or 4 cups fresh spinach, cooked, chopped and squeezed dry
4 egg yolks
4 stiffly beaten egg whites
Mushroom Sauce
Parsley, for garnish

1. Grease 4-cup ring mold with 1 Tablespoon butter. Sprinkle with bread crumbs. Set aside.
2. In large saucepan, melt remaining 3 Tablespoons butter.
3. Sauté onion until tender.
4. Stir in flour, salt and nutmeg. Cook until mixture is smooth and bubbly.
5. Gradually add half-and-half, cooking until mixture boils and thickens, stirring constantly.
6. Stir in spinach.
7. Blend small amount of hot mixture into egg yolks and return to saucepan. Cook only until mixture begins to bubble, stirring constantly.
8. Fold beaten egg whites into spinach mixture.
9. Spoon spinach mixture into prepared ring mold.
10. Place mold in pan containing about 1 inch hot water.
11. Bake at 325 degrees for 25-35 minutes or until knife inserted comes out clean.
12. Cool 5 minutes.
13. To serve, loosen edges of soufflé. Turn onto serving platter. Spoon Mushroom Sauce into center of ring. Garnish with parsley.

Mushroom Sauce.

2 4½-ounce jars drained, sliced mushrooms
3 Tablespoons butter
2 Tablespoons flour
¼ teaspoon salt
1½ cups half-and-half
2 Tablespoons chopped parsley

1. In saucepan, sauté mushrooms in butter. Stir in flour and salt.
2. Cook until mixture is smooth and bubbly.
3. Gradually add half-and-half. Cook until mixture boils and thickens, stirring constantly.
4. Stir in parsley.

Preparation Time:	**30 minutes**	**Serves:**	**6**
Baking Time:	**25-35 minutes**		
Cooking Time:	**15 minutes**		

329

SPINACH TORTILLA CASSEROLE

1 16-ounce can vegetarian burger
1 chopped onion
1 package taco seasoning mix
1 cup water
Garlic powder to taste
Salt to taste
1 cup medium taco sauce
10 corn tortillas
2 10-ounce packages frozen, chopped spinach, thawed and squeezed dry
3 cups shredded Monterey Jack cheese
1 cup sour cream

1. Combine burger, onion, taco seasoning mix and water. Cook 10 minutes.
2. Add garlic powder and salt.
3. In 9 x 13-inch baking dish, pour ½ cup taco sauce to cover bottom.
4. Coat 5 tortillas with taco sauce and place in baking dish.
5. Add ½ spinach to burger mixture. Spread on tortillas in dish.
6. Layer ½ cheese.
7. Add layer of 5 tortillas dipped in remaining taco sauce.
8. Spread sour cream on tortilla layer.
9. Spread remaining spinach and then remaining cheese.
10. Bake at 375 degrees for 25 minutes with dish covered with foil and another 25 minutes uncovered.

Preparation Time: 25 minutes   **Serves:** 8-10
Baking Time: 50 minutes

VEGETABLE BURRITOS
"A gardener's delight"

Filling

2 Tablespoons oil
1 thinly sliced, large onion
2 pressed garlic cloves
1 large green pepper, cut in thin strips
4 medium zucchini, cut in ¼-inch slices
½ pound sliced mushrooms
2 thinly sliced, medium carrots
4 diced, medium tomatoes
1 4-ounce can drained, diced green chiles
½ teaspoon chili powder
1 teaspoon salt
½ teaspoon oregano leaves
¼ teaspoon ground cumin
1 2½-ounce can drained, sliced olives
12 flour tortillas

Toppings

Salsa
Sour cream
Thinly sliced green onions
Sunflower seeds
1½ cups grated Monterey Jack cheese or jalapeño cheese
1½ cups grated Cheddar cheese

1. In 12-inch fry pan, add oil and place over medium heat. Add onion and garlic. Sauté until onion is limp.
2. Add vegetables and seasonings. Bring to boil, cover and lower heat. Simmer until vegetables are barely tender, about 5 minutes. Uncover and gently boil, stirring occasionally, until all liquid has evaporated and vegetables are tender, about 5-10 minutes.
3. Add olives to vegetable mixture.
4. To heat tortillas, wrap in foil and place in 350-degree oven until hot, about 20 minutes.
5. To serve, place ¼ cup Filling in flour tortilla and roll up. Place burrito on plate, seam down, and cover with favorite Toppings.

Preparation Time:	1 hour	**Yield:**	12 burritos
Cooking Time:	30 minutes	**May do Filling 1 day ahead**	
Heating Time:	20 minutes		

VEGETABLE TORTA
"Striking to the eye and palate"

1 pound frozen puff pastry sheets

Egg Layer

12 eggs
¼ cup half-and-half (milk may be used)
Pinch each of oregano, marjoram, thyme and basil
½ teaspoon salt
2 Tablespoons butter

1. Lightly beat eggs, half-and-half and seasonings.
2. Scramble in butter. Set aside.

Spinach Layer

3 Tablespoons chopped, fresh parsley
3 Tablespoons minced, fresh chives
1 Tablespoon butter
3 10-ounce packages frozen, chopped spinach, thawed and squeezed dry
1 teaspoon salt
¼ teaspoon nutmeg

1. Sauté parsley and chives in butter.
2. Add spinach and seasonings. Mix well. Set aside.

Cheese Layer

¾ pound thinly sliced Swiss cheese
¼ cup grated, fresh Parmesan cheese

Pepper Layer

1 diced, large red bell pepper
⅓ cup chopped pimentos
1 Tablespoon butter

Sauté bell pepper and pimentos in butter. Set aside.

Mushroom Layer

1 pound sliced, fresh mushrooms
2 minced garlic cloves
1 Tablespoon butter

Sauté mushrooms and garlic in butter. Set aside.

Continued

VEGETABLE TORTA — Continued

Puff Pastry

1. Roll out 1 sheet plus ⅓ of second sheet to ¼-inch thickness.
2. Line bottom and sides of lightly greased 8-inch springform pan, leaving ½-inch overhang.

To Assemble

1 beaten egg white

1. Layer in pan in order listed:
   ½ Egg Layer mixture
   ½ Spinach Layer mixture
   ½ Cheese Layer mixture
   All of Pepper Layer mixture
   ½ Cheese Layer mixture
   ½ Spinach Layer mixture
   ½ Egg Layer mixture
2. Roll remaining pastry.
3. Cut into 8-inch circle.
4. Place on top of torta.
5. Pull up overhanging pastry to seal to the top and make a fluted edge.
6. Create air vents.
7. Decorate with scraps of puff pastry in shapes of leaves, etc.
8. Brush with beaten egg white.
9. Bake at 425 degrees for 10 minutes.
10. Reduce heat to 400 degrees for 45 minutes.
11. Remove from oven and cool slightly.
12. Release from pan to serve.
13. Cut with electric knife or thin, sharp knife. Serve warm or at room temperature.

Preparation Time: **45-60 minutes**   **Serves:**   **12**
Baking Time: **55 minutes**   **May do ahead**

TORTILLA DRY SOUP

12 corn tortillas
⅓ cup plus 2 Tablespoons vegetable or olive oil
1 cup minced onion
1 4-ounce can diced green chiles
1 cup half-and-half or evaporated milk
1 cup tomato purée
Salt to taste
½ pound shredded Monterey Jack cheese
2 Tablespoons butter

1. Cut tortillas into thin strips. Sauté in ⅓ cup oil until crisp, but not brown. Drain on paper towel.
2. Sauté onion in 2 Tablespoons oil until transparent. Add chiles, cream and tomato puree. Simmer 10 minutes. Add salt.
3. Grease 9 x 13-inch baking dish. Cover bottom with half of tortilla strips. Pour half of sauce over tortillas and add half of shredded cheese.
4. Repeat layers, ending with shredded cheese. Dot with butter.
5. Bake at 350 degrees for 30 minutes.

Preparation Time:	**30 minutes**	**Serves:**	**6**
Baking Time:	**30 minutes**		

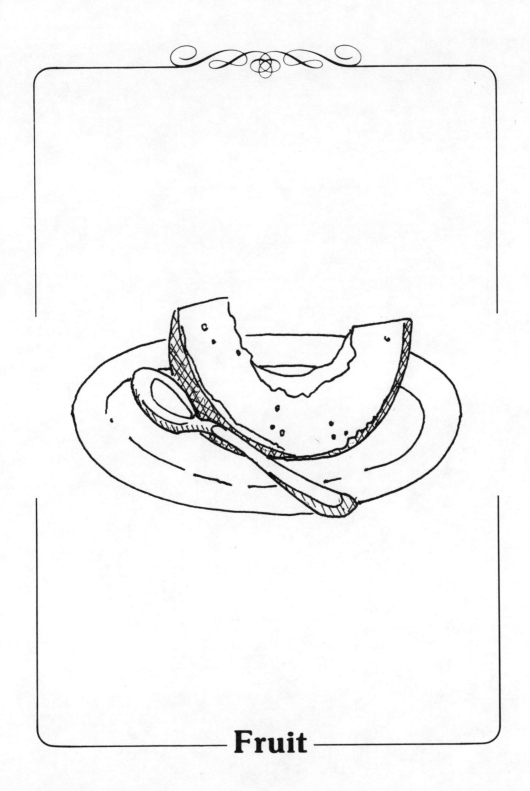

Fruit

APPLE ON A STICK

8 medium, red apples
8 wooden skewers
3 cups sugar
½ cup light corn syrup
½ cup water
1 drop oil of cinnamon (available at pharmacy)
1 teaspoon red food coloring

1. Wash and dry apples. Remove stems and insert skewers into stem end.
2. In saucepan, combine sugar, corn syrup and water. Cook over medium heat until temperature is at soft crack stage, 285 degrees. Remove from heat.
3. Add oil of cinnamon and coloring. Mix.
4. Dip each apple by skewer, covering apple with syrup.
5. Place on lightly buttered baking sheet to cool.

Preparation Time: **30 minutes** **Yield:** **8 apples**

HOT CURRIED FRUIT

"Unusual - especially good for fall or winter days"

1 16-ounce can each of pears, apricots, peaches, pineapple chunks and seedless bing cherries
6 Tablespoons butter
1 cup brown sugar
2 teaspoons curry powder
½ teaspoon nutmeg
½ cup 7-UP
Sour cream, optional

1. Drain fruit well. Cut into large pieces.
2. Over medium heat, melt butter, brown sugar, curry powder and nutmeg. Cook 3-5 minutes.
3. Grease 2-quart casserole dish with butter.
4. Spoon half of fruit for first layer and pour half of brown sugar sauce over fruit. Repeat 1 time.
5. Pour 7-UP over all layers.
6. Bake at 325 degrees for 1 hour.
7. Serve hot with sour cream as topping.

Preparation Time: **20 minutes** **Serves:** **10-12**
Baking Time: **1 hour** **May do ahead and refrigerate**
Tip: *Reheat on stove over low heat, stirring gently to avoid breaking up fruit.*

SPECIAL APPLESAUCE

1 16-ounce jar applesauce
6 finely chopped, dried apricots
¼ cup dried black currants

Combine all ingredients. Refrigerate overnight.

Preparation Time:	**15 minutes**	**Yield:**	**2½ cups**
Standing Time:	**6-8 hours**	**Must do ahead**	

SPICED PEACHES

1 pound sugar
1 cup white vinegar
2 sticks cinnamon
2 teaspoons whole cloves
2½ teaspoons whole allspice
½ cup peach juice
3 16-ounce cans peach halves

1. In saucepan, mix sugar and vinegar. Stir until sugar is dissolved.
2. Tie spices in cheesecloth.
3. Add juice and spice to sugar and vinegar. Boil 5 minutes.
4. Add peaches and boil a few minutes longer.
5. Let stand in syrup overnight or longer.
6. Remove spices.

Preparation Time:	**25 minutes**	**Serves:**	**10-12**
Standing Time:	**10-12 hours**	**Must do ahead**	

Pizza

BROCCOLI-ONION PIZZA

"You were wondering what to do with the broccoli"

1 cup frozen broccoli cuts, thawed and drained
¼ cup chopped onion
2 minced garlic cloves
2 Tablespoons olive or vegetable oil
1 large frozen cheese or vegetable pizza
½ cup shredded Cheddar cheese

1. In skillet, sauté broccoli, onion and garlic in oil until crisp-tender.
2. Spoon hot mixture evenly over frozen pizza.
3. Sprinkle with cheese.
4. Bake at 450 degrees for 8-10 minutes or until center is hot.

Preparation Time: **15 minutes**   **Serves:**   **4**
Baking Time: **8-10 minutes**
Tip: *For crispier crust, sprinkle a little cornmeal on baking sheet.*

FRENCH BREAD PIZZA

"This loses nothing in the translation"

1 pound loaf French bread
1 6-ounce can tomato paste
1 teaspoon oregano leaves
1 teaspoon basil leaves
1 Tablespoon olive or vegetable oil
1 minced garlic clove
1 2½-ounce jar drained, sliced mushrooms
8 ounces sliced mozzarella or provolone cheese, cut into triangles
1 green pepper, sliced into rings
1 medium red onion, sliced into rings

1. Slice bread in half lengthwise. Place on ungreased cookie sheet, cut-sides up.
2. In small bowl, combine tomato paste, oregano, basil, oil and garlic.
3. Spread tomato mixture on cut surface of bread halves. Top with mushrooms.
4. Arrange cheese, overlapping and alternating with green pepper and onion rings.
5. Bake at 375 degrees for 15-20 minutes or until cheese is melted.

Preparation Time: **20 minutes**   **Serves:**   **6**
Baking Time: **15-20 minutes**

MINI-PIZZAS

"A teenage favorite"

½ pound grated Colby cheese
½ pound grated Monterey Jack cheese
1 8-ounce can tomato sauce
5 chopped green onions
1 4-ounce can chopped green chiles
1 6-8-ounce jar chopped pimento-stuffed olives
1 minced garlic clove
Salt to taste
12 halved English muffins

1. Mix all ingredients and spread on halved muffins.
2. Broil in 300-degree oven for 5 minutes, until lightly browned.

Preparation Time: **15 minutes**   **Yield:**   **24 mini-pizzas**
Broiling Time: **5-15 minutes**
Tip: *Toast muffins before covering with toppings.*

MUSHROOM-ARTICHOKE PIZZA

"An exciting marriage of flavors"

1 6-ounce jar marinated artichoke hearts
1 4½-ounce jar drained, sliced mushrooms
1 thinly sliced, small onion
1 minced garlic clove
3-4 sliced cherry tomatoes
1 large frozen cheese or vegetable pizza
½ cup grated, fresh Parmesan cheese
1 Tablespoon chopped fresh parsley, optional

1. Drain artichokes, reserving 2 Tablespoons marinade.
2. Cut artichokes into ½-inch pieces.
3. In skillet, sauté mushrooms, onion and garlic in reserved marinade until crisp-tender. Stir in tomatoes and artichoke pieces. Heat 1 minute.
4. Spoon hot vegetable mixture over frozen pizza.
5. Sprinkle with cheese and parsley.
6. Bake at 450 degrees for 8-10 minutes or until center is hot.

Preparation Time: **20 minutes**   **Serves:**   **4**
Baking Time: **8-10 minutes**
Tip: *For crispier crust, sprinkle a little cornmeal on baking sheet.*

OLIVE-AVOCADO PIZZA
"Cholesterol special"

1 2¼-ounce can drained, sliced ripe olives
1 large frozen cheese or vegetable pizza
½ cup shredded Cheddar cheese
8 slices avocado
Alfalfa sprouts, optional

1. Sprinkle olives evenly over frozen pizza. Top with cheese.
2. Bake at 450 degrees for 8-10 minutes or until center is hot.
3. Arrange avocado slices on pizza. Garnish with alfalfa sprouts, if desired.

Preparation Time:	**15 minutes**	**Serves:**	**4**
Baking Time:	**8-10 minutes**		

Tip: For crispier crust, sprinkle a little cornmeal on baking sheet.

PIZZA MUFFINS
"More, more"

12 halved English muffins
1 14-ounce jar pizza sauce
1 cup grated mozzarella cheese
1 cup grated Cheddar cheese

Toppings

    Olives
    Diced green chiles
    Chopped onion
    Diced tomatoes

1. Cover each muffin half with pizza sauce, cheese and Toppings.
2. Broil until cheese melts.

Preparation Time:	**20 minutes**	**Yield:**	**24 pizza muffins**
Broiling Time:	**3-5 minutes**		

Tip: Toast muffins before covering with toppings.

ZUCCHINI PIZZA
"Surprise"

¾ cup thinly sliced onions
¾ cup sliced zucchini
1 minced garlic clove
½ teaspoon basil leaves
2 Tablespoons margarine
1 large frozen cheese or vegetable pizza
½ cup grated Parmesan cheese

1. In skillet, sauté onions, zucchini, garlic and basil in margarine until vegetables are crisp-tender.
2. Spoon hot vegetable mixture over frozen pizza.
3. Sprinkle with cheese.
4. Bake at 450 degrees for 8-10 minutes or until center is hot.

Preparation Time: **20 minutes**   **Serves:**   **4**
Baking Time: **8-10 minutes**
Tip: *For crispier crust, sprinkle a little cornmeal on baking sheet.*

Potpourri

BLUEBERRY CREAM

¾ cup sour cream
Brown sugar to taste
1 cup fresh blueberries

1. Mix cream with sugar.
2. Gently fold in blueberries.

Preparation Time: 5 minutes   **Yield:** 1¾ cups
Serving Suggestion: *Serve with sweet bread.*

DEVONSHIRE CREAM

"This would be great for dipping strawberries"

1 3-ounce package softened cream cheese
½ cup Cool Whip or ½ cup whipped cream
¼ teaspoon vanilla
3 Tablespoons powdered sugar

1. In small bowl, beat cream cheese until smooth.
2. Add Cool Whip or whipped cream, vanilla and sugar.

Preparation Time: 5-10 minutes   **Yield:** ¾-1 cup

GARLIC BUTTER

½ cup softened butter
½ cup softened cream cheese
2 crushed garlic cloves

Mix all ingredients until creamy smooth.

Preparation Time: 5 minutes   **Yield:** 1 cup
Serving Suggestion: *Serve with hot sourdough bread or French bread.*

LEMON BUTTER

1 cup melted butter
1 Tablespoon lemon juice
2 Tablespoons grated, fresh Parmesan cheese

Combine ingredients and stir until well-blended.

Preparation Time: 5 minutes   **Yield:** 1⅓ cups
Serving Suggestion: *Serve with Mushroom-Artichoke Crepes or use for dipping artichoke leaves.*

RASPBERRY-LEMON CREAM

"So-o-o good over fruit"

1 3-ounce package cream cheese
1 Tablespoon sugar
1 teaspoon grated lemon peel
1 Tablespoon lemon juice
½ cup frozen raspberries, thawed and drained (reserving syrup)
½ cup whipped cream

1. Beat cream cheese until light and fluffy.
2. Add sugar.
3. In separate bowl, combine lemon peel, lemon juice, raspberries and 1 Tablespoon reserved syrup.
4. Fold raspberry mixture into cream cheese.
5. Fold in whipped cream. Refrigerate to chill.

Preparation Time: **15 minutes**   **Yield:**   **1½ cups**
Chilling Time: **30 minutes**
Tips: *Do not prepare day before serving. Bananas, peaches, strawberries, melons, apples and pears may be used.*

STRAWBERRY DEVONSHIRE CREAM

"Delicious and extravagant"

½ cup chilled whipping cream
2 Tablespoons brown sugar
½ cup sour cream
1 cup diced fresh strawberries

1. In small bowl, combine cream and brown sugar. Whip until peaks form.
2. Fold in sour cream and strawberries. Refrigerate until cold.

Preparation Time: **10 minutes**   **Yield:**   **2 cups**
Chilling Time: **30 minutes**
Serving Suggestion: *Serve on sweet bread.*

SWEET LEMON BUTTER

4 beaten eggs
1¾ cups sugar
½ cup butter
Juice and grated peel of 2 lemons

1. Combine all ingredients.
2. Cook until thickened.

Preparation Time: **15 minutes**   **Yield:**   **2½ cups**
Tip: *Will keep several weeks in refrigerator.*

ALMOND SANDWICH FILLING

½ cup almonds
½ cup finely chopped celery
½ cup mayonnaise
½ teaspoon salt, or to taste

Grind almonds and mix with remaining ingredients.

Preparation Time: 10 minutes   **Yield:** 1-1½ cups
Serving Suggestion: *Trim crust from white bread slices. Spread filling on bread and slice into finger sandwiches.*

CHICKEN SALAD FILLING

2½ cups ground soyameat chicken
2 cups chopped celery
6 chopped, hard-boiled eggs
1 cup chopped, salted peanuts
2 teaspoons curry powder
1 teaspoon garlic powder
2 teaspoons onion powder
Salt to taste
1½-2 cups mayonnaise
Sweet pickle relish to taste

Mix all ingredients.

Preparation Time: 15 minutes   **Yield:** 8 cups salad filling
Serving Suggestion: *Spoon mixture into 6 luncheon-size or 72 bite-size puffs. Replace lid.*

CURRY-CREAM CHEESE FILLING

3 8-ounce packages cream cheese at room temperature
2 4-ounce cans chopped, drained olives
2 Tablespoons horseradish
2 teaspoons curry powder
Dill weed to taste
2-3 Tablespoons sour cream, if necessary

Mix all ingredients and blend well. Thin with sour cream, if necessary.

Preparation Time: 20 minutes   **Yield:** 3 cups filling
Serving Suggestion: *Trim crusts from colored bread sliced lengthwise, 5-6 slices per loaf. Spread with filling and cut into finger sandwiches.*
Tip: *Order colored bread sliced lengthwise from bakery.*

NUTEENA FILLING

1 19-ounce can mashed Nuteena
1 cup sweet pickle relish with juice
1 bunch finely chopped green onions
Dijon mustard to taste
Garlic powder to taste
Salt to taste
Mayonnaise, if necessary

Mix all ingredients and blend well. Thin with mayonnaise, if necessary.

Preparation Time: 20 minutes   **Yield: 3½ cups filling**
Tip: *Makes enough filling for 2 bread loaves.*   **May do ahead and freeze**

PINEAPPLE-CREAM CHEESE FILLING

1 3-ounce package cream cheese
¼ cup drained, crushed pineapple
2 Tablespoons chopped pecans
¼ teaspoon salt

Mix all ingredients and blend well.

Preparation Time: 15 minutes   **Yield: ¾ cup filling**
Serving Suggestion: *Trim crust from white bread slices. Spread filling on bread and slice into finger sandwiches.*

CHINESE NOODLES

3 cups flour
1 teaspoon salt
2 large eggs
9 Tablespoons cold water
½ teaspoon sesame oil
Cornstarch for dusting and rolling

1. Place flour and salt in food processor with metal blade. Add eggs, 1 at a time. Pulse 2-3 times.
2. Turn on food processor and gradually add water until mixture forms ball.
3. Form dough into ball and rub with sesame oil. Cut ball into quarters. Wrap in plastic wrap and let rest for 10 minutes.
4. Using ¼ dough at a time (keep remaining quarters in plastic wrap), press into flat 4 x 6-inch rectangle. Rub with cornstarch. With lightly floured rolling pin or pasta machine, roll into very thin sheets ⅛-inch thick. Repeat with remaining quarters of dough.
5. Cut into desired-size strips or cut with pasta machine according to appliance directions.
6. Cook in large pot of boiling, salted water for 1-2 minutes until tender.

Preparation Time: 2 hours   **Serves: 6-8**
Tips: *Fresh pasta cooks much faster than dry pasta and care must be taken not to overcook it. May be dried or frozen.*

HOMEMADE PASTA

"Ronzoni, eat your heart out!"

3 cups flour
4 large eggs

1. Place flour in food processor with metal blade. Add eggs, 1 at a time. Mix until ball of dough forms.
2. Remove from bowl. Cut dough ball into quarters. Wrap in plastic wrap and let rest for 10 minutes.
3. Using ¼ dough at a time (keep remaining quarters in plastic wrap), press into flat 4 x 6-inch rectangle. With lightly floured rolling pin or pasta machine, roll into very thin sheets ⅛-inch thick. Cover with clean towel and let stand 15 minutes.
4. Cut into desired strips or cut with pasta machine according to appliance directions.
5. Repeat with remaining quarters of dough.
6. Cook in large pot of boiling, salted water for only 1-2 minutes until tender.

Preparation Time: 2 hours   **Serves: 6-8**
Variations: *To make tomato pasta, add 4 Tablespoons rich tomato paste to egg pasta. To make spinach pasta, add ½ cup finely puréed spinach to egg pasta. Any vegetable may be added to pasta dough.*
Tips: *Fresh pasta cooks much faster than dry pasta and care must be taken not to overcook it. Fresh pasta may be dried or frozen.*

CHINESE PANCAKES

1½ cups flour
¼ teaspoon salt
2 beaten eggs
1½ cups milk
1 cup water

1. Sift flour and salt into mixing bowl.
2. In separate bowl, combine eggs, milk and water.
3. Add to dry ingredients and beat until smooth. Cover and let stand for 30-60 minutes.
4. Lightly oil teflon skillet and place over low heat.
5. Stir batter and, with skillet off the heat, pour in small amount. Rotate pan to cover bottom with batter. Pour out any excess. Cook until set, but not browned. Turn and cook other side.
6. Remove and let cool on paper towel.
7. Continue until all batter is cooked, brushing skillet with oil as necessary.
8. Place stack of pancakes in foil or plastic wrap and seal.

Preparation Time: 45 minutes   **Yield: 12-16 pancakes**
Standing Time: 30-60 minutes   **May do ahead and freeze**
Cooking Time: 5-8 minutes
Serving Suggestion: *Serve with Moo Shu Vegetables.*

CREPES

15 Servings

2 eggs
⅛ teaspoon salt
1 cup flour
1 cup plus 2 Tablespoons milk
2 Tablespoons melted butter

1. In medium bowl, combine eggs and salt.
2. Gradually add flour alternating with milk. Beat with electric mixer or whisk until smooth.
3. Beat in melted butter.
4. Refrigerate batter at least 1 hour.
5. Cook on upside-down crepe griddle or in traditional pan.

Preparation Time:	**20 minutes**	**May do ahead and freeze**
Chilling Time:	**1 hour**	
Cooking Time:	**20 minutes**	

Tip: *Freeze cooked, cooled crepes between waxed paper sheets. Thaw to use.*

30 Servings

4 eggs
¼ teaspoon salt
2 cups flour
2¼ cups milk
¼ cup melted butter

50 Servings

6 eggs
⅓ teaspoon salt
3 cups flour
3¼ cups plus 2 Tablespoons milk
6 Tablespoons melted butter

100 Servings

12 eggs
¾ teaspoon salt
6 cups flour
6¾ cups milk
¾ cup melted butter

SOFT CREPE TORTILLAS

2 eggs
2 Tablespoons white cornmeal
2 Tablespoons liquid butter
1 cup cornstarch
1 teaspoon salt
½ cup milk

1. Mix all ingredients until smooth.
2. In hot, 10-inch, teflon skillet, swirl ⅓ cup batter around bottom of pan making complete circle.
3. Cook on both sides until golden.

Preparation Time: **5 minutes**   **Yield:**   **6 tortillas**
Cooking Time: **10 minutes**
Variation: *Use for soft tacos or enchiladas.*

SOFT TACOS

2 packages Spanish rice and sauce mix
12 Soft Crepe Tortillas (see recipe)
4 cups refried beans
2 cups grated Colby cheese
3-4 cups chopped lettuce
2-3 diced, small tomatoes
4-6 sliced green onions
2 cups salsa
Sour cream
Guacamole

1. Cook Spanish rice and sauce mix according to package directions.
2. Place remaining ingredients in individual serving containers.
3. Layer desired fillings inside soft crepe tortillas. Roll up and eat like a burrito.

Preparation Time: **30 minutes**   **Yield:**   **12 tacos**

PARTY POPCORN
"This will keep several days"

6 Tablespoons butter or margarine
3 cups miniature marshmallows
3 Tablespoons orange jello
3 quarts popped popcorn

1. Melt butter and marshmallows over low heat.
2. Blend in jello and pour mixture over popcorn.
3. Shape into balls.

Preparation Time: **30 minutes**   **Yield:**   **15 balls**
Variation: *Any flavor jello may be used.*
Tips: *To make jack-o-lanterns, shape popcorn into balls. Insert skewers for "neck" handles. Press on black gumdrops for eyes and nose and black licorice whip for mouth. Wrap in clear plastic wrap and twist tightly around skewer. Slip small doily over handle, gather up and tie in place with orange or black ribbon.*

POPPYCOCK
"Popcorn lover's delight"

1⅓ cups sugar
½ cup light corn syrup
1 cup butter
½ teaspoon salt
8 heaping cups popcorn
1 cup roasted pecans
1 cup roasted almonds

1. Cook sugar, corn syrup, butter and salt until soft-ball stage, 236 degrees.
2. Pour immediately over popcorn and nuts.
3. Mix well and spread on cookie sheet to cool.
4. Break into bite-size pieces when cooled.

Preparation Time: 30 minutes   **Yield:** 10-12 cups poppycock
Cooking Time: 10-15 minutes

RAINBOW POPCORN

9 cups popped white popcorn
1 cup light corn syrup
½ cup sugar
1 3-ounce package fruit-flavored jello
1⅔ cups coarsely chopped peanuts

1. Place popcorn in large, lightly buttered bowl.
2. Combine corn syrup and sugar in saucepan. Bring to boil. Remove from heat.
3. Add jello. Stir until dissolved.
4. Add peanuts.
5. Pour over popcorn. Mix until popcorn is well-coated.
6. Spread popcorn on large, greased cookie sheet. Let cool completely. Break into small clusters.

Preparation Time: 15 minutes   **Yield:** 10 cups popcorn clusters
Variation: *Several batches may be done using different flavored jellos.*

MERINGUE MUSHROOMS

½ cup egg whites (about 4 eggs)
¼ teaspoon cream of tartar
¼ teaspoon salt
1 cup superfine sugar
1 teaspoon vanilla
Cocoa powder
Chocolate chips

1. In bowl, beat egg whites, cream of tartar and salt until soft peaks form.
2. Slowly add sugar and vanilla. Beat until meringue does not feel sugary, about 15 minutes.
3. Place parchment paper on baking sheets.
4. Place meringue in pastry bag with large plain tip.
5. Pipe stems by squeezing small amounts of meringue mixture on sheet, lifting to a peak. Squeeze out rounds for mushroom caps, matching size of stems.
6. Bake at 225-250 degrees for 1 hour. Turn off heat and leave for 2-3 hours or overnight.
7. Lightly dust tops with sifted unsweetened cocoa powder.
8. Attach stems to caps with melted chocolate chips.

Preparation Time:	1 hour	**Yield:**	24 mushrooms
Baking Time:	1 hour		
Standing Time:	3 hours		

Serving Suggestion: *Serve as decorations.*
Tip: *May cover loosely for up to 1 week at room temperature.*

SOUR CREAM WALNUTS
"Will disappear before your eyes"

MICROWAVE RECIPE

1½ cups sugar
½ cup sour cream
1½ teaspoons vanilla
3 cups chopped walnuts

1. Mix sugar and sour cream in large batter bowl. Stir to combine. Microwave on high, stirring every 2-3 minutes until sugar is dissolved, approximately 7-9 minutes.
2. Add vanilla and walnuts. Stir until creamy.
3. Quickly turn out onto greased waxed paper and separate into pieces.
4. Store in tightly sealed plastic bags.

Preparation Time:	15 minutes	**Serves:**	15
		May do ahead 1 week and freeze	

Variations: *Any variety of nuts may be used. Substitute 1 cup brown sugar plus ½ cup granulated sugar for 1½ cups sugar.*

COOKIE CRUST FRUIT BASKET

¼ cup butter
½ cup sugar
¼ cup light corn syrup
¼ cup light molasses
7 Tablespoons flour
1 cup finely chopped nuts
2 teaspoons vanilla
Plain yogurt
Sliced, seasonal fresh fruit

1. Melt butter in saucepan over low heat.
2. Add sugar, corn syrup and molasses. Cook over high heat until liquid boils, stirring constantly. Remove from heat.
3. Stir in flour, nuts and vanilla.
4. For each basket, spoon 2-3 Tablespoons batter onto center of well-greased baking sheet.
5. Bake, 1 at a time, at 325 degrees until golden brown, about 10-11 minutes. Batter will become thin and spread considerably.
6. Cool until cookie firms up slightly, about 1 minute.
7. When edges are just firm enough to lift, but still warm and pliable, lift cookie. Turn and drape over glass that measures 2 inches across bottom. Gently cup cookie around base. Let shaped cookie cool until firm.
8. To serve, place scoop of yogurt in each basket and top with sliced fruit.

		Yield:	8-10 baskets
Preparation Time:	1½ hours		
Cooking Time:	15 minutes		
Baking Time:	10-11 minutes		

Tip: *Timing is very important. If cookie is lifted too soon, it will continue to spread and fall apart. If cookie is allowed to cool too long, it will lose flexibility and stick to the pan. Anticipate losing a few "practicing." Baskets may be stored in airtight container at room temperature up to 1 week.*

Salads

GARLIC DRESSING

2-3 finely minced garlic cloves
Juice of 4 lemons
⅔ cup olive oil
Salt to taste
Minced parsley, optional

Combine all ingredients in pint jar. Shake well.

Preparation Time: 5 minutes   **Yield:** 2 cups
Serving Suggestion: *Serve with Greek Salad.*
Tip: *For best results, prepare 3-4 hours or a day ahead.*

NUT TREE SALAD DRESSING
"Best on fruit salad"

1 cup sugar
⅔ cup light corn syrup
½ cup hot water
2 egg whites
Dash salt
¼ teaspoon vanilla
¼ cup mayonnaise
1 Tablespoon grated orange peel

1. Combine sugar, corn syrup and hot water. Heat slowly until sugar dissolves. Boil without stirring until firm ball or long thread stage, 248 degrees on candy thermometer.
2. Beat egg whites with salt until very stiff.
3. Gradually beat in hot syrup, beating until thick and fluffy.
4. Add vanilla.
5. Fold in mayonnaise and orange peel.

Preparation Time: 25 minutes   **Yield:** 3 cups
Variation: *Substitute orange juice for hot water.*   **May be frozen**
Tip: Add a little orange juice if not quite thawed or if stored in refrigerator a long time.

PARISIAN DRESSING

⅔ cup rice vinegar
1 Tablespoon dry mustard
1 teaspoon garlic powder
1 teaspoon salt
Dash tarragon
2 cups salad oil

1. Blend vinegar, mustard, garlic powder, salt and tarragon. Stir in salad oil.
2. Let dressing stand 2 hours, then refrigerate.

Preparation Time: 5 minutes   **Yield:** 2⅔ cups
Standing Time: 2 hours
Chilling Time: 1 hour
Tip: *Refrigerate up to 2 weeks.*

POPPY SEED SALAD DRESSING
"Outstanding"

1 chopped, small, white onion
1½ cups sugar
⅔ cup cider vinegar or lemon juice
2 teaspoons dry mustard, optional
1½ teaspoons salt
2 cups vegetable oil
2-3 Tablespoons poppy seeds

1. In electric blender or food processor, add chopped onion and blend on medium speed until onion is slushy.
2. Add sugar, vinegar, mustard and salt.
3. With motor running, slowly pour oil through top of blender. Mixture will be thick.
4. Add poppy seeds and blend a few seconds longer.
5. Store in refrigerator.

Preparation Time: **10 minutes**   **Yield:**   **4 cups**
Chilling Time: **30 minutes**   **May do ahead**

VINAIGRETTE DRESSING

1 cup olive oil
2 Tablespoons lemon juice
4 Tablespoons vinegar
2 Tablespoons Dijon mustard
1 minced garlic clove
1 Tablespoon chopped, fresh basil
1 Tablespoon chopped, fresh tarragon
1 Tablespoon chopped, fresh oregano
Season to taste

Combine above ingredients. Mix well.

Preparation Time: **15 minutes**   **Yield:**   **2 cups**

CRANBERRY SALAD

1 12-ounce package finely ground cranberries
2 cups sugar
1 cup halved, seeded Tokay grapes
1 cup chopped, toasted pecans
1 cup unsweetened whipping cream

1. Combine cranberries and sugar. Let stand overnight.
2. Drain for several hours.
3. Fold in remaining ingredients. Chill.

Preparation Time:	15 minutes	**Serves:**	10-12
Standing Time:	6-8 hours	**Must do ahead**	
Chilling Time:	3 hours		

RAINBOW FRUIT CUP

"Delightful for a summer luncheon"

½ cup sliced strawberries
½ cup blueberries
1 sliced kiwi
½ cup pineapple chunks
1 sliced banana
1 8-ounce carton piña colada yogurt
½ cup shredded coconut

1. In large bowl, combine strawberries, blueberries, kiwi, pineapple and banana.
2. Place in individual serving bowls.
3. Top each with 1 Tablespoon yogurt.
4. Sprinkle with coconut.

Preparation Time: 15 minutes   **Serves:** 4
Variation: *Any other fruits in season may be used.*
Tip: *If preparing fruits ahead, add banana just before serving.*

RAINBOW FRUIT SALAD

10 Servings

1 head lettuce
1½-2 red apples
5 canned pineapple slices (reserve syrup)
10 canned peach halves
⅔ cup Miracle Whip salad dressing
30-40 red raspberries

1. Arrange lettuce leaves on plates.
2. Slice apples very thin and dip slices in pineapple syrup.
3. Arrange half-slice pineapple, peach half (cut side up) and several apple slices for each serving.
4. Fill peach half with approximately 1 Tablespoon salad dressing. Top with a few fresh raspberries.

Preparation Time: 20 minutes

50 Servings

6 heads lettuce
8 red apples
3 20-ounce cans drained, sliced pineapple
1½ #10 cans peach halves (18 cups)
3 cups Miracle Whip salad dressing
1 quart red raspberries

100 Servings

12 heads lettuce
16 red apples
6 20-ounce cans drained, sliced pineapple
3 #10 cans peach halves (24 cups)
6 cups Miracle Whip salad dressing
2 quarts red raspberries

APRICOT SALAD
"A crowd pleaser"

1 6-ounce package apricot jello
2 cups boiling water
1 20-ounce can undrained, crushed pineapple
1 8-ounce package softened cream cheese
1 junior-size jar apricot baby food
½ pint whipping cream, whipped

1. Add apricot jello to boiling water and dissolve.
2. Add crushed pineapple and refrigerate until partially set.
3. In blender, combine cream cheese and baby food. Add small amount of strained liquid from jello.
4. Add cream cheese mixture to cooled jello. Fold in whipped cream.
5. Pour into 8-cup jello mold and chill until set.

Preparation Time:	20 minutes	Serves:	16
Chilling Time:	4-6 hours	Must do ahead	

Variation: *Substitute orange or lemon jello.*

CINNAMON JELLO

¾ cup red cinnamon candies
1 cup boiling water
1 3-ounce package lemon jello
1 cup applesauce
1 cup drained, crushed pineapple
½ cup chopped nuts
Dash salt

1. Melt candies in boiling water.
2. Add jello and dissolve.
3. Add applesauce, pineapple, nuts and salt.
4. Place in 1-quart serving bowl.
5. Chill until set.

Preparation Time:	15 minutes	Serves:	8-10
Chilling Time:	3-4 hours		

Tip: *This is soft-set jello. Do not try to mold. Jello should be served from bowl.*

CRANBERRY JELLO

Cranberry Relish

1 pound cranberries
2 oranges
1 medium apple
1½ cups sugar
Pinch of salt

1. Grind together cranberries, oranges and apple.
2. Stir in sugar and salt.
3. Allow to stand overnight.

Jello

2 6-ounce packages strawberry Jello
4 cups boiling water
1 quart Cranberry Relish
1 pint small curd cottage cheese
1 cup whipping cream, whipped

1. Mix Jello with water. Add Cranberry Relish.
2. Pour half of mixture into 9 x 13-inch dish. Refrigerate to set Jello. Set aside remaining half of Jello-Relish mixture.
3. Fold together cottage cheese and whipped cream. Spread evenly over set Jello.
4. Spoon remaining Jello-Relish mixture over cottage cheese layer.
5. Refrigerate overnight.

Preparation Time:	**30 minutes**	**Serves:**	**24**
Chilling Time:	**Overnight**	**Must do ahead**	

Tip: *Makes 2 6-cup molds.*

HONEYDEW SALAD

"You will find this a remembered delight"

1 6-ounce package red jello
2 cups hot water
1 cup cold water
1 honeydew melon
Whipped cream

1. Make jello according to directions on box, using water amounts indicated above.
2. Peel and cut honeydew in half. Scoop out seeds. Melon cavity should be dry. Flatten bottom so melon sits level.
3. Fill cavity with jello. Place in refrigerator until firm.
4. Slice in wedges and top with dollop of whipped cream.

Preparation Time:	**25 minutes**	**Serves:**	**8**
Chilling Time:	**3 hours**		

Serving Suggestion: *Serve on bed of lettuce, surrounded by fruits in season.*

JELLIED CRANBERRY SALAD

1 3-ounce package raspberry jello
1 cup hot water
½ cup cold water
1 peeled, diced orange
½ cup drained, crushed pineapple
1 16-ounce can whole cranberry sauce
¼ cup chopped nuts

1. Dissolve jello in hot water.
2. Add cold water and chill until partially set.
3. Mix in orange, pineapple, cranberry sauce and nuts.
4. Pour into 9 x 13-inch dish. Chill until firm.
5. To serve, cut into squares.

Preparation Time:	20 minutes	**Serves:**	12-15
Chilling Time:	6 hours	**Must do ahead**	

RASPBERRY-CRANBERRY SALAD

"Everyone's favorite"

First Layer

1 3-ounce package raspberry jello
¾ cup boiling water
1 16-ounce can cranberry sauce
1 20-ounce can drained, crushed pineapple

1. Dissolve jello in boiling water.
2. Add cranberry sauce and pineapple. Mix.
3. Pour into 9 x 13-inch dish. Chill until set.

Second Layer

1 pint sour cream

Spread sour cream over First Layer. Chill in refrigerator 1 hour.

Third Layer

1 6-ounce package raspberry jello
1½ cups boiling water
1 20-ounce package frozen raspberries, thawed

1. Dissolve jello in boiling water.
2. Add raspberries. Pour over Second Layer. Chill at least 4 hours.

Preparation Time:	30 minutes	**Serves:**	12
Chilling Time:	6-8 hours	**Must do ahead**	

EGG SALAD MOLD

13 chopped, hard-boiled eggs
1 cup chopped celery
1 teaspoon Worcestershire sauce
Dash of hot pepper sauce
1 Tablespoon grated onion
2 Tablespoons chopped parsley
¼ cup pickle relish
2 Tablespoons lemon juice
¼ cup chopped green pepper
1 envelope unflavored gelatin
½ cup cold water
2 cups mayonnaise
¾ teaspoon salt
Olives for garnish
Pimento for garnish

1. Combine eggs, celery, sauces, onion, parsley, relish, lemon juice and green pepper.
2. Soften gelatin in cold water. Dissolve over boiling water.
3. Beat mayonnaise into gelatin.
4. Add egg mixture and salt. Mix well.
5. Place in 6-cup mold and chill until firm.

Preparation Time:	**20 minutes**	**Serves:**	**12**
Chilling Time:	**4-6 hours**		

FROZEN BERRY SALAD

"An elegant salad"

1 8-ounce can drained, crushed pineapple (reserve syrup)
1 10-ounce package frozen strawberries or raspberries, thawed and drained
1 cup miniature marshmallows
¼ cup chopped pecans
1 puréed banana
1 envelope unflavored gelatin
2 Tablespoons cold pineapple syrup
½ cup hot pineapple syrup
¼ cup mayonnaise
1 cup whipping cream, whipped, or 2 cups Cool Whip

1. Combine pineapple, strawberries, marshmallows, pecans and banana purée.
2. Soften gelatin in cold pineapple syrup.
3. Dissolve softened gelatin in hot pineapple syrup.
4. Add to fruit-nut mixture.
5. Combine mayonnaise and whipped cream and fold into fruit-nut mixture.
6. Fill 10 paper baking cups placed in muffin tin or 1½-quart jello mold. Freeze.

Preparation Time:	**20 minutes**	**Serves:**	**10**
Freezing Time:	**4 hours**	**Must do ahead**	

LIME-PINEAPPLE SALAD

1 6-ounce package lime jello
1 cup hot water
1 cup miniature marshmallows
1 cup mayonnaise
1 cup crushed pineapple
1 cup finely shredded cabbage
½ cup chopped almonds
1 cup whipping cream, whipped

1. Mix jello, hot water and marshmallows. Stir until thoroughly dissolved. Let stand in refrigerator until thickened.
2. Add mayonnaise, pineapple, cabbage and almonds.
3. Fold in whipped cream.
4. Pour into 6-cup mold. Refrigerate until set.

Preparation Time:	**15 minutes**	**Serves:**	**8-10**
Standing Time:	**2 hours**	**Must do ahead**	
Chilling Time:	**4-6 hours**		

Variation: *Cabbage may be omited.*

ORANGE-LEMON CUSTARD JELLO

Jello

1 6-ounce package orange jello
1¾ cups boiling water
1 20-ounce can undrained, crushed pineapple
1 6-ounce can frozen orange juice concentrate

1. Dissolve gelatin in water.
2. Add pineapple with juice and frozen orange juice concentrate. Stir until well-blended.
3. Pour into 9 x 13-inch dish. Refrigerate until firm.

Custard Topping

1 4¼-ounce package lemon pudding and pie filling mix
2 slightly beaten eggs
⅓ cup sugar
1¾ cups cold water
1 cup sour cream
1½ cups grated Cheddar cheese

1. Combine pudding mix with eggs, sugar and ½ cup cold water. Stir until smooth. Add remaining cold water.
2. Cook over medium heat, stirring constantly until mixture comes to full boil and is thick.
3. Cool, stirring occasionally.
4. Add sour cream.
5. Spread over jello. Sprinkle grated cheese over Custard Topping, pressing down very lightly.
6. Chill thoroughly.

Preparation Time:	**30 minutes**	**Serves:**	**12-15**
Cooking Time:	**10-15 minutes**	**Must do ahead**	
Chilling Time:	**4-6 hours**		

PEACH BAVARIAN SALAD
"Heavenly"

1 3-ounce package lemon or peach jello
1 cup boiling water
¼ teaspoon almond extract
2 cups Cool Whip or whipped cream
2 cups fresh or canned peaches, sliced or cut in small pieces

1. Dissolve jello in boiling water and let partially set.
2. Add almond extract and Cool Whip.
3. Fold in peaches. Pour into 6-cup mold.
4. Chill until set.

Preparation Time:	**20 minutes**	**Serves:**	**10**
Chilling Time:	**4 hours**		

PERSIMMON SALAD

1 3-ounce package orange jello
1 cup hot water
1 cup persimmon pulp
1½ Tablespoons lemon juice
1½ cups fresh orange slices
½ cup toasted, sliced almonds

1. Dissolve jello in hot water.
2. Combine remaining ingredients and add to jello.
3. Pour into 8 x 8-inch dish. Chill until set.

Preparation Time:	**15 minutes**	**Serves:**	**6**
Chilling Time:	**4 hours**	**Must do ahead**	

Variation: *May add 1 cup drained, crushed pineapple.*

RIBBON JELLO
"Plan ahead"

1 3-ounce package lime jello
1 3-ounce package lemon jello
1 3-ounce package strawberry jello
1 3-ounce package orange jello
4 cups boiling water
2½ cups cold water
2 cups milk
1 cup sugar
2 envelopes unflavored gelatin
2 Tablespoons vanilla
2 cups sour cream

1. In separate bowls, dissolve each package of jello in 1 cup boiling water.
2. Add ½ cup cold water to each and let stand at room temperature.
3. In saucepan, boil milk and sugar until sugar is dissolved. Stir often.
4. In bowl, dissolve unflavored gelatin in ½ cup cold water.
5. Add gelatin mixture to milk and sugar.
6. Add vanilla and sour cream to gelatin and milk mixture.
   Blend with beaters.
7. Pour lime jello into 9 x 13-inch dish. Chill ½ hour.
8. Spread 1½ cups of white mixture over jello. Chill ½ hour.
9. Repeat layers, spooning remaining jellos and white mixture, ending with jello on top.
   Chill 5 hours.
10. Cut into 3-inch squares and serve on lettuce.

Preparation Time:	**1 hour**	**Serves:**	**12**
Chilling Time:	**6-8 hours**	**Must do ahead**	
Cooking Time:	**15 minutes**		

Serving Suggestion: *For garnish, top each serving with 1 Tablespoon whipped cream. Add slice of lemon cut in half to resemble a rainbow.*
Variation: *Any flavor jello may be used.*

STRAWBERRY MOLDED SALAD

1 6-ounce package strawberry jello
2 cups boiling water
1 10-ounce package frozen strawberries
2 mashed bananas
1 8-ounce can drained, crushed pineapple
1 8-ounce carton sour cream

1. Dissolve jello in boiling water.
2. Add frozen strawberries and its juice.
3. Let stand, stirring occasionally until berries are thawed.
4. Add bananas and crushed pineapple.
5. Pour ½ of jello into 9 x 13-inch dish. Refrigerate until set.
6. Spread sour cream over jello layer.
7. Spoon remaining jello mixture over sour cream. Refrigerate until set.

Preparation Time: 45 minutes   Serves: 12
Chilling Time: 4 hours
Variations: *Substitute raspberry jello for strawberry jello and raspberries for strawberries.*

MACARONI AND CHEESE SALAD

1 12-ounce package macaroni or salad-roni
1½ cups mayonnaise
2 cups diced sharp cheese
6 diced, hard-boiled eggs
3 thinly sliced green onions
1 10-ounce package frozen petite peas
Salt to taste

1. Cook macaroni 8-10 minutes. Avoid overcooking. Drain and rinse with cold water.
2. Add mayonnaise to macaroni.
3. Toss in remaining ingredients.
4. Refrigerate at least 4 hours before serving.

Preparation Time: 30 minutes   Serves: 10-12
Chilling Time: 4 hours

PASTA SALAD

1 pound thin spaghetti
1 8-ounce bottle Italian salad dressing
2¾-ounce jar Salad Supreme salad seasoning
2 chopped celery stalks
1 chopped green pepper
1 thinly sliced red onion
1 pint cherry tomatoes
1 6-ounce can pitted ripe olives

1. Cook spaghetti according to package directions. Drain and rinse in cold water.
2. Combine spaghetti, salad dressing and salad seasoning.
3. Add celery, green pepper and onion.
4. Chill 3-4 hours.
5. Just before serving, add tomatoes and olives.

Preparation Time:	**15 minutes**	**Serves:**	**8**
Chilling Time:	**3-4 hours**	**May do 3-4 days ahead**	

PASTA PRIMAVERA SALAD
"One dish meal"

1 12-ounce package rotelle pasta
1 16-ounce package frozen broccoli, cauliflower and carrot mix
½ sliced, medium green or red bell pepper
½ sliced, medium red onion
1 package Classic Herb or Good Seasons salad dressing mix, mixed according to package directions
Salt and seasoning to taste

1. Cook pasta according to package directions. Drain and rinse in cold water.
2. Run hot water over frozen vegetables for several minutes. Drain and rinse in cold water.
3. Toss pasta with vegetables, pepper and onions.
4. Add prepared dressing, salt and seasonings to taste.
5. Refrigerate overnight.

Preparation Time:	**30 minutes**	**Serves:**	**16**
Chilling Time:	**6-8 hours**	**Must do ahead**	

MACARONI SALAD

16 Servings

Dressing

⅔ cup mayonnaise
⅔ cup Miracle Whip salad dressing
1 Tablespoon lemon juice
2 Tablespoons cream or evaporated milk
1 teaspoon sugar
½ teaspoon salt or to taste
1 teaspoon Spice Island salad seasoning
2 teaspoons catsup

Salad

1 pound macaroni
½ cup chopped celery
½ cup diced green or yellow onions
½ cup diced green pepper
2 diced, medium dill pickles
1 Tablespoon chopped pimento
4 chopped, hard-boiled eggs
1 Tablespoon sweet pickle relish, optional

1. Cook macaroni according to package directions. Drain and rinse.
2. Mix Dressing ingredients.
3. Add to Salad ingredients.
4. If needed, moisten with extra cream and mayonnaise.
5. Chill well.

Preparation Time:	45 minutes	**Yield:**	2 quarts
Chilling Time:	4 hours or overnight	**Must do ahead**	

50 Servings

Dressing

1⅓ cups mayonnaise
1⅓ cups Miracle Whip salad dressing
2 Tablespoons lemon juice
¼ cup cream or evaporated milk
2 teaspoons sugar
1 teaspoon salt or to taste
2 teaspoons Spice Island salad seasoning
4 teaspoons catsup

Continued

MACARONI SALAD — Continued

Salad

3 pounds macaroni
1½ cups chopped celery
1½ cups diced green or yellow onions
1½ cups diced green pepper
6 diced, medium dill pickles
3 Tablespoons chopped pimento
1 dozen chopped, hard-boiled eggs
3 Tablespoons sweet pickle relish, optional

Yield: 6 quarts

100 Servings

Dressing

2⅔ cups mayonnaise
2⅔ cups Miracle Whip salad dressing
¼ cup lemon juice
½ cup cream or evaporated milk
4 teaspoons sugar
2 teaspoons salt or to taste
4 teaspoons Spice Island salad seasoning
2 Tablespoons catsup

Salad

6 pounds macaroni
3 cups chopped celery
3 cups diced green or yellow onions
3 cups diced green pepper
12 diced, medium dill pickles
3 Tablespoons chopped pimento
2 dozen chopped, hard-boiled eggs
⅓ cup sweet pickle relish, optional

Yield: 3 gallons

SPAGHETTI SALAD

1 10-ounce package spaghetti
¾ cup mayonnaise
2 minced garlic cloves
½ teaspoon cumin seeds
Salt to taste
2 8-ounce jars medium-hot salsa
¼ cup chopped green onion
¼ cup diced celery
½ cup sliced, pimento-stuffed olives

1. Cook spaghetti according to package directions. Drain and rinse in cold water.
2. In blender, combine mayonnaise, garlic cloves, cumin seeds, salt and 1 jar salsa. Purée.
3. Combine mayonnaise mixture with remaining jar salsa, onion, celery and olives.
4. Add spaghetti. Toss until spaghetti is well-coated. Chill at least 4 hours.

Preparation Time: 25 minutes   **Serves:**   8-10
Chilling Time: 4 hours   **May do ahead**

ENGLISH BIBB SALAD

"English down to the radish"

1 teaspoon dry mustard
1 teaspoon seasoned salt
1 teaspoon Lawry's Pinch of Herbs
¼ teaspoon Lawry's Garlic Powder with Parsley
⅓ cup rice vinegar
1 cup olive oil
2 heads Bibb lettuce, torn into bite-size pieces
¾ cup walnut quarters
1-2 Tablespoons imitation bacon bits
½ cup grated Gruyère cheese
1½ cups croutons
¼ cup sliced radishes

1. Combine seasonings and vinegar in jar. Shake well.
2. Add olive oil and shake for 30 seconds.
3. Refrigerate several hours.
4. Toss remaining ingredients.
5. Add dressing, toss and serve immediately.

Preparation Time: 20 minutes   **Serves:**   6-8
Standing Time: 3-4 hours   **Must do ahead**

GREEK SALAD
"A classic"

½ head chopped iceberg lettuce
¼ bunch thinly cut endive
1 bunch romaine lettuce, torn into bite-size pieces
1 thinly sliced cucumbers
3 sliced green onions
8 sliced radishes
3 tomatoes, cut into eighths
18 Greek or ripe green olives
12 ounces crumbled feta cheese

1. On large platter, preferably wooden and rubbed with garlic, arrange greens in center.
2. Cover greens with row of sliced cucumbers.
3. Sprinkle cucumbers with sliced onions.
4. Surround them with sliced radishes.
5. Encircle edge of platter with tomato wedges.
6. Garnish with olives and sprinkles of feta cheese.

Preparation Time: **20 minutes**   **Serves:**   **6-8**
Serving Suggestion: *Serve with Garlic Dressing.*

INTERNATIONAL SALAD

½ pound spinach, torn in bite-size pieces
1 cup stemmed watercress
½ peeled, thinly sliced, small jicama
1 thinly sliced red onion
½ cup Parisian Dressing (see recipe)
½ teaspoon soy sauce

1. Toss spinach and watercress together in large bowl.
2. Add jicama and onion rings.
3. Blend Parisian Dressing and soy sauce.
4. Pour over salad and toss. Serve at once.

Preparation Time: **20 minutes**   **Serves:**   **4**

ITALIAN GREEN SALAD

1 bunch romaine lettuce
1 bunch leaf lettuce
2 tomatoes, cut in wedges
½ sliced green pepper
½ cup sliced radishes
¼ cup sliced green onion

1. Tear greens in bite-size pieces in salad bowl.
2. Add tomatoes, green pepper, radishes and green onion. Toss lightly.

Preparation Time: **15 minutes**   **Serves:**   **6-8**
Serving Suggestion: *Garnish with extra tomato wedges. Serve with Poppy Seed Dressing.*

MANDARIN SALAD
"A refreshing surprise"

Salad

¼ **cup toasted, sliced almonds**
1 **teaspoon sugar**
1 **Tablespoon butter**
¼ **head chopped iceburg lettuce**
½ **bunch chopped romaine letuce**
1 **cup chopped celery**
2 **chopped green onions**
1 **11-ounce can drained mandrin oranges**

1. Cook almonds and sugar in butter until almonds are browned and sugar is dissolved. Place almonds on waxpaper and cool.
2. Combine remaining Salad ingredients.

Dressing

2 **Tablespoons sugar**
2 **Tablespoons rice vinegar**
¼ **cup oil**
½ **teaspoon salt and seasoning to taste**
1 **Tablespoon minced parsley**

1. Combine all Dressing ingredients.
2. Toss with Salad when ready to serve.

Preparation Time: **30 minutes**   **Serves:**   **10-12**

SPINACH-BERRY SALAD
"A most unusual combination"

Salad

2 bunches fresh spinach, washed and drained
1 pint fresh strawberries, washed, hulled and halved

Poppy-Sesame Seed Dressing

½ cup sugar
2 Tablespoons sesame seeds
1 Tablespoon poppy seeds
1½ Tablespoons minced onion
¼ teaspoon Worcestershire sauce
¼ teaspoon paprika
½ cup vegetable oil
¼ cup rice or cider vinegar

1. Place sugar, sesame and poppy seeds, onion, Worcestershire sauce and paprika in blender.
2. With blender running, slowly add oil and vinegar until thoroughly mixed and thickened.
3. Drizzle over strawberries and spinach. Serve immediately.

Preparation Time:　　**30 minutes**　　　　　　　**Serves:**　　**6-8**
Variation: *Substitute pomegranate seeds and avocados for strawberries.*

AVOCADO SALAD
"Simply . . . good"

6 lettuce leaves
3 ripe avocados
2 4¼-ounce cans diced ripe olives
3-4 sliced, medium tomatoes
6-8 sliced mushrooms
Salad dressing (thousand island and ranch dressings are good)

1. Place lettuce leaf on salad plate.
2. Cut each avocado in half. Peel and seed.
3. Place ½ avocado on lettuce.
4. Fill center of each avocado with diced ripe olives.
5. Place 2-3 slices of tomato and mushrooms on lettuce.
6. Drizzle salad dressing lightly over avocado, tomatoes and mushrooms.

Preparation Time:　　**15 minutes**　　　　　　　**Serves:**　　**6**

BEAN SALAD

30 Servings

Salad

1 15½-ounce can red kidney beans
1 15½-ounce can garbanzos
1 15½-ounce can green beans
1 15½-ounce can yellow wax beans
1 diced, large green pepper
4 sliced green onions
2 4-ounce cans sliced, black ripe olives
2 Tablespoons chopped pimento

Dressing

⅓ cup vegetable oil
⅓ cup lemon juice
⅓ cup honey
2 Tablespoons soy sauce
2 teaspoons Spice Island salad seasoning

1. Place Dressing ingredients in glass jar and shake to mix.
2. Drain all beans.
3. Combine Dressing with Salad ingredients. Toss well.
4. Marinate in refrigerator for 6 hours or overnight. Toss occasionally.

Preparation Time:	**30 minutes**	**Yield:**	**2½ quarts**
Marinating Time:	**6-8 hours**	**Must do ahead**	

100 Servings

Salad

3 15½-ounce cans red kidney beans
3 15½-ounce cans garbanzos
3 15½-ounce cans green beans
3 15½-ounce cans yellow wax beans
3 diced, large green peppers
12 sliced green onions
3 4-ounce cans sliced, black ripe olives
¼ cup chopped pimento

Dressing

1 cup vegetable oil
1 cup lemon juice
1 cup honey
6 Tablespoons soy sauce
2 Tablespoons Spice Island salad seasoning

Yield:	**7½ quarts**

CABBAGE SALAD

"This is a yummy colorful cabbage salad"

Salad

1 shredded, large cabbage head
½ cup finely chopped green pepper
¼ cup finely chopped onion
¼ cup chopped pimento

1. Combine all ingredients.
2. Gently stir in Dressing. Refrigerate.

Dressing

¾ cup vegetable oil
1 cup sugar
½ cup lemon juice
1 teaspoon salt
1 teaspoon dry mustard
1 teaspoon celery seed

1. Mix all salad dressing ingredients in small saucepan.
2. Bring to boil and cook 2 minutes. Do not overcook.
3. Cool and pour over salad.

Preparation Time:	**15 minutes**	**Serves:**	**12**
Cooking Time:	**2 minutes**	**May do ahead**	

Tip: *May keep 9 days in refrigerator.*

COLESLAW

"Easy to make for a crowd"

1 grated cabbage head
6 grated carrots
1 finely chopped green pepper
1 minced green onion, optional
¼ cup chopped parsley
½ cup Miracle Whip salad dressing
2 Tablespoons sugar
1 Tablespoon dill weed
1½ teaspoons celery seed
1 Tablespoon rice vinegar
Salt to taste

Mix all ingredients. Refrigerate.

Preparation Time:	**20 minutes**	**Serves:**	**8-10**

COTTAGE CHEESE-POTATO SALAD
"Picnic special"

6-8 diced, boiled, chilled potatoes
1½ cups diced celery
1 diced, medium onion
1 Tablespoon oil
1½ teaspoons salt
1 cup mayonnaise or salad dressing
1 pint cottage cheese
Season to taste

1. Mix all ingredients.
2. Chill.

Preparation Time:	**25 minutes**	**Serves:**	**10-12**
Chilling Time:	**2-3 hours**	**May do ahead**	

HOT GERMAN POTATO SALAD
"Wonderful dish for a crowd - doubles or triples well"

2 Tablespoons butter or margarine
2 Tablespoons flour
1 cup milk
2-3 drops liquid smoke
½ cup mayonnaise
1½ teaspoons salt
1 finely chopped onion
6 cooked, diced, medium potatoes
⅓ cup imitation bacon bits

1. Melt butter in saucepan. Add flour and stir until bubbly. Add milk slowly, stirring until thickened. Remove from heat.
2. Add remaining ingredients. Mix well.
3. Spoon into 9 x 13-inch baking dish.
4. Bake at 350 degrees for 30 minutes or until bubbly.

Preparation Time:	**30 minutes**	**Serves:**	**10**
Baking Time:	**30 minutes**	**May do ahead**	
Tip: *Warm to serve.*			

ELEVEN-LAYER SALAD

"Be glad you can make this ahead"

Salad

4 cups chopped iceberg lettuce
2-3 cups chopped fresh parsley (reserve 2 Tablespoons for garnish)
8 diced, hard-boiled eggs
2 sliced green or red bell peppers
1 10-ounce package frozen green peas
2 cups shredded carrots
1 6-ounce can, sliced colossal pitted olives
2 cups sliced radishes
2 cups grated sharp Cheddar cheese
1 cup diced red onions
3 cups Green Salad Dressing

1. In 5-inch deep bowl, layer ingredients in listed order except Green Salad Dressing.
2. Spoon Green Salad Dressing over top of salad. Sprinkle with 1 Tablespoon parsley.
3. Refrigerate at least 6 hours or overnight.

Preparation Time:	30 minutes	**Serves:**	15
Chilling Time:	6-12 hours	**Must do ahead**	

Tip: *May do up to 6-24 hours ahead, 12 hours being best.*

Green Salad Dressing

2 cups mayonnaise
½ cup minced parsley
1 teaspoon basil
1 teaspoon dill weed
1 Tablespoon sugar
½ cup sour cream

Mix all ingredients. Blend until smooth.

Preparation Time:	5 minutes	**Yield:**	2½ cups

Tip: *Double recipe, using 1 recipe to spoon over Eleven-Layer Salad and second recipe to place in serving bowl for extra dressing.*

LAYERED VEGETABLE SALAD

1 cup diced red onion
1 8-ounce can diced water chestnuts
1 cup diced celery
1 10-ounce package frozen green peas
6 diced, hard-boiled eggs
1 teaspoon salt
1 medium head shredded lettuce
¾ cup mayonnaise
¾ cup sour cream
½ teaspoon garlic powder
2 teaspoons sugar
½ cup shredded sharp Cheddar cheese

1. Combine red onion, water chestnuts, celery, peas, eggs and salt.
2. In crystal bowl, starting with lettuce, layer alternately with vegetables.
3. Mix mayonnaise, sour cream, garlic powder and sugar.
4. Cover salad with mayonnaise mixture, sealing edges.
5. Chill overnight.
6. Just before serving, sprinkle cheese over top of salad.

Preparation Time:	**30 minutes**	**Serves:**	**10-12**
Chilling Time:	**6-8 hours**	**Must do ahead**	

Variations: *Substitute green onions for red onion. Substitute 2 cups mayonnaise for mayonnaise-sour cream mixture. Substitute grated, fresh Parmesan cheese for Cheddar cheese. Garnish with 2 medium tomatoes, cut in wedges, ripe olives and parsley.*

ENGLISH CUCUMBERS

3 cucumbers
Salt to taste
Sugar to taste
¼ cup fresh lemon juice
¼ cup water
Chopped parsley
Radish slices

1. Cut unpared cucumbers into thin slices.
2. Sprinkle with salt and sugar to taste.
3. Combine lemon juice and water. Pour over cucumbers to barely cover.
4. Chill 1 hour.
5. To serve, drain well. Garnish with chopped parsley and thinly sliced radishes.

Preparation Time:	**15 minutes**	**Serves:**	**6-8**
Chilling Time:	**1 hour**		

FRESH GREEN BEAN AND YELLOW BELL PEPPER SALAD

"If you like fresh green beans, you will love it!"

2 pounds fresh green beans, sliced in 2-inch pieces
5 Tablespoons oil
2 large yellow bell peppers, cut in thin strips
2 Tablespoons rice vinegar
2 Tablespoons lemon juice
1 Tablespoon sugar
1 Tablespoon minced, fresh basil
½ teaspoon salt
1 cup small, pitted, ripe olives

1. In 5-quart saucepan in 1-inch boiling water, heat green beans to boiling. Reduce heat to low. Cover and simmer about 10 minutes or until beans are crisp-tender. Drain. Place beans in large bowl.
2. In same saucepan over medium-high heat in 2 Tablespoons hot oil, cook yellow peppers, stirring frequently until crisp-tender. Add to green beans.
3. Combine vinegar, lemon juice, sugar, basil, salt, olives and 3 Tablespoons oil. Pour over vegetables and toss to coat.
4. Cover and refrigerate at least 1 hour to blend flavors, stirring mixture occasionally.

Preparation Time:	**30 minutes**	**Serves:**	**10**
Cooking Time:	**30 minutes**		
Chilling Time:	**1-2 hours**		

Variations: *Substitute 2 Tablespoons additional lemon juice for rice vinegar. Omit salt and substitute ¾ teaspoon seasoned salt. Green or red bell peppers may be used.*
Tip: *If using dried herbs, use ⅓ of amount.*

MARINATED BROCCOLI SALAD
"Color in every bite"

Salad

2 cups fresh broccoli flowerets
1 cup chopped tomatoes or halved cherry tomatoes
1 cup chopped cucumber
1 cup coarsely chopped red onion
1 cup grated Cheddar cheese

Dressing

¼ cup salad oil
⅛ cup lemon juice
½ teaspoon salt
¼ teaspoon cayenne pepper
Black olives, optional

1. Blanch broccoli 2 minutes in boiling water. Rinse in cold water.
2. Combine all Dressing ingredients.
3. Combine vegetables. Marinate 4-6 hours in Dressing.
4. Before serving, add cheese and toss well.

Preparation Time:	**20 minutes**	**Serves:**	**8**
Marinating Time:	**4-6 hours**	**Must do ahead**	

Variation: *Omit cucumber and cheese, adding 2 cups broccoli pieces. Marinate in 1 8-ounce bottle ranch dressing.*

TABOULI
"Unusual and delightful - a pleasant surprise"

1 cup bulgur wheat
1½ cups lemon juice
5 chopped, fresh tomatoes
3 peeled, chopped cucumbers
2 bunches chopped green onion
3-4 bunches finely chopped, fresh parsley
2 teaspoons salt
1 cup olive oil

1. Place wheat in bowl. Soak in 1 cup warm lemon juice for at least 1 hour.
2. Squeeze moisture out of wheat with hands.
3. Toss with chopped vegetables, salt, remaining lemon juice and olive oil.
4. Let stand in refrigerator at least 4 hours before serving.

Preparation Time:	**45 minutes**	**Serves:**	**10**
Soaking Time:	**1 hour**	**May do 1 day ahead**	
Chilling Time:	**4 hours**		

Variation: *May add ½ finely chopped green pepper to step 3.*

MARINATED CARROTS
"The color is beautiful"

2 1-pound packages frozen carrots
Salt to taste
1 thinly sliced, medium onion
1 diced, small green pepper
1 11-ounce can tomato soup
½ cup salad oil
¾ cup cider vinegar
1 cup sugar
1 teaspoon prepared mustard
1 teaspoon Worcestershire sauce

1. Boil carrots until crisp-tender. Drain. Immediately salt carrots to taste.
2. Alternate layers of carrots, onion and green pepper.
3. Boil remaining ingredients until thick.
4. While hot, pour sauce over carrot mixture.
5. Marinate at least 12 hours to a week or more.
6. Serve cold.

Preparation Time:	25 minutes	Serves:	15
Cooking Time:	15 minutes	Must do ahead	
Marinating Time:	12 hours		

Variations: *Add 1 sliced, medium red onion and 1 10-ounce package frozen peas. Alternate layers of carrots, peas, onion rings and green pepper.*
Tip: *Will keep in refrigerator 3-4 weeks.*

TOMATOES WITH MUSHROOM-ARTICHOKE FILLING
"No cooking"

8 firm, large tomatoes
Seasoned salt
2 6-ounce jars drained, marinated artichoke hearts
2 8-ounce jars drained mushroom stems and pieces
1 cup mayonnaise
⅔ cup sour cream
2 teaspoons curry powder
2 teaspoons lemon juice
2 Tablespoons minced onion
Paprika

1. Dip tomatoes in boiling water for 30 seconds, then run under cold water.
2. Peel and scoop out pulp and seeds to form a cup.
3. Sprinkle generously with seasoned salt and fill with artichokes and mushrooms. Refrigerate.
4. In bowl, combine mayonnaise, sour cream, curry powder, lemon juice and onion. Refrigerate.
5. To serve, top each tomato with mayonnaise mixture and sprinkle with paprika.

Preparation Time:	20 minutes	Serves:	8
Chilling Time:	1 hour	May do ahead	

SPRING ASPARAGUS SALAD

Dressing

1 package Italian salad dressing mix
¼ cup water
¼ cup olive liquid from pimento-stuffed olives
⅓ cup oil

Mix above ingredients in jar, shake and chill.

Salad

2½ pounds asparagus
2 cups boiling water
1 3-ounce jar pimento-stuffed olives
¾ cup pepitas
Romaine lettuce

1. Cut cleaned asparagus into ½-inch diagonal slices. Cook covered 3 minutes. Drain and rinse in cold water. Cool.
2. Slice olives and add with Dressing to asparagus. Chill at least 1 hour. Add pepitas just before serving.
3. Drain off excess dressing. Serve on bed of romaine lettuce.

Preparation Time:	**25 minutes**	**Serves:**	**6-8**
Cooking Time:	**3 minutes**	**May do ahead**	
Chilling Time:	**1-2 hours**		

WILD RICE-ARTICHOKE SALAD

2 cups cooked wild rice
1 10-ounce package frozen green peas
1 pint cherry tomatoes, cut in half
1 16-ounce can drained, diced artichoke hearts
½ cup olive oil
2 Tablespoons vinegar
2 Tablespoons minced green onion

Mix all ingredients. Chill.

Preparation Time:	**15 minutes**	**Serves:**	**6-8**
Chilling Time:	**4-6 hours**	**May do ahead**	

TOMATO-CHEESE SALAD WITH CUCUMBERS
"Lovely to look at - delightful to eat"

Salad

3-4 sliced, medium tomatoes
½ pound sliced, smoked gouda cheese
24 slices cucumbers (run fork tines down cucumbers to decorate)
1 bunch watercress

1. On individual salad plates, place 3 slices of tomato. Top with slice of cheese, then with cucumber slices.
2. Pour Dressing over Salad and garnish with sprigs of watercress in the center.

Dressing

1-2 quartered garlic cloves
½ cup salad oil or olive oil
½ teaspoon salt
Cavender's Greek Seasoning and other seasonings to taste
3 Tablespoons fresh lemon juice
¼ cup seasoned rice vinegar

1. Marinate garlic in oil overnight or at least 1 hour.
2. Just before serving, remove and discard garlic.
3. Combine oil, salt and seasonings in small bowl.
4. Mix lemon juice with vinegar. Gradually add to oil and whisk to combine.

Preparation Time: **15 minutes**   **Serves:**   **6-8**

CURRY CHICKEN SALAD

2½ cups diced soyameat chicken
1 8-ounce can sliced water chestnuts
1 13½-ounce can drained pineapple chunks
¼ cup sliced celery
¼ cup sliced ripe olives
½ cup sour cream
½ cup mayonnaise
2 teaspoons curry powder
3 Tablespoons mango chutney
1 5-ounce can chow mein noodles
½ cup chopped pecans

1. Mix chicken, water chestnuts, pineapple, celery and olives.
2. Blend sour cream, mayonnaise, curry powder and chutney.
3. Mix chicken mixture and sour cream mixture together. Let chill overnight in refrigerator.
4. Just before serving, add noodles and nuts.

Preparation Time: **15 minutes**   **Serves:**   **8-10**
Chilling Time: **6-8 hours**   **Must do ahead**

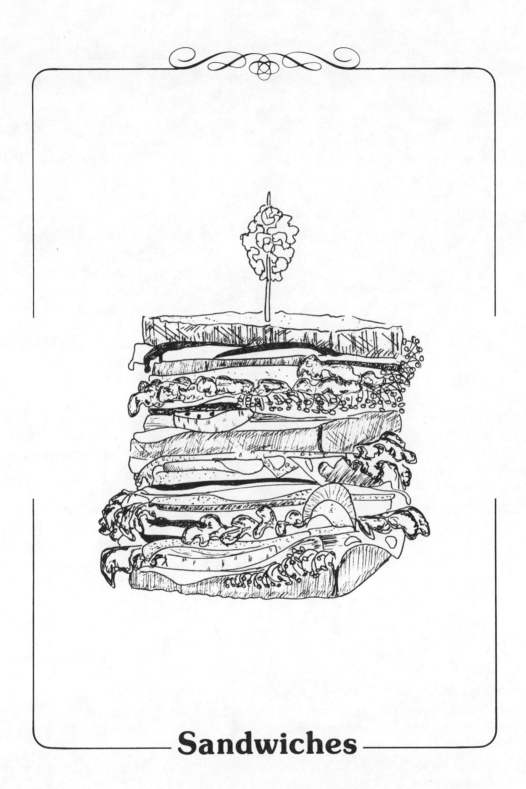

Sandwiches

BROILED CHEESE ROLLS
"These disappear quickly"

1 cup grated Cheddar cheese
½ cup grated Monterey Jack cheese
2 Tablespoons chopped green onions
2 Tablespoons chopped olives
1 Tablespoon chopped parsley
2 Tablespoons imitation bacon bits
½ cup mayonnaise
6 sourdough rolls

1. Mix all ingredients with mayonnaise to moisten.
2. Let mixture stand for at least 1 hour.
3. When ready to serve, cut sourdough rolls in half.
4. Spread rolls with cheese mixture.
5. Place rolls under broiler until bubbly.

Preparation Time:	20 minutes	**Serves:**	6
Standing Time:	1 hour		
Baking Time:	3-10 minutes		

Variation: *May use English muffins.*
Tip: *Rolls may be toasted before spreading cheese mixture.*

FRENCH BREAD GARLIC LOAF
"A meal in itself"

1 pound loaf French bread
½ cup butter
6 crushed garlic cloves
2 Tablespoons sesame seeds
1½ cups sour cream
2 cups cubed Monterey Jack cheese
¼ cup grated, fresh Parmesan cheese
2 Tablespoons dried parsley flakes
2 7-ounce cans drained artichoke hearts
1 cup grated Cheddar cheese
1 6-ounce can drained, pitted, ripe olives
Tomato slices and parsley sprigs for garnish

1. Cut bread in halves lengthwise. Place halves on aluminum foil-covered baking sheet.
2. Tear out inner portion of bread in large chunks, leaving crusts in tact.
3. Melt butter in large skillet. Stir in garlic and sesame seeds. Add bread chunks and fry until bread is golden and butter is absorbed. Remove from heat.
4. Combine sour cream, Monterey Jack cheese, Parmesan cheese and parsley flakes. Stir in artichoke hearts and toasted bread mixture. Mix well. Spoon into bread crust shells and sprinkle with Cheddar cheese.
5. Bake at 350 degrees for 30 minutes.
6. Remove bread from oven. Arrange tomato slices and parsley sprigs down center and olives around edges.

Preparation Time:	25 minutes	**Serves:**	8
Baking Time:	30 minutes		

MEXICAN ROLLS

"A tasty meal in itself"

12 sourdough rolls
1 bunch chopped green onions
½ cup mayonnaise
1 teaspoon Worcestershire sauce
3 dashes hot pepper sauce
¾ cup grated Cheddar cheese
½ cup grated Monterey Jack cheese
1 2-ounce can chopped green chiles

1. Cut "V" lengthwise in roll. Remove wedge and small amount of bread center.
2. Mix remaining ingredients. Fill rolls with cheese mixture.
3. Place in foil-covered pan.
4. Bake at 350 degrees until cheese is melted and bubbly. Serve hot.

Preparation Time:	**25 minutes**	**Yield:**	**12 rolls**
Baking Time:	**12-15 minutes**		

ONION BREAD

2 cups coarsely chopped onion
2 cups grated Monterey Jack cheese
1 cup mayonnaise
1 pound loaf French bread

1. Mix onion, cheese and mayonnaise.
2. Cut French bread lengthwise into halves.
3. Spread onion-cheese mixture over bread.
4. Bake at 350 degrees for 15 minutes or until cheese begins to brown.

Preparation Time:	**15 minutes**	**Serves:**	**8**
Baking Time:	**15 minutes**		

ONION ROULADES

"Great party sandwich"

1 package refrigerated crescent rolls
Melted butter
4 teaspoons dry onion soup mix
1 3-ounce package cream cheese
1 separated egg
Grated Romano cheese

1. Separate and roll out crescents. Brush with melted butter.
2. Combine soup mix, cream cheese and egg yolk. Spread evenly on each crescent.
3. Roll each jellyroll fashion and place seam down on ungreased pan.
4. Brush with egg white and sprinkle with Romano cheese.
5. Bake at 375 degrees for 10-13 minutes. Serve warm.

Preparation Time:	20 minutes	**Serves:**	8 roulades
Baking Time:	10-15 minutes		

Serving Suggestion: *To make roulades diploma style, just before serving place strip of pimento across center of roll like a ribbon. Arrange on tray to serve.*

PETITE FRENCH ROLLS WITH CHEESE

"If you love cheese, you will love these"

2 dozen petite French rolls
½ pound grated Monterey Jack cheese
½ pound grated Cheddar cheese
4-5 chopped green onions
Mayonnaise, enough to hold mixture together

1. Cut hole in top of each roll. Remove section from center large enough so each roll will hold 1½ Tablespoons of filling.
2. Mix cheeses, green onions and mayonnaise. Stuff rolls.
3. Bake at 350 degrees until cheese melts, about 10 minutes.

Preparation Time:	30 minutes	**Yield:**	24 rolls
Baking Time:	10 minutes	**May do ahead**	

PINWHEELS
"Very colorful"

1 loaf unsliced bread
Parsley Butter
7 ounces pimento-stuffed olives

Parsley Butter

½ cup butter or margarine
1½ Tablespoons minced fresh parsley
½ teaspoon lemon juice

1. Cut bread lengthwise into ⅜-inch slices. Most bakeries will do this.
2. With electric knife, trim crusts from bread loaf.
3. Flatten slices with rolling pin.
4. Spread each slice with Parsley Butter.
5. Place stuffed olives at end of each slice. Roll up starting with olives.
6. Wrap in waxed paper and refrigerate.
7. To serve, place seam-side of roll against cutting board and slice.

Preparation Time: **1 hour**	**Yield:** **120 pinwheel appetizers**
	May do ahead

Variations: *Nuts, ripe olives, chopped green pepper, chopped dill pickle, thinly sliced radishes, chopped cucumber with onion salt, chopped green onions or chives, chopped dates, or cooked prunes, jelly and jam may be blended with cream cheese. Food coloring may also be added.*

SLOPPY JOES

Sauce

1 chopped onion
2 Tablespoons butter
2 cups hot water
1 cup dry burger granules
½ cup catsup
⅓ cup barbecue sauce
1 Tablespoon Worcestershire sauce
1 Tablespoon mustard
¼ cup sweet pickle relish
2 slices lemon
12 burger buns, split in halves

1. Saute onion in butter.
2. Add remaining ingredients.
3. Slow cook for 1-2 hours.
4. Remove lemon slices before serving.
5. To serve, spoon sauce over split buns. Replace tops.

Preparation Time: **20 minutes**	**Serves:** **12**
Cooking Time: **1-2 hours**	

STUFFED HOT DOG ROLLS
"Everybody's favorite"

1 pound grated Colby or Cheddar cheese
1 4½-ounce can chopped olives
1 grated, medium onion
1 minced garlic clove
4 chopped, hard-boiled eggs
6 Tablespoons tomato sauce
3-4 Tablespoons soy sauce
¼ cup oil
24 hot dog rolls

1. In bowl, mix all ingredients except hot dog rolls.
2. Cut each roll in half. Fill with stuffing.
3. Wrap stuffed roll in foil.
4. Heat at 250 degrees for 20 minutes.

Preparation Time:	30 minutes	Yield:	24 rolls
Baking Time:	20 minutes	May do ahead and freeze	

STUFFED CHEESE BUNS

1 pound grated mild Cheddar cheese
1 4½-ounce can chopped olives
3-5 chopped green olives
2 grated, hard-boiled eggs
1 4-ounce can chopped green chiles
1 8-ounce can tomato sauce
12 sourdough rolls

1. Combine all ingredients except rolls. Mix thoroughly.
2. Cut 3-inch slot in top of roll. Pull out portion of center.
3. Fill rolls with cheese mixture.
4. Wrap in foil and bake at 325 degrees for 15 minutes.

Preparation Time:	25 minutes	Yield:	12 rolls
Baking Time:	15 minutes	May do ahead and freeze	

Variation: *Hollow out large sourdough loaf. Fill, bake and serve as above.*

SURPRISE FRENCHIES
"C'est bon!"

1 7½-ounce can drained, pitted ripe olives
6 chopped green onions
2 minced garlic cloves
3-4 diced, hard-boiled eggs
1 4-ounce can chopped green chiles
1 pound grated cheese
1 8-ounce can tomato sauce
⅓ cup oil
1 teaspoon salt
30 small French rolls

1. Combine all ingredients except rolls. Mix well.
2. Hollow out rolls and fill with mixture.
3. Wrap individually in foil.
4. Heat in oven at 300 degrees for 30 minutes, just before serving.

Preparation Time:	**20 minutes**	**Serves:**	**15**
Baking Time:	**30 minutes**	**May do ahead and freeze**	

Soups

ASPARAGUS-LEEK CHOWDER
"Soup lovers salute this winner"

3 cups sliced, fresh mushrooms
3 sliced, large leeks
1 10-ounce package frozen cut asparagus, thawed
6 Tablespoons butter
3 Tablespoons flour
½ teaspoon salt
2 cups chicken-style broth
2 cups half-and-half
1 12-ounce can white corn

1. In large saucepan, sauté mushrooms, leeks and asparagus in butter until just tender, but not browned, about 10 minutes.
2. Stir in flour and salt.
3. Add broth and half-and-half. Cook and stir until mixture is thickened and bubbly.
4. Stir in corn.
5. Heat thoroughly, but do not boil.

Preparation Time:	**20 minutes**	**Serves:**	**6-8**
Cooking Time:	**30 minutes**	**May do ahead**	

AVOCADO SOUP
"Creamy and mild"

3 diced, large avocados
1 cup half-and-half
2 cups chicken-style broth

1. In blender, mix avocado and half-and-half until smooth.
2. Heat broth in saucepan.
3. Add avocado mixture and barely heat through.

Preparation Time:	**15 minutes**	**Serves:**	**6**
		May do ahead	

Serving Suggestion: *Serve hot or cold. Garnish with extra diced avocado, imitation bacon bits, chopped green onions or dollop of whipped cream.*

CHILI-NOODLE SOUP
"Noodles olé"

1 15-ounce can stewed tomatoes
1 quart water
1 20-ounce can prepared chili or 2½ cups chili and beans
1 minced, large onion
2 Tablespoons oil
2 eggs
3 bay leaves
1 Tablespoon chicken-style seasoning
Accent to taste
Garlic salt to taste
2 cups dry noodles
1 cup half-and-half

1. Place tomatoes, water and chili in kettle. Heat to boiling.
2. Sauté onion in oil and add eggs. Scramble until lightly browned.
3. Add bay leaves and seasonings to tomato-chili mixture.
4. Bring to boil and add dry noodles and scrambled eggs.
5. Simmer slowly for 45 minutes.
6. Just before serving, add 2 Tablespoons half-and-half to each bowl.

Preparation Time:	**20 minutes**	**Serves:**	**8**
Cooking Time:	**1 hour**	**May do ahead**	

CREAM OF MUSHROOM SOUP

2 cups chopped onion
4 Tablespoons butter
12 ounces sliced, fresh mushrooms
1-2 teaspoons dill weed
2 cups chicken-style broth
1 Tablespoon soy sauce
1 teaspoon paprika, or to taste
3 Tablespoons flour
1 cup milk
1 teaspoon salt
2 teaspoons fresh lemon juice
½ cup sour cream

1. Sauté onions in 2 Tablespoons butter.
2. Add mushrooms, dill weed, ½ cup chicken-style broth, soy sauce and paprika.
3. In separate saucepan, melt 2 Tablespoons butter. Add flour and milk. Stir until thickened.
4. Combine white sauce, mushroom mixture and remaining 1½ cups chicken-style broth. Cover and simmer 10 minutes.
5. Just before serving, add salt, lemon juice and sour cream.

Preparation Time:	**20 minutes**	**Serves:**	**4**
Cooking Time:	**20 minutes**		

CURRY-CARROT SOUP
"Just a dash of curry makes the difference"

2 cups sliced carrots
4 cups chicken-style broth
1 8-ounce package cream cheese
$^1/_2$ teaspoon curry powder
8 chopped green onions

1. Cook carrots in chicken-style broth for 5 minutes.
2. While hot, put in blender or food processor.
3. Add cream cheese, curry and green onions. Blend thoroughly.
4. Serve immediately.

Preparation Time: **15 minutes**   **Serves:**   **8**
Tip: *Do not bring to boil.*

EGG-RICE LEMON SOUP

9 cups chicken-style broth
3 Tablespoons butter
1 cup rice
4 separated eggs
Juice from 2 lemons

1. Bring chicken-style broth to boil. Add butter and rice. Simmer, covered, for 30 minutes. Remove from heat.
2. In bowl, beat eggs whites until stiff. Add yolks, 1 at a time. Beat well.
3. Slowly add lemon juice to eggs, beating continuously.
4. Add 2 cups of broth and do NOT stop beating! (The constant beating is the secret to preventing curdling of this delicate soup).
5. When eggs and broth are well mixed, pour this mixture into remaining broth and rice. Stir well over heat, but do NOT allow to boil.
6. Serve at once in bowls, garnished with thinly sliced lemons.

Preparation Time: **20 minutes**   **Serves:**   **8**
Cooking Time: **35 minutes**

GAZPACHO
"You'll never guess it's low cal"

1 8-ounce can tomato juice
1 16-ounce can stewed tomatoes
1 chopped, large tomato
2 chopped zucchini
4 chopped green onions
1 chopped green pepper
¼ cup sliced black olives
Sour cream

1. In large saucepan, combine tomato juice, tomatoes, zucchini, onions and green pepper.
2. If serving hot, simmer 30 minutes. If serving cold, chill ½ hour.
3. To serve, place in individual soup bowls. Garnish with black olive slices and dollop of sour cream.

Preparation Time:	30 minutes	Serves:	6
Chilling Time or		May do ahead	
Cooking Time:	30 minutes		

Variation: *Any fresh vegetables may be used.*

OLD-FASHIONED VEGETABLE STEW
"Very good and different"

8 cups water
2 diced, medium onions
4 chopped, large stalks celery
¾ teaspoon crumbled basil leaf
2 minced garlic cloves
½ cup tamari or soy sauce
4 cups carrots, sliced in ½-inch rounds
3 unpeeled, large potatoes, cut into 1-inch cubes
1 20-ounce package frozen green peas
½ pound tofu, frozen, thawed and cubed into ½-inch pieces
2 Tablespoons flour
½ cup cool water

1. In 6-quart pot, bring to boil water, onion and celery.
2. Add basil, garlic, tamari and carrots. Simmer, covered, stirring occasionally until carrots are slightly tender, about 15 minutes.
3. Add potatoes and simmer, covered, stirring occasionally, until potatoes are tender but still intact, about 10-15 minutes.
4. Add peas and tofu. Reduce to lowest heat.
5. Whisk flour into water until smooth. Gently, but quickly, stir into mixture. Continue simmering on low heat until stew thickens, about 5 minutes.
6. Add additional tamari to taste.

Preparation Time:	45 minutes	Serves:	10-12
Cooking Time:	50 minutes	Yield:	5 quarts
		May do ahead	

HOBO STEW

"Delicious! Sounds complicated, but really isn't"

PRESSURE COOKER RECIPE

6 medium potatoes
1 finely chopped, large onion
3 stalks celery, cut in 1-inch pieces
2 Tablespoons plus ¼ cup butter
1½ pounds fresh green beans, cut in pieces
2 cups water
1 Tablespoon herb salt
1 teaspoon summer savory
½ teaspoon thyme
1 Tablespoon chicken-style seasoning
1 teaspoon onion powder
½ teaspoon garlic powder
2 Tablespoons hickory smoked yeast
1 bay leaf (discard before serving)
1 teaspoon salt
¼ cup flour
1 2-ounce jar diced pimentos
½ pound tofu, frozen, thawed and cubed

1. Cook unpeeled potatoes 10 minutes in pressure cooker at 15 pounds pressure. Cool slightly. Peel and cut into eighths. Set aside.
2. In pressure cooker, sauté onion and celery in 2 Tablespoons butter for 5 minutes.
3. Add green beans, 1½ cups water and seasonings.
4. Cook 1½ minutes at 15 pounds pressure.
5. Add ¼ cup butter to melt in beans and ½ cups water blended with flour. Cook until thickened.
6. Add cooked potatoes.
7. Add pimento and tofu cubes. Heat to serving temperature.

Preparation Time: **1 hour**   **Serves:**   **8**
Cooking Time: **20 minutes**
Tip: *May do ahead up to step 7.*

PICKLE BEAN-VEGETABLE SOUP
"Where's the pickle?"

1¼ cups dry navy beans
6 cups water
2 cups water mixed with 3 packets G. Washington's Rich Brown Seasoning and
   Broth
1 cup sliced celery
1 cup shredded cabbage
1 cup thinly sliced carrots
½ cup thinly sliced onion
1 24-ounce jar thinly sliced, kosher dill pickles
¾-1 cup dill pickle juice
1 teaspoon salt
⅛ teaspoon cayenne pepper
1 teaspoon marjoram
½ teaspoon basil
1 28-ounce can tomatoes

1. Sort and rinse beans.
2. Place in large saucepan. Add 6 cups water. Boil for 2 minutes. Remove from heat and soak
   1 hour. Drain and reserve liquid.
3. Return beans to large pan. Add all remaining ingredients plus 2 cups of reserved bean liquid.
   Cover and simmer 45 minutes, adding extra bean liquid if necessary.

Preparation Time:	**30 minutes**	**Serves:**	**4-6**
Standing Time:	**1 hour**	**May do several days ahead**	
Cooking Time:	**50 minutes**		

POTATO, CHEESE AND CHILE SOUP
"A unique twist to an old favorite"

4 diced, medium potatoes
3 cups water
1½ cups chopped onion
1 Tablespoon butter
1 Tablespoon olive oil
1¾ teaspoons salt
1 teaspoon cumin
1 teaspoon basil
2 crushed garlic cloves
Cayenne pepper to taste
1½ cups diced green pepper
2 4-ounce cans diced green chiles
1 cup milk
¾ cup sour cream
1 cup grated Monterey Jack cheese
2 minced green onions

1. Cook potatoes in water in partially covered pan until tender. Cool to room temperature while in cooking water.
2. Sauté onions in butter and oil in large skillet. Add salt, cumin, basil, garlic and cayenne pepper. Continue to sauté over medium heat for 5-8 minutes. Add diced pepper and sauté a few additional minutes.
3. Using blender, purée potatoes in cooking water. Return purée to saucepan. Add sautéed mixture, green chiles and milk. Whisk until well-blended.
4. Heat over low setting.
5. Stir in sour cream, Monterey Jack cheese and green onions.

Preparation Time: **50 minutes**   **Serves:**   **6-8**
Cooking Time: **45 minutes**
Tip: *Flavor is best if made 1 day ahead.*

POTATO-QUESO CHOWDER

2 cups cubed, unpeeled, raw potatoes
¾ cup chopped onion
½ cup coarsely chopped celery
2½ teaspoons salt
2½ cups boiling water
4 Tablespoons margarine
4 Tablespoons flour
1½ teaspoons soy sauce
2 cups milk
¼-½ pound grated Cheddar cheese
1 cup canned, chopped tomatoes
2 or more Tablespoons chopped parsley

1. In deep kettle, combine potatoes, onion, celery, 1 teaspoon salt and boiling water. Simmer 15 minutes or until tender.
2. In separate saucepan, melt margarine. Stir in flour until smooth. Add remaining 1½ teaspoons salt and soy sauce. Cook, stirring constantly, for about 1 minute.
3. Add milk gradually, stirring constantly. Cook until thickened.
4. Add cheese and stir until well-blended.
5. Stir into potato mixture. Add tomatoes and parsley.

Preparation Time:	30 minutes	Serves:	6-8
Cooking Time:	25 minutes	May do ahead	

PUMPKIN-LEEK SOUP

"A real surprise - yummy!"

½ pound diced, fresh pumpkin or banana squash
1 diced, medium potato
2 Tablespoons butter
1 sliced, small onion
3 cups chicken-style broth
½ teaspoon garlic powder
1 cup water
1 16-ounce can unsweetened pumpkin
1½ teaspoons chopped parsley
½ cup thinly sliced leeks
1 cup heavy cream
Salt to taste

1. In large saucepan, stir fresh pumpkin, potato and butter over moderate heat.
2. As mixture begins to brown, add onion and continue to stir until onion softens.
3. Add broth, garlic and water. Bring to boil, reduce heat and simmer 35 minutes.
4. Add canned pumpkin, parsley and leeks. Simmer 20 minutes.
5. Purée soup in food processor.
6. Reheat in saucepan.
7. Before serving, stir in heavy cream. Season with salt. Serve hot.

Preparation Time:	30 minutes	Serves:	8
Cooking Time:	1 hour	May do ahead	

SPICY TOMATO-RICE SOUP

1 11-ounce can tomato-rice soup
1 11-ounce can tomato soup
1 11-ounce can nacho cheese soup
1 15½-ounce can Chilli Man Vegetarian Chilli or 2 cups homemade chili, optional
2 cans water
1 can milk

1. Mix all ingredients.
2. Heat and serve.

Preparation Time: **10 minutes**   **Serves:**   **8**

WATERCRESS SOUP

3 quarts chicken-style broth
2 bunches watercress
1 cup shredded Chinese cabbage
4 Tablespoons cornstarch dissolved in 4 Tablespoons water
12 dried Chinese mushrooms, soaked for 10 minutes in 1 cup very hot water
    (discard stems)
2 thinly sliced green onions

1. Boil broth.
2. Add watercress and cabbage. Simmer 2 minutes.
3. Stir in cornstarch. Cook 1 minute.
4. Stir in mushroom caps and green onions.
5. Serve hot.

Preparation Time: **20 minutes**   **Yield:**   **3½ quarts**
Cooking Time: **10 minutes**

ZUCCHINI SOUP

"A gardener's delight"

12 medium zucchini
6 packets G. Washington's Golden Seasoning and Broth
2 cups water
6 stalks chopped celery
1 chopped large onion
1 chopped green pepper
4 crushed garlic cloves
2 cans evaporated milk or 3 cups half-and-half
2 Tablespoons chopped parsley for garnish

1. On low heat, cook all ingredients except milk and parsley for 45 minutes.
2. Put mixture into blender and purée.
3. Return mixture to large kettle. Add milk. Stir well. Heat through.
4. To serve, garnish with parsley.

Preparation Time: **30 minutes**   **Serves:**   **8**
Cooking Time: **45 minutes**   **May do ahead**
Variation: *Add 1 teaspoon curry powder.*
Tip: *May be frozen at end of step 2.*

Vegetables

CHINESE ASPARAGUS

"Welcome asparagus season with this"

3 cups sliced asparagus
1 Tablespoon vegetable oil
½ teaspoon salt
2 Tablespoons soy sauce
2 minced garlic cloves
2 cups cherry tomatoes

1. Snap off woody base of asparagus stalk at breaking point where tender part begins. Slice on extreme diagonal, approximately 1½ inches long.
2. Heat oil in large skillet. When hot, add asparagus pieces.
3. Mix salt, soy sauce and garlic. Pour over asparagus. Cover and heat 4-5 minutes until asparagus is crisp-tender.
4. Add cherry tomatoes. Stir to heat tomatoes slightly.

Preparation Time: **15 minutes**   **Serves:**   **6**
Cooking Time: **5-6 minutes**
Variation: *Fresh pea pods may be substituted for asparagus.*

HERBED ASPARAGUS WITH PARMESAN CHEESE

2 pounds fresh asparagus, tough ends removed
4 Tablespoons unsalted butter
1 Tablespoon chopped parsley
1 Tablespoon chopped, dried chives
1 teaspoon rosemary
1 teaspoon dill weed
1 cup grated, fresh Parmesan cheese

1. Blanch asparagus in boiling water for 1½-2 minutes or until just crisp-tender. Remove to paper towel and pat dry.
2. Just before serving, in small saucepan, combine butter with parsley, chives, rosemary and dill weed. Heat thoroughly. Remove from heat.
3. Place asparagus in herb-butter mixture. Let stand 2-3 minutes.
4. Remove to serving platter. Sprinkle cheese over asparagus. Serve immediately.

Preparation Time: **15 minutes**   **Serves:**   **8**
Cooking Time: **1-2 minutes**

BROCCOLI CASSEROLE
"Tastes like Stouffer's'

1 20-ounce package frozen, chopped broccoli or 4 cups fresh broccoli flowerets and pieces
1 cup mayonnaise
1 cup sour cream
1 cup grated Cheddar cheese
1 diced, medium onion
1 egg
1 cup saltine cracker crumbs

1. Cook broccoli and drain well.
2. Mix with all other ingredients except cracker crumbs.
3. Pour into 9 x 13-inch baking dish. Top with cracker crumbs.
4. Bake at 350 degrees for 30 minutes.

Preparation Time:	**15 minutes**	**Serves:**	**8**
Baking Time:	**30 minutes**	**May do ahead**	

Variation: *Substitute 1 11-ounce can cream of mushroom soup for sour cream. Cheese-flavored cracker crumbs may be used for topping.*

BROCCOLI WITH ORANGE SAUCE
"Different and delicious"

1½ pounds (5 cups) broccoli, cut into serving-size pieces
6 ounces cream cheese
¼ cup milk
½ teaspoon salt
½ teaspoon grated orange peel
¼ teaspoon thyme
¼ cup orange juice
2-3 Tablespoons pecans or almonds

1. Cook broccoli in boiling, salted water until crisp-tender. Drain well.
2. In separate saucepan, combine cream cheese, milk, salt, orange peel and thyme.
3. Cook over medium heat until smooth, stirring occasionally.
4. Add orange juice and mix well.
5. Place hot broccoli in serving dish. Pour orange sauce over broccoli. Sprinkle with nuts.

Preparation Time:	**20 minutes**	**Serves:**	**6-8**
Cooking Time:	**20-30 minutes**		

Variation: *Garnish with orange slices.*

BROCCOLI WITH PARSLEY VINAIGRETTE
"Something different"

2½-3 pounds well-trimmed broccoli, cut into flowerets with 1-2 inch stems
6 Tablespoons rice vinegar
1½ teaspoons Dijon mustard
¾ cup vegetable oil
½ cup snipped, fresh chives
¾ cup minced fresh parsley
3 Tablespoons finely minced shallots
1 teaspoon salt

1. Cook broccoli in boiling, salted water 8-10 minutes, until stems are easily pierced with fork. Drain well.
2. Combine vinegar and mustard in small bowl. Slowly whisk in oil. Continue whisking until vinaigrette is emulsified.
3. Add chives, parsley, shallots and salt. Mix well.
4. Pour enough dressing over hot broccoli to coat. Serve warm or let cool to room temperature.

Preparation Time:	20 minutes	Serves:	8
Cooking Time:	8-10 minutes		

BABY CARROTS WITH GREEN ONIONS
"Perfect party vegetable"

1 16-ounce package frozen whole baby carrots
4-5 sliced green onions
3-4 Tablespoons butter
Salt to taste

1. Place carrots in boiling water. Cover and cook until crisp-tender.
2. Remove from heat. Drain.
3. Add green onions, butter and salt to taste.

Preparation Time:	5 minutes	Serves:	6-8
Cooking Time:	5-10 minutes		

GLAZED CARROTS WITH ORANGE SLICES

8-10 Servings

⅓ cup margarine
1 cup sugar
2-3 unpeeled, thinly sliced oranges
2½ 10-ounce packages frozen carrots, cooked

1. Melt margarine and sugar. Cook on low approximately 5-10 minutes.
2. Remove seeds from orange slices and add to sugar mixture.
3. Add drained carrots. Simmer 5 minutes.

Preparation Time: **10 minutes**
Cooking Time: **30 minutes**

50 Servings

1½ cups margarine
5 cups sugar
13 unpeeled, thinly sliced oranges
13 10-ounce packages frozen carrots, cooked

100 Servings

3 cups plus 2 Tablespoons margarine
10 cups sugar
25 unpeeled, thinly sliced oranges
25 10-ounce packages frozen carrots, cooked

PARSLEYED CAULIFLOWER

1 head cauliflower, about 1¾ pounds, trimmed and cut into flowerets
4 cups water
¼ cup milk
1¼ teaspoons salt
5 Tablespoons butter
1 hard-boiled, peeled, finely sieved egg
2 Tablespoons minced parsley

1. In large saucepan, bring cauliflower, water, milk and ¼ teaspoon salt to boil. Simmer 10 minutes or until barely tender. Drain.
2. In skillet, melt 1 Tablespoon butter. Add cauliflower and toss until flowerets start to take on color. Transfer to serving dish and keep warm.
3. Melt remaining 4 Tablespoons butter. Add egg and remaining 1 teaspoon salt. Pour over cauliflower. Sprinkle with parsley.
4. Serve immediately.

Preparation Time: **20 minutes**   **Serves:**   **4-6**
Cooking Time: **20 minutes**
Tip: *After step 1, cauliflower may be set aside and final preparation done later.*

CORN STRADA

12-15 slices French bread without crusts
Butter
1 16-ounce can creamed corn
1 16-ounce can drained, whole kernel corn
1 7-ounce can diced green chiles
2 cups grated Monterey Jack cheese
6 beaten eggs
2 cups milk
1 teaspoon salt

1. Butter both sides of bread.
2. Line bottom of 9 x 13-inch baking dish with ½ of buttered bread slices.
3. Combine creamed corn and whole kernel corn. Spread evenly over layer of bread.
4. Add layer of green chiles, then 1 cup of cheese.
5. Repeat layers 1 time.
6. Beat eggs, milk and salt. Pour over layers. Cover and refrigerate overnight.
7. Bake at 350 degrees for 1 hour.

Preparation Time:	**20 minutes**	**Serves:**	**12-15**
Baking Time:	**1 hour**	**Must do ahead**	

CREAMED GREEN BEANS

MICROWAVE RECIPE

1 8-ounce jar pasteurized process cheese spread
1 11-ounce can cream of mushroom soup
Hot pepper sauce to taste
1 Tablespoon soy sauce
1 chopped, medium onion
3 Tablespoons butter
5 chopped, fresh mushrooms
1 8-ounce can drained, sliced water chestnuts
2 16-ounce cans drained, French-style green beans
Slivered almonds

1. In glass bowl, combine cheese spread, soup, hot pepper sauce and soy sauce. Microwave 3-5 minutes, stirring halfway through cooking time.
2. In 1½-quart glass casserole, microwave onion and butter 3-4 minutes, stirring halfway through cooking time until onions are transparent. Stir in mushrooms and water chestnuts and microwave 1 minute.
3. Add green beans and soup mixture to mushroom mixture. Stir to blend. Garnish with almonds.
4. Microwave 5 minutes, rotating dish ¼ turn halfway through cooking time.
5. Rest 5 minutes before serving.

Preparation Time:	**10 minutes**	**Serves:**	**6-8**
Cooking Time:	**12-15 minutes**		
Standing Time:	**5 minutes**		

GREEN BEANS WITH CASHEWS
"Easy and flavorful"

2½ pounds fresh green beans
⅓ cup butter
1½ teaspoons lemon juice
¾ cup salted cashews
Salt and seasoning to taste

1. Trim ends of beans and cut into 1-1½-inch pieces.
2. Bring large pot of salted water to boil.
3. Add beans and boil on medium heat, uncovered, about 10 minutes or until crisp-tender.
4. Pour into colander and run under cold water 3-4 minutes.
5. Spread beans on towel and pat dry.
6. Before serving, allow beans to cool to room temperature. Melt butter in skillet and add beans, lemon juice and cashews. Cook and toss on medium-high heat until heated thoroughly. Add salt and seasoning to taste.

Preparation Time:	**10 minutes**	**Serves:**	**6-8**
Cooking Time:	**10 minutes**		

Tip: *May cover and refrigerate overnight until ready to serve.*

MARINATED GREEN BEANS

1½ pounds green beans

Marinade

¼ cup minced dry onions
2 minced garlic cloves
¼ cup olive oil
¼ cup safflower oil
1 Tablespoon fresh lemon juice
½ cup rice vinegar
½-¾ cup sugar
2 teaspoons Dijon mustard
½ teaspoon tarragon
½ teaspoon dill weed
½ cup fresh, minced parsley
½ cup toasted, slivered almonds

1. Cook green beans until crisp-tender, about 5-6 minutes. Drain. Rinse in cold water.
2. Mix Marinade ingredients together. Pour over green beans. Marinate overnight.
3. When ready to serve, toss in almonds.

Preparation Time:	**20 minutes**	**Serves:**	**8**
Cooking Time:	**5-6 minutes**	**Must do ahead**	
Standing Time:	**Overnight**		

CREAMED MUSHROOMS AND ARTICHOKES

2 Tablespoons butter
1 pound sliced, fresh mushrooms
½ cup sliced green onion
2 Tablespoons flour
1 teaspoon chicken-style seasoning
¼ teaspoon thyme
½ teaspoon salt
Dash nutmeg
2 cups milk
½ cup sour cream
1 9-ounce package frozen artichoke hearts, thawed
½ cup grated Swiss cheese

1. In saucepan, melt butter. Sauté mushrooms and onion.
2. Add flour and seasonings. Mix well.
3. Gradually add milk. Heat until mixture thickens, stirring constantly.
4. Add sour cream until just blended.
5. Fold in artichokes and cheese.

Preparation Time: **15 minutes**   **Serves:**   **4-6**
Cooking Time: **15 minutes**
Serving Suggestion: *Serve over fettuccine noodles or rice. Sprinkle with grated Swiss cheese.*
Tip: *May thin with a little milk, if necessary.*

PEAS WITH WATER CHESTNUTS

2 10-ounce packages frozen green peas
1 8-ounce can sliced water chestnuts
Butter
Seasoned salt to taste

1. Cook peas in boiling water until just tender, about 2-3 minutes.
2. Add water chestnuts, butter and seasoned salt.

Preparation Time: **2 minutes**   **Serves:**   **6-8**
Cooking Time: **2-3 minutes**

PETITE PEAS PIQUANT

2 16-ounce packages frozen petite peas
¼-¼ cup Piquant Dressing

1. Prepare peas according to package directions.
2. Lightly toss with Piquant Dressing just before serving hot.

Piquant Dressing

1 cup oil
½ cup rice vinegar
1 minced garlic clove
1 teaspoon salt
1 teaspoon dry mustard
2 teaspoons basil
2 dashes nutmeg
1 Tablespoon sugar

Combine all ingredients. Shake well before using.

Preparation Time: 5 minutes   **Yield: 2 cups**
Tip: *Leftover dressing is great for salads.*

SNOW PEAS WITH ALMONDS
"The ultimate"

¼ cup chopped green onions
2 Tablespoons butter
½ pound fresh snow peas
1 cup sliced, fresh mushrooms
2 Tablespoons cornstarch
1 teaspoon chicken-style seasoning
⅔ cup water
2 teaspoons soy sauce
2 Tablespoons toasted, slivered almonds

1. In large skillet, sauté onion in butter until tender.
2. Add snow peas and mushrooms. Toss and cook over high heat for 1 minute. Remove from heat.
3. Combine cornstarch, chicken seasoning, water and soy sauce. Mix into snow peas and mushrooms. Cook until mixture thickens and bubbles.
4. To serve, toss with almonds.

Preparation Time: 15 minutes   **Serves: 6-8**
Cooking Time: 15 minutes

GOLDEN POTATO CASSEROLE
"Even the kids will like this"

6 medium potatoes
½ cup melted butter
1 cup grated Cheddar cheese
2 cups sour cream
2 cups thinly sliced green onions, including tops
1 teaspoon salt
2 Tablespoons butter

1. Cook unpeeled potatoes in salted water. Chill and peel. Grate into large bowl.
2. Add remaining ingredients except 2 Tablespoons butter. Mix thoroughly.
3. Pour into 9 x 13-inch baking dish. Dot with 2 Tablespoons butter.
4. Bake at 350 degrees for 45 minutes.

Preparation Time:	**15 minutes**	**Serves:**	**6**
Baking Time:	**45 minutes**	**May do ahead**	

HASH BROWN CASSEROLE

1 2-pound package frozen hash brown potatoes
1 8-ounce package diced Velveeta cheese
½ cup melted butter
1 cup sour cream
1 11-ounce can cream of mushroom soup

1. Mix all ingredients. Pour into 9 x 13-inch casserole dish.
2. Bake at 350 degrees for 1 hour.

Preparation Time:	**15 minutes**	**Serves:**	**8-10**
Baking Time:	**1 hour**	**May do ahead**	

Variations: *Add ½ cup onion and substitute mild or sharp Cheddar cheese. Extra cheese may be added as topping during last 10 minutes of baking.*

LEMON-BUTTERED NEW POTATOES

10-12 small new potatoes
⅓ cup butter
1 teaspoon chopped parsley
1 teaspoon grated lemon peel
½ teaspoon salt
3 Tablespoons lemon juice

1. Trim 1-inch strip around center of each potato.
2. Cook potatoes in small amount of boiling water until tender. Drain well.
3. Melt butter in separate pan. Add remaining ingredients and potatoes. Heat thoroughly.
4. To serve, place hot potatoes in serving dish. Pour butter mixture over potatoes.

Preparation Time:	**15 minutes**	**Serves:**	**6**
Cooking Time:	**15-20 minutes**		

POTATO-CHIVE SQUARES

3 peeled, grated, cooked potatoes
¼ cup chopped chives
2 eggs
2 Tablespoons flour
½ teaspoon baking powder
Salt to taste

1. Combine all ingredients. Mix well.
2. Pour into well-greased 9 x 9-inch baking dish.
3. Bake at 350 degrees for 45 minutes.
4. Cut into squares.

Preparation Time:	15 minutes	**Serves:**	5-6
Baking Time:	45 minutes		

Serving Suggestion: *Serve with dollop of sour cream and Special Applesauce.*
Tip: *Grate potatoes just before using so batter does not darken. If grated earlier, cover with cold water and drain before using. Pat dry with paper towels.*

TATER TOTS SUPREME

4 cups frozen Tater Tots
1 16-ounce can stewed tomatoes
¼ teaspoon oregano
1 cup sour cream
2 Tablespoons milk
1 4-ounce can diced green chiles
1 teaspoon salt
½ cup grated Cheddar cheese

1. Place Tater Tots in 9 x 9-inch baking dish.
2. Mix tomatoes with oregano. Pour over potatoes.
3. In small bowl, mix sour cream, milk, green chiles and salt.
4. Spoon over tomatoes.
5. Sprinkle with cheese.
6. Bake at 375 degrees for 25 minutes.

Preparation Time:	15 minutes	**Serves:**	6
Baking Time:	25 minutes		

SQUASH CASSEROLE

"Even non-squash eaters go for this"

2 pounds summer squash
1½ sliced, medium onions
1 11-ounce can cream of mushroom soup
1 cup sour cream
1 cup grated carrots
½ cup melted margarine
1 8-ounce package herb stuffing mix

1. In saucepan, cook squash and onion in boiling water 5 minutes. Drain.
2. In mixing bowl, combine soup and sour cream.
3. Stir carrots into soup-sour cream mixture.
4. Fold in squash and onions.
5. Pour melted margarine over stuffing mix.
6. Spread ½ stuffing in bottom of 8 x 8-inch baking dish.
7. Spoon vegetables over stuffing.
8. Cover with remaining stuffing.
9. Bake at 350 degrees for 30 minutes.

Preparation Time:	20 minutes	**Serves:**	6-8
Baking Time:	30 minutes		

SWEET POTATO SOUFFLE

"Good as punkin' pie"

Potatoes

3 cups cooked, mashed sweet potatoes
1 cup sugar
2 eggs
½ cup milk
½ teaspoon salt
1 teaspoon vanilla

Topping

1 cup brown sugar
½ cup flour
½ cup chopped pecans
¼ cup butter

1. Combine potato ingredients. Mix well.
2. Pour into buttered 8 x 8-inch baking dish.
3. Combine topping ingredients. Spread over potato mixture.
4. Bake at 350 degrees for 30-40 minutes or until brown on top.

Preparation Time:	15 minutes	**Serves:**	6
Baking Time:	30-40 minutes		

SWEET POTATOES WITH COCONUTTY TOPPING

Sweet Potatoes

4 cups mashed sweet potatoes
1 cup sugar
½ cup milk
⅓ cup melted butter
2 slightly beaten eggs
1 teaspoon vanilla
½ teaspoon salt

Combine all ingredients and place in 9 x 13-inch baking dish.

Coconutty Topping

1 cup shredded coconut
1 cup chopped pecans
1 cup brown sugar
⅓ cup melted butter
⅓ cup flour

1. Combine all ingredients and sprinkle over top of Sweet Potatoes.
2. Bake at 350 degrees for 40 minutes.

Preparation Time:	**15 minutes**	**Serves:**	**10-12**
Baking Time:	**40 minutes**		

YAMS IN ORANGE CUPS

4 cups hot, mashed yams
¼ cup butter
½ cup orange juice
½ teaspoon salt
4 oranges
Maraschino cherries for garnish

1. Whip all ingredients except oranges and cherries.
2. Cut oranges in half crosswise. Clean out oranges. Trim edges in decorative scallop.
3. Fill orange cups using pastry bag with large star tip.
4. Bake at 350 degrees for 20 minutes.
5. Garnish with maraschino cherries.

Preparation Time:	**30 minutes**	**Serves:**	**8**
Baking Time:	**20 minutes**		

BROILED TOMATOES

"This is even better if you have grown your own tomatoes"

3 large tomatoes
1½ Tablespoons herb-garlic salad dressing
⅓ cup melted butter
1⅓ cups soft bread crumbs
1 Tablespoon chopped parsley
1 crushed garlic clove
½ teaspoon salt
½ cup grated, fresh Parmesan cheese

1. Cut stems from tomatoes. Cut tomatoes in half crosswise.
2. Brush salad dressing over cut sides of tomato halves.
3. In small bowl, combine butter, bread crumbs, parsley, garlic and salt. Toss until well-mixed.
4. Spoon evenly over tomatoes. Sprinkle with Parmesan cheese.
5. Place on broiler pan. Broil 5 inches from heat 2-3 minutes or until topping is lightly brown.

Preparation Time:	**20 minutes**	**Serves:**	**6**
Broiling Time:	**2-3 minutes**		

TOMATOES STUFFED WITH MUSHROOMS

"The perfect combination"

4 ripe, firm, medium tomatoes
1 teaspoon salt
¼ teaspoon sugar
6 thinly sliced green onions
2 Tablespoons butter
¾ pound thinly sliced, fresh mushrooms
1½ Tablespoons fresh lemon juice
1 Tablespoon tarragon vinegar
1 teaspoon paprika
¾ cup half-and-half
3 Tablespoons grated, fresh Parmesan cheese
3 Tablespoons grated, fresh Gruyère cheese

1. Cut tops off tomatoes and scoop out pulp. Chop pulp and set aside to drain.
2. Sprinkle entire tomato shell lightly with salt and sugar.
3. Stand tomatoes upside down to drain for 30 minutes.
4. Sauté green onions in butter until softened. Add mushrooms and sauté until golden.
5. Stir in tomato pulp, lemon juice, tarragon vinegar, paprika and salt to taste. Continue cooking for 2 minutes.
6. Turn heat to high and add half-and-half. Cook, stirring until liquid is reduced and thickened.
7. Place tomato shells in greased, shallow baking dish and fill with mushroom mixture. Top each with Parmesan and Gruyère cheese.
8. Bake at 400 degrees for 10 minutes. Place under broiler to brown.
9. Serve immediately.

Preparation Time:	**1½ hours**	**Serves:**	**4**
Baking Time:	**10 minutes**		
Broiling Time:	**1-2 minutes**		

MOO SHU VEGETABLES

½ cup sliced, dried black mushrooms
½ cup boiling water
6 Tablespoons oil
1 diced green onion
1 Tablespoon minced ginger root
3 Tablespoons soy sauce
½ teaspoon sugar
½ teaspoon cornstarch
2 cups shredded cabbage
¼ cup bamboo shoots
½ cup chopped water chestnuts
½ teaspoon salt
4 slightly beaten eggs
3 Tablespoons hoisin sauce
8 Chinese Pancakes (see recipe)
Plum Sauce (see recipe)

1. Place mushrooms in bowl and cover with boiling water. Soak 20 minutes.
2. In wok or large skillet, heat 2 Tablespoons oil. Add green onion and ginger root. Stir fry 1 minute.
4. Add 1 Tablespoon soy sauce, sugar and cornstarch. Remove from wok and set aside.
5. In wok, heat 2 Tablespoons oil. Add cabbage, bamboo shoots, mushrooms, water chestnuts and salt. Stir fry 2 minutes. Remove from wok and set aside.
6. In wok, heat 2 Tablespoons oil. Pour in eggs and scramble very fine.
7. Return vegetables to wok. Heat thoroughly. Add 2 Tablespoons soy sauce and stir fry quickly for 1-2 minutes.
8. To serve, place steamed Chinese Pancake on plate. Spread 1 teaspoon hoisin sauce in center of pancake. Scoop 2 Tablespoons filling on top of sauce. Roll pancake, folding ends. Place seam down. Serve with Plum Sauce.

Preparation Time:	**30 minutes**	**Serves:**	**8**
Soaking Time:	**20 minutes**		
Cooking Time:	**8 minutes**		

STIR-FRIED VEGETABLES

2 Tablespoons soy sauce
½ cup water
1 teaspoon sugar
1 teaspoon chicken-style seasoning
2 Tablespoons vegetable oil
2 cups broccoli flowerets
1 sliced, medium onion
1 Tablespoon minced garlic clove
1 teaspoon minced ginger root
2 Tablespoons sesame oil
8 ounces fresh snow peas
1 cup sliced, fresh mushrooms
2 cups fresh bean sprouts
2 teaspoons toasted sesame seeds or ¼ cup unsalted cashews

1. In small bowl, combine soy sauce, ¼ cup water, sugar and chicken-style seasoning. Set aside.
2. In wok or heavy skillet, heat vegetable oil until it ripples. Add broccoli, onion, garlic and ginger root. Stir fry 1 minute.
3. Add remaining ¼ cup water. Steam covered until crisp-tender. Remove vegetables. Set aside.
4. Reheat wok. Heat sesame oil. Add snow peas and mushrooms. Stir fry 1 minute.
5. Return broccoli mixture to wok. Add bean sprouts and soy sauce mixture. Stir 1-2 minutes until just warm.
6. Sprinkle with sesame seeds or cashews. Serve immediately.

Preparation Time:	**30 minutes**	**Serves:**	**6**
Cooking Time:	**10 minutes**		

ZUCCHINI WITH KASSERI CHEESE

8 medium zucchini, about 2 pounds
2 chopped medium onions
4 Tablespoons butter
4 beaten eggs
Salt to taste
1-2 cups grated Kasséri cheese

1. Cut zucchini into ¼-inch slices. Salt. Drain in colander.
2. Grease 8 x 8-inch casserole dish.
3. Steam zucchini for about 8 minutes or until just tender. Drain. Place in casserole dish.
4. Sauté onions in hot butter over medium heat until soft, but not browned.
5. Combine beaten eggs, onions, salt and cheese. Pour over zucchini.
6. Bake at 375 degrees for 20 minutes or until cheese is golden and bubbly.

Preparation Time:	**25 minutes**	**Serves:**	**6**
Baking Time:	**20 minutes**		

ZUCCHINI WITH CHEESE-NUT STUFFING

"No one will guess it's zucchini"

6 large zucchini
1 chopped, large onion
2 cups chopped mushrooms
2 Tablespoons oil
2½-3 cups cooked brown rice
1 cup chopped walnuts
2 beaten, large eggs
2 teaspoons curry powder
Salt to taste
3 cups grated Swiss cheese

1. In large pot of boiling water, parboil zucchini until soft, not mushy, about 10 minutes. Drain and cool.
2. Slice off a lid lengthwise. Scoop out interior, leaving ¼-inch shell. Chop pulp.
3. Saute onion and mushrooms in oil until soft. Drain off any liquid. Transfer mixture to bowl.
4. Add zucchini pulp, rice, nuts, eggs, curry powder, salt and half the cheese.
5. Spoon into zucchini shells. Sprinkle with remaining cheese.
6. Place in greased 9 x 13-inch baking dish.
7. Bake at 325 degrees for 20-30 minutes until stuffing is set.

Preparation Time:	1 hour	Serves:	6
Cooking Time:	10 minutes	May do ahead	
Baking Time:	20-30 minutes		

Variations: *Substitute macadamia nuts or cashews for walnuts. Use 1 12-inch zucchini about 3 inches in diameter. Slice to serve.*

BROCCOLI-CHEESE SAUCE

"A tasty topping"

1 cup fresh broccoli
2 Tablespoons butter or margarine
2 Tablespoons flour
1 cup milk
4 ounces grated Cheddar cheese
¼ teaspoon salt

1. Cut broccoli into ½-inch pieces. Steam. Set aside.
2. In medium saucepan, melt butter over low heat and stir in flour. Stir until bubbly.
3. Add milk gradually. Cook over medium-high heat, stirring constantly until thickened. Remove from heat.
4. Stir in cheese and salt. Mix until cheese is melted.
5. Gently stir in broccoli.

Preparation Time:	15 minutes	Yield:	Topping for 4 baked potatoes
Cooking Time:	5-8 minutes		

CHEESE SAUCE

2 Tablespoons margarine
3 Tablespoons flour
1 cup milk
1½ cups shredded sharp Cheddar cheese
2 Tablespoons chicken-style broth
¼ teaspoon Worcestershire sauce

1. In medium saucepan, melt margarine.
2. Stir in flour. Cook until mixture is smooth and bubbly.
3. Gradually add milk. Cook until mixture boils and thickens, stirring constantly.
4. Add cheese, chicken-style broth and Worcestershire sauce. Stir until cheese is melted.

Preparation Time:	10 minutes	Yield:	1½ cups
Cooking Time:	10 minutes		

PERK-UP-A-POTATO

1 11-ounce can cheddar cheese soup
1 cup cooked broccoli flowerets
2 Tablespoons sour cream
½ teaspoon Dijon mustard
Chopped pimento

1. Stir soup in medium saucepan over medium heat.
2. Stir in broccoli, sour cream and mustard. Heat thoroughly, stirring occasionally.

Preparation Time:	5 minutes	Yield:	Topping for 4 baked
Cooking Time:	5-8 minutes		potatoes

Index

A

415

INDEX

INDEX

INDEX

INDEX

INDEX

INDEX

INDEX

Very Innovative Parties Cookbook

Loma Linda University Dental Auxiliary
P.O. Box 382
Loma Linda, California 92354
1-800-841-3838

Please send ____ copies of **Very Innovative Parties Cookbook** @ $24.95 each $ _____
Postage and handling U.S. residents @ 5.00 each $ _____
Postage and handling Non-U.S. residents @ 7.00 each $ _____
Sales tax per book (California residents only) @ Applicable $ _____
TOTAL $ _____

Please make checks payable to **Loma Linda University Dental Auxiliary.**
NAME _____
ADDRESS _____
CITY_____STATE_____ZIP_____

- -

Very Innovative Parties Cookbook

Loma Linda University Dental Auxiliary
P.O. Box 382
Loma Linda, California 92354
1-800-841-3838

Please send ____ copies of **Very Innovative Parties Cookbook** @ $24.95 each $ _____
Postage and handling U.S. residents @ 5.00 each $ _____
Postage and handling Non-U.S. residents @ 7.00 each $ _____
Sales tax per book (California residents only) @ Applicable $ _____
TOTAL $ _____

Please make checks payable to **Loma Linda University Dental Auxiliary.**
NAME _____
ADDRESS _____
CITY_____STATE_____ZIP_____

- -

Very Innovative Parties Cookbook

Loma Linda University Dental Auxiliary
P.O. Box 382
Loma Linda, California 92354
1-800-841-3838

Please send ____ copies of **Very Innovative Parties Cookbook** @ $24.95 each $ _____
Postage and handling U.S. residents @ 5.00 each $ _____
Postage and handling Non-U.S. residents @ 7.00 each $ _____
Sales tax per book (California residents only) @ Applicable $ _____
TOTAL $ _____

Please make checks payable to **Loma Linda University Dental Auxiliary.**
NAME _____
ADDRESS _____
CITY_____STATE_____ZIP_____

The name and address of a book store or gift shop in your area would be appreciated.

Name _____

Address _____

City _____ State _____ Zip _____

Phone Number (_____) _____

- -

The name and address of a book store or gift shop in your area would be appreciated.

Name _____

Address _____

City _____ State _____ Zip _____

Phone Number (_____) _____

- -

The name and address of a book store or gift shop in your area would be appreciated.

Name _____

Address _____

City _____ State _____ Zip _____

Phone Number (_____) _____

Very Innovative Parties Cookbook

Loma Linda University Dental Auxiliary
P.O. Box 382
Loma Linda, California 92354
1-800-841-3838

Please send _____ copies of **Very Innovative Parties Cookbook** @ $24.95 each $ _____
Postage and handling U.S. residents @ 5.00 each $ _____
Postage and handling Non-U.S. residents @ 7.00 each $ _____
Sales tax per book (California residents only) @ Applicable $ _____
TOTAL $ _____

Please make checks payable to **Loma Linda University Dental Auxiliary.**

NAME _____
ADDRESS _____
CITY_____STATE_____ZIP_____

Very Innovative Parties Cookbook

Loma Linda University Dental Auxiliary
P.O. Box 382
Loma Linda, California 92354
1-800-841-3838

Please send _____ copies of **Very Innovative Parties Cookbook** @ $24.95 each $ _____
Postage and handling U.S. residents @ 5.00 each $ _____
Postage and handling Non-U.S. residents @ 7.00 each $ _____
Sales tax per book (California residents only) @ Applicable $ _____
TOTAL $ _____

Please make checks payable to **Loma Linda University Dental Auxiliary.**

NAME _____
ADDRESS _____
CITY_____STATE_____ZIP_____

Very Innovative Parties Cookbook

Loma Linda University Dental Auxiliary
P.O. Box 382
Loma Linda, California 92354
1-800-841-3838

Please send _____ copies of **Very Innovative Parties Cookbook** @ $24.95 each $ _____
Postage and handling U.S. residents @ 5.00 each $ _____
Postage and handling Non-U.S. residents @ 7.00 each $ _____
Sales tax per book (California residents only) @ Applicable $ _____
TOTAL $ _____

Please make checks payable to **Loma Linda University Dental Auxiliary.**

NAME _____
ADDRESS _____
CITY_____STATE_____ZIP_____

The name and address of a book store or gift shop in your area would be appreciated.

Name _____

Address _____

City _____ State _____ Zip _____

Phone Number (   )_____

— —

The name and address of a book store or gift shop in your area would be appreciated.

Name _____

Address _____

City _____ State _____ Zip _____

Phone Number (   )_____

— —

The name and address of a book store or gift shop in your area would be appreciated.

Name _____

Address _____

City _____ State _____ Zip _____

Phone Number (   )_____

Very Innovative Parties Cookbook

Loma Linda University Dental Auxiliary
P.O. Box 382
Loma Linda, California 92354
1-800-841-3838

Please send ____ copies of **Very Innovative Parties Cookbook** @ $24.95 each $ _____
Postage and handling U.S. residents   @   5.00 each $ _____
Postage and handling Non-U.S. residents   @   7.00 each $ _____
Sales tax per book (California residents only)   @   Applicable $ _____
                                                                              TOTAL $ _____

Please make checks payable to **Loma Linda University Dental Auxiliary.**

NAME _____

ADDRESS _____

CITY_____STATE_____ZIP_____

- -

Very Innovative Parties Cookbook

Loma Linda University Dental Auxiliary
P.O. Box 382
Loma Linda, California 92354
1-800-841-3838

Please send ____ copies of **Very Innovative Parties Cookbook** @ $24.95 each $ _____
Postage and handling U.S. residents   @   5.00 each $ _____
Postage and handling Non-U.S. residents   @   7.00 each $ _____
Sales tax per book (California residents only)   @   Applicable $ _____
                                                                              TOTAL $ _____

Please make checks payable to **Loma Linda University Dental Auxiliary.**

NAME _____

ADDRESS _____

CITY_____STATE_____ZIP_____

- -

Very Innovative Parties Cookbook

Loma Linda University Dental Auxiliary
P.O. Box 382
Loma Linda, California 92354
1-800-841-3838

Please send ____ copies of **Very Innovative Parties Cookbook** @ $24.95 each $ _____
Postage and handling U.S. residents   @   5.00 each $ _____
Postage and handling Non-U.S. residents   @   7.00 each $ _____
Sales tax per book (California residents only)   @   Applicable $ _____
                                                                              TOTAL $ _____

Please make checks payable to **Loma Linda University Dental Auxiliary.**

NAME _____

ADDRESS _____

CITY_____STATE_____ZIP_____

The name and address of a book store or gift shop in your area would be appreciated.

Name _____

Address _____

City _____ State _____ Zip _____

Phone Number (   ) _____

The name and address of a book store or gift shop in your area would be appreciated.

Name _____

Address _____

City _____ State _____ Zip _____

Phone Number (   ) _____

The name and address of a book store or gift shop in your area would be appreciated.

Name _____

Address _____

City _____ State _____ Zip _____

Phone Number (   ) _____

Notes

Notes